TOWARD TRANSFIGURED LIFE

Also by Stanley S. Harakas

Living the Liturgy, 1976
Contemporary Issues: Orthodox Christian Perspectives, 1976
Something is Stirring in World Orthodoxy, 1978
The Melody of Prayer, 1979
Guidelines for Marriage in the Orthodox Church, 1979
For the Health of Body and Soul, 1980
Contemporary Moral Issues Facing the Orthodox Christian, 1982
Let Mercy Abound: A Chronicle of Greek Orthodox Social Concerns, 1983

TOWARD TRANSFIGURED LIFE

The *Theoria* of Eastern Orthodox Ethics

Stanley Samuel Harakas

Come, let us rejoice, mounting up
from the earth to the highest
contemplation of the virtues: let
us be transformed this day into a
better state and direct our minds to
heavenly things, being shaped anew
in piety according to the form of
Christ. For in His mercy the Saviour
of our souls has transfigured
disfigured man and made him shine
with light upon Mount Tabor.

> *Sticheron,* Small Vespers,
> Feast of the Transfiguration

1983

Light and Life Publishing Company
P.O. Box 26421
Minneapolis, Minnesota 55426-0421

Copyright © 1983
Light and Life Publishing Company
Library of Congress Card No. 82-083078

ISBN 0-937032-28-X

DEDICATION
To Him

who "is not God of the dead, but of
the living; for all live to Him" (Luke 20:38)

and

To my *Alma Mater,*
Holy Cross Greek Orthodox School of Theology,
Brookline, MA, U.S.A.

ACKNOWLEDGEMENTS

Those who have directly contributed to the making of this volume are too numerous to mention. However, I wish to acknowledge some who, in contributing to my interest in and understanding of the discipline of Christian Ethics, have made this volume possible: my first teacher of Ethics, the Rev. John Papadopoulos at Holy Cross Greek Orthodox School of Theology; Dean Walter G. Muelder, my major Professor at Boston University School of Theology; Professor Panagiotes Demetropoulos at the School of Theology of the University of Thessalonike, Greece; and Professor George Mantzarides of the University of Thessalonike whose writings have been a constant magnet to the patristic sources of Orthodox Christian Ethics.

Others have made it possible for me to study, research and teach in the discipline of Orthodox Christian Ethics at Holy Cross Greek Orthodox School of Theology. For this, I am grateful to the Dean, Fr. Alkiviadis Calivas and my colleagues on the Faculty and to the administration, embodied in its President, Dr. Thomas Lelon. Most importantly, I am grateful to the Chairman of the Board of Trustees of Hellenic College and Holy Cross Greek Orthodox School of Theology, Archbishop Iakovos, who has provided funds for the preparation of the manuscript and for assistance in its publication, through the Taylor Foundation. Further, he has constantly affirmed the necessity of the theologian's role in the growth and program of the Church. For this, I'm most grateful.

I wish, as well, to acknowledge the hospitality of Boston College during a sabbatical semester when much of this volume was written in second draft.

Special expressions of gratitude are due to my wife, Emily G. Harakas and my former secretary Cathy Lazarides, who typed and retyped many of the early drafts of these pages; to Jean Finnigan, who typed the manuscript in its entirety; and to Pauline Pavlakos who has secretarily seen the book through to its conclusion. Deep appreciation goes as well to all the students of Orthodox Christian Ethics who taught me much over the years and who have contributed more than they know to the final form of this book.

Finally, many thanks to Fr. Anthony Coniaris of Light and Life Publishing Company for his constant support and encouragement in the vicissitudes involved in publishing such a work.

Clean Monday,
March 21, 1983
Brookline, MA

TABLE OF CONTENTS

INTRODUCTION

This book has its origin in the teaching of Orthodox Christian ethics in the course of theological studies at Holy Cross Greek Orthodox School of Theology, Brookline, Mass. Student reactions and comments, as well as the deepening understanding and perception of the author have served to provide the impetus for continued revision of its contents.

Probably, this process could go on forever. There is much that can be refined and more carefully stated. Yet, after many years of teaching the subject of Orthodox Christian Ethics at Holy Cross, I believe that the approach and ideas of the first volume of this work can be placed before the public in general at this time for evaluation.

One of the hesitancies I have felt about the publication of this book is the difficulty and complexity of the subject. It is not alone the particular issues in ethics which are of necessity controversial in character; it is the question of the discipline itself. It is well known that as a discipline of Theology, Christian Ethics is of relatively recent origin. It appears that the discipline of Christian Ethics, perceived as formally separate from the discipline of Christian Doctrine, was established only in the seventeenth century by the Protestant theologian Georg Calixtus. However, as one historian of doctrine notes, "the distinction between doctrine and life had been in force long before that division of labor was effected."[1] The key to this issue is the word "distinction." For Orthodox Christianity, doctrine and ethics may be distinguished but they may never be separated. It is only the "division of labor" in which some theologians of the Church turn their attention to the things, which in the words of St. Athanasios "make known the word concerning Christ, and the mystery regarding him," on the one hand, while other theologians concern themselves primarily with the Christian teaching, again in the words of St. Athanasios, whose intention it is "to point to the correction of habits."[2] Cyril of Jerusalem thus says, "the method of godliness consists of these two things, pious doctrines and virtuous practice."[3] Theodore of Mompsuestia noted in his comment on Jesus' words, "Go therefore and make disciples of all nations, baptizing them in the name of the Father and of the Son and of the Holy Spirit, teaching them to observe all that I have commanded you" (Matthew 28:19) that this referred to a distinction of the subject matter of the Christian faith into two parts, "the ethical part and the precision of dogmas."[4] It would thus appear that the distinction between the discipline of ethics and the discipline of dogmatics (the systematic exposition of the doctrines of the Christian Faith) is rooted in the tradition of the Church.

1

The mistake, for Orthodox Christian theology, would be to separate them. In this work, a strenuous effort is made to keep the faith of the Church not only in contact with the ethical issues, but as their fundamental source and inspiration.

However, the problems of ethics are not always the problems of the systematic exposition of the doctrines of the faith. In a substantive sense, the discipline of ethics, even Orthodox Christian Ethics, must deal with issues and concerns which are not immediately the subject matter of doctrine. There is, in ethics, a vocabulary, a set of concerns, and a body of terminology peculiar to it. The student of the subject will do well to expect a different orientation from that of his doctrinal studies. The *Theoria* of Orthodox Christian Ethics is, without question, inextricably bound up with the doctrinal formulations of the Church. But the theoretical foundations of Orthodox Christian Ethics have their own emphases, foci, and problematics. It is a *Theoria* of Orthodox Christian Ethics, and not merely the repetition of a course in Dogmatics.

It is this specific *Theoria* which, in turn, provides the guidelines and the direction for the determination of the *Praxis,* i.e., the "virtuous practice" and the "correction of habits" and the "ethical part" of the Christian life, referred to by Cyril of Jerusalem, and St. Athanasios and Theodore of Mompsuestia, as noted above.

Thus, in this work we remain in the tradition of the recent past in Orthodox Christian Ethics, which sees as legitimate the "division of labor" which assigns to one area of Systematic Theology the exposition of the content of the saving knowledge of the revelation of God, and which reserves to another area of Systematic Theology the exposition of the "works" of the Christian life. The assumption in this work is that a separation between them is fatal, a distinction unavoidable. The aim of this book is to provide an exposition of ethical themes from a distinctively Eastern Orthodox Christian perspective.

¹ Jaroslav Pelikan, *The Christian Tradition: A History of the Development of Doctrine.* Volume I, *The Emergence of the Catholic Tradition* (100-600). Chicago: The University of Chicago Press, 1971), p. 3.

² *Festal Epistles,* 11.3.

³ *Exposition of Ephesians,* 1:114.   ³ *Catechetical Lectures,* 4.2.

⁴ *Jaroslav Pelikan,* op. cit., p. 2.

Chapter One

THE DISCIPLINE OF
ORTHODOX CHRISTIAN ETHICS

"The life of Christians . . . is a sort of system of rational acts."
(Clement of Alexandria, The Instructor, *1,13.)*

The Importance of the Ethical Life

Orthodox Christian ethics deals with the living of the Christian life, attempting to interpret in an orderly fashion the basic principles which underlie it and the specific application of the Orthodox Christian ethical teachings in the human situation. In the most general of ways, it can be affirmed that the Christian life flows out of faith in Christ and participation in the life of the Church: Baptism, Eucharist, sacramental life in general, prayer and Christian love.

Yet in the concrete and specific circumstances of the Christian life, that is, the experience of the Church, neither is the Christian way of life lived and realized automatically, nor is it unambiguously clear precisely what is appropriate to the Christian ethos. Thus, in addition to basic calls to faith in God and to belief in the saving and redeeming work of Christ and to incorporation of the believer into the body of Christ which is the Church, the earliest Christian teaching also included directives and exhortation on issues specifically related to the living of the Christian life. An example is St. Paul's reaction to the case of a Christian who was cohabitating with his step-mother as described in the fifth chapter of St. Paul's first letter to the Corinthians. Such behavior was not to be tolerated, since it was perceived as totally incompatible with being a follower of Christ as well as with the existence of the Church of Christ itself.

Christianity has always had an ethical character and an ethical teaching. The second part in all of St. Paul's major epistles, for example, the Sermon on the Mount and other discourses by Jesus Christ, the early patristic emphasis on the "two ways" and on Christian behavior in general, witness to that fact. Ignatios of Antioch, for instance, in his *Epistle to the Magnesians* writes "Let us learn how to live according to Christ." The New Testament passage Matthew 19:16-22 which describes the quest of the Rich Young Man for salvation, prefaces the discussion with the request "Teacher, what good deed must I do to have eternal life?" Jesus' response is "If you would enter life, keep the commandments." It is significant that a number of ten commandments are then described as necessary for obtaining eternal life. Another New Testament passage which indicates the importance of ethical behavior for Christianity is the passage describing the Last Judgment (Matthew 25:31-46). In this passage, the final judgment of mankind is described as taking place not on the basis of Faith, nor of worship, nor of sacramental participation, but rather, on the basis of loving acts for the welfare of the neighbor: "In as much as ye have done these things unto these the least of my brethren, you have done them unto me." Feeding the hungry, taking in the stranger, clothing the naked, visiting the sick and imprisoned cannot be classified other than as ethical acts. One cannot deprecate this dimension of the Christian Life as "mere moralizing," without having the weight of both Holy Scripture and Holy Tradition to contend with.

Thus from the beginning, Christianity has had clear-cut ethical dimensions. There seems to be, however, a constant struggle within Christianity as to the importance of those ethical dimensions for the Christian life. Thus, there is a tendency for Theology to swing from an over-emphasis to an under-emphasis on the dimension of ethics in the Christian life. In our day, in Orthodox Theology, we are presently under the powerful influence of liturgy and mystical experience in Theology which tend to weaken the role of ethical concerns and interest in ethical living within the larger concept of what it means to be an Orthodox Christian. For Orthodoxy this is erroneous, just as it would be erroneous to define Orthodox Christianity in exclusively ethical terms. There is need for a proper understanding of the ethical life in Christianity. It is a task of Orthodox Christian ethics to provide this understanding.

The Need for the Discipline of Christian Ethics

Thus, generally, for the Christian ethical life, there is need for reflection, theological study and explication of the ethical dimensions of the Orthodox Christian faith. However, today, a study of the major resources in Orthodox Christian teaching as they apply both to the foundational principles of ethics as well as to their practical application in the life of the Church, is not merely an academic exercise. It is, as well, an imperative.

This imperative is not particularly felt in places and in times when the social milieu in which the Church lives is stable, imbued with the Christian spirit and based on a Christian world-view. In some measure, Byzantium and Holy Russia may have represented such a situation in the past. However, it is quite clear that the Orthodox Church does not enjoy such a status anywhere in the world today. In the Communist dominated lands the Church suffers a sometimes veiled, sometimes open persecution, coupled with severe and consistent propaganda attacks. In the western capitalist nations the secularistic spirit flies in the face of the Christian ethos, a confrontation perhaps even more insidious than the open opposition of the Communistic ideology.

Other forces contribute as well to the lack of clarity and sureness about the content of the Christian ethic. Among these are pluralism and

4

rapid scientific advance. The isolated closed community is rapidly becoming a thing of the past. Pluralism of culture, religions, and life-styles is a fact of life in many nations, particularly as they become more and more urbanized. As Orthodox Christians join in this process, and contribute to it by their very presence, questions and problems arise which they have never had to face before. In such instances, proximity to others who hold to differing opinions and life-styles also puts into question opinions and teachings previously considered "obvious" or "natural," and consequently, unexamined.

Further, rapid scientific advances in our time have given totally new dimensions to some old issues and, in addition, raised problems for the behavior of Orthodox Christians which have never existed before. An example of the former is the influence of the awesome destructiveness of nuclear weapons on all Christian thinking regarding war. Examples of the latter are the many advances in the sphere of medicine, including procedures such as artificial insemination, organ transplants, conception control methods, sex-change operations and genetic manipulation.

All of these factors, and others as well, call for a careful examination of the fundamental principles as well as the specific guidelines for the living of the Orthodox Christian life. In other words, the need for Orthodox Christian ethical study and the development of the discipline is a spiritual imperative and a demand on the part of the Church. Those who take seriously their Orthodox Christian commitment will, then, of necessity seek answers to a multitude of unresolved questions. But the answers may not be expressed in mere pronouncements. They must be theologically solid at their foundation, firm yet compassionate in their formulation, capable of application, and explicable either by identity or contrast in the terms of the societies, and value systems in which Orthodox Christians live.

In short, there is a great need for an organized study of Orthodox Christian ethics.

Non-Revelatory Ethics and Christian Ethics

As Orthodox Christian Ethics undertakes the task, it confronts immediately the fact that many others have dealt with ethical issues. In the early period of the Church, the confrontation of Christian ideas and the Greek philosophical world served as a catalyst for the development and formulation of the Orthodox Christian teaching. Thus, even though Christianity never felt itself bound by philosophical categories and perspectives, it always dealt with them.

In our time, non-revelatory approaches to the issues which concern us as Orthodox Christians are not only those of the philosophers of antiquity, such as Plato and Aristotle, with whom the great Fathers of the Church dealt. Ethical responses, as well as the formulations of the problems themselves are often the products of more recent ethical schools of thought. Orthodox Christian ethics cannot function as if these teachings, positions and ethical systems did not exist, for oftentimes they provide the rationale and argumentation in support of the antithetical non-Orthodox views. Further, however, they often contain insights and truths which are compatible and supportive of the Orthodox Christian ethical teaching.

Thus, while it is conceivable that Orthodox systematic Theology may be written and studied without direct reference to current theological and secular world-views, it is not possible to adequately deal with ethical issues in isolation from the world and the thinking in and about the world in which Orthodox Christian ethics is to be practiced.

This does not mean that the various systems of non-revelatory ethics ought to be confused with Christian ethics. Yet, non-revelatory ethics addresses many of the same issues and problems which form part of the human experience with which Christian Theology is concerned as well. This is because they reflect in some measure, the divine image in human life. Consequently, the various approaches to basic ethical questions may not be ignored by Orthodox Christian ethics.

Philosophers and theologians give definitions of non-revelatory ethics which are very close to each other. One philosophical ethicist defines ethics as "the normative science of human conduct" and conduct as a "collective name for voluntary actions." Panagiotes Demetropoulos[1] defines ethics as "the name of that science which concerns itself with the treatment of human actions." In both cases, the discipline of ethics is considered to be a "science." We are entitled to ask the question, "In what sense is ethics a science?" Most of us are familiar with the application of the word "science" to the positive sciences, in which there is observation of phenomena, without prejudgment regarding their value as good or evil. Positive sciences are usually experimental in method and arrive at conclusions which may be tested by others through experimentation. Ethics, by its very nature is not easily adapted to the experimental method. Normative sciences, such as ethics, aesthetics and logic are obviously of a different category. It is only proper to distinguish between the two. Therefore, in using the word science, we preface it with the word "normative" when it is used to describe or characterize ethics. Thus, we can say that "ethics is a normative science." However, it is necessary for us to recognize that in this special case, we are using the word "science" in the sense of "an organized body of knowledge" rather than as a description of a discipline which uses the experimental method. Thus, Demetropoulos comments: "If it is true that the Christian life can be studied, it follows that Christian ethics, as a study concerned with the history of the life according to Christ, the sources of that life and the rules which govern those relationships in this very unqiue mode of living, can truly be called a science."[2] However, if we leave the issue there, it would appear that Christian ethics is simply a sectarian type of study. Just as one might be able to develop—on the basis of socialist theory—a socialistic ethic, and—on the basis of the religion of the Koran—a Mohammedan ethic, and—on the basis of communist philosophy—a Communistic ethic, and—on the basis of business activity—a business ethic, one would then produce a very narrowly conceived ethic which could be called "Christian

Ethics" which applies to the behavior of those persons in the world who might want to live according to the Christian faith.

It is necessary to proceed from such an understanding and to investigate the relationship of Christian ethics to the totality of reality. We must, therefore, ask what the relationship of Christian ethics is to non-revelatory ethics. It is important, first of all that we be able to relate Christian ethics to general knowledge and especially the views of the world that characterize philosophical and metaphysical theory.

A strong philosophical view which is widely accepted among non-specialists is that the nature of the good depends on the nature of reality. However, certain philosophers have questioned this and have attempted to maintain a sharp differentiation between what the world *is* and how people *ought* to behave; that is, the so-called "is-ought bifurcation." The classic exponent of this view is the English philosopher, G. E. Moore, who taught that identifying reality with ought statements was a logical fallacy, which he termed the "naturalistic fallacy." He holds a metaphysical view that the good itself does not depend on its relationship with other things. He teaches that the good is a quality in and of itself which may not be reduced to any other thing. His classic example is the color "yellow." Just as "yellow" cannot be defined in any other terms, but simply as what it is, so it is with the good. The good, in the thinking of G. E. Moore, is irreducable to any other term. Thus the good cannot be defined as pleasure, or evolution or any other "natural" reality. We will examine the claim for the "independence" of the good further in our discussion, especially in relationship to certain theories of the good from the Orthodox point of view. Suffice it to say that for Orthodox Christian ethics, God does not depend for His goodness on any other thing.

Christian ethics, further, is closely related to non-revelatory ethics and philosophy in general because it, too, is subject to examination of the validity, coherence and consistency of its judgments and evaluations. If Orthodox Christian ethics is true, it must in some way come to terms with acceptable standards of validation, though this in no way means that the ultimate apophatic and transrational character of Orthodox Christian Theology is compromised. In addition, non-revelatory ethics and philosophy in general will be seen as requiring ultimate grounding in order to be acceptable by human beings generally. Further, the relationship of philosophical ethics and Christian ethics is seen in the fact that both provide data for general philosophical reasoning and for knowledge in general.

What we must conclude is, that it is not possible to do Christian ethics in a vacuum. The ethical thinking of non-Christian ethicists and philosophical, scientific, sociological, psychological knowledge are of necessity related to Christian ethics. This is true because Christian ethics is not a sectarian ethic. It claims to speak to all of mankind and to speak to human beings in the whole human condition. It is a dimension of the catholic truth of the faith and as such directs itself to all of mankind. In doing this it must take into consideration general human knowledge.

The Relationship of Philosophical Ethics and Orthodox Christian Ethics

In practice, how does this relationship between Christian Ethics and philosophical ethics take place? In his *Systema Ethikes,* Chrestos Androutsos identifies philosophical ethics and Christian ethics. He states, "philosophical ethics and Christian ethics are identical, and the only additional contribution of Christian ethics is to provide the necessary motivation for the doing of the good."[3] This, perhaps might be true if there was one generally accepted philosophical world view and that this one generally accepted world view shared basic metaphysical presuppositions with that of Christianity. However, the fact is that this is not the case. Demetropoulos is more correct when he writes "there are as many kinds of philosophical ethics as there are philosophical systems." "Thus," he notes, "in a great number of points, Christian ethics differs fundamentally from the various philosophical systems."[4] Specifically, he notes six areas of difference. He refers to the humility by which Christian ethics approaches its task and the elitist character of most philosophical ethical systems; its generally balanced approach as opposed to one-sided approach by philosophical ethical and systems; the contrast between love and grace on the Christian side and justice and honesty on the philosophical side; the Christian recognition of God as the source of true ethical living and thinking, in comparison to this-world presuppositions of the varying views of philosophical ethics; the universal appeal and application of the Christian ethic as compared to many philosophical views which are more or less aristocratic; and finally, the intent on the part of Christian ethics that its teachings be applied to life and not remain, as is the case with philosophical ethics, a subject of theoretical inquiry.[5]

The Discipline of Orthodox Christian Ethics

We may use P. Demetropoulos' definition of Christian ethics as a working definition as we proceed with this inquiry and exposition of Orthodox Christian ethics. His definition of Christian ethics has the virtue of comprehensiveness, avoiding the more or less narrow and sectarian understandings of the discipline which characterizes some contemporary views of the discipline. However, this definition also avoids the other view which sees little or nothing unique about the discipline of Christian ethics. It is both universal and specific, appealing to the generally recognized validity of non-revelatory knowledge as well as the uniqueness of the revelatory experience. He defines it as follows:

> Christian ethics is that unique ethic having divine validity which concerns itself with the study of the whole of morality, including the natural moral law and all ethical values, both absolute and relative which may or may not be available to the ethically sensitive non-Christian, as well as the ethical dimension existing in the holy human nature of Christ and in those men and women in whom Christ has been formed—the saints.[6]

8

The consequences of this definition indicate that Christian ethics provides us with a new world of ethical values, which however, include the ethical values of common ethical life and its philosophical understanding. Christian ethics, however, has its authority and its roots in God. It therefore is an ethic which is founded on the very nature of ultimate reality. It is more Orthodox to think of Christian ethics as the completion, or the fulfillment of a natural, non-revelatory ethic, and it, as an introduction to Christian ethics, without separating them into two distinct and unrelated ethics. Eastern Orthodox ethics will emphasize the continuity between natural ethics (creation) and revealed ethics (redemption). What is emphasized here is the existence of the personal, free Triune God who is the source of the moral experience, and consequently, the source of all reflection and teaching about the discipline of ethics.

There are minor and major sources for the discipline of Christian Ethics. Characteristic of the first are the non-revelatory sources. The chief non-revelatory source for Christian Ethics are the philosophical moral sciences. There are six moral disciplines which deal with the experience of morality. The positive science of morals provides a historical description of human behavior as it relates to moral standards. It describes how people have behaved in the past, or, how people are behaving in the present. Thus, a "Moral History of the United States" could be written in which American behavior through the decades could be described as it refers to the moral standards dominant throughout its history. The second moral science is ethics. As we have understood it, it is a "normative science," which has as its task to provide analysis and reasoning on ethical norms and to prescribe what men ought to do, and what men ought not to do. A third moral science is moral philosophy, or what might also be called philosophical ethics. In this discipline the metaphysical and metaethical questions are discussed on exclusively non-revelatory bases. The fourth moral science is casuistry, in which standards are applied to particular and concrete cases. It seeks to give concrete and specific moral directions in particular situations. The fifth may be characterized as moralizing, or practical ethics, whose goal and purpose is the improvement of the conduct of the person or persons receiving the instruction. Usually this is done in the home, school and the pulpit. The final "moral science" is the art or the practice of living the good life. The ancient Greeks called this the art *(techne)* of living well *(ev zein)*. Additional sources for Christian ethics from the non-revelatory sphere, which provide much data for Christian ethics are the disciplines of psychology, anthropology, sociology, economics, political science, the philosophy of history, biology, physics, medicine, literature, language, semantic studies, etc.

The revelatory, or Christian sources for Orthodox Christian ethics are of much more importance than any of those previously discussed. A primary source for Orthodox Christian ethics is Holy Scripture and especially the New Testament. The Old Testament is studied and drawn upon by Christian ethics in relationship to the New Testament and is interpreted in the light of the New Testament. Orthodox Christian ethics equally draws upon Holy Tradition as the conscience of the Church, especially in its normative historical statements. We have several excellent examples of such normative historical statements. They are found, of course, in the patristic understandings of the Scripture, in sermons of the Fathers, and also, in a unique way, in the canon law of the Orthodox Church, as well as throughout all of the varied expressions of Holy Tradition as the witness to divine revelation.

Christian ethics is also in relationship with the disciplines of Theology. Orthodox Christian ethics is totally dependent upon the doctrines, theological teachings and dogmas of the Orthodox Christian Church. Numerous Orthodox systematic theologians have made this point. Some are the following. Zekos Rossis wrote, "Christian ethics is based on dogmatics and the activities (energies) of God in relationshp with mankind. It examines these energies as well as the actions of man, indicating what ought to be done by man. . ."[7] Chrestos Androutsos says, "The theoretical science of Christianity is the mother of the practical theological sciences. Dogmatics provides the beginnings of Christian ethics."[8] Panagiotes Trembelas writes, "Christian ethics is based on a doctrinal foundation, borrowing its basic principles from Dogmatics."[9]

The relationship of Christian ethics to practical theology is very clear since its teachings are embodied in preaching, in religious education, in counseling, in the sacrament of Holy Confession, in canon law, etc.

Canon law is unique as a source for Orthodox Christian ethics because it is the only place where the consciousness of the Church has expressed itself in extremely concrete and even quantative ways in reference to ethical issues. However, Orthodox Christian ethics will draw on the canonical tradition without blind literalism. The changing conditions of the times, from the Patristic period to our own, do not permit literal application of patristic statements to the ethical life without some consideration of the altered circumstances. As noted previously, Orthodox Theology will serve as the fundamental source for Orthodox Christian ethics. Finally, the virtuous life of the saints, the great ecclesiastical personalities will be important for Christian ethics, in that their lives embodied the experience of the Christian ethic. One very useful source of the lives of the saints will be found in the worship services of the Church, especially in its hymnology, where the consciousness of the Church has been able to identify virtues and modes of behavior which are especially appropriate to the Christian life.

The History of Orthodox Christian Ethics

These comments lead easily to a discussion of the history of Christian ethics, with special reference to Greek Orthodox ethics. The history of Christian ethics may be divided into three periods according to Professor John Karmiris.[10] First, the Ancient or Patristic period, from the end of the Apostolic period to the Great Schism of the ninth century. Second, from the schism to the reformation in the sixteenth century. And third, the

Modern Period, from the appearance of Protestantism to the present day. The first period, from the second through the ninth centuries provide very few—and these elementary—writings regarding ethics. We find that these ethical discussions during the first three centuries take place in larger contexts with special reference to dogmatic issues. In spite of that fact, there were serious concerns with ethical questions by the early Fathers of the Church. These concerns arose from various causes. The criticisms directed against the Christians by both Jews and pagans gave opportunity to Christian apologists to respond. Some of these charges were of an ethical character and the responses which they elicited from the defenders of the faith argued for the ethical purity of the members of the Church, their high idealism and the example of their teaching. Another cause for the writing of ethical works during the fourth and fifth centuries was the weakening of Christian enthusiasm and life. The influx of new converts from paganism meant that the new converts brought their non-Christian life styles with them which had to be reformed and corrected. This became the cause for some writings on Christian ethics. Also, the specific ethical failures of Christians caused some legislation by the Church. We have a number of canons by the Church throughout the centuries of this period which deal with primarily ethical questions. In addition, we have seen the rise of the Confessional on a personal basis, which required Father Confessors to have some idea of moral questions and how to treat them. Thus, in addition to the ethical teaching of the New Testament, which as we know was "occasional"—that is, it dealt with specific situations as they arose and was not systematic—we have early Fathers (the Apostolic Fathers) dealing with ethical questions, such as Ignatius, in his epistle, Hermas and the *Didache,* the author of the *Epistle to Diognetos.* After the Apologists reference should be made to Clement of Alexandria *(Stromata, Paidagogos, Who is the Saved Man?).* Origen made a contribution to ethics in his *On Prayer* and his *Logos Protreptikos eis Martyrion.* Also, of great importance for some parts of Christian ethics are the writings of Justin, the Philosopher, Tertullian and Cyprian.

From the fourth century we have an increase in the writings on Christian Ethics, just as we do in all fields of theology. During this period we have many ethical writings, sermons, ascetic works, confessions of Fathers in which we find a great deal of ethical material. However, in fact, we do not have a formal treatise on ethics, that is, a structured treatment of Christian ethics as separate from other disciplines of Theology. Here of course, the great Fathers of the Golden Age of the Church are prominent; Makarios of Egypt, Basil, the two Gregories, Methodios of Olympus, John Chrysostom, Cyril of Alexandria, Isidore Pelusiotes, Efraim and Isaac the Syrians, Hesychios of Jerusalem, John of the Ladder, John the Faster, Anastasios of Sinai, Symeon the Stylite, Theodore of Tyron and should we be so inclined, we can place Dionysios the Areopagite in this period, and others in the East. In the West, major figures during this period are Ambrose, Jerome, Augustine, and Pope Gregory the Great.

Of special interest to ethicists are two writings, which deal with ethical questions, but of course, not in a purely systematic way. These are the writings of Maximos the Confessor in his *Chapters on Love,* and St. John Damascus' *Iera Parallela,* as well as his *Exposition of the Orthodox Faith.*

During the second period, the ninth through the sixteenth centuries, we have little creative work. Anthologies predominate, ethical teachings of the Fathers of the first period are gleaned from the earlier writings. A few did concern themselves with ethical questions, such as Theodore the Studite, Theodore of Edessa, Philotheos of Sinai, Gregory of Sinai, Neketas Stethatos, and Nicon the Monk. In the West we have the so-called *Sententiae* or "opinions" of Peter of Lombard, and especially books II and III of the *Summa Theologica* of Thomas Aquinas. All of these combine doctrinal and ethical teaching and provide this pattern for a contemporary Orthodox ethic.

Of importance for this period are the writings of the Byzantine Mystics, such as Symeon Metaphrastes, Symeon the New Theologian, Nicholas Kabasilas and Gregory Palamas and his supporters. These men emphasized the mystical traditon of Dionysios Areopagite. In the West, we also have some mystical writers during this period. It seems to be the major characteristic of ethical writings during this time. Mystical tendencies sought to revitalize, so to speak, the formalistic and legalistic tendencies which had overtaken much of Christian life during this period, in which the mere following of rules and the mere attendance at services were divorced from personal involvement and a personal relationship with God. The ethic of the mystical theologians can be characterized as an ascetic ethic, which is cultivated primarily in the monastic life.

Of importance for ethics during this period are the *Exomologetaria* or *Libri Penitentalia,* prepared for Father Confessors to deal with various sins, especially as to how they are to be "canonized." We have several examples of this kind of book in the East. One of the earliest was written by John Scholasticus in 578. They are of interest to us because they, together with the canons, develop quantifications of ethical judgments. For instance, in the canons of the Church we have some which speak to the question of Christians who have committed murder. A murderer is "canonized," that is, is prohibited from receiving Holy Communion for a period of three years if the act was involuntary,[11] ten years if voluntary,[12] and other such distinctions, such as parricide which is canonized for thirty years. In these judgments we see considerations of motive, proximity of relationship, external circumstances, etc. Thus, the penitential books and the canons of the Church have significance for us as we seek to make ethical judgments. Of course from the point of view of Orthodox Christian ethics we cannot say that the canons are of absolute significance for our discourse.

In both the East and the West, the use of the canons and the penitential books led to the wide spread casuistic approach to Christian ethics. This "Periptosiologia" (*Periptosis* in Greek is the "circumstance" and thus the application of the moral rule to specific cases), tended to become legalistic in the West, attempting to foresee and deal with and categorize every act and every motive which might be conceived. Appropriate punishments and penances were devised in every situation and case and applied in a rather rigid and legalistic manner. Scholars feel that the penitential books which were written for Father Confessors were used differently in the East. They are thought rather to be exercises in theology, rather than actually enforced in practice.

The third period of the history of Christian Ethics is from the sixteenth century to the twentieth century. Here we will turn our attention primarily to Greek Orthodox writers. During this modern period, we have developing in all of Christianity a new theological discipline, the discipline of Christian ethics which distinguishes itself from both dogmatics on the one hand and pastoral theology on the other. It becomes what might be termed an independent discipline of Theology. Roman Catholics and Protestants led in this development, though among Greek Orthodox writers we have the development of a small bibliography, usually not of significant value until the appearance of several writers who will be discussed below in reference to the present situation.[13]

All of the early 19th century works were short, popular catechetical writings. They make no claims to serious and detailed treatment of ethical issues nor with the major theoretical questions of Christian ethics. We need to turn to the more serious authors of the early 20th century in our concern to determine the present status of Greek Orthodox ethics.

It is possible to address the scholarly attempts to write Orthodox ethics by theologians of the Greek Orthodox Church in a manner which would permit us to categorize these men and their writings in three basic groups or schools. When we explore the development of the discipline of Christian ethics in Greek Orthodoxy we may discern three basic "schools" or approaches to ethics within Greek Orthodoxy: the Athenian, the Constantinopolitan and the Thessalonian.

Mid-nineteenth century treatments of Christian ethics reflected a strong Western, even Kantian influence especially in the direction of emphasizing moral law. The first "school" of Christian ethics, the Athenian School, developed primarily by Chrestos Androutsos, emphasized that there is no vital difference between Christian and philosophical ethics precisely because ethics are based on human rational nature. His treatment of ethics reflects strongly the influence of philosophical Idealism. The "good" is that which is identical with the will of God. Other examples of this school adhere to this major assumption with some differences in emphasis. In general, Athenianism underscores the scientific and scholarly character of ethics, draws very little from the patristic fathers and only marginally from Scripture, prefering instead philosophical sources.

Professor John Karmiris represents a trend toward another direction in that he draws heavily from patristic sources and Scripture, attempts to separate Christian from philosophical ethics and holds Christian ethics to

13

be higher. However, his fundamental assumptions are still within the Athenian position, i.e., the basic identity of philosophical and Christian Ethics.

The highly influential Basil Antoniades is the strongest representative of the Constantinopolitan School. His approach is Christocentric. Ignoring philosophical definitions, Antoniades concentrates on the personal relationship to Christ and its effects on actions. Thus, "the discipline of Christian ethics is primarily an examination of the life appropriate to this redeemed of man."[14] His sources are primarily biblical and patristic, especially the Greek and Latin Fathers of the first four centuries, including extensive reference to Augustine. Thus, his focus is on the Golden Age of the Patristic Period rather than on philosophy on the one hand, or the late Byzantine period on the other. He also draws upon Thomas Aquinas rather extensively. Other examples of this general evangelical and Christ-centered approach may be documented. The ethics of this approach are not uniquely Orthodox.

The third approach, the Thessalonian School, is apophatic in character and draws from later Byzantine sources. Contributors are Panagiotes Chrestou, Theodore Zeses, John Romanides, Christos Giannaras and George Mantzarides, especially the latter two. Giannaras' emphasis is existential and personalistic. He teaches that humanity exists in a state of separation from God and is less than human. As one relates as an individual to Christ (personhood) and as a part of the Kingdom of God in Society (Church), one becomes more fully human or what he or she is meant to be—in the image of God. George Mantzarides also represents Thessalonianism but differs in that he seeks to rely on more purely Orthodox sources rather than communicating the tradition through existential categories. Philosophy is impotent in achieving salvation. Good is a reality not an idea. It is a personal existence, ". . . true nature is the reality of man and world transfigured in the likeness of God, understood within a trinitarian relational framework."[15]

In this work on Orthodox Christian ethics we seek to incorporate all that is valuable in the three "schools" and hope to avoid the failures and shortcomings of each and a one-sided dependence on any of them. From the Athenian School we will emphasize through these pages the claim to universal validity of Orthodox Christian ethics. Orthodox Christianity speaks the truth of the whole human condition in both its doctrine and ethics and may not be perceived as a merely sectarian ethic applicable only to members of the Orthodox Church. It is catholic and universal in application. From the Constantinopolitan School we will draw a strong rootage for our ethics in the scriptures and in the Cappadocian tradition. It is a tradition which is clearly Christ-centered, but realistically in touch with the world, its institutions, its problems, its reality. The Constantinopolitan School is a school of order, pattern and structure. From the Thessalonian School we will seek to draw upon the mystical tradition and monastic resources of Orthodoxy. The Apophatic approach to Theology, and the inherent trinitarianism and personalistic perspective

14

strongly embodied in this school, will give unique perspectives to our treatment of Orthodox ethics.[16]

Again, in conclusion, it must be re-emphasized that as we approach the specifics of ethical theoretical problems and concrete issues we will be in constant touch with Orthodox doctrine especially the doctrines of man and the Holy Trinity.

[1] Panagiotes Demetropoulos, *Orthodox Christian Ethics*, Athens, Greece, 1970, p. 1.

[2] *Ibid.*

[3] Chrestos Androutsos, *Systema Ethikes*, Athens: Basil Regopoulos Publishing House, 2nd ed. 1964, p. 22.

[4] *Op. cit.*, pp. 7-15.

[5] *Ibid.*, pp. 20-26.

[6] *Ibid.*, p. 5.

[7] Zekos Rossis, *Systema Dogmatikes tis Orthodoxou Katholikes Ekklesias*, Athens: Aneste Konstantinidou Press, 1903. Vol. I. pp. 34-35.

[8] Chrestos Androutsos, *Dogmatike tis Orthodoxou Anatolikes Ekklesias*, Athens: Astor Publishing House, 2nd ed., 1956.

[9] Panagiotes Trembelas, *Dogmatike tis Orthodoxou Katholikes Ekklesias*, Athens: Zoe, 1959. Vol. I, p. 19.

[10] John Karmiris, *Christianike Ethike*, University Lectures (mimeographed) Athens: 1967, pp. 29-32.

[11] St. Basil, Canon 55.

[12] St. Basil, Canon 11.

[13] Some of these men who first wrote were: Misael Apostolides, *A Handbook on Christian Ethics*, (1849), K. A. Moschopoulos, *Introduction to Dogmatics and Ethics*, (1851), Robotou, *Christian Ethics*, (1855), Gregory Gogos, *Christian Ethics: The Duties of a Christian*, (1877), Gregory Palamas, *Orthodox Christian Ethics*, (1877), Constantine Paritses, *Handbook of Orthodox Christian Ethics*, (1889), Diomides Kyriakos, *Christian Ethics*, (1900), A. Protopapadakis, *Christian Ethics Handbook*, K. Nestorides, *Kathekontologia*, or *The Duties of Man as Christian and Citizen*, (1892), T. N. Byzantiou, *Christian Ethics Drawn from the Confessions of St. Augustine*, T. Psyscharis, *Christian Ethics: The Major Christian Duties*, (1961), M. Daskalakis, *Handbook of Christian and Social Ethics: Part Three, Christian Social Ethics*, (1934), Elias Tsakos, *The Ethical Ideal According to Christ*, (1967).

[14] *Enchriridion Kata Christon Ethikes* (Constantinople: Fazilet Press, 1927. Vol. I, pp. 24-25-.

[15] Stanley S. Harakas, "Greek Orthodox Ethics and Western Ethics," *Journal of Ecumenical Studies*, Vol. 10, No. 4, 1973, for references to works and other authors as well as for a more detailed presentation of this typology.

[16] The discipline of Orthodox Christian Ethics as taught in the seminaries of Romania seem to be in the tradition based on western manuals, and appear to be written without a focus on the unique doctrinal sources of Eastern Christian theology. As such, they are in the tradition of the Athenian school. See Alf Johansen, *Theological Study in the Rumanian Orthodox Church under Communist Rule*, London: The Faith Press, 1961, pp. 29-32. Russian Ethics, as exemplified in the texts used in the Leningrad and Moscow Academies are doctrinally based on the redemptive work of Jesus Christ and seen as a therapeutic for fallen man. This approach is very much in harmony with the Constantinopolitan school.

The ethical teaching in the Theological Academy of Sophia, as exemplified in three text books is of great interest, in that, like this work, it tends to include all three approaches, even though it be in an attenuated and divided form. *Orthodox Christian Ethics* by Metropolitan Nikodirm Xristov and Ivan Pantchovski (1955) is written in the Athenian style and closely parallels the Rumanian work. Ivan Pantchovski's *The Methodology of Ethical Theology* (1962) relates Orthodox Ethics both to theology and philosophy. Here Orthodox ethics is in dialogue with both in relationship to many contemporary currents of thought. Most significant, however, is Ivan Pantchovski's work *Introduction to Moral Theology* (1958). The first four chapters relate the essence of religion to the essence of ethics. The final two make the significant relationship between God as the source of ethics and the creation of humanity in the image and likeness of God—a first step in the approach to ethics we have characterized as Thessalonian. See Alf Johansen, *Theological Study in the Russian and Bulgarian Orthodox Churches Under Communist Rule*, op. cit., pp. 43-46.

Chapter Two

THE ORTHODOX CHRISTIAN THEOLOGICAL FOUNDATION FOR ETHICS

"Why do you ask me about what is good? None is good except one-God." *(Matthew 19:16.)*

As we begin our inquiry into the study of Orthodox Christian ethics there are several possible patterns and courses open to us. There is the course which would have us repeat and explicate the Biblical and Patristic images and affirmations as the Scriptures and Holy Tradition have recorded them. This approach to ethics makes pronouncements and articulates positions on the ethical teaching of the Orthodox Church, with persuasiveness and strong emotional appeal, but without careful theological and ethical analysis. Yet it has an important advantage; it is familiar, kerygmatic, and pastoral. It touches the heart and succeeds in obtaining commitment, devotion and obedience, speaking as it does to the human condition with love, compassion and grace. This is the voice of the Church as it speaks in sermon and teaching to the people of God, and this is the voice of the Church as it speaks for the flock to God and in His Name. In the parish, in the confessional, in the family and the marketplace, this is the language of the Church. It must never be forgotten nor substituted by any other approach.

Yet, in a study such as this, the kerygmatic, pastoral approach also has certain serious deficiencies. When the purpose is to clarify and separate out for study and scrutiny the foundational concepts and principles at the basis of Orthodox Christian ethics, then a more careful, critical and organized approach is needed. When, further, the purpose of the discipline is to assist the Church not only in clarifying its existing ethical teaching, but also to apply that teaching in new circumstances and to articulate authentic Orthodox Christian responses to previously unheard of ethical issues, such as those in the bioethical field, then the more careful, analytical, theological approach is required. On the basis of the effort to clarify Orthodox Christian ethical principles and standards, the Church will be able to expand and deepen its kerygmatic and pastoral approach.

Thus, the first choice in the doing of Orthodox Christian ethics is the decision to approach the subject matter theologically, as an organized discipline of knowledge, seeking to present a systematized description of Orthodox Christian ethics in the light of the teaching and ethos of Orthodoxy. This method requires keeping the discussion in touch with the main currents of ethical thought in our culture. Consequently, this book is a step removed from the pastoral engagement with the issues. It in fact precedes that engagement by addressing the foundational questions, the methodological issues, and substantive principles which underlie the Church's personalist concern with the life of the people of God and the life of the world in general.

Such a method, however, is not without its own dilemma. Several different major categories of approach confront anyone who begins this ethical inquiry. In the history of ethical thought, there are three general ways of approaching the subject matter. These are a) good/evil, b) right/wrong and c) fitting/unfitting or appropriate/inappropriate.

Ethical systems which are based primarily on good/evil categories form a general conception of the foundations of ethics. They often seek to identify a single basic source of principle upon which all other ethical categories and judgments depend. As these systems proceed to particularize ethical judgments, they tend to do so either by promulgating sets of ideals which persons are called upon to realize, or to focus on the kind of character which expresses through numerous virtues what the good is. The strength of this good/evil approach is that it provides an inclusive and universal standard and foundation for the ethical endeavor. It is orderly and comprehensive and, in general, speaks to the quality of life rather than to specific acts and deeds.

On the other hand, ethical approaches which are based on right/wrong categories focus on acts and deeds. This kind of ethic emphasizes the intrinsic value of the act itself. It is easy to see, then, why such an ethic will tend to emphasize specific rules and prohibitions; it will be clear-cut and specific, concrete and practical. Virtue will not consist so much in one's general character, as in doing the right thing. Right/wrong ethics tend, consequently, to be rule ethics. The strength of this approach lies in its directness, concreteness and specificity. A third group of ethical systems is based on the category of fitting and appropriate/unfitting and inappropriate. This is a common approach in traditional social groups where the idea of the "good" is not fully articulated and consciously identified, though in some way acknowledged. Concurrently, in this approach, there are many "right/wrong" prescriptions which, again are not always reasoned through and justified. An ethic of the "appropriate and fitting" has a certain aesthetic and wholistic appeal which speaks less to the mind (as does the "good/evil" ethic) and less to the will (as does the "right/wrong" ethic) but more to feelings. The ancient Greek identification of the good and the beautiful, *"kalokagathos,"* seems to be embodied in this ethic. The "appropriate and fitting" applies to attitudes as well as actions related to the foundational principles and to the circumstances in which they take place. The sense of harmony, balance

17

and inter-dependence as they relate to morality characterize this approach and provide it with its major strength.

Though these are identifiable as separate approaches to ethics, none seems to be fully adequate alone. For instance, the Bible includes examples of ethical teaching from each of these approaches. Thus, from the first, we read in both Testaments "Be ye holy for I am holy, says the Lord God."[1] In a passage such as this, the good is defined in terms of God. The right/wrong ethical approach is seen in the numerous commandments such as the Decalogue in the Old Testament. Similarly, in the New Testament it is seen in the Lord's injunctions; for example, "Judge not, that you be not judged"[2] and in St. Paul's teachings, such as "live in harmony with one another; do not be haughty, but associate with the lowly; never be conceited."[3]

The "fitting and appropriate" can be illustrated in the Old Testament from the question in the book of Job, "Is it fitting to say to a king, thou art wicked?"[4] Here, the honor and respect due to the political ruler is perceived to be a major obstacle to identifying evil acts on the king's part: hence, the dilemma. Thus, also, Jesus comments, "No one who puts his hand to the plow and looks back is fit for the Kingdom of God."[5] The Greek word for "fit" in this case is *"euthetos"* (εὔθετος) which literally means "well or appropriately placed." Other Greek words which carry this meaning are *"harmozon"* (ἁρμόζον), *"prosekon"* (προσῆκον), and *"anekon"* (ἀνῆκον). St. Paul uses the latter in the following moral instruction, "Let there be no filthiness, nor silly talk, nor levity, which are not fitting (ἀνήκοντα)."[6] Elsewhere, more positively and generally, he writes, "I am bold enough in Christ to command you to do what is required (ἐπιτάσσειν σοι τό ἀνῆκον)."[7]

Each of these approaches is more appropriate to some of the issues of Christian ethics than to others. One well-known ethicist, in speaking about the first two has commented, "Christian morality has at various times and in various societies combined elements of both types—as must any satisfactory morality."[8] It is safe to say that Orthodox Christianity combines elements of all the approaches described above. The question of the good is primary, however, because it provides ethics with its basic and sure foundation. That is why the issue of the nature of the good needs to be addressed first. It is an essentially theological issue, as the question is responded to by Eastern Orthodox Christianity. To ask, "what is the good" means that one is searching to discover if there is, in fact, a source and identifiable foundation for ethics, including right or wrong and the fitting or the inappropriate. To ask, "what is the nature of the good" is to raise the question of absolutism or relativism in ethics for the question assumes that there is an answer which can provide, in practice, a sure criterion for the moral life. There are some approaches to ethics which do not deal with such an issue—but that is because from the outset they despair of ever identifying a fundamental standard for the ethical life. Not so, Orthodox Christianity. Our first task, then, is to seek to identify the good as a foundation for the doing of ethics.

The Triune God: The Source of the Ethical Life
God and the Good

Orthodox Theology identifies the good with God. The Triune God is not only *good,* but also *the good.* This fundamental theological affirmation is the foundation of Orthodox Christian ethics.

Both Scriptures and Holy Tradition provide abundant evidence of this theological truth.

Though the Old Testament does not approach the question of the good from a systematic point of view, numerous passages in it support the view that God is not only good, but *the* good. The same is true in the New Testament. Neither Testament is by any stretch of the imagination an ethical textbook, philosophical or otherwise. But that God is the good is abundantly clear from its passages. Thus, the Old Testament teaches: "The Lord is good." Jesus' response to the inquiry of the young rich man is well known: "None is good, save one, that is God."[9]

The patristic tradition is rich with reference to the unique goodness of God. For the Fathers of the Church the *Summum Magnum* is God. Thus, Tertullian says, "God is the great Supreme, existing in eternity, unbegotten, uncreated, without beginning, without end. . . ." and he also teaches that in God, goodness is "natural and inbred," "eternal," "perpetual and unbroken" and is "stored up and kept ready in the treasures of His natural properties" and this goodness of God "underlies every first material cause."[10] Clement of Alexandria writes more specifically:

> God is confessed to be good; therefore God does good. The good, since it is good, does nothing other than to do the good. Therefore, God does all good . . . But the good is not called good because of its having virtue, just as justice is not called good because of its having virtue (for it is virtue itself), but because in itself and for itself it is good.[11]

St. John of Damascus speaks of God "Who is good and brought us out of nothing into being that we might share in His goodness." He adds: "The Deity is good and more than good, and so is His will."[12] St. Gregory of Nyssa confirms the patristic view; saying that "the most beautiful and supreme good of all is the Divinity itself."[13]

In discussing the goodness of God, Panagiotes Trembelas provides us with a series of similar affirmations by the Fathers of the Church. He writes:

> In brief, God is the supreme good. . . God is good in a fashion which is unique and appropriate to Him alone. In other words He is "the primary and main good, whose very nature is goodness," "he who is good by nature, being the source and fountain of all other goods," and unlike human beings "who easily move away from that which is good" whose goodness "compared to the goodness of God, could be thought of as evil *(poneria)*." For

"only in the Divine Trinity, which created all things does goodness exist essentially *(enyparhei ousiodos e agathotes),"* while others have it conditionally and subject to loss.[14]

But it is extremely important that we note some additional dimensions of the affirmations regarding the good which we have made. One is an apophatic concept and the other a consequence of the personal character of God. The apophatic approach to the doctrine of God in Eastern Orthodox teaching is the negative approach, affirming the inability of the creature to comprehend the reality of the uncreated God. Apophaticism notes that even our purported positive knowledge of God's being (Kataphatic Theology) tends to be negative in character, i.e., "eternal" really means "not limited by time." This negative approach is seen more obviously in such theological attributes—*in*finite, limit*less, un*searchable, *in*corruptible, *im*mortal, *im*mutable. These terms, and others like them, refer to the divine *ousia,* i.e., essence. It is precisely the divine essence which Orthodox Christian theology strongly affirms as absolutely unknowable and incomprehensible. In the words of St. John of Damascus, "God is infinite and incomprehensible: and all that is comprehensible about Him is His infinity and His incomprehensibility."

John of Damascus, however, proceeeds to point out that "all that we can affirm concerning God does not show forth God's nature, but only the qualities of His nature."[15] Later, in the history of Orthodox Theology, the concept of "qualities of His nature" would be generally referred to as the "energies" of God, that is, God's relationship with His creation, and especially His relationship with humanity.

Apophaticism and The Good

Thus, apophatically speaking, Professor George Mantzarides correctly notes that the "good must not be sought as a simple idea. . . . The good must be a reality."[16] Yet we have seen that the good is the reality whom we call God. Strictly speaking, from an apophatic point of view, God is beyond any human conception, category of thought or name devised by man. Consequently, God is also beyond the "very meaning or name of the good."[17] This understanding has led theologians and Fathers of the Church to use the word "hyperagathos"—the "goodness above goodness" to refer to the reality of Divine Goodness.

Thus, apophatic theology teaches that God is not good—in the sense that He is not good as is any other good within the created world. In the *Mystical Theology* attributed to Dionysios the Areopagite the following is said about God:

> The cause of all things, existing above all things is not without essence, nor is He lifeless, nor without reason, alogos, nor without mind, nor is He body; Yet He is not form, nor type, nor quality, nor quantity and He has no mass . . . Nor does He live, Nor is He life. Neither is He essence, nor eternity, nor time. Nor is He rational content or contact, nor knowledge, nor truth, nor

20

kingdom, nor wisdom. Nor is He one, nor unity, neither divinity nor goodness, nor is He spirit, as we know these things.''[18]

The key to interpreting this passage is the phrase ''as we know these things.'' Mantzarides notes: ''The characterization of God as good is not an attempt at definition, consequently limiting God to human rational forms but the expression of the innermost desire of man, that he comprehend God and speak concerning Him. Because we love God and we wish to know Him and to say something about Him, it is for this reason that we call Him good, etc.''[19]

We cannot know in its fullness the good which is God since the essence of God is, in itself, undefinable and incomprehensible. Yet we know the goodness of God because as human beings we have some experience of this good. This experience comes only through the energies of God. We know something of the good only inasmuch as God has revealed Himself through His actions and His activity in relationship to us, His creatures. Thus, even if the good as God is essentially beyond any human comprehension, it is comprehensible in part inasmuch as it relates through the Divine energies (activities and actions) of God to creation in general and to human beings in particular.

Our creation in the divine image is a central theological linch-pin for Orthodox Christian ethics. This central Orthodox doctrine connects the ultimate good intimately with the human moral experience.

Thus, what is methodologically required—that the good be transcendent to the human situation— is in practice made known to us by the energies of God and realized in human beings for their own sake. From this perspective, the good is both transcendent to man, yet at the same time since man is created in the image and likeness of God, it is also immanent to our human existence contemporaneously.

This also addresses the issue regarding the heteronomy and autonomy of the good. If the good were only transcendent to the empirical natural experiences of human persons, then it would come as a rule of law which was imposed from outside, i.e., heteronomy (*heteros* = other, *nomos* = law). It would rightly then be an external imposition by a more powerful being (in this case, God) upon a weaker and relatively indefensible being (in this case, humanity). There is a generally held view that for an act to be ethical it must express the will of the ethical agent. This is called ''autonomy'' in ethics. But if the good is foreign in nature, character, and demand to the ethical agent, then the good is either imposed upon him or the only virtue is to submit to the superior authority.

The Orthodox Christian view, however, identifies the good with human purpose, intent and potential. Since human beings are truly human insomuch as they become like God, the Divine good cannot be limited to human categories. Thus, the good for human beings is both transcendent and immanent, which means that the good of God is man's good; it is not heteronomous at all; it is not strange and foreign but precisely identical with what it means to be human in its fullness. In the deepest, most existential sense, human nature is "theanthroponomous," that is, in order to become fully human, we must become God-like.

Some Eastern Orthodox ethicists have sought to use certain categories to identify these varying dimensions of the good from the perspective of Orthodox Theology. Thus, in these efforts, the only *absolute good* is God Himself. The *absolute ethical ideal* is that which we are able to perceive from God's energies. Otherwise stated, the absolute ethical ideal for human beings is the will of God in accordance to which a human being must conform him or herself to achieve goodness for his or her own human fulfillment and perfection. Thus, the Scriptures admonish, "Don't let the world around you squeeze you into its own mold, but let God remold your minds from within, so that you may prove in practice that the plan of God for you is good, meets all His demands and moves (you) to the goal of true humanity."[20]

"Don't let your character be molded by the desires of your ignorant days, but be holy in every department of your lives, for the one who has called you is Himself holy."[21] An *ethical good,* consequently is anything which conforms to the will of God as expressed to us in His energies. More particularly, in matters of choice and behavior, all the ethical good which has been perceived by humanity has been embodied in various codes, precepts, counsels and philosophical systems, and these are to be understood as being within this category.

The Good as Personal

Mention of the will of God has led some speculative minds, still influenced by the hope for an objective, impersonal good which could be "abstracted," so to speak, from God to raise the question: "Is the good good in itself, or is it good because God so wills it?" The demand is for a concept of the good which is absolute and unchanging—not to be influenced by the will of another, even if that other were God Himself. A clear statement of the issue, and an adequate resolution is to be found in the ethical writings of Vasilios Antoniades, whose argument is reproduced in the following paragraphs.

In Antoniades' view on this question, the issue of the relationship of the moral good with the divine will is very similar to the issue in platonic philosophy concerning the relationship between the idea of the good, as the supreme idea, to God Himself as the supreme being and creator of all. The issue is whether the good is to be identified with God; or, to be distinguished from Him as either subject to Him or He subject to it or if they are of co-equal authority and honor; or, whether the good serves God as a pattern and example for His creative task. Thus, we also are required to treat the question of the relationship of the good to God and His will.

In the case of the good and the divine will, the question is whether the good is the same or different than the will of God, either as something derived from it and gaining its authority from it, or, as something self-contained and independent from the divine will. In this latter case the good functions as a law for God which directs His will and activities.

This last view has found some supporters in the Christian tradition led by Thomas Aquinas and among some more recent philosophers. This view holds that the good as honored and recognized by men is not good because God so wills and orders, but because the good is good in itself, having its value in itself. God approves it and commands it to men for the governance of their lives as the best for them.

On the contrary, those who follow Duns Scotus, Occam, Descartes and others, hold that the moral good has no value which is self-authenticating and independent of the will of God. Rather, for them, the good is good and is honored as such because God has so willed and ordered. In such a case, God as the Supreme Being is both able and has the authority to will otherwise and define what ought to be done and what ought not to be done as He wishes and desires.

Both of these views are one sided. Both indicate a deficient view of God's perfection and energies as we can know them. The first view sees the good as if it were some sort of constitutional document or sacred law parallel to and independent of God imposing itself upon God. The second understands the good as if it were something indifferent as to content, taking on value as far as and in so much as God desires it.

The patristic approach addresses this problem in an unforced manner in the same manner as it treats the issue of the relationship of God's freedom and omnipotence to man's freedom of the will.

Just as the freedom of God stands above any sort of force and need, yet is not irrational and arbitrary, thus the moral good which is honored as worthy of respect among men is neither thought of as good because God so arbitrarily chooses (in which case a simple change of choice could cause that which He now considers shameful and wrong and vile and evil to be considered as obligatory and to be praised as good and virtuous and respectful) nor is it something standing outside of God which imposes itself upon Him, governing His will and activity.

Rather, the moral good is what it is, because it is the will of *God,* and God wills as he wills and not otherwise because thus willing is the only possible way for God to will in accordance to His own perfection. In other words, the moral good is an expression and reflection of the very holiness and perfection of God. As such it is of absolute value, eternal validity, inalienable beauty.[22]

Consequently, God's will is an expression of His whole being. He, being goodness itself, cannot but express Himself in His energies and in His will for humanity other than as goodness. To do otherwise would in effect cause God to cease being Himself—an incoherent and self-denying syllogism! This means, in effect, that we cannot escape the conclusion that at heart the good is personal in character. A personal God alone can will the good.

But we can ask what the nature of God's will is; that is, what characterizes the energies, actions, will, demands, prohibitions, and aspiration of God as they appear to us His creatures as ethical norms? In practice what is the ethical ideal for human beings? In its broadest, yet most simple and precise identification it is this: "God is love" (1 John 4:8). Our love is based on *His* being and energies of love. "Herein is love, not that we loved God, but that He loved us, and sent His Son to be the propitiation of our sins. Beloved, if God so loved us, we also ought to love one another."[23]

Later in this study we will seek to deal with the question of the meaning of Christian Love, i.e., agape-love, especially as it is expressed in God as a pattern and example of the kind of love which humanizes human beings and makes them realize their potential to become the image and likeness of God. At this point, it is enough to point to the most direct and simple expression of that divine agape-love which manifested itself in God's redemptive love for mankind: "For God so loved the world that He gave His only begotten Son, that whosoever believes in Him will not be lost, but will have life eternal" (John 3:16). At heart, love means to willingly and freely act for the benefit of others without seeking one's own personal advantage through the act. Notice that love as we understand it here refers to the "energies" of God, not His essence. Jesus has taught the Christian what God's will is for human beings: they are to love. His command to love is all encompassing and shows that love is at the heart of the Christian understanding of the good.

> You shall love the Lord your God with all your heart, and with all your soul, and with all your mind. This is the great and first commandment. And a second is like it. You shall love your neighbor as yourself. On these two commandments depend all the law and the prophets.[24]

Thus, love for God, love for neighbor and love for self are included in the understanding of the good, which has its source, its being and its force in the good that is God Himself. Central to the concept of the good, is the way of love which has its source as an ethical norm in God and which serves to focus on the fact of the personal character of the good.

More specifically, God's love for humanity can be articulated as His will that all human beings become members of His kingdom. If love is seen primarily as an act (though not exclusively so), then for the human being, membership in God's Kingdom is an existential condition and may serve as a general statement of the good as it is related to the human condition. It refers both to the present life and to life after death. It is the framework of the human good, which in the language of the Church is called "eternal life." The concept of God's Kingdom, and our membership in it also emphasizes the communal and corporate dimension of moral life, since the casting of the human moral good in terms of the Kingdom of God is relational both in the vertical dimension (God) and the horizontal dimension (neighbor). When seen in close conjunction with the

God-given *telos* of each person to realize the potential of the image and likeness of God and to achieve Theosis, the full dimension of what we have described above as the *ethical good* is manifested for human beings. The kingdom of God is the embodiment of God's will for mankind. Its chief expressions are love for God, love for neighbor and love for self.

The personal life toward Theosis and the life of the Kingdom, however, are closely inter-related and mutually aspects of each other. The Orthodox doctrine of the Holy Trinity and the Orthodox doctrine of the Church are at the heart of this affirmation. Just as God is a Trinity—that is, a community of persons in relationship while at the same time uniquely one, the individual and personal growth toward Theosis cannot be separated from communion with persons, both divine and human. Theosis requires love for God-in-Trinity and our fellow human beings, as well. But realization of this capacity for communion with others requires personal commitment to growth in communion with God. One can be social without having personal experience of God, in some measure. And one can have personal communion with God without relationship to others, in some measure. But to have each in full measure, requires the realization of both.

Thus, an important aspect of the personal dimension of good from an Orthodox perspective is the fact that God is Trinity. The Orthodox insistence of the primacy of the Triune nature of God points to the fact that ultimate reality—God—is interpersonal relationship. Good, then, is equally interpersonal relationship. This relates not only to the realization of the image and likeness of God in persons, but also to the communal dimension of human existence, in the Kingdom. That the ultimate and supreme good is not an abstract principle, ideal, concept or impersonal "thing" is affirmed by the fact that God is above all a Trinity of Persons. Thus, the realization of the divine image within us is of necessity possible only in personal relationship with God, and, by extension, in relationship with our fellows, especially those of the "household of God."

The doctrine of the Church affirms this same dynamic. We are Christians as individuals only because of the fact that there are others whom God has set apart and constituted as His people. In the first instance, the Church is the Church because God in His grace has formed it and called it to be His bride, in communion with Him. The individual commits himself to faith in what God has done, only because the word of salvation is taught and preached and the experience of grace is mediated to him in the sacramental life in the Church. Yet if there were no individual believers who accepted and participated in the life of grace, there would be no Church either, though we can conceive of this only in a hypothetical fashion.

Thus, the Church itself is a witness, as well, to the personal character of the good, and the ethical life which is based on it.

But this is only the first statement of the good; a basic orientation and starting point. God is the absolute good. His essence as good is in fact beyond our understanding and comprehension. We know of His goodness through His energies, His actions: creation, providence, redemption in

Jesus Christ. All these are characterized by self-less love for the welfare of others. God has no need which either requires Him to love nor makes Him to love to gain something in return for Himself. Since human-kind is created in God's image and can achieve wholeness only by realizing that image, the ethical ideal for humanity is found in God, and more specifically in His will for mankind. The will of God for mankind is characterized by outgoing unselfish, other-directed benevolence— agape-love. On the individual, one-to-one basis, the ethical good for human beings is love, because God is love. In the complex, multifaceted, interpersonal, experiential plane, the will of God for all human beings is that they enter into a personal relationship of love in the Holy Trinity, the Kingdom. It is partially realized (and partially unrealized) now in the Church and in the World and we await its fulfillment in the fulfillment of the *eschaton,* the coming of the Kingdom in its fullness.

The Theological Foundations of Orthodox Christian Ethics

The explication of Orthodox Christian ethics is based upon the doctrines, beliefs, and practices of the Orthodox Christian Church. The derivative character of the Orthodox ethics however, does not arise from the confusion of an empirical "is" with a prescriptive "ought." At the heart of the Orthodox Christian ethics are doctrines held by the Church which relate the "telos" of human existence with a perception of ultimate reality which is theological in the most significant of ways. These doctrines pertain to God, Creation, Anthropology, Christology, Ecclesiology, and Eschatology. Together, they provide a "Heilsgeschichte" which expresses itself in many different ways, including expression in terms of normative discourse, i.e., ethics. Some of these are deliniated below.

The Doctrine of the Holy Trinity

As we have seen, Orthodox Theology identifies the good with God. The Triune God is not only *good* but also *the good.* This fundamental theological affirmation is the foundation of Orthodox Christian ethics. It is the distinctive mark of Orthodox Christian ethics that it takes this truth seriously and bases its theoretical and practical ethic upon it. More specifically, the Orthodox doctrine of the Holy Trinity provides the working principles of an Orthodox Christian ethic.

As noted above, "only in the Divine Trinity . . . does goodness exist essentially." The Holy Trinity is the source of our understanding of the Good. The Trinity provides us with a foundational insight to Christian ethics because the doctrine of the Trinity points to the fact that ultimate reality is not an idea, principle, force or other inanimate existence, but that ultimate reality—God—is interpersonal relationship. The interpersonal relationships of the Holy Trinity are of two kinds. The Orthodox have long insisted on the importance of the *Filioque* as a serious error in Trinitarian theology. The *Filioque* controversy is based on the Western Christian insertion of the phrase "and the Son" (Filioque), in the Nicene Creed, referring to the procession of the Holy Spirit. The Orthodox have rejected this, not only as an unwarranted innovation in the doctrine of the Holy Trinity, but also as a dangerous teaching which has the effect of depersonalizing the person of the Holy Spirit and consequently weakening the main thrust of the trinitarian emphasis on the personal inter-relatedness of the Holy Trinity. Thus, the Orthodox have tended to see in the *Filioque* a tendency to stress the unity of the nature of God at the expense of a true distinction among the persons of the Trinity.[25] Opposition to the *Filioque* points to the need for a correct view of the "structure" of the inter-personal relationship of the Trinity. There is a correct and an incorrect view of the relationship of the Father with the Son, the Father with the Holy Spirit, and the Son with the Holy Spirit. The inter-personal relationships of the persons of the Holy Trinity have a certain pattern, order, fittingness and appropriateness. For ethics, the importance of the *Filioque* controversy in Trinitarian theology points to a structured pattern for inter-personal relationships in God, and therefore for moral rules and morally fitting patterns of behavior for human beings. But we also know that the relationships of the persons of the Trinity are characterized by love: a more free, caring, supportive mutuality and sharing which goes beyond "structures." Further, we know about Divine love, from the Energies of God as expressed in Creation, Providence, and particularly in the Divine Economy of Salvation (John 3:16). We know the good inasmuch as we know God in Trinity.

The mystery of the Holy Trinity points to the relational character of the good. We are created in the image and likeness of a Trinity of Persons. Thus, ultimate truth is a community of divine persons. The ethic, then, of the Gospel which is based on *that* goodness, will not point to some merely objective, transcendent ideal, but will see the very nature of goodness as a living reality which is personal, and as a consequence, relational and communal. Chrestos Yannaras has stated it so well "God is man's ethos."

Fr. Thomas Hopko has pointed to the specifically ethical aspect of the divine ethos for humanity when he writes in another context, "What humans must do *in community* and not as isolated individuals, is to acquire and activate ever more perfectly, all of the spiritual and moral attributes of God."[26]

The Creation of Humanity in the Image and Likeness of God

Whatever pertains to human existence is related to God through the fact that human beings are created in the image and in the likeness of God. Human purpose and human nature (human ontology) are related to the fundamental fact of our human *telos* to become "like God." This also points to an additional reason why attempts to base the ethical good on nature or empirical human nature are bound to fail: because of sin (original and committed) we are not yet fully human. Therefore, attempts to argue from what man is to what man ought to be are bound to fail as starting from an inadequate base.

God as the good, is however, intimately related to human good because human beings are destined to become "like God," to realize the "image and likeness of God" and to achieve "Theosis" *in order to achieve and realize their own humanity!*

The Orthodox Christian view, relates the good with human purpose, intent and *telos*. Since human beings are truly human insomuch as they become like God, the Divine good and human good are identifiable, at least in part (since, as we have seen, the Divine good cannot be limited to human categories). Thus, the good for human beings is both transcendent and immanent, which means that the good of God is man's good; it is not heteronomous to him; it is theonomous—not strange and foreign but precisely identified with what it means to be human in its fullness.

Thus the creation of the human race in the divine image means that our *telos,* the goal which embodies our proper humanity is directly commensurate with our beginning in God. Lossky thus notes that "Man created 'in the image' is the person capable of manifesting God in the extent to which his nature allows itself to be penetrated by divine grace."[27] We are

> to become as much as is humanly possible like God. This happens when our thoughts are like His thoughts, our desires coincide with His desires, our will chooses as He chooses, our actions are reflections of His actions. In other words, we become like God when our ways of thinking, feeling, acting and doing are united with God's ways of doing things. We fulfill our purpose as human beings when we are thus united with God.[28]

Theosis

A prominent aspect of Orthodox Christian theological anthropology is the teaching concerning "Theosis" or deification. It is in fact another way of stating the doctrine of man's creation in the image and likeness of God. While "image" emphasizes the ontological beginning of man, "theosis" emphasizes the ontological end or *telos* of man. Both say that "true man," "true humanity," "perfect and complete humanity," is realized only in relationship with the divine prototype of humanness. This is closely related with the doctrine of the perfection of human nature. In the Sermon on the Mount, which will be discussed below, Jesus teaches, "Be ye perfect as your Father in heaven is perfect." That injunction—as impossible as it sounds—is an imperative which includes within it the implication that human perfection is intimately and fundamentally related to divine perfection. When the doctrine of the image, especially in its patristic form, and the doctrine of Theosis are related to this call for perfection, they form a coherent whole.

Incarnation

The doctrine of the Incarnation is critically important for ethics, especially as it deals with those issues connected with the "this-worldly" concerns of the Christian ethos. The Incarnation for Christians in the

Orthodox tradition is one of the major and crucial doctrines of the faith. The doctrine of the Incarnation teaches that the second person in the Holy Trinity assumed a full human nature in time and thus became "theanthropos," a fully human and fully divine being. The implications of this for Orthodox Christian ethics may be perceived on at least two levels. The first deals with the question of human purpose about which we have spoken before. Human purpose and *telos* are to be achieved in Theosis and yet Theosis is not understood to be a totally "spiritual" phenomenon. The doctrine of Theosis refers to the sanctification of the body as well as of the spirit. Thus, the whole sacramental structure of the Orthodox Church uses material things to be vehicles for spiritual realities. The sanctification of the human beings includes the sanctification of the physical as well as the spiritual. The implications for this in ethics are very important, since it prohibits a dualism that would separate the spiritual dimension of life from the physical dimensions. This unity of the psychosomatic reality of man is reflected in the unity of the divine and of the human in the incarnate Christ. It is brought together in its fullness eschatologically speaking, in the doctrine of the Resurrection. The Orthodox Church goes beyond a mere understanding of human existence which speaks of "the eternal soul" because the doctrine of the Resurrection emphasizes that eternal life is a gift from God which begins in this life and which is to be fully realized in the future when the body will be resurrected and will partake of the Kingdom eternally as a result of divine grace, as a gift. However, it is also meant that full and complete human existence is not located just in the spirit but in the spirit and the body together. Therefore, the teachings of the Church and of the Christian life refer not only to spirit but to spirit and body; not only to the future, but to the present, as well.

A second level of approach regarding this brings it much closer to ethical concerns specifically. The Church has always made a rough distinction between *soma* and *sarx* (σῶμα - σἀρξ). *Soma* has been used as a rather neutral word which refers to the physical body as created. Since it is the result of God's creative activity, it is good. *Sarx* has been used generally to refer to the inordinate and sinful passions of body. The first is praised, the second is condemned. The first is a given which is part of our humanity and also part of our eternal destiny as resurrected beings. The second is distortion of our humanity and this should be battled against. In this sense both *soma* and *sarx* have important places in Orthodox ethical thought. *Sarx* is the object of spiritual struggle and the Christian is called upon to battle what is referred to in Scripture and in the Fathers as σαρκικόν φρόνημα or "the mind of flesh." On the other hand, *soma* becomes an important determinate in Orthodox Christian ethics especially in reference to those issues which refer to medical concerns and the myriad of social issues which deal with human material needs. Thus, the unity of body and spirit form a basis for ethical thinking and ethical decision making for the Orthodox.

The Kingdom of God

The Kingdom of God, or the Kingdom of Heaven is a chief image in the Orthodox ethic. The Kingdom is given by the redeeming acts of the Father, in the work of Jesus Christ and through the power of the Holy Spirit. In the first instance it comes into being and we share in it by Divine, not human initiative.

God establishes His Kingdom and invites humanity to respond by accepting what He has done. The sign of acceptance is Baptism. Baptism creates a new condition for man. It creates a certain discontinuity between the old condition of man and the new condition of man in the Kingdom. The images of "new cloth," "new wine," and "new heaven and a new earth," "new commandment," "new name," and "new song" in the Scriptures refer to this discontinuity. "He said, behold, I make all things new." [29]

The Kingdom is concurrently both personal and corporate. It is personal in that the Christian has direct and personal—we would say today, experiential and existential—relationships of a new order both with God and with man. The interpersonal existence of the Holy Trinity calls for personal relationship and communion with God in order that the person may achieve his or her own fulfillment. The Trinity also is a paradigm of human society. What is seen as inadequate in the first case is atomistic individualism. What is seen as inadequate in the second case is mere institutionalism and formal structure. The Kingdom points to what it means to be authentically human, both as person and as community, within our individuality and our corporateness. The chief embodiment of the Kingdom in this world is the Church, but it is not limited to the Church.

Ethically speaking, membership in the Kingdom of God demands certain kinds of behavior. Image, Theosis, Perfection, Life in the Spirit, conformity to the will of God and other such characteristics of the Kingdom, refer, in ethical perspective, to both overt acts and internal dispositions. An example of the first is St. Paul's clear reference to certain types of overt behavior which simply do not conform to the idea of the Kingdom of God (1 Cor. 6:9-10). An example of internal dispositions is Jesus' reference to little children as a paradigm for the Christian life. The *new* dimension of the Christian ethic is in the dispositions, and these are directly related to the new condition and restored relationship with God caused by His gracious acts for the redemption and sanctification of mankind, i.e., the establishment of His Kingdom.

The Kingdom idea, so inseparably bound with the Church is also the major theme and foundation for the Church's social ethic. If the fullness of salvation of the individual person can take place only within the framework of the Church, then in so much as the Church seeks the transformation of the world imbuing it as much as possible with its own ethos, it exercises its responsibility for the transformation of the world from what is not the Kingdom, to what is the Kingdom. As long as the forces, powers, institutions and life of the world do not reflect the Kingdom, they are in need of transformation in as much as they are able, "taking every thought captive, to obey Christ."

Sacramental Life and Eschatology

The realization of the Kingdom is both present and future. We are, in one sense, already in the Kingdom, already saved, already united with God. We experience and manifest the Kingdom in this life primarily in the life of the Church and most vividly in the Sacramental life. The Eucharist, especially, is the experience of the Kingdom in which we manifest the unique relationship of God and His people. The intimate, profound experience of the reception of the very Body and Blood of the Incarnate God makes the Kingdom a reality for us *now*. But, it is also true that the Kingdom is not fully here. It is to come in power and in glory. Here, yet not here. This truth also has its influence on ethics. Our acts and our dispositions manifest the Kingdom. When we become in spirit and in behavior *"douloi Kyriou,"* i.e., servants of the Lord, submitting our lives to Him; when we obey His will; when we are not "conformed to this world, but . . . transformed by the renewal of (our) mind;"[30] when we are in some measure "conformed to the image of (God's) Son,"[31] the Christian ethic is realized. Yet, it is in fact not fully realized, nor will it be ever fully perfected in this life. Only with the Second Coming, the Resurrection, the Final Judgment and our entrance into the Eternal Kingdom will sin be fully vanquished and will the good be fully triumphant. Clement of Alexandria thus writes: "Perfection lies ahead, in the resurrection of the faithful, but it consists in obtaining the promise already given to us."[32]

It lesser measure Christians are able to direct that which is not Church, i.e., the "world" in the direction of the Kingdom. As long as the world is not responsive to the whole message of salvation it will not, indeed, it cannot respond in any measure of fullness to the Christian ethic. Yet, it need not be devoid of aspects of it either. The Church needs to reach out to it, to heal it where it can, to convert it where it can, and to influence its structures where it can. This is the "Liturgy after the Liturgy" of which we speak. As Father Bria says

> . . . the Liturgy is not a self-centered service and action, but is service for the building up of the one Body of Christ within the economy of salvation which is for all people of all ages. . . There is a double movement in the Liturgy: on the one hand, the assembling of the people of God to perform the memorial of death and resurrection of our Lord "until He comes again." It also manifests and realizes the process by which "the *Cosmos* is becoming the ecclesia."[33]

Growth

Between the new condition proclaimed in Baptism and its full realization in the Kingdom there is a process of moral and spiritual growth in which we are involved. We are not called simply to accept a forensic

31

justification, but to change, to develop, to grow, to mature, to be transformed and transfigured. We are, in Saint Paul's phrase, to grow "from glory to glory." St. Paul articulated this powerfully in the fourth chapter of the Epistle to the Ephesians. In large part, growth into our "new nature" is ethical in character—"true righteousness and holiness." St. Gregory of Nyssa writes characteristically:

> Though it may not be possible completely to attain the ultimate and sovereign good, it is most desirable for those who are wise to have at least a share in it. We should then make every effort not to fall short utterly of the perfection that is possible for us, and try to come as close to it and possess as much of it as possible. For it may be that human perfection consists precisely in this constant growth in the good.[34]

Salvation of the World

This movement is a movement of salvation *from* brokenness and sin *for* wholeness and fullness of life. Like all of these faith affirmations salvation is incapable of full definition, but it certainly includes victory over death, sin and evil, it is the first fruit and foretaste of the general resurrection, it is the liberation of captive nature from the forces of the devil and the restoration of the creation in Christ. As such, it has direct impact upon the life of those who directly share in the saving work of Christ through the commitment of faith, the sharing in the death and resurrection of Christ in the Sacraments and the life which seeks conformity to his will, as we have seen above in the discussion on the Orthodox doctrine of Theosis. But salvation is offered for all of mankind — and even when it is not accepted consciously by the world the Holy Spirit works in it and sustains it while every Christian of necessity must involve him or her self in the task of the world's salvation. Dumitru Staniloae in his remarkable article "the Orthodox Doctrine of Salvation and its implications from Christian Diakonia in the world" shows the connection

> Everything which Christ did — his incarnation, his teaching, his life of obedience to the Father and loving service of us in the trials of our earthly lives, his sacrifice in the world — all these things emphasize . . . the value of human life on earth. No path toward eschatological perfection exists which bypasses life on earth and the struggles which accompany that life. Every single aspect of eternal happiness is promised by the Lord as the result of certain ways of living and acting in this life, as the fruit of certain seeds sown and nurtured in the fields of this world.

> . . . .

> The Christian has a duty, therefore to fight on behalf of justice because the presence of injustice can appear to provide a justification for eternal death, while the removal of injustice deprives eternal death of any such justification. One who

32

struggles to end injustice follows in the path of Christ who was the first to use justice as a means to deprive death of its justification.[35]

Thus, salvation for the world grants a cosmic and catholic perspective to the ethic of Eastern Christianity; growth gives the dynamic dimension to Orthodox Christian ethics; eschatology explains its limitations, yet at the same time gives it hope and power; the Kingdom gives it the dimension of communality in the Church, rescuing it from individualism; the Incarnation redeems it from shallow "spiritualisms"; Theosis gives it its content and its telos; the image and likeness give it its beginning and foundation; and the Triune God determines it forever as objective, relational, and interpersonal, at once.

A Synopsis of Orthodox Christian Ethics

The teachings just sketched out, provide the essential framework for Orthodox Christian ethics. The reciprocal relationships of God and true human life provide for an "ought" based not on the "facts" of a fallen humanity, but on a "telos" or goal toward which we are called to strive in order to achieve our authentic humanity. Within this framework, it is possible to sketch out a theory of ethics which in brief can be summarized as follows; forming a synopsis of the theoretical concerns of Orthodox Christian ethics.

The Good

The affirmation that the Triune God is the supreme good does not exclude, but in fact includes aspects of all other understandings of the good developed by ethicists throughout history. Thus the good as in-born, as law, as pleasure, as evolution, as perfection, as value, as existential and as love are included in a complete perception of the good. In its anthropology, the Orthodox Church perceives humanity as endowed with a number of in-born ethical capabilities. There is a particular Orthodox understanding of the natural moral law which is reflected in some law theories of ethics; further, the Orthodox ethic recognizes an important place to rules as indicated above in the discussion of the relations of the persons of the Holy Trinity. Pleasure, both as the effect of a good conscience and physical and psychological enjoyment are the outcomes, in part of a properly lived human life. Even evolutionary theories have a resonance in Orthodox ethics since they recall the Orthodox emphasis on development and growth toward the fulfillment of the divine image. Perfectionist theories are represented in the Orthodox ethic by the imperative to achieve Theosis, thus providing the critical *telos* needed by all perfectionist views, as well as providing the rationale for the ethical struggle, i.e., the process of *ascesis,* i.e., spiritual exercise which contributes on the human side, to the achievement of that goal. Value ethics are given concrete and objective content by the Orthodox ethics and become a serviceable means for "doing ethics." Though there is much to be concerned with by a wholesale adoption of an existential understanding of ethics, the relational character of Orthodox ethics is in part expressive of the existential perspective in ethics. While the "absolute" place given to love by many Protestant ethicists cannot be accepted (only God is absolute good), love *(agape-theion eros)* is central to Orthodox ethics. All of these ethical theories find their place and status within the larger framework which comes from the identification of the good with God alone. Each of the non-revelatory views shares in a portion of the truth of that which St. Maximos the Confessor calls "the good by nature" *(physei agathon)*, i.e., God.

Evil and Sin

The problem of evil for all Christian believers is well known. The Orthodox ethic identifies evil in an ultimate sense as "meonic" *(meon = non-being)* since evil is perceived as not having a reality of its own but as being the "absence of the good." Empirically, of course, evil is experienced in a multitude of forms. As sin, it is the willful rejection on the part of created beings of the fitting and appropriate relationship between God and themselves. The Orthodox hold that evil is a result of the choice of free creatures to reject communion and proper relationship with God. The result is that as persons we are in fact "less than human" not fully living up to our potential and that as societies our human structures are of necessity distorted and incomplete. Even physical nature shares in this distorted and fallen condition. Such a view might lead to a general moral pessimism which would require a position akin to the Protestant *sola gratia* emphasis. In Orthodoxy, however, it does not. The description of the human condition as outlined above speaks of the distortion and darkening of the image of God and the loss of the potential to achieve the human destiny of Theosis, but it does not speak of the obliteration of human moral capabilities. Much of the image remains. Thus, human beings are still able to do good in measure. Consequently, Orthodox ethics is neither overly optimistic nor overly pessimistic considering the moral capacities of unredeemed humanity.

Human Moral Capacities

Part of the divine image in man is understood to be the universal existence of human moral capacities, a phenomenon so commonly assumed, that its importance for ethics is often overlooked. Humanity is inextricably bound up with the ethical imperative. Some Orthodox ethicists thus speak of a "Moral Drive" by which they understand the universal human practice of seeing events and situations in ethical categories. They also speak of an "Ethical Sense," by which they mean the universal human penchant for making moral judgments. These both are perceived to be a part of the basic and essential meaning of our humanity as the image of God. Arising from these is the ability of human beings to be ethically self-determining. The favorite patristic term for this capability is *"autexousion."* Usually the Fathers reserve the term *"eleutheria,"* i.e., freedom, for the condition reached in Theosis where there is no conflict or struggle in acting in a fully human, divine-like fashion.

The Conscience

The conscience is another of the human moral capacities. It is not perceived as a faculty, but rather as the moral expression of the functioning human personality depending on the Moral Drive and Sense, the autexousion, the intellect, emotions, and human relationships and experience. That which holds them all together and identifies the conscience is the sense of moral obligation. The imperative character of the conscience is its distinguishing characteristic. It is, of course, subject to development or deforming pressures. Thus it needs to be cultivated and educated, trained and developed. Thus, conscience is central to the moral life. It is through the conscience that the "objective" good which is God is appropriated "subjectively" by the individual. The good as made known by God in creation and in revelation is, so to speak, external to us until there is a personal meeting, an inner experience, which brings the objective good into direct, intimate, responsible, felt and personal relationship with ourselves. As we have seen, the Orthodox ethic affirms that the human good is intimately related with the divine "objective" good because humanity is not only created in the image of God (the only absolute good) but also designed to become—ought to become—"like God" thereby achieving and realizing true and full humanity, i.e., Theosis. The conscience, thus, is the chief locus for the moral life. In a sense, the conscience may be understood as a process or ability to discern, to distinguish, to evaluate and to judge moral realities, as distinguished from the standards of what is in fact good, or what is in fact evil. It is the human capacity to function ethically. We now turn to the content of ethics—its specific normative imperatives.

The Natural Moral Law

Those who hold that the content of the conscience is wholly learned would deny that there is any pan-human standard of ethics. Orthodox ethics, in contradistinction, affirms that part of the "given" of our common humanity, the "image of God" in all human beings includes a basic perception of what is good and what is evil in content. The name usually applied to the specific inborn content of our ethical nature is the natural moral law. For the Greek Fathers, the natural law is universal and expressed in numerous ways throughout human culture. However, they also hold that "an excellent expression" of it is to be found in the Decalogue. For the Fathers, the Decalogue is a "low level" ethic whose main purpose is the basic maintenance of human society. Thus, none of its prescriptions may be reversed and made into a moral imperative without doing serious damage to any society and in effect destroying it. Thus, it has an empirical, universal application and effect which justifies its designation as a *natural* moral law. However, it is "low level" and provides only for a minimal social existence. Societies and religions have developed, in consequence, various other kinds of ethical systems, values, injunctions, ideals, etc. That which the Christian Church teaches is of divine origin and most fully appropriate to the human condition as created in the image and likeness of God. It may be described as the "Evangelical Ethic."

The Evangelical Ethic

The Evangelical ethic must be seen as within the context of the whole "Christian story" of humanity's creation in the divine image and the destiny to achieve Theosis. This context points to the need for the saving work of Jesus Christ, participation in the Divine Energies through Faith and the Sacramental life, by membership in the Body of Christ, the Church, communion with God and the eschatological hope. The content of the Evangelical ethic focuses, on one hand, on the teaching of Christ which demands a coherence between inner dispositions, intents, and motives and external, overt behavior. On the other hand, the content of the Evangelical ethic focuses on agape-love. Agape-love is perceived as concern and action for the welfare of the neighbor, for his or her benefit, without self-serving interests. God expressed this agape-love especially in the Incarnation of the Son of God for the salvation of humanity. The caring, mutual relationship of fatherly love, described in the Gospels and experienced by Christians is reciprocated and communion in its fullest is achieved in love for God. The Fathers did not hesitate to call this *theion eros,* and to characterize it as the highest spiritual and moral activity of which human beings are capable, thereby participating in the divine life of the Holy Trinity. The Sermon on the Mount is perceived to be an "excellent expression" of the Evangelical ethic and it is seen in Eastern Orthodox Christianity as a program for life and not as an ideal assigned to convict us of sin or as an image of the Kingdom, unrealizable in this life.

The Evangelical ethic, as a reflection of man's true life in the Trinity points both to modes of behavior which are seen as almost universal and objectively describable fitting and appropriate ways of behavior for the life leading to Theosis, and to a freer and more experiential interpersonal relationship and communion. The first of these reflects the modes of relationship in the Trinity as expressed in the filioque controversy—these "relatively absolute" standards of behavior are the rules of ethics, as embodied in the canon law, the ethical teaching and the penitential discipline of the Church. The second is Christian practice of "agape" for the neighbor and "theion eros" for God. The conscience focuses the content of the ethic upon the empirical reality of our lives, by which our moral being is formed, our ethical decision-making is guided and in acting ethically, concretely and specifically.

Being Moral: Conformed to the Image of God

The road to Theosis demands a transfiguration and transformation of life. On the personal level this refers to the development of character so that it embodies in our "being" a God-like mode of existence. The cultivation of the virtues and elimination of the vices is seen in the light of "Christian being." The virtues and vices are perceived as modes of that being, the fitting (in the case of the virtues) or the inappropriate (in the

36

case of the vices) modes of being are respectively characterized as virtues and vices. There is a tradition in Eastern Christianity calling for the Imitation of Christ and the Saints, not of course, in a slavish external way, but in a deep inner fashion which speaks to the issue of "being" rather than doing. The focus on "being" i.e., character, virtues, and the imitation of Christ and the Saints, does not exclude the possibility or requirement to respond to the radical demands of the Gospel. Yet these radical demands are perceived to be occasional incidents in a stable, developing ethos of life which characterizes the Christian's life as a whole.

Ethical Decision-Making

In order to make appropriate decisions which are fitting and appropriate to the Orthodox Christian ethic, there is need to develop the virtue of "diakrisis" or discernment. The purpose of every ethical judgment is to discern, in the words of Maximos the Confessor, "what is bad or what is good, according to which participation or non-participation in the divine life is naturally produced." Included in consideration in the process of decision-making are the following:

The Right (law and rules)
Consequences (good and evil results)
Intent (what is to be accomplished)
Motives (that which moves us to action)
Means (appropriate methods)
Values and Disvalues (dimensions of being)
The Perception of the Situation.
Decision-making as an Ecclesial-Corporate process.

The "Politeia of Theosis"

The end of all ethical theory and teaching must be action, expressed in a life or a community existence which struggles against evil and for the doing of the good. Evil is overcome when the passions are attacked and battled against. This is accomplished on the personal level through repentance, conversion, the uprooting of the causes of evil in us, primarily self love. More concretely, evil is overcome by a complex set of practices known as *askesis* in the Orthodox tradition, including prayer, worship, fasting, attentiveness, struggle *(agona),* temperance, confession of sins, participation in the Sacramental life and particularly the Eucharist.

All of these help also in the positive doing of the good. Moreover, love for God of necessity implies living in communion with Him and expressing that communion in a life marked, in the words of St. Basil, by a "painstaking zeal to do the will of God." The Fathers speak of the need to make a pledge *(orkos)* to this effect, to struggle to accomplish it *(askesis* and *agona),* to do it in an ecclesial context and with a full understanding that it takes place only in cooperation with the Divine Energies. The Orthodox doctrine of the "synergy" of the human will with divine grace, places great emphasis on the divine component.

The doing of the good, finally is never a private, solitary experience. It always has a communal, ecclesial, and social dimension to it. This means not only that the individual is aided in the doing of the good by the communal experience, but that ethics also has as its proper object the social life lived in common by Christians as well as the life lived in society by all people. Thus there is an ethic of Church life, of the family, of concern for nature, of the state, of the socio-economic sphere and of all manner of social concerns. It is the task of the remainder of this volume to develop and explicate this synopsis of the foundations of Orthodox Christian ethics.[36]

[1] 1 Peter 1:16, Leviticus 11:44-45.

[2] Matthew 7:1.

[3] Romans 12:16.

[4] Job 34:18.

[5] Luke 9:62.

[6] Ephesians 5:4.

[7] Philemon 8.

[8] R. M. Hare, "Right and Wrong" in John Macquarrie, *Dictionary of Christian Ethics,* Philadelphia: The Westminster Press, 1967, p. 299.

[9] I Chronicles, 16:34, 2 Chronicles 5:13, Psalms 100:5, 106:1, 107:1, 118:1, 29, 135:3, 136:1, 145:9, Jeremiah 33:11, Lamentations 3:25, Nahum 1:7. Luke 18:19, see also Matthew 19:17.

[10] *Tertullian, Adv. Marcionem* I, III and I, XXII.

[11] *Instructor* I, VIII.

[12] John of Damascus *An Exact Exposition of the Orthodox Faith,* Book I, Chapters iv, ix, xii. *Nicene and Post-Nicene Fathers,* Grand Rapids, Mich.: Wm. B. Eerdmans Publishing Co., 1955, Volume IX.

[13] Gregory of Nyssa *Peri toy Biov Moyseos.* Migne PG 44, 301.

[14] Gregory of Nyssa, *Peri Tou Biou Tou Moyseos Migne* P G 44, 301. Didymos as quoted by Ecumenios on Acts 11:24, *Migne* P G 123, 353. *Origen Peri Archon* I, 6, 2. Trembelas *Dogmatike Tis Orthodoxou Katholikes Ekklesias,* Athens: "ZOE," 1959, Vol. 1, p. 222 and footnote 54.

[15] *An Exact Exposition of the Orthodox Faith,* Book I, Ch. iv. *Ibid.,* Chapter xii, p. 14 and Chapter xxii, p. 94.

[16] *Christianike Ethike, University Notes,* Thessalonike: Pournara, 1971, p. 33.

[17] *Ibid.,* p. 37.

[18] *Migne,* P G 3, 1040-1048.

[19] *Op. cit.*

[20] Romans 12:2. J. B. Phillips translation, *The New Testament in Modern English.*

[21] 1 Peter 1:14. *Ibid.*

[22] Vasileios Antoniades, *A Handbook of Ethics According to Christ.* Vol. 1. Constantinople: Fazilet Press, 1927, pp. 102-104. For a contemporary, philosophical treatment of the same subject see, Burton F. Porter, *Deity and Morality: With Regard to the Naturalistic Fallacy,* London: George Allen and Unwin Ltd., 1968, especially Chapter VIII, "'God is Good': An Analytic."

[23] 1 John 4:10-11. *American Revised Standard New Testament* translation.

[24] Matthew 22:37-40 RSV.

[25] There is a vast literature on this subject. A few representative authors are: Vladimir Lossky, *The Mystical Theology of the Eastern Church,* London: James Clarke and Co., 1957, Chapter 3. Jaroslov Pelikan, *The Spirit of Eastern Christendom,* Vol. 2 of *The Christian Tradition: A History of the Development of Doctrine,* Chicago: The

University of Chicago Press, 1974, Chapter 4. John Meyendorff, *Byzantine Theology: Historical Trends and Doctrinal Themes,* New York: Fordham University Press, 1974, Chapter 13, 14. Michael H. Fahey and John Meyendorff, *Trinitarian Theology: East and West,* Brookline, Mass.: Holy Cross Orthodox Press, 1977.

[26] "On the Male Character of the Christian Priesthood," *St. Vladimir's Theological Quarterly,* 19:3, 1975, p. 153.

[27] Vladimir Lossky, *In the Image and Likeness of God,* Ed. by John H. Erickson and Thomas E. Bird. Tuckahoe, N.Y.: St. Vladimir's Seminary Press, 1974, p. 139.

[28] Stanley S. Harakas, *Living the Liturgy,* Minneapolis: Light and Life Publishing Co., 1974, p. 13.

[29] Revelation 21:5.

[30] Romans 12:2.

[31] Romans 8:29.

[32] *Paidagogos,* Book I, 28.

[33] *Martyria/Mission: The Witness of the Orthodox Churches Today.* Geneva: WCC Commission on World Mission and Evangelism, 1980, p. 68.

[34] 2 Corinthians 3:18. *The Life of Moses,* PMG 44, 300B-3010, tr. in Jean Danielou & Herbert Musurillo, *From Glory to Glory,* New York: Scribners, 1961, p. 81.

[35] Dumitru Staniloae, *Theology and The Church,* Crestwood, N.Y.: St. Vladimir's Seminary Press. 1980, p. 207, 211.

[36] Portions of this chapter originally appeared in the *Journal of Ecumenical Studies.* Fall 1978, Vol. 15, No. 4, pp. 614-646.

Chapter Three
DIMENSIONS OF THE GOOD

"If then, there is some relationship of the teachings (Christian and philosophical) to each other, the knowledge of them is useful to us. If, on the other hand, there is no such relationship, then the understanding of the differences which comes from their comparison, is of no small value, since it will show which is the better."

(*St. Basil,* Exhortation to Youth as to How They Shall Best Profit by the Writings of Pagan Authors)

The attempt to identify the source and basic foundation for the ethical life is not restricted to the Church. All major religions have ethical teachings. In addition, as we have seen, the human effort to understand existence, to interpret life's meaning, i.e., philosophical inquiry, has also produced efforts at making sense of the ethical experience of life.

Just as all persons, nations, societies, classes and special groups have their own experiences of the moral, so also have they made efforts to clarify and understand that moral experience. Thus, in history there have been many different efforts to understand and explicate the meaning of the moral life on the basis of human experience. We refer to these non-revelatory efforts of the philosophical understanding and interpretation of the general human, moral experience as "philosophical ethics." There is, however, no single identifiable and exclusive philosophical ethic: there are many different attempts by essentially non-revelatory means to identify the good, the right and the appropriate/fitting source of the ethical dimension of human existence.

The question, then, cannot be avoided by anyone who wishes to fully comprehend the Orthodox Christian understanding of the ethics, and particularly the Orthodox Christian understanding of the good: How do these basically non-revelatory approaches to ethics[1] relate to the Orthodox Christian ethic?

The issue is not merely one of ethical curiosity. It is one aspect of the larger theological question of the relationship of the Christian Faith with the world. The Orthodox doctrines of Revelation, Creation, Human Nature, Original Sin, Redemption in Jesus Christ, and Theosis, all acknowledge to human existence a certain capacity for ethical reflection and moral responsibility which can be exercised in a non-revelatory fashion. The classic biblical expression of this reality is to be found in St. Paul's letter to the Romans:

> When Gentiles who have not the law do by nature what the law requires, they are a law unto themselves, even though they do not have the law. They show that what the law requires is written on their hearts, while their conscience also bears witness . . .[2]

This passage is of great importance for Orthodox Christian ethics and will be dealt with extensively in the chapter below on Natural Law. Suffice it to note that St. Paul here is referring to the ethical dimensions of life which are uninformed by divine revelation, as recorded in Scripture and experienced in the Tradition of Faith. Subsequently, in the history of the Church there were a number of efforts to understand the place of such non-revelatory understandings of the ethical life. One of the most influential and well-known is Justin Martyr's doctrine of the "spermatic logos." This teaching is important "because it forms a bridge between pagan philosophy and Christianity."

> . . . Justin teaches, that although the Divine Logos appeared in his fullness only in Christ, 'a seed of the Logos' was scattered among the whole of mankind long before Christ . . .[3]

For Justin, those who are not Christians, may be seen as sharers in the Logos if they have in fact taught and lived in accordance with the teaching and life of the Logos—Christ. Justin writes:

> For whatever either law-givers or philosophers uttered well, they elaborated by finding and contemplating some part of the Logos. But since they did not know the entire Logos, which is Christ, they often contradicted themselves . . .[4]

To survey the scene of philosophical ethics today from the perspective of Orthodox Christian ethics, is to find vindication of that statement. Many philosophical approaches to ethical theory exist today, side by side. They all[5] begin with a non-revelatory acknowledgement of the existence of a sphere of life which is uniquely moral and treated in a discipline appropriate to it, the philosophical discipline of ethics. There is a history of the non-revelatory attempt to deal with this reality of human nature and human society. And in that history, Orthodox Christian ethics will be able to discern much that is to be rejected as an inadequate view of the good. But what philosophers and others have given central importance to in their views of the good, may in fact, however, have a significant, though not central, place in Orthodox Christian ethics. We are to be guided here by Justin Martyr's famous dictum "Whatever all men have uttered aright is the property of us Christians."[6]

We turn first to the affirmations of *intuitive ethics*. In the elaboration of ethical theory in the western world a view was developed, primarily in England, which emphasized the source of the good as inborn in human nature. Writers such as Lord Schaftesbury (1671-1731), Francis Hutcheson

(1694-1746) and Joseph Butler (1692-1752) understood a certain innate human ability to perceive the good, as the primary data of ethics. Each of these ethicists felt that people knew intuitively what was right and wrong by some measure of introspection. Their emphases, indeed, were different. One held that moral right and wrong is ascertained by the reason or intellect, or a "reflected sense." Another opposed this view by holding that the insights of moral values are more instinctual, and insightful, rather than a rational process. The most well known form of this view, however, was articulated by Bishop Butler. Butler's main emphasis was on the conscience, which he perceived to be a critical and cognitive ability to pass judgment on motives and intentions, as well as a power which determines actions. It is less a reasoning process than an immediate and direct awareness of what is right and wrong.

Generally speaking, inborn or intuitive ethical theories focus on the direct insight into the moral nature of things rather than on rational reflection and the use of discursive reason. This is what is central to their view.

When we examine this ethical theory from an Orthodox Christian point of view, we note that this is a far from adequate ethical theory. First, it is not a helpful theory for determining the origin of the good, since empirically, people's intuitions about the good oftentimes differ radically. Further, it is impossible to pinpoint the line dividing what is inborn from what is learned, since in our experience what is inborn or intuitive is always found in conjunction with experience, instruction and learning, as well as with our rational ability. Further, from a strictly Eastern Orthodox perspective, the human nature which is the source of this intuition, is a fallen human nature, distorted by being in the condition of original sin, as well as by the developed passions. How can the good be known with clarity by intuition when it is drawn from a distorted and fallen human nature? For these reasons, this theory cannot be accepted as an adequate central and foundational explanation of the good.

Yet, in the intuitive theory of ethics there seems to be a seed of truth, as well. For, in spite of our fallenness and the haziness of the intuitions themselves, it does appear that there is something in human nature which is consistently and universally apprehensive of moral relationships. This reality is taken into account by Orthodox Christian ethics on the basis of the Orthodox Christian anthropological doctrine which understands the creation of human beings as being in the image and the likeness of God. Traditionally, this has been understood to mean some perception of the good "naturally" by human beings. To want to "be good;" to avoid condemnation as an "evil person" is an elementary human experience. In subsequent chapters, under the heading of "Human Moral Capabilities" we will discuss concepts formulated by modern Greek Orthodox ethicians which point to an inner moral capacity in human beings which coincides with the major thrust of the intuitive school of ethics; that as human beings we have certain inborn moral potentialities. The technical terms used by Greek Orthodox authors to describe these inborn, moral capacities are

42

"The Ethical Drive," "The Ethical Sense," "The Conscience" and "The Autexousion" (self-determination). Thus, there is a certain affinity between Eastern Orthodox concepts of the human being as a creature made in the image and likeness of God, and the reality described by intuitive ethical theories. This general ethical approach to the question of the good is not rejected; it is incorporated into the larger concept of the good which identifies the good with God. The same pattern of incorporation into the larger scheme and pattern holds true with other non-revelatory identifications of the good.

The *good as law* is an important and highly influential ethical theory. Distinguished from positive, or enacted law, and descriptive, or scientific law, moral law is normative, i.e., it commands on the basis of presumed objective moral criteria which are discovered to exist in the nature of things. Moral Law theories take several forms. One is the "Divine Command" theory recently described and supported by Janine Marie Idziak.[7] In this view, the good is what God commands. It does not particularly matter what it is that God commands; it is sufficient and central that God commands it and this creates the obligation. The objection to this view is quite obvious. It is an overly legalistic view, which seems to permit a potentially capricious God to order opposite things as the good or right at different times. If it be countered that God only orders that which is good, then the true source of the good would not be the command of God, but what it was to which God Himself conformed His own will. That would require us to go beyond the divine command to some other source of the good. Consequently, it is not an adequate theory of the good for ethics.

The Natural Law Theory of the good seeks to overcome such criticism. This theory holds that there is, in fact, a morality built into the nature of things. This view of morality is very widely held and is found in many diverse cultures. Far Eastern religions, such as Hinduism and Taoism have elements of natural law teachings, for example. Ancient Greek philosophers such as Plato and Aristotle articulated rational views of the Natural Law. For Aristotle, Natural Law is "reason unaffected by desire," and that it was fully independent of enacted laws. He further taught that the natural law was permanent and changeless. However, it was the Roman Stoics who developed natural law into a central ethical teaching. Cicero's definition is a classic expression of this view.

True law is right reason conformable to nature, universal, unchangeable, eternal, whose commands urge us to duty, and whose prohibitions restrain us from evil. Whether it enjoins or forbids, the good respect its injunctions, and the wicked treat them with indifference. This law cannot be contradicted by any other law, and is not liable to derogation or abrogation. Neither the senate nor the people can give us any dispensation for not obeying this universal law of justice. It needs no other expositor and interpreter than our own conscience. It is not one thing at Rome, and another in Athens; one thing today, and another

43

tomorrow; but in all times and nations this universal law must forever reign, eternal and imperishable. It is the sovereign master and emperor of all beings. God Himself is the author, its promulgator, its endorser. And he who does not obey it, flies from himself, and does violence to the very nature of man. And by so doing, he will endure the severest penalties even if he avoids the other evils which are usually accounted punishments. [8]

This strong rationalistic approach to the natural law was adopted and given a central emphasis in western, scholastic ethical systems. Thus, for Thomas of Aquinas, reason and law are seen to be inseparable and ethics takes on a character of rational discovery of the law and deduction from it. For Thomas, reason is the source of morality; the source of reason is the mind of God; the law then is the eternal law of God in the mind of God. Though it is in God's mind, God cannot and does not change it in any way. He conforms to it Himself.

There are two major criticisms of this view. If there is a law, which in truth is natural to all persons, then there would be a universally recognized content to the law. However, the rationalist approach, in fact, does not supply such a universally recognized and acknowledged rationally discovered and defined moral law. Secondly, because of its insistence in identifying the natural moral law with reason it has serious effects on Theology. It tended to introduce a certain dualism or diarchy into ethics: the good as a rational principle on the one hand, and God as the good on the other. In the end, God is presented as conforming Himself to an abstract rational principle; a view which does violence to the Christian understanding of a sovereign and free God.

One way of resolving such a dilemma, is to accept the rational principle whole heartedly without concern for its consequences on Theology. Such was the theoretically secularist view of Emmanuel Kant. Kant sought to formulate the natural law in a purely formal affirmation: "there is nothing in the world or out of it that can be called good without qualification except a good will." Kant defined a good will as one which willed in accordance with rational principles and that whatever is willed be willed for its own sake, and not for its consequences. He sought to cast the moral law in purely formal (contentless) imperatives such as these maxims.

Act only on that maxim which you can at the same time will to become universal law.

Treat others as an end, never as a mere means.

This expression of the natural moral law as a formal rational and exceptionless principle, described as the "categorical imperative," however, has been criticized. For example, the phrase "you can will," may mean "you can will logically" or it may mean "you can will after you take into consideration the consequences." In the first case, logical relations are the good, a questionable assertion because they are contentless (as in a syllogism "A is to B as C is to D") and may be used to serve any number of conflicting values or premises. In the second, if "you can will," implies the consideration of consequences, the formal character of the definition is lost.

In and of themselves, these views as understandings of the good are seen to be deficient. Yet, Orthodox theological ethics is able to recognize some important and necessary elements in natural law theories. Particularly appreciated in the natural law tradition of ethics is the search for an objective basis for ethical judgment; for the association between the principles of the good and what it means to be a human being and to live humanly; for the claim to universality and the effort to relate the good to God in a significant way. Though we are not able to accept any of the various forms of the good as law theories, the concept of law is not excluded from the Orthodox Christian understanding of ethics. As we shall see in a subsequent chapter, there is a distinctive patristic and scriptural understanding of the natural moral law. Further, much of the will of God has been articulated to us in Scripture, in the writings of the Fathers and in the Church's Canons, in the form of commandments, rules and laws. That the law is not central to Eastern Orthodox Christianity is a widely known fact. But it is not true that the existence of the law is eliminated from the Orthodox way of life or from its ethics. Nor does the law have to be conceived as an imposition upon human nature, for from our discussion of the autonomy and heteronomy of the good, it is expressed in the will of God. For example, the book of Hebrews quotes with approval and with application to the Christian, the words of the Prophet Jeremiah[9] "This is the covenant that I will make with them after those days, says the Lord: I will put my laws on their hearts, and write them on their minds."[10] The inter-relatedness of the commandments of God and love as an ethical expression of the good is strikingly emphasized by Christ Himself who is quoted as saying: "He who has my commandments and keeps them, he it is who loves me; and he who loves me will be loved by my Father, and I will love him and manifest myself to him."[11]

One of the most wide-spread approaches to the good is the view which identifies it with one or another form of *pleasure or happiness*. In the popular mind, it is widely accepted without careful understanding.

In addition, many theorists have sought to identify the good with pleasure. The simplest of these theories is Ethical Hedonism. Ethical Hedonism teaches that pleasure is the only quality because of which an experience is good or valuable. It says that whatever actions a person does, they are good only inasmuch as they provide him or her with pleasurable experiences. Therefore, the determinant is not the motive or the intention, but the consequences alone. If one performs an act for the purpose of obtaining pleasure, but in fact does not experience pleasure, it is not good. Usually, this basic theory of the good as pleasure emphasizes the idea of *immediate* pleasure and the avoidance of *immediate* pain. In this view, it is obvious that evil is by definition pain and suffering.

The basic criticism of this ethical view is that it is self-destructive. This is the case because the immediate seeking out of pleasure—that is, the pleasure of the moment—usually destroys the possibility of continuing that search for pleasure. In addition, there are some theoretical criticisms of the theory, in that it is difficult to measure pleasure. How does a person distinguish between pleasures which may potentially be experienced at the same time? If you must choose between pleasures, you need some criterion of measurement which will permit you to know which will be the greater pleasure. Since there is no known objective standard or criterion of pleasure, the moral duty of ethical hedonism to maximize pleasure is incapable of fulfillment. Further, intuitively, people do not usually see it as a *duty* to seek their own pleasure.

But if everyone did this, it would become self-destructive. It would quickly lead to a situation of chaos in which everyone's opportunity for personal pleasure would be destroyed. Further, not all pleasures can be defined in terms of the immediate experience of the pleasure. This fact has led to another theory of the good as pleasure, which assumes a slightly larger perspective.

A more sophisticated view of the good as pleasure is the theory of Egoistic Ethical Hedonism. This view does not call for the seeking after immediate physical pleasure, but sets the "personal happiness" of the individual as its goal. "Personal happiness" is defined as the "good." The emphasis in this theory is on the well-being of the self, the individual. All arguments opposed to the pleasure principle seen above would also apply in reference to this view. However, we must add that this view ignores the intimate relation of community to personal happiness. It is a denial of society and community, and everything good which can and does come from the relationship of persons which are found in every social group. In practice, it leads to a selfish a-moralism. The present day theory which embodies this view and has been given widespread exposure is the so-called "Playboy Philosophy." Because of these rather serious criticisms, and even more broadly based hedonistic theory of the ethical good has been developed.

Utilitarianism, or "Social Happiness" theories hold that the objective, or material end of good conduct is "the greatest happiness for the greatest number." This theory has been widely taught in England and the United States. The writers who have supported this theory are Jeremy Bentham, James Mill and John Stuart Mill. There is significance in the fact that the description of the system and the emphasis in the system moves from "pleasure" to "happiness" to "utility," so as to make it appear more acceptable. In this it has been successful.

Utilitarianism has wide acceptance. It is used very often in social policy arguments in politics. Many laws of the nation and state are formulated on the basis of a utilitarian rationale.

In criticism of this view, it can be first noted that John Stuart Mill, in his book *Utilitarianism,* argues from what people *do* do to what people *ought* to do. Thus he says, people *are* concerned about their happiness; therefore, people *ought* to be concerned about their happiness. The distinction between descriptive language and normative language is blurred by this kind of argumentation. That the argument is not valid is evident, for by substituting "happiness" with another term such as "telling falsehoods" we could argue fallaciously that "People tell falsehoods; therefore people ought to tell falsehood." Secondly, we observe that people do not always act on the exclusive motive of pleasure. This view is also subject to the same criticisms of the less complex forms of hedonism, in that there can be no superior pleasure, because the good, in this view, is only pleasure itself. Thus, there is no criterion to distinguish between kinds or qualities of pleasure. Further, this theory can be criticized because it seems to equate individually maximized pleasure with social good. But that does not necessarily follow. Because a small percentage of the population enjoy many luxuries does not mean that society is better off for it. Individual pleasures do not necessarily translate themselves into general happiness.

Further, in spite of the efforts of some proponents of this view, such as Jeremy Bentham, who have attempted to develop a "calculus of pleasure," seeking to apply various criteria with the goal of measuring the magnitude of differing pleasures, it is generally agreed that it is next to impossible to critically compare pleasures and to determine in any objective way their rank in value. An additional criticism of Utilitarianism is that we have no real principle of distribution in it. By what measure should the greatest number of people receive the pleasure or happiness? If the criterion of distribution was to be described, then this would subject pleasure and happiness to that criterion. This would mean that pleasure and happiness would not be the ultimate criterion of the good, but that principle of distribution would be the criterion of the good. For instance, if it were argued that "absolute equality" was the criterion of distribution of pleasures, *it* would be the ultimate good or at least superior to pleasure. From the Orthodox perspective it is possible to understand pleasure within the framework of the good as we have identified it. It is true that "the pleasures of this life" (Parable of the Sower) may choke and finally kill the good growth of the spiritual life and that many of us are "lovers of pleasure, more than lovers of God."[12] Yet, it is also true that the good person is reputed to also be a happy person. Ethics recognizes many pleasures in life as fitting and appropriate to living in God's image and likeness. Surely, pleasure is not our goal, but it accompanies many of our morally appropriate and fitting actions. God has so created mankind that pleasure is associated with many and varied acts of obedience to His will: the moderate and temperate pleasures which attach themselves to food, to creative work, to chaste marital relations and to friendships, are examples of appropriate pleasure. Even more is the joy the Christian experiences in relationship to God. As the Psalmist put it: "let all those that put their trust in thee rejoice: let them ever shout for joy, because thou defendest them: let them also that love thy name be joyful in thee."[13] And on the mystical plane, the pleasure *(hedone)* of our relationship with God is widely praised by the Fathers of the Church. In one of his passages defining love, St. Maximos the Confessor describes it as "the unfailing pleasure *(adiaptotos hedone)* and inseparable union of those who with longing partake in that which is good by nature *(physei agathon)*'' which of course, is God alone.[14]

Thus, the utilitarian motto, if understood within the Orthodox Christian world-view and its understanding of love with special reference to the will of God that ''all persons coming into the world, not perish but have life eternal'' in His Kingdom, finds a place in the over-all Christian ethic. Further, there is much possible good in this theory in the light of the Christian concern for philanthropy, economic and social justice and in the Social Ethic of Eastern Orthodox Christianity.

According to theories of Personal *Perfection* ''each human being ought to develop his own potentials to the most perfect possible level.'' In this ethical system the good is whatever contributes to the perfection of the individual; the ultimate good is the achievement and fulfillment of this perfection in the individual. At the heart of personal perfectionist ethical theories is the conviction that there is some inborn quality or capacity in human beings which through human effort and direction ought to be fulfilled and perfected. However, this emphasis raises serious questions about the adequacy of this view. Either the specific potential must be identified or one must choose among many potentials. However, if one human potential is identified as the good which is to be brought to perfection, then in fact, it is no longer a perfectionist theory of the good, but simply an ethical command to do the good, which is otherwise defined. For example, if it were deteremined that of all our human potentials, the intellect was the most noble and worthy of perfection, the intellect or mind or gnosis will have been identified as the good. The process of the perfection of this good then is incidental and not central to its identification. ''Intellect'' would be the good, not the process of achievement.

But, it appears that we are born with many undeveloped potentials. The same person often has many talents and abilities and not just one. The question is raised then, which ought to be developed? If one responds, ''All talents and potentials should be perfected,'' this becomes practically impossible, since neither the time nor the resources are available to each of us. If a choice must be made, of the many talents a person may have, the issues of a criterion arises, which is a mortal blow to the theory. As a result, some concept of human perfection is usually imposed from the outside, or introduced into the perfectionist system. Most often, in practice it has been the intellectualistic-gnostic views mentioned above. Perfectionist theories also tend to be individualistic in character. They are subject to the same criticism as the hedonistic views. In order to avoid these criticisms, universalist, general, catholic or social perfectionist theories expand perfectionism beyond the sphere of the individual to the social and historical whole. The good is ''catholic progress leading to universal perfection.'' The bearer of this good, consequently is not the individual but the totality of the human race. The philosopher George Hegel (1770-1831) propounded a theory of the dialectical progress of mankind, expressed in the formula of "Thesis-Antithesis-Synthesis" according to which the all-inclusiveness of the synthesis is considered to be ethically as well as historically and metaphysically superior. Thus the good is seen to be the perfection of the whole of society and mankind.

However, this view is also subject to the criticisms which are directed toward personal or individual perfectionism. Mainly that the concept of progress toward perfection, whether individual or social, implies a telos or goal. But once this is defined *it* becomes the good and not merely the process itself.

We can summarize Orthodox objections to all perfectionist views in the following six points. First, these theories tend to absolutize relatively unimportant activities by seeing them all as "contributing to the growth" of the society or the individual toward perfection. Secondly, these views tend to completely ignore the formal (intent and motive) dimensions of the good. Thirdly, the point made above concerning the need for identification of perfection itself is to be noted: what Demetropoulos calls the "inspecificity of progress." Further, the place of those who cannot contribute to progress, such as the aged, the weak, the ignorant, the feeble, the sick, the feeble-minded lose ethical value in such a system. The implications of such a theory for such persons, are fearsome indeed. A further point which follows from such a view is the observation that in fact, for perfectionist ethics, what is important is not an act of will, but the natural capabilities of the ethical agent — a questionable foundation for ethics. Finally, from an empirical point of view we might well doubt that the moral life of individuals and societies of the "civilized nations" is higher than that of less advanced cultures, i.e., destructiveness of weapons in war, etc.

Perfectionism as a theory has one major fault: it is unable to satisfactorily identify the nature of perfection itself. In Orthodox Christian ethics, the nature of the perfect is identified: it is God Himself who is the perfect good. That is why the perfectionist teaching of Christ and his Apostles is the fitting fulfillment of this philosophical view. "You, therefore, must be perfect, as your heavenly Father is perfect," Jesus instructed.[15] The thrust of Orthodox theological anthropology, in seeking to lead human beings toward the fulfillment of the image of God in their lives, to achieve Theosis, is the embodiment of a perfectionist ethic. In Orthodoxy, however, it avoids the legalism which characterizes sectarian perfectionism, because with John, it takes seriously the relationship of love and perfection: "God is love; and he that dwelleth in love dwelleth in God and God in him. Herein is our love made perfect, that we may have boldness in the day of judgment: because as he is, so are we in this world"[16] and "Beloved, if God so loved us, we also ought to love one another . . . ; if we love one another, God abides in us and his love is perfected in us."[17] The perfectionist pattern is not unrelated to Orthodox Ethics — but it receives content only from the Orthodox central affirmation that God is the good.

49

In 1859 Charles Darwin published his revolutionary study, *The Origin of the Species,* in which he propounded a theory of *evolution,* including the evolution of man. The major postulates of his view were the principles of natural selection and the survival of the species.

This theory and its many different interpretations and understandings has been attacked by many religious people, especially those who tend to understand Scripture in literalistic terms. In the Orthodox Christian world, such literalistic approaches to the question still exist. Yet, parallel with them are more reasoned and empirical understandings, which seek to relate the "facts" upon which evolutionary theory is based, and the "interpretations" which are always made from a particular metaphysical position. Panagiotes Trembelas, in a series of articles first published in the Greek periodical, *Aktines,* and subsequently published as part of his *Apologetical Studies,* has taken a careful and critical look at the phenomenon of evolution. After carefully evaluating the evidence, this Orthodox theologian concludes that there is no question that an evolutionary process is at work. However, he rejects all interpretations which would undermine a spiritual interpretation of human development. He holds that it is possible to include some forms of evolutionary theory within the Orthodox Christian theological framework.[18]

The reverent attitude counselled by Professor Trembelas has not characterized all those who have taken evolutionary theory seriously. It was not long after Darwin, that a number of persons began to explicate the philosophical consequences of evolutionary theory, including many who sought to develop ethical theory on the basis of evolutionary concepts. Common to all of these views is the idea that conduct at a later stage in history, is, by necessity, more evolved conduct and therefore "good" and "right." The inadequacy, however, of identifying the good with anything that is chronologically later, is evident. Thus, most proponents of evolution as the ethical good maintain that as a matter of fact, later or more developed conduct is better than that which precedes it, without however, holding that chronological development is the good in itself. More important is the fact that Darwin's theories connect survival with good conduct. Thus, in practice, evolutionists hold that what prolongs or assists life to develop is good.

The first theorist to develop an ethic on the basis of evolution was Herbert Spencer (1820-1903). Spencer saw life as a continual play between internal and external factors, and conduct as the adjustment of actions to specific ends. Good conduct is relatively more evolved. The proper adjustment of acts to ends prolongs and increases life. Good life is pleasant. Rules leading to good and bad behavior obtain their authority from punishment and reward (extinction or survival). Specific moral rules change to fit the circumstances of a given society; obedience to them leads to success, disobedience leads to failure. In Spencer's society, (the period of the Industrial Revolution) the ethically approved conduct fits the factory and merchandising system of the time. Persons are free to choose their own advantage provided they do not infringe on the rights of others.

Thus, in this "evolutionary" theory we see several factors at work: Utilitarianism (social hedonism), Victorian *Laissez Faire* economics, and biological evolution. This theory is found to be inadequate for several reasons. Though we can agree that life is good, is it not possible to speak of a good life which is short and a long life which is bad? Further, this theory does not provide an explanation which would require the individual to act in a way which would further development (evolution) since it speaks only of the present society in which a person lives. In addition, it should be noted that the concept of progress is useless without a goal toward which a person is to move. Spencer provides three goals, prolongation of life, increase (complexity and "abundance") of life and pleasure. With these, he not only departs from a purely evolutionary theory of the good, but he provides no guidance or criterion for choosing among three alternative goals when they conflict, as they must.

Three other writers have sought to ground the concept of the good in evolutionary processes. They are Lloyd Morgan, LeCompte du Nouy and Pierre Teilhard de Chardin. Lloyd Morgan[19] developed a theory of "Emergent Evolution" according to which he saw a step by step development of life from non-life, mind from living matter and, now in process, ideal free moral conduct from determined conduct. Though his views were criticized as being in themselves mechanical and determined, this pattern of thinking was taken over by others.

LeCompte du Nouy, a winner of a Nobel Prize in biology, articulated his ethical views in the book, *Human Destiny*.[20] He holds that the physical dimensions of human evolution have now ceased because man adjusts his environment (culture, civilization, technology) to fit him as he is. Evolution is now moral and spiritual. On these presuppositions he develops a "telefinalist hypothesis of evolution" which sees man's end in remarkably Christian terms. He felt that the evolutionary process was directed ever onward and upward by a "Will" which manifests itself through evolution. Its goal is the realization of morally perfect beings, completely liberated from human passions, such as egotism, greed, the lust for power, etc. Thus, "anything which opposes this evolution in the moral and spiritual realm, anything which tends to bring about a regression toward the animal, to replace man under the dictature of the body is contrary to the directing Will and represents absolute Evil. On the contrary, anything which tends to deepen the chasm between man and beast, anything which tends to make man evolve spiritually is Good."[21] In du Nuoy's view, the contribution of man to his own evolution depends on his use of his own freedom.

The philosophical consequences of this approach are that—at least in theory—the whole human race is united in the effort to achieve the proposed spiritualized future, evolutionary goal. However, it also tends to separate and disassociate the body from the human spirit or soul. On the human and social level, each person is enjoined to realize within himself the ideal of all humanity, and consequently, evil is within us, since each has absolute freedom to either conform or not conform to the directing "Will" of evolutionary process.

There is an obvious attraction to this view for the Christian, providing, as it does, a scientific setting for some surprisingly Christian-like values. Especially for the Orthodox, the emphasis on will and the ideas of development and growth have some appeal. Yet closer attention to the theory leads to an evaluation of it as basically rationalist: there is no place in it for forgiving and saving divine grace, and no need for the person or work of Jesus Christ. Like other evolutionary theories of the good it tends to shift its major emphasis in development. It is not cohesive as a theory.

Pierre Teilhard de Chardin, a Jesuit priest who was also an anthropologist of world renown wrote three books on human evolution: *The Phenomenon of Man* (1955, French edition), *The Appearance of Man* (1956, French edition) and *The Future of Man* (1959, French edition). All these books were acclaimed upon their publication in English translation. The most significant for our study is *The Future of Man.*[22]

As an evolutionist, de Chardin sees a progressive development in the Cosmos, leading to an ultimate goal.

In a chapter entitled, "From the Pre-Human to the Ultra-Human" de Chardin develops his views on the future of man:

> . . . the human multitude is moving as time passes not towards any slackening but rather towards a superstate of psychic tension. Which means that it is not any sluggishness of the spirit that is ahead of us, but on the contrary, an eventual critical point of collective reflection. Not a gradual darkening, but a sudden blaze of brilliance, an explosion in which thought, carried to the extreme, is volitized upon itself . . .[23]

This ultimate achievement of man is what de Chardin calls "Christogenesis." He writes: "The unique business of the world is the physical incorporation of the faithful in Christ, who is of God. This major task is pursued with the *rigour and harmony of a natural process of evolution* . . ."[24]

In spite of this, the will of man must cooperate with evolutionary processes; this then qualifies his view to be included in a survey of evolutionary ethical theories. "No evolutionary mechanism can have any power over a cosmic matter if it is entirely passive, still less if it is opposed to it." Should mankind fail to cooperate "the psychic mechanism of evolution would come to a stop . . . shattered." Ultimately the evolutionary goal is Christogenesis, a "sort of trans-humanity at the ultimate heart of things."[25]

The Orthodox Christian, with the doctrine of Theosis in mind, cannot help but be moved by such projections. Yet upon attention, certain flaws appear in this Christian-Scientific synthesis. Primarily, we emphasize the Christian truth that Christ is a Christ of history; many have achieved that which de Chardin only projects as the end point of a long evolutionary process. Christ's redeeming work is available now, not only in ages to come. Again, the evolutionary process is first presented as central, but then it is transformed by the introduction of a new element; in this case, Christ. The first and main criticism of all evolutionary approaches to ethics, and especially regarding the concept of the good, is the formal observation that "development," "progress," "process" and other such terms are in fact without meaning until a goal is posited *toward which* the development or progress moves. However, once this goal is posited, it becomes the real criterion of the good, and not development, progress or process.

Another observation is based on the fact that a strict understanding of most evolutionary theories implies a mechanistic process. It is a problem, as we have seen, to these theorists to combine the mechanistic, inevitable movement of evolution with the freedom of action implied in any ethical theory. In Christian doctrine, it is God who is leading humanity toward its ultimate fulfillment, and not a mechanical process. It would appear that when human freedom is introduced into an evolutionary ethical theory, its distinctive character of an *evolutionary theory* is removed, or severely compromised.

Further, these theories have a very high estimation of human progress and development. They are characterized by the "progress mentality" of early capitalism. Recent events seem to indicate that this optimism concerning human development is not so easily justified. The energy crisis, the ecological crisis, the population boom, the sharpening of economic disparities, terrorism, high-jackings, increased political instability, etc., tend to discount predictions of an evenly and progressively achieved better future. From a Christian point of view, evolutionary theories tend to underplay and even discount the power of sin and evil. A tendency which leads us to question the adequacy of evolutionary ethical theories.

The dynamic form of perfectionism in ethical theory is evolutionary ethics. From an Orthodox Christian point of view, this mode of thought has a certain appeal, since it emphasizes growth, development and a teleological perspective. We have seen the inadequacies of this approach. Yet, that each Christian is not yet perfected, not yet fully the image of God, has not yet achieved Theosis and is in the process of *askesis* in the achievement of that goal, does have ethical affinity with evolutionary ethical views. St. Paul, in making a personal confession that he has not yet achieved perfection, emphasizes the process of dynamic growth with which Eastern Orthodox Christian ethics has much affinity:

> Not that I have already obtained this or am already perfect; but I press on to make it my own, because Christ Jesus has made me his own; . . . but one thing I do, forgetting what lies behind and straining forward to what lies ahead, I press on toward the goal for the prize of the upward call of God in Christ Jesus. Let those of us who are mature be thus minded. . .[26]

For St. Paul, each has received gifts of varying nature "for building up the body of Christ" and he continues in this same dynamic, evolving, growth toward the divine image, a mode of thought so characteristic of evolutionary ethical theories. He then points forward: "until we all attain to the unity of the faith and of the knowledge of the Son of God, to mature manhood, to the measure of the stature of the fullness of Christ, so that we may no longer be children . . . Rather, speaking the truth in love, we are to grow up in every way into him who is the head, into Christ."[27]

Some ethicists seek to develop the idea of the good around the concept of *value*. Simply defined, value is "a good thing" whether it be an internal disposition, or an act, or an object or an end. Evangelos Theodorou, Frankena and others distinguish between the moral and non-moral sense of value. Theodorou says, for instance, that a value is "everything which from a certain perspective (material, intellectual, social, asethetic, etc.) satisfies us because it responds to certain needs, inclinations, prejudices, or tendencies of man."[28]

However, we can distinguish between values which are desired by people to satisfy their wants and those ethical values which would be "goods" which *ought* to be desired or realized by human beings in general and by mankind as a whole. A more careful approach to moral value, however, would identify moral values as "ends," i.e., as experiences, attitudes, consequences and/or goals which *ought* to be realized. This then would be either a consequence ethic, if it were concerned with relatively proximate values, or a teleological ethic if it were concerned with distant goals.

Some ethicians, and most value theorists, tend to see value in subjective, naturalistic terms, however. Value, for these theorists, is subjective in that what is valued is determined by the ethical agent either in terms of admiration or satisfaction. In the first case, what is valued by the subjective ethical agent is deemed praiseworthy. This may be a subjective ethic or may claim to discover value within the action or object, which it praises, admires, and presents as morally obligatory. In the case in which value is an object of satisfaction of desires, it is clear that we are dealing with an essentially subjective ethic. In fact, much of modern value theory is of this second type.

It is clear that a purely subjective value theory of the good would also be relativistic. It is this theory which, in large part, informs much of contemporary sociological, anthropological and psychological teaching. It makes no claim at identifying the ultimate criterion of the good. As a consequence much of value theory is inadequate for our inquiry.

Yet, "value-language" can still be helpful to us. If it be supposed that there is an objective good which was independent of any other thing, we could call it the *Supreme,* or *Absolute Value.* Other values might be sufficient in themselves, needing no other factor outside of themselves to define their goodness. Such values would be *"intrinsic* values."

Some ethicians have sought to give examples of intrinsic values. Sidgwick held, for instance, that pleasure was an intrinsic value. G. E.

Moore taught that in fact intrinsic values are complex in structure and are to be found rather in "organic wholes," such as family and nation. Some values are important and classified as such not because of themselves, but because they lead to other values. These are called *instrumental values*. Money may be considered an instrumental value, since as paper and metal it is of little intrinsic worth: but as a means of exchange it is instrumental for the obtaining of values which may be good in themselves. Further, of use to ethical thinking is the concept of the *hierarchy of values*. It is clear, upon the slightest reflection, that we rank our various experiences, attitudes, consequences and/or goals as being of greater or lesser importance. The famous passage of St. Paul does this, for example: "Now there remains faith, hope and love. But the greatest of these is love." Whenever we must make a choice between several alternatives, we may unconsciously rank the possible courses of action on a hierarchy of values from higher to lower, thus helping us make a decision. It is easier to do this when we think of various alternatives in terms of what we consider *worthy* ends, consequences, experiences, motives or intents.

Those who discuss value as the ethical good often seek to comprehend it intuitively as that which is morally fitting and which carries a sense of moral obligation. Thus values may be seen as present in organic wholes, and as discernable by intuition rather than by logical deduction. Theodorou writes ". . . the order of values is not rational and it does not have direct relation with reason, but with the feelings . . . values are perceived through special activities (energies) of the spirit *(tou pnevmatos)."* He refers to something he calls a "value sense" *(axiologikon synaisthema)*. He also emphasizes its obligatory character: "values do not say 'what is' but rather 'what should be'."[29]

Though the confusion existing among value theorists, with the majority opting for a subjective, relativistic position ought to be enough to discredit it, the use of value-language is helpful to all ethicians and others. The positivist value theorists do not provide us with a solid and concrete understanding of the good. Some may object to the thorough-going intuitive character of this theory, implying that the good does not share in the experience of reason. Whatever the value of this perspective on the good, it fails to satisfy us in our quest for the nature of the good.

The *good as "Agape"* (love) is based on Christian revelation. It is included here because in much ethical writing today it is used as an independent ethical principle. If it is true that traditional Roman Catholic ethics emphasized natural law as a necessary basis of the good, it can be said that in contrast, Protestant ethics have tended to emphasize the source of the good as *agape* or Christian love. The founders of this approach are the Reformation leaders, Martin Luther and John Calvin. However, in more modern times, the figure who set the tone for Protestant ethical identification of the good was Anders Nygren in his monumental *Agape and Eros*.[30] Nygren's concern was to sharply delineate *agape* (Christian love) from *eros* (human desire): ". . . to represent two quite distinct ideas of love, one of them prevalent in the ancient Hellenistic world where it was called *eros* and the other characteristic of primitive Christianity, to which it was known as *agape* . . . the question under discussion is not how the Greeks or primitive Christians loved, but what they thought about love."[31]

Nygren is intent in keeping the two as separate as possible. It helps us to see the sharp differentiation characteristic of subsequent Protestant thought on the subject in the following:

> Religion is fellowship with God. But two different conceptions are possible of the way in which this fellowship with God is brought about. It can be thought of as achieved by the raising up of the human to the Divine—and that is the contention of egocentric religion of Eros; or else it is held to be established by the gracious condescension of the Divine to man—and that is the contention of theocentric religion, of Agape.[32]

For our purposes, what is significant in Nygren's view is the place he gives to Agape in ethical thought.

> "What is the good, the good in itself? . . . the good is Agape and the ethical demand finds summary expression in the commandment of Love, the commandment to love God and thy neighbor."[33]

It seems that as Natural Law functions for traditional Roman Catholic ethics, Agape serves as the foundation of Protestant ethics. Of course, Protestant theology is very diverse. A case in point is the meaning of Agape. Among modern Protestant writers on Agape we obtain numerous understandings. A sampling of some views follows. As an ethical good, Protestant ethical writings emphasize love for neighbor rather than love for God. This passage from Paul Ramsey's book *Basic Christian Ethics* is a case in point.

> "God's love for man is "first love," man's for God is "second love." On account of the strength and direction gained from God's love, man's love for neighbor is again in relation to him, "first love." "First love takes the lead; it gives what is needed, *it does not first seek what the agent himself needs or desires*. Christian responsive love stands in no need of seeking, *desires nothing,* but *out of gratitude* obediently loves the neighbor. "In this is love, not that we loved God but that He love us . . . we love, because He first loved us." (1 John 4:10, 19). No man ought to *"use himself or his neighbor even for the sake of union with God;* yet every man ought to "treat humanity" in himself *as a means used in his neighbor's service.* Underneath these terminological considerations lies an exceedingly important issue, an issue arising from the fact that "on the whole, God's love for us is a much safer subject for us to think about than our love for Him."[34]

For Ramsey, "Christian love means an entirely neighbor-regarding concern for others."[35] Norman Geisler, an evangelical protestant in a chapter entitled "Love: the Only Absolute" states that "Love is the only candidate for moral absoluteness which is not self-defeating."[36] For him however, love is found in God and specifically and explicitly is found in and derived from Holy Scriptures. In practice this becomes a biblical legalism. For Geisler the love principle is the summary of the laws of Scripture. Alone love does not guide us in specific behavior unless it is seen as a summary of specific laws. For this author "law is Love put into words."

Another recent Protestant author on the subject is Gene Outka, in his study *Agape: An Ethical Analysis*.[37] "Agape is regard for the neighbor which in crucial respects is independent and unalterable."[38] Several times he approvingly quotes Karl Barth saying that neighbor-love means "identification with his interests in utter independence of the question of his attractiveness, of what he has to offer, of the reciprocity of the relationship."[39] And because this concern "extends to everyone alike," he chooses to define Agape as "equal regard." The emphasis on Agape as the highest standard of the good is exemplified in a further comment by Paul Tillich: "I have given no definition of love. This is impossible because there is no higher principle by which it could be defined."[40]

But Agapism as the the definition of the highest good is subject to serious criticism. Of course, its value and importance for ethics cannot and must not be minimized. Yet as an understanding of the good in an ultimate sense it is subject to serious flaws. The comment above by Tillich creates a serious problem. The ultimate good is undefined, for him. Others define it, as we have seen it, only in terms of its object, (neighbor). Most seriously of all we are not given an adequate, self-sufficient reason *why* we should concern ourselves with the good of the neighbor. Those who would argue that it is because God commands it, then would have to agree that there is a "higher principle by which it could be defined" and that would be "Obey God" which then in fact would be the ultimate good.

If Agapism is the ultimate good, then we should be able to easily justify why it is ethical to seek the welfare and benefit of the neighbor and unethical to seek our own benefit and welfare. It is possible for this to be done. But it will be done on the basis of some other criterion, i.e., the benefit of society, which in turn would be the good.

Further, Agapistic ethical systems are often incapable of determining the "welfare" of the neighbor to be accomplished. Act-agapism narrows the welfare of the neighbor to specific acts which meet expressed desires or wants of the neighbor. Rule-agapism looks rather to the large view of human welfare, and acts according to principles and precepts for the neighbor welfare.

Further, the whole issue of love for God and love for oneself as implied in the two-fold love-commandments of Christ find little response in this view.

57

The most thorough going attempt to work out a completely other-regarding ethic based on Christian Agape was by Joseph Fletcher. His system of thought has become known by the name "situationalist ethic," or the so-called "new morality."[41]

Fletcher sees his method as resting midway between the two extremes of legalism and antinomianism. There are two major emphases in situationalist ethics. The first is that the good as objective, permanent and unchanging is rejected and that the primacy of the situation in the making of moral decisions is emphasized. The second is that the goal of ethical decision-making is to "serve love." As a consequence, this ethic is case-centered or "neo-casuistic" as Fletcher terms it and does not anticipate or prescribe any decisions outside of concrete and specific situations. The only stable factor "that is binding and unexceptionable, always good and right regardless of the circumstances,"[42] is agape.

According to this view it is impossible to forsee what is right in any given future situation. Thus, "Love's decisions are made situationally, not prescriptively." According to Fletcher, ethics is not a system but a method. What is required is an open-ended approach to situations. Thus, this ethical approach becomes totally based on love, to the point that traditional rules of morality are easily put aside. One example may suffice to show what is meant. A married woman in a POW camp has herself impregnated by a guard so that, according to camp rules, she can return to her family in Germany, the implication is that this was right even though it was formally adultery. This view point has been criticized by many ethicists as to the adequacy of Fletcher's understanding of the "situation," his methodology, the theological inadequacy of this approach and its social inadequacy.[43]

> "Love," like "situation," is a word that runs through Fletcher's book like a greased pig . . . nowhere does Fletcher indicate in a systematic way his various uses of it. It is the only thing that is intrinsically good; it equals justice; it is a formal principle, it is a disposition, it is a predicate and not a property, it is a ruling norm etc., etc.[44]

But the criticism of Fletcher's understanding of agape is not limited to this. The coldness of his agape is the target of some of its critics. It is described as "so unsentimental as to be nearly void of feeling" and another author describes his ethic as "a blood chilling application of love by a process of cool reasoning."

From an Orthodox point of view agape can be identified with the Christ-like, God-like telos which we seek to realize. Like Fletcher, Orthodox ethics would emphasize its relational character. Agape is how God has dealt with us. He has concerned Himself for our welfare, He has redeemed us through Christ Jesus. He cares. But who can read the Prophets and view the compassion and tenderness of Jesus as He dealt with people and call that relationship an "agapeic calculus?" We must agree that calculation alone is not agape. God cares about us not coldly and calculatedly, but rather because of the fellowship and communion which arises because we are His creation made in His own image and likeness. There is an essential, redeemable worth in us, in spite of our sinful condition which does not permit us to claim anything of God, however. For this reason, true agape goes beyond "selfless benevolence" (i.e., doing something for another's welfare without trying to get anything out of it for yourself). It is this, but it mellows into the compassion and feeling which signals respect. Christian agape is God-like. It is like Christ who exemplified in His own life what He taught saying "greater love hath no man than this, that a man lay down his life for his friends." (John 12:13) Situationalism is right when it speaks of the supreme value of agape. But the understanding of it is lacking; and in lacking, it becomes a distortion. For love is an energy, an activity of God, not a calculus but a divine-human relationship. Situationalism belittles agape when it tries to make it do all things in all situations. Agape characterizes the Christ-like goal, purpose and destiny of man. It presupposes the willing, unstrained living of the natural moral law. Fletcher's "agape" does not reach high enough as it seeks to spread out over everything. But this is not the "second story" of a natural/supernatural universe as taught by Scholasticism. Agape, even as agape, requires the fulfillment of the natural moral law.

Love contains and protects God's commandments; it does not violate them. Fletcher's peculiar understanding of love as permitting the violation of God's essential and basic commands for mankind is neither scriptural nor patristic. Love transfigures the law of God; it does not abrogate it.

Thus, it must be concluded that attempts to make agape-love into the supreme good fail. Yet, to demonstrate the central importance of agape-love in Orthodox Christian ethical thinking is unnecessary. Scripture and Holy Tradition affirm it abundantly. It is only that Orthodox ethics cannot find it possible to consider love the good in itself; love is good because God—who is good in itself—is loving and has created us so that we find our fulfillment in being like Him. The motive for living the life of love is not a cold altruism which cannot rationally sustain itself, but the loving energies of the good God: "In this is love, not that we loved God but that he loved us and sent his Son to be the expiation for our sins. Beloved, if God so loves us, we also ought to love one another."[45] It is the goodness of God which makes love an imperative. Love in itself is not the good, but, as we have seen and shall see in even more detail later, it stands at the core and heart of the ethical imperatives for Christian behavior.

Existentialist ethics is generically different from almost all other theories of ethics "in that it is not really a 'theory' but an attitude (or set of attitudes) toward human life and its problems."[46] Some call the attraction of Existentialism a "mood" rather than a coherent and defensible system of thought.[47] Whatever the case, it cannot be denied that existentialism is important, for existentialist perspectives provide the key to understanding much of what passes for contemporary thought.

The "attitude" and "mood" of existentialism can be summarized in three points. The first is the existentialist *opposition to systems*. In the philosophical context this meant the origin of existentialism in opposition to Hegelian "essentialism." The existentialist theories of knowledge all locate significant knowledge in the consciousness of the individual. Since each individual is unique, perceiving reality subjectively, this means for existentialism that no real or significant knowledge can be "objective." This leads to an anti-rationalist mood which abhors "grand schemes," "over-all views," "systematic presentation," "world views," and the like. It, of course, rejects by and large systematic expositions of doctrine and organized presentations of ethical theory.

The second aspect of the existentialist mood is that existentialists tend to see human existence in an almost absolute frame of reference of *subjective individuality*. For nearly all existentialists the sharp dividing line is placed between essence and existence. Essence is the totality of the characteristics of a thing over which it has no determination or control. Thus, to define something is to describe its essence. On the other hand, existence is the self's consciousness and its freedom to determine its own course of action; existence means to be fully conscious of one's self, to perceive things in one's own way, to own one's own private truth, to devise projects consciously and deliberately and to put them into practice. The focus of existentialist thinking is on this very private and personal decision-making in which one "assumes responsibility for himself."

The only absolute value of the existentialist position is freedom. By freedom is meant the self's own determination of the course of its own life. To "consciously choose" and not to accept or conform to, or submit to, or adopt the views of others is that which permits us to "exist." Freedom thus understood has no content, no substantive and specific referents. For ethics this means that each of us has "to devise his *own* morality, and make his *own* choices without the help of rules or principles."[48]

To function this way is variously described as "true existence," living with "good faith," and achieving "authentic existence."

The opposite, that is, not acting consciously and decisively (regardless of what one does) is called "false existence," "non-existence," living with "bad faith" and being "inauthentic." "Bad faith" is, more generally, the taking from people the opportunity to choose for themselves. Any "objective principles, standards, ethical criteria, etc." are, thus, by definition "bad faith," and productive of "inauthentic existence."

A third aspect of the existentialist stance is the *assessment* about human personal and social reality which it makes. The key words here are "absurdity," "other people" and "atheism." If there are no general truths, no objective existence, no ultimate reality which have meaning for human beings it means that life for each individual is totally ambiguous. At heart there is a nothingness about the human being who "makes meaning" through his choices, but who also knows that this meaning has no meaning outside himself. His efforts to transcend himself are doomed to

60

fail. The effect is, for the individual, in total despair of significance for himself to "create" reality as a rebellious assertion which he knows in his consciousness is a lie. Thus the very act of achieving "existence," "authenticity," and living in "good faith" is acknowledged as absurd.

This absurdity and ambiguousness is heightened when the existentialist turns to "other people." In such an individualistic and subjective perspective "other people" have a significance which is only marginal. The significance of "other people" for the strictly existential approach is that they help the individual modify his own acts and his own self-perception of his existence. More negatively, "other people" are those who seek to limit, restrict, control and dominate the individual. Thus they are seen as the main force which restricts the development of the individual's "authentic existence." Consequently, it is easy to understand why one of the most important existentialist spokesmen, Jean Paul Sartre, in his *Being and Nothingness*, could write that "the enemy is other people" and human existence, thus "of necessity means, that we are always in conflict with others."[49]

The issue of "other people" raises, as well, the question of the possibility of an ethic, any ethic.

Existentialism faces a contradiction; it needs people to achieve the individual's own authenticity, yet it cannot deal with the equally valid claim of the freedom of others in any principled way, since it cannot appeal to any objective criterion and standard. It must of necessity reject any this-worldly effort to assert that some things are good in themselves, or that some acts are good because they always have good consequences. But in the same fashion, Existentialism must of necessity reject belief in any idealistic, non-naturalistic, or theistic belief in an transcendent good or system of values. Thus, most existentialists seem to reject the development of anything which might be called a discipline of ethics.

Further, the "internal transcendence" of the existentialist mood leads to atheism. Those most closely related to the philosophical existentialist movement such as Heidegger, Sartre, de Beauvoir and Nietzsche either completely rejected God as He is normally understood in the Judeo-Christian tradition or, in deistic fashion consider God irrelevant or neutral. There is however, a group of believers who may be called existentialist theologians and who, affirm a place for God in a generally existential mode of thought. The most important of these was the Danish writer Soren Kierkegaard. Reflecting his own personal experience, Kierkegaard spoke of three alternative ethical life styles, the aesthetic, the ethical and the religious. The aesthetic life style is one of pleasure seeking, self-interested concern with individual happiness and one's own personal security. The ethical life style is the decision to obey moral commands, to live intensely and to follow through, to be involved with other people. The religious, for Kierkegaard is the highest level in which there is a full consciousness of one's sin, the acceptance of forgiveness in faith and the acceptance of suffering. Kirkegaard's prototype is Abraham's willingness to sacrifice his son at the command of God, which he described as "the theological suspension of the teleological."[50]

Kierkegaard was unimpressed by theological doctrine, churchly institutions, creeds, and considered that

> . . . an objective acceptance of Christianity is paganism or thoughtlessness . . . Christianity protests against every form of objectivity; it desires that the subject should be infinitely concerned about himself. It is subjectivity that Christianity is concerned with, and it is only in subjectivity that its truth exists, if it exists at all; objectively, Christianity has absolutely no existence. If its truth happens to be only in a single subject, it exists in him alone; and there is greater Christian joy in heaven over this one individual than over universal history and the System.[51]

Christian existential ethics usually posit love as the only "ethical criterion." Though there are other foci as well. Thus the early Paul Ramsey spoke of "an ethic without laws," Paul Tillich of a "trans-moral conscience," Fletcher of a "new morality" in which only love and the situation are central. In this same mood, Nicholas Berdyaev, who has some connection with Eastern Orthodoxy, spoke of an "ethic of creativity."

Within the Orthodox tradition several writers have tended, more or less, to identify with the existentialist stance. Thus, it is possible to understand Feodor Dostoevsky as a fore-runner, at least, of existentialism where themes of absurdity of life, free and unfettered choice, and the focus on will as manifesting the whole life characterize his writings.

Closer to the theological sphere is Chrestos Giannaras. Writing from within the Orthodox tradition, Giannaras finds much in common between the mystical tradition of the Desert Fathers and Dionysios the Areopagite with the existentialist philosopher, Heidegger. In a series of writings he has described parallels in the two historically disparate traditions and sought to interpret Eastern Orthodox Christianity in the light of existentialism. Giannaras, thus, is much opposed to any systematic, principled approach to ethics. Characteristic is the title of his major work on ethics, *The Freedom of Ethos*.[52] For Giannaras, any attempt to "objectify" Christian ethics through the articulation of rules, commands and standards to which people are to conform their lives is a "bourgeoisie ethic" *(astike ethike)* which is denial of the free, interpersonal, unstructured and undefinable relationship of the human person with the free, interpersonal (Trinitarian), undefinable divine reality. For Giannaras an "objective" Christian ethic is an impossibility and a denial of the deepest insights of Eastern Orthodox Christianity.[53]

In a general evaluation of these approaches, it must be first noted that the existentialist denial of meaning to human life flies in the face of the ordinary understanding of the Christian gospel. Not only must it reject the atheism of the philosophical existentialists, but even the pre-occupation with the "absurd," and "ambiguity" and the ultimate "meaninglessness" of life needs to be criticized in the light of the Christian hope. The teaching of the Christian faith regarding victory over death, sin and evil in the person and work of Jesus Christ are and always have been perceived in traditional Christianity not only as events of the deepest significance for the world, but as true (one would say "objective") events, not merely as symbols of renewal or potentiality.

The eschatological emphasis of early Christianity precisely countered the values of this life and the presently experienced existence, with the values of the "Kingdom to come." It is impossible to conceive of traditional Christianity as presented in the Bible, further, as espousing an exclusive subjectivist, hopeless, individualistic approach to life. The total incompatability of the central concept of Christian love is in direct and irrevocable conflict with such a view. The Christian Church has never felt that there was something "inauthentic" and inappropriate about providing ethical direction to others. As we have seen, obedience to God and His commands is a standard Christian injunction.

Further the restriction of all that is genuinely human to the conscious subjective experience is unwarranted. It fails to take into account that all perception, experience and life needs a reality outside of itself in order to find its own identity. Others, on the other hand, cannot be merely occasions for my existence. Pushed to its extreme as in existentialism, subjectivity becomes a privatism of knowledge and experience in that it becomes impossible either to communicate, share, or live in harmony with one another. This subjectivity becomes then a form of individualism ("atom-ismos," in Greek) which, as in all egoistic systems of thought tends to be self-defeating. Human beings are social by nature and may not exist only to exploit others for his own ends. In the interface of persons in community we fulfill ourselves in large measure. Service, sacrifice, mutuality, all are characteristic of a human maturity which transcends mere atomistic pursuit of one's own interests. Human communality, mutuality and brotherhood are essential aspects of existing humanly. They refute an exclusive emphasis on subjective individualism.

As if to prove the point, it has been observed that existentialism is notoriously unstable. It is well known that Sartre was led to adopt Marxism as a philosophy for living. Numerous existentialists needing content for their lives, not content with the bare "authenticity" of choosing "anything" for themselves have committed their lives to "causes." Often these causes are worthwhile endeavors. If, however, they become, as they often do, ends in themselves, they not only become "idols" from a Christian perspective, they also refute the basic adequacy of the existentialist vision, for they become, in practice, "objective" criteria, standards and principles.

More can be noted in this view, from a specifically Orthodox perspective. The pessimism characteristic of the existentialist assessment of the human condition reflects more of a Protestant, Calvinist anthropology than it does an Eastern Orthodox view of humanity which takes the image of God and the movement to "theosis" seriously. It is impossible to affirm the "absurdity of human existence" together with the ideas in Eastern Orthodoxy of "growth toward perfection."

One is at a loss to reconcile the Orthodox respect and reverence for tradition with the existentialist emphasis on individualistic isolation. Even when we adopt a view of Holy Tradition such as that espoused by Georges Florovsky, which points to the "patristic spirit" including both the "mind of the Scriptures and the mind of the Fathers," one cannot do this without sensing the impact of communion with that spirit which is "authoritative" and a source of truth which is not original to our subjective experience but comes from without as a revelation from God. The first chapter of the Gospel of John is the ultimate refutation of the existentialist refusal to accept truth as substantive reality:

> In him (the Word) was life, and the life was the light of men . . . the true light that enlightens every man was coming into the world . . . yet the world knew him not . . . But to all who received him, who believed in his name, he gave power to become children of God . . . from his fullness have we all received, grace upon grace . . . grace and truth came through Jesus Christ.[54]

We may also see the non-existentialist bent of Orthodox Christianity in both Sacramental Theology and the monastic spiritual tradition. Suffice it to note in the first case the rejection of the heretical Donatist view about the dependence of the validity of the sacraments on the personal virtue of the celebrant provided to the sacraments an "objectivity" totally out of line with existentialist categories. Even more striking is the Jesus Prayer, the goal of its practice being that it "pray itself" within the practitioner without a conscious, active effort on the part of the monk, so that it is the Holy Spirit which prays within us and not ourselves. By definition, in existentialist terminology, that is "inauthentic existence!"

Though the existentialist mood helps Christians focus upon the genuine experience of the presence of God in the life of each person and the "personal" dimension of the Orthodox Christian spiritual and moral life, there is a major difference. For Eastern Orthodox Christianity all virtues such as freedom, self-realization, anti-legalism, the absence of hypocrisy focus not on the exclusive subjective consciousness of the individual, but on the person's communion with God-in-Trinity who through His divine energies leads us to become authentically ourselves by becoming more and more God-like. It is precisely for this reason that the one thing which Eastern Orthodox Christianity cannot do, is accept the "theological suspension of the teleological." Rather, it will affirm it as central for its ethics.

This has meant that ethical norms were never absent from Orthodox teaching, or that obedience to them was in some way "inauthentic." It is impossible to read any portion of the sources of Orthodox Christian ethics from the Old and New Testaments through the Cappadocian Fathers and to the *Philokalia* without seeing that there is, in Orthodox Christian ethical tradition, an important place for rules and commands of an "objective" character.

Existentialist ethical approaches, however, do raise up some dimensions of the ethical life which are important for Orthodox Christian ethics and which sometimes have not been focused upon by modern treatments of Orthodox Christian ethics. Because existential approaches tend to emphasize personal responsibility, the need for moral decision making and a conscious, personally committed ethical and moral life, they serve to challenge more traditional and customary understandings. Often, in Orthodox ethical teaching and preaching, mere blind and unreflective obedience, without personal assent, understanding and commitment, has been presented as desirable. Without question obedience to God's Will will always be virtuous for the Christian. But a totally submissive mentality—outside of certain short-term conditions (the young child, the novice monk, the new convert, etc.)—cannot be reflective of the spirit of Eastern Orthodox Christianity. The focus on Christian freedom is important, and is legitimately identified in the tradition — especially in the writings of the mystical tradition.

Because this contribution is so important for a genuine Orthodox approach to ethics, there is included in this treatment of Orthodox Christian ethics a chapter on ethical decision-making, a subject generally absent from the usual Orthodox ethics textbooks. However, we have sought to treat this topic from the perspective and practice of the Eastern Orthodox tradition.

Existentialism, though not an adequate foundation for ethics, does reflect some of the important truths of a genuine Orthodox Christian ethic.

———————

Our discussion of the various attempts to identify the good by philosophers and others led us to reject each as inadequate understandings of the good. We noted that the very empirical nature of many of them ("is" statements) is based on a distorted reality and therefore these views are at heart incapable of providing a sure foundation for the identification of the good. We sought to show that only a transcendent inter-personal being, God-in-Trinity, could provide the link between "is" and "ought" for human ethics since human beings are created in the very image and likeness of God, Himself. God's "is" is our "ought." Yet, as we have seen, the non-revelatory identifications of the good, precisely because they reflect some part of what God has created and what He had done—His energies—also relate to the good in positive ways, even though they may not be identified with the good itself. What this means is, that each of the non-revelatory identifications of the good, though not the good itself, shares in the good, and in part, expresses the moral good in our empirical human moral experience.

All of the ethical theories which have been examined above find their place and their status within the larger framework which comes from the

65

correct identification of the absolute good with the Triune God alone. Much of our understanding is clouded since the essence of God, apophatically speaking, is beyond our comprehension as finite creatures. But God has seen fit to act through His energies in many multifaceted ways. It is in these energies of a God who is goodness itself (or should we say "goodness Himself" or even better "goodness in Trinity"), that we find sufficient illumination to understand what the good is and to distinguish it from that which is evil. Each of the philosophical views shares in a portion of the truth of that which St. Maximos the Confessor called the "good by nature" *(physei agathon)* i.e., God. Thus, non-revelatory ethical thought is of assistance to us in our attempt to clarify and delineate the ethical imperatives of an eternal and constant good in relation to a constantly changing and fluid world in which we live, as well as to understand and participate in the public debate of moral issues of each place and time. But with the firm anchor of our understanding of the good as God-in-Trinity and Him alone, Orthodox ethics is able not only to separate the valid from the invalid, but also to find direction for ethical judgments, evaluations, decisions, commitments and actions for Christian life first, and for the world as well.

The world passes away, and the lust of it; but he who does the will of God abides forever.

(1 John 2:17)

---

[1] In the treatment which follows on different philosophical identifications of the good, I have also included some views which are clearly biblically based. However, I have included them here because in their function they tend to be used in a fashion similar to the philosophical systems with which they are included. I prefer the term "non-revelatory" to "natural" since the latter term needs very careful definition in a total doctrinal context.

[2] Romans 2:14-15.

[3] Johannes Quasten, *Patrology:* Vol. I, *The Beginnings of Patristic Literature,* Utrecht, Antwerp: Spectrum Publishers, 1966, p. 209.

[4] *Apologia* 2,10.

[5] See Note 1.

[6] *Apologia* 2,13.

[7] *Divine Command Morality: Historical and Contemporary Readings.* Lewiston, N.Y.: Edwin Mellen Press, 1980.

[8] *On The Commonwealth.*

[9] Jeremiah 31:33-34.

[10] Hebrews 10:16.

[11] John 14:21; see also John 15:9-11.

[12] Luke 8:14.

[13] Psalm 5:11.

[14] *Chapters on Theology,* 5:13.

[15] Matthew 5:48.

[16] 1 John 4:17. KJV.

[17] 1 John 4:11-12. RSV.

[18] *Apologetikai Meletai,* Vol. 3 - Sec. 4, *The Theory of Evolution,* Athens, Zoe Publications, 1938. For a few more reflections on this topic see my book, *Contemporary Moral Issues Facing the Orthodox Christian.* Minneapolis: Light & Life Publishing Co., 1982. Chapter 6.

[19] C. Lloyd Morgan, *Emergent Evolution.* New York: Holt & Co., 1931.

[20] Pierre LeCompte du Noüy, *Human Destiny,* New York: Longmans, Green and Co., 1947.

[21] *Ibid.,* pp. 225-226.

[22] Pierre Teilhard de Chardin, *The Future of Man,* trans. by N. Denny, New York: Harper and Row, 1964.

[23] *Ibid.,* p. 295.

[24] *Ibid.,* p. 305. (Emphasis mine.)

[25] *Ibid.,* p. 297.

[26] Philippians 3:12-15.

[27] Ephesians 4:13-14, 15.

[28] Evangelos Theodorou, *Threskevtike kai Ethike Encyclopedia.* Athens: A Martinos, 1963, Vol. 2, p. 1010.

[29] *Ibid.*

[30] Anders Nygren, *Agape and Eros.* New York: Harper and Row, 1969 in the paperback edition.

[31] *Ibid.,* p. xvi.

[32] *Ibid.,* pp. 206-207.

[33] *Ibid.,* p. 38.

[34] Paul Ramsey, *Basic Christian Ethics,* New York: Charles Scribner's Sons, 1953, pp. 130-131. (Emphasis mine.) The final quotation is from C. S. Lewis, *Christian Behavior,* Macmillan, 1943, p. 53.

[35] *Ibid.,* p. 95.

[36] Norman Geisler, *The Christian Ethic of Love,* Zondervan Publishing House, 1973.

[37] Gene Outka, *Agape: An Ethical Analysis,* New Haven: Yale University Press, 1972.

[38] *Ibid.,* p. 9.

[39] *Ibid.,* pp. 11, 214.

[40] Paul Tillich, *The Protestant Era,* trans. and with a concluding essay by James Luther Adams, Chicago: University of Chicago Press, 1958, p. 160.

[41] See Harakas, "An Orthodox Christian Approach to the New Morality," *Greek Orthodox Theological Review,* Brookline, Mass.: Vol. XV, No. 1, Spring, 1970, p. 107.

[42] Joseph Fletcher, *Situation Ethics: The New Morality,* Philadelphia: The Westminster Press, 1966, p. 30.

[43] Harakas, "An Orthodox Christian Approach to the New Morality," *op. cit.,* pp. 115-125.

[44] Harvey Cox, ed., *The Situation Ethics Debate,* Philadelphia: Westminster Press, 1968, p. 81.

[45] 1 John 4:10-11.

[46] Vernon J. Bourke, *History of Ethics,* Garden City, N.Y.: Doubleday and Co., Inc., 1968, p. 295.

[47] Mary Warnock, *Existentialist Ethics,* New York: St. Martins Press, 1967, p. 57.

[48] Warnock, *op. cit.,* p. 26.

[49] Jean Paul Sartre, *Being and Nothingness: An Essay of Phenomenological Ontology,* trans. Hazel E. Barnes, Methuen, 1957, p. 364.

[50] Kierkegaard, *Concluding Unscientific Postscript,* trans. by D. G. Swenson, with Introduction and Notes by W. Lowrie, Princeton: Princeton University Press, 1941, pp. 118, 119.

[51] Mantzarides, *Christianike Ethike: University Lectures,* Thessalonike: Pournaras Publication, 1974.

[52] Chrestos Giannaras, *The Freedom of Ethos.* The second edition of this work has been published. Unfortunately it comes too late for reference and comment here.

[53] Michael Dahulich, *The Extent of Historical, Cultural, Sociological and Theological Influences Responsible for the Underdevelopment of Systematic Moral Theology in the Orthodox Church.* M.A. Dissertation, Duquesne University, Pittsburgh, Pa.

[54] John 1:4, 9, 12, 16, 17.

Chapter Four

EVIL AND SIN

"Thou are not a God who delights in wickedness; evil may not sojourn with thee."   *(Psalms 5:4.)*

The Existence of Evil

The discussion of the good which we have just concluded requires that we give attention to its opposite; "Evil." That evil exists hardly needs documentation. Evil can be thought of as a condition on the one hand, and an act, or series of acts on the other. When injustice, hunger, starvation, tornadoes and hurricanes, accidents, tragedies of various sorts, oppression, wars, crimes, illnesses, hatreds, take place all around us, we very much feel the presence of evil as a condition which goes beyond the will or choice of the individual. Evil is often thought of in this larger context. It is seen as systemic. When evil takes place on the more limited scale of interpersonal relationships, when the evil can be seen in a limited context and when the responsibility for the evil is easily pin-pointed to one or more persons, we tend to use the word sin to describe evil acts, situations or consequences.

The words are frequently interchangeable, but the general distinction is useful. Wars, for instance are usually of such huge dimensions, that we speak of them as *evil*. A lie, on the other hand, is more than likely to be seen as a *sin*. Yet, the important point is that experientially, existentially, human beings clearly identify certain experiences, conditions, acts, attitudes, motives, intentions and deeds as non-good, as evil. Only a thoroughly convinced amoralist (if such exists) can deny that evil exists existentially.

The scriptures often identify both evil and sin with the term "the world." What is meant, of course is not the world as created by God, for what He has created is good since its source of existence is goodness itself, the Triune God. Christians are warned of the existence of "the world" which is seen as opposed to the goodness of the life in Christ. "Be not conformed to this world: but be ye transformed by the renewing of your mind that ye may prove what is that good and acceptable and perfect will of God."[1] Here, it is clear that St. Paul is identifying the world as something evil, the opposite of the good and acceptable and perfect will of God. I John also shows the contrast: "Love not the world, neither the things that are in the world. If any man love the world, the love of the

Father is not in him[2] . . . and . . . the lust of the world passeth away, and the lust thereof: but he that doeth the will of God abideth for ever."[3]

Whether we call it evil or sin, there is a reality empirically known which is identifiable as opposed in some way to the good as we have identified it. 3 John instructs Christians in terms of this empirical reality. "Beloved, follow not that which is evil, but that which is good. He that doeth good is of God: but he that doeth evil hath not seen God."

Generally speaking, then, evil is that which ought not to be, which ought not to exist, or if it does exist in fact, should not continue to do so. In value terms, evil is a dis-value, that which is not valued, that which is not desired or ought not to be desired.

The Problem: Evil and Reality

Beyond the question of the existence of evil, philosophers and theologians have sought to understand the relationship of evil to reality. For Christians, the problem, oftentimes considered the most weak element in Christian doctrine, is the question of the relationship of the existence of evil with God. There are many varying views on the subject of the nature of evil and its relationship to reality.

One approach to the question of the relationship of evil to reality is *Relativism*. In this case, evil is that which opposes one's purposes. For example, a study of Lenin's works reveals a view which identifies as evil anyone or anything which opposes the communist revolution. He justified the robbing of banks if the purpose was to aid the "revolution." Many persons, with other viewpoints, often find themselves functioning practically with this understanding of evil: "evil is whatever stands in the way of the accomplishment of my own purposes."

A more sophisticated and metaphysical approach to the issue of evil and reality, is to see it as a *necessary element* of existence. Evil is seen as part of an organic whole which is reality. Consequently, evil *must* exist; it is a necessity. Good and evil are seen as two sides of the same coin. In some forms of Stoic pantheism, both good and evil exist side by side to form the harmony of the created world which is all that is, since Stoicism was pantheistic. In Chinese philosophy, reality was described graphically as a circle with an "S"-like line drawn within it. Each portion of the circle had its characteristics. One side was masculine, active, light, *good;* the other side was feminine, passive, dark, *evil*. But both were required to make up the whole of reality. More recently, the philosopher, Edgar Sheffield Brightman, developed the idea of a "finite God" in whom evil existed as a sort of uncontrolled deposit which he called the "surd." God struggled with the surd-evil within Himself. As such, evil had a metaphysical reality which, as part of God, had real existence, even though God "struggled" with it.[4]

This view is only one step away from another approach to the nature of evil in relation to morality, that of *Dualism*. According to this view, both good and evil exist side by side in a never-ending contest. The two principles are not seen as necessary complements to each other, but as rival principles in an antagonistic relationship. In Plato's *Republic,* for instance, good and evil are sharply distinguished.

. . . the truth is that nature is good and must be described as such.

Unquestionable.

Well, nothing that is good can be harmful; and if it cannot do harm, it can do no evil; and so it cannot be responsible for any evil.

I agree.

Again, goodness is beneficient, and hence the cause of well-being.

Yes.

Goodness, then, is not responsible for everything, but only for what is as it should be. It is not responsible for evil.

Quite true.

It follows, then, that the divine, being good, is not, as most people say, responsible for everything that happens to mankind, but only for a small part; for the good things in human life are far fewer than the evil, and whereas the good must be ascribed to heaven only, we must look elsewhere for the cause of evils . . .
If our commonwealth is to be well-ordered, we must fight to the last against any member of it being suffered to speak of the divine, which is good, being responsible for evil.

This passage not only sharply differentiates the good from evil as opposing and opposite forces, but also introduces the issue of the relationship of God with evil. This problem is known as *Theodicy* and will be judged below more fully. But it also leads us to mention the most thorough of dualistic systems, the religious teachings of Zoroastrianism. Though this religion has gone through many developments, one of its cardinal emphases is that there are two kingdoms in reality, one of light, the other of darkness. The kingdom of light is presided over by Ahura Mazda, the god of goodness. The god of darkness and evil, Angra Mainyu, is in constant struggle with the good god Ahura Mazda. It is a question of debate whether finally, the good will overcome the evil. Two ancient Christian heresies also had dualistic teachings. Manichaeism was "based on a supposed primeval conflict between light and darkness combined with ascetic beliefs." Marcion was another heretic, attacked by many Church Fathers who taught the existence of two gods, one of the Old Testament and one of the New Testament. Characteristically, he expounded his teaching in a work entitled, *Antitheses.* "The Creator God or Demiurge, revealed in the Old Testament from Gen. I onwards as wholly a God of Law, had nothing in common with the God of Jesus Christ . . . he was fickle, capricious, ignorant, despotic, cruel. Utterly different was the Supreme God of Love whom Jesus came to reveal. It was His purpose to overthrow the Demiurge."[5]

Evil may also be seen as the *non-fulfillment of the purposes of all philosophical systems*. Thus, serially, for the intuitist, it would be to stamp out the intuitions of the good and not to cultivate them; for natural law ethics, it would be to ignore or violate its commands (for Kant, it would be to fail to obey the Categorical Imperative); for the hedonist, it would be not to seek personal pleasure or happiness; for the utilitarian it would be not to seek, or to frustrate the greatest good for the greatest number of people; for the perfectionist, it would be to violate or not fulfill the goal of perfection depending on how it was conceived; for the evolutionist, it would be not to contribute to the evolutionary process of mankind.

Another view is that in fact, *evil is illusory,* i.e., it in fact does not exist. Among those who teach this view are the Christian Scientists. For them, evil does not exist. If it exists it is not evil. Physical evil, or rather, that which people call physical evil (sickness, tidal waves, earthquakes, etc.) is not evil even though it exists, because it is seen as a necessary part of the functioning of the created world: in itself, it is not evil. Some who hold this view, say that ethical evil does not exist simply because nature is blind and knows no purposes. What we call evil, the amoralist contends is convention and the denial of our own relative purposes and goals.

A deeper form of this view is that evil is *meonic* (Greek, *me* = not, and *on* = being). This view argues that physical evil does not exist because the events which are called evil are in fact neutral. They take place, of course, but since ethical evil must involve choice and volition, these events cannot be properly called evil. As far as moral or ethical evil is concerned some teach that it does not exist because it is in fact just the absence of the good, hence, it is *meon* or *meonic*. But since the fact of evil seems to be quite real, this view tends to translate itself into the view we described above, that evil is an organic aspect of the good, a necessary requirement for good to exist. One gets this impression from Berdyaev's treatment of evil in his book, *The Destiny of Man*. This meonic view of evil is in fact a distortion of the Eastern Orthodox Christian view of evil.

The Orthodox Christian Position on Evil

The beginning of evil is understood in Orthodox Christian thinking and teaching as having its source in the self-determination *(autexousion)* of created rational beings. Basically, it is understood as being separation and apostasy from the source of goodness in Trinity, God Himself.

It is the teaching of the Church that what God created, He created good, for nothing evil can come from the good God. St. Athanasios says, "There was a time when there was no evil" *(ouk en kakia)*. Consequently, Orthodox Christian thought would reject those views which would identify evil dualistically as created matter. It also, rejects, on a more metaphysical plane the idea that evil has substance in itself, that it is an essence, or something which might be called a "thing." Nor does the Eastern Christian position accept that evil is a necessary constituent of good.

71

However, only in an ultimate sense, the Fathers of the Church tended to see evil as *meonic,* as not existing in a metaphysical sense, as ultimate. In the words of Demetropoulos:

> God is not the author of evil. St. Basil teaches ". . . nor is it reverent to say that evil has its beginning from God, because of the principle that opposites cannot create each other. Neither does life give birth to death, nor is light the beginning of darkness, nor is sickness the creator of health . . ."[6]

> Insofar as everything was created by God, evil was not created by God at the outset, nor does it exist within Him, nor is it some kind of essence. In consequence, it is by necessity characterized as meonic, which men, instigated by the devil, "began to conceive of themselves, having lost the vision of the good" according to St. Athanasios.[7] St. John of Damascus even more clearly defines the essence of evil when he says that "Virtue was given by God to nature and He is the beginning and cause of every good," but "evil is nothing other than the withdrawal of the good, just as darkness is the withdrawal of light," or, in other terms, "it is not in man's nature to sin, but rather, in his choice."[8]

> Consequently, moral evil, or sin, does not exist as some kind of being in the organic nature of man, but rather it is only possible for evil to exist in man's power of self-determination *(autexousion).*[9]

Thus, evil is ontologically *meonic,* it does not exist in any ultimate, metaphysical sense. Strictly speaking the whole question of good and evil from the human point of view is dependent on the existence of freedom of the will, or as we have already noted, on *autexousion.* The self-determination which characterizes the ethical life demands the possibility of denying the good as well as the decision and effort to cultivate the good and to choose for it. Thus, evil is not to be found in any essential way in our humanity. Contrary to the commonplace phrase, "after all, I'm only human" which implies that imperfection, evil and sin are components of our inner nature, our true humanity does not necessarily involve evil.

A question then arises. Since evil does not have its source in God, nor does it have its source in human existence, where *does* it come from? The traditional answer is that the source of evil is the Devil, the first and chief fallen angel and those angels who followed him. The Devil is presented as the first creature who rebelled in pride against God and led humanity into the same state of rebellious pride against God. Thus Gregory of Nyssa refers to the Devil as the "inventor of evil" (*kakias euretin*).[10] St. Gregory Palamas describes the fall of the Devil and his angels thusly:

> Satan pridefully desired to rule, in spite of the decision of the Creator. He abandoned his rightful place, together with those of

his fellow angels who rebelled with him, and in consequence he himself was justly abandoned by the Fount of True Life and light, thus taking on to himself death and eternal darkness. Because man was so ordered so as not only to be ruled but also to rule over all things upon the earth, the Prince of Evil *(o archekakos)* looking upon him with jealous eyes, used every trick to take away from man his dominion. Devoid of force, which was denied to him by the Ruler of All, Who, however, created rational nature both free and self-determining *(eleutheron te kai autexousion),* the Devil offered to man the advice which destroyed his dominion . . . He convinced human beings to look about themselves without restriction and to be open to violation, or to rebel and to do the opposite of the commands and counsels given by Him who was greater. Since man had participated in the apostasy, he consequently also had to participate within himself of the eternal darkness and death.[11]

This is, without question, an acceptable response regarding the source of evil. But, more philosophically the source of evil is not primarily the Angel gone bad, but the mis-use of the freedom given to the Angel. That mis-use originated in the "desire to rule" which was not quashed, but fanned so that it led to rebellion. The source of evil, then, in both men and angels is the mis-use of our freedom, an improper use of our *autexousion.*

Thus St. Augustine writes:

If we ask the cause of the misery of the bad (angels, i.e. devils), it occurs to us, and not unreasonably, that they are miserable because they have forsaken Him who supremely is, and have turned to themselves who have no such essence . . . For when the will abandons what is above itself, and turns to what is lower, it becomes evil, not because that is evil to what it turns, but because the turning itself is wicked. Therefore, it is not an inferior thing which has made the will evil, but it is itself which has become so by wickedly and inordinately desiring an inferior thing.[12]

Thus, we can say that the real source of evil in the world is the inappropriate exercise of free will, of self-determination *(autexousion)* in separating the creature from God. The mis-use of self-determination, both of angels and men, is the basic cause of evil in the world, in that it causes an abandonment from the source of goodness, who is God-in-Trinity. This, however, raises another question which has great significance for the Christian faith. It is the question of *Theodicy (Theos* and *dike,* i.e., the justification of God). Theodicy seeks to answer the question "If God is good, why is there sin and evil in the world which He has created? Or, put more forcefully in the form of a trilemma, "Evil exists because God does not know how to make a better world, did not want to make a better world, or was not able to make a world without evil." But for Christianity none of these alternatives is acceptable; since God is all-wise, all-good and all-powerful. How then do we justify God in the face of empirical evil? Evil is usually distinguished as existing in two forms, ethical evil and physical evil.

Ethical evil clearly exists because of the misuse of the *autexousion* of rational, created beings. Thus, the question is in fact, why did God create beings who were free to choose evil? However, if we contemplate the consequence of this question, we see that if rational creatures were created without this ability of self-determination, they would in fact be *automata,* a sort of living robot, to which it would be impossible to ascribe human and angelic attributes. For example, God could have created humanity immutable. That would mean that there would be no growth, no change, no choosing of right and wrong, no need for personal self-discipline. God could even have created us with a penchant for worshipping and adoring Him. But such worship and adoration is worthless and would be insulting to God. Our ability to choose, to repent, to praise God freely and in a manner determined by ourselves is what gives our praise and worship of God significance, both to ourselves and to Him. As Jesus said, ''I tell you, there will be more joy in heaven over one sinner who repents than over ninety-nine righteous persons who need no repentance.'' (Luke 15:7) It is this mutability, this ability to change, to choose, to decide which causes this joy and which consequently merits praise. Of course, to be able to choose the good means also the ability not to choose it, to choose its opposite, evil. The very ability to change for the good, necessitates the ability to choose evil, also. St. Gregory of Nyssa, however, emphasizes the former aspect in the following passage:

> The perfection of the Christian life—and I mean that life which is the only one the name of Christ is used to designate—is that in which we participate not only by our mind and soul but in all the actions of our lives, so that our holiness may be complete, in accordance with the blessing pronounced by Paul, in our *whole body and soul and spirit* (I Thess. 5.23), constantly guarded from all admixture with evil.

> Now it may be objected that such a good is hard to achieve, seeing that only the Lord of creation is constant and that human nature is mutable and prone to change. How then is it possible to establish in our changeable nature this permanence and immutability in good? To this then we answer: there can be no crown unless the contest is fair, and the contest is fair only if there is an adversary to fight with. Thus, if there is no adversary, there is no crown. There is no victory unless there is conquest. Let us then struggle against this very mutability of our nature, coming to grips as it were with our adversary in spirit; and we become victors not by holding our adversary down but rather by not allowing him to fall. For man does not merely have an inclination to evil; were this so, it would be impossible for him to grow in good, if his nature possessed only an inclination

towards the contrary. But in truth the finest aspect of our mutability is the possibility of growth in good; and this capacity for improvement transforms the soul, as it changes, more and more into the divine . . .

One ought not then to be distressed when one considers this tendency in our nature; rather let us change in such a way that we may constantly evolve towards what is better, being *transformed from glory to glory* (2 Cor. 3. 18), and thus always improving and ever becoming more perfect by daily growth, and never arriving at any limit of perfection. For that perfection consists in our never stopping in our growth in good, never circumscribing our perfection by any limitation.[13]

Thus we see that freedom to do the good, which makes the choice of the good a praiseworthy and self-realizing thing, implies the possibility of choosing evil. The gift of self-determination comes to us from God so that we might be free to choose to become gods. It is not God who causes evil, it is we who exercise that self-determination who are the sources of sin and evil. Ethical evil is not caused by God. Brief reflection on ethical evil shows this clearly. God does not pull the trigger of the murderer's gun, a human being does. God does not press the accelerator of a speeding auto which causes an accident, a self-determining person does. God does not cause greedy and prideful nations to wage war upon each other, diplomats, rulers and officials do. Very few of the moral evils we experience are without traceable causes to the actions of human beings: free, self-determining human beings. Thus, the major issue of concern is not ethical evil, but what we call natural evil.

Natural evil is understood to be that evil which occurs without apparent human cause. It presents itself to us as unrelated to human willing and therefore as a different class of evil. Examples of natural evil are storms, earthquakes, plagues, etc. With some reflection, some of the so-called natural evils can be perceived to be ethical evils dependent upon human choice. For example, in the Alps there are villages which are periodically struck by avalanches, yet people continue to go back to the same place to rebuild the village. An avalanche is a natural phenomenon which is not considered evil in and of itself. It simply obeys the physical laws of the universe; e.g. laws of weight, stress, tension and gravity. We would not want to live in a world that was governed by capricious physical laws which worked sometimes, but not all the time. The ancient Greeks properly referred to the world as *"kosmos,"* that is, "order." In and of itself an avalanche is amoral, that is, it is not evil nor particularly good other than being an example of the reliability of the laws of our physical universe. What does make an avalanche evil is when human beings are hurt by it, socially, and physically. But, oftentimes it is human choice which permits this to happen. The wrong choice on the part of human beings, then, is the primary cause of this kind of human death and destruction. The same holds true regarding the building of cities in close

75

proximity to known earthquake prone areas. Thus, much of what appears as natural evil, is, in fact, moral evil for which human choosing is responsible.

But not all of it. Evils of nature often occur without such extenuating circumstances, beyond the pale of human choice. Not only is our human situation affected by sin, but the creation is infected by it, also. Evil has mixed itself up with the creation as a result of human sin. This mysterious truth is taught by St. Paul in his epistle to the Romans.

> I consider the sufferings of this present time are not worth comparing with the glory that is to be revealed to us. For the creation waits with eager longing for the revealing of the sons of God; for the creation was subjected to futility, not of its own will but by the will of him who subjected it in hope; because the creation itself will be set free from its bondage to decay and obtain the glorious liberty of the children of God. We know that the whole creation has been growing in travail together, until now; and not only the creation, but we ourselves, who have the first fruits of the Spirit, groan inwardly as we wait for adoption as sons, the redemption of our bodies. [14]

This remarkable passage has much to teach us about the existence of physical evil. The first point is that the natural world, in addition to its basic order and *kosmos,* is also subject to evil, is "subjected to futility," and it "waits with eager longing" for its redemption "from its bondage to decay." What this says is that evil is empirically part of the natural world. It shows that this evil has arisen as a result of the sin and disobedience of angels and human beings. This is hard to accept unless we understand it as being the human disharmony which resulted from sin. Just as sin caused a breakdown of the relationship of humanity with God, and the human with the fellow human, in like manner is caused a break in the relation between the human and the physical world. Just as a color-blind person cannot perceive and relate with the true colors in the world, in the same fashion all of humanity stands in a condition of disharmony with aspects of the world in which we live. At heart, sin is the cause of natural evil, and that evil has real effect upon us.

In spite of that, evil *can* be an occasion for good in our lives, if we so choose to so interpret it. Demetropoulos says

> In spite of all this, the wisdom of God uses natural evil in service of the good as a means of judgment and fatherly concern, by which he punishes or educates and maintains humanity in the good. [15]

But this passage also points to the ultimate victory over natural evil as well. This eschatological emphasis does not mean that evil will disappear (the doctrine of *apokatastasis*) but that it will be contained and will no longer be free to influence creation. This victory over evil and sin and death will take place in the second coming of Christ. "Then the lawless one will be revealed, and the Lord Jesus will slay him with the breath of his mouth and destroy him by his appearing and his coming.''[16]

Until then, evil has been permitted by God to influence us as a test. *(parahoresis)*. In this ''time between the times'' evil occurs and is real. But in no case is it of necessity overwhelming.

> But while the liberty to attack man has been granted to (devils), they have not the strength to overmaster anyone, for we have it in our power to receive or not receive the attack.[17]

But until the Second Coming, Christians will struggle with evil so as to remove it as much as possible from their personal life, from the community of the faithful, considered as a human institution, from the society in which they find themselves and in the whole of human existence.

They do this strengthened by the eschatological reality which has already come to us in Christ.

> Through the saving work of Jesus Christ the power of evil is broken; that is to say, not that sin and death no longer exist, but that, the devil having been once and for all conquered by Christ, His triumph is in principle universal, and His redemptive work can go forward everywhere, through the Spirit who unites men with God and ''deifies'' them . . .[18]

The Experience of Sin

As we have noted, the personal or individual dimension of evil is frequently characterized as sin. This reality of evil pervades the teaching of the Old and New Testaments. As an authority notes:

> The Bible takes sin in dead seriousness. Unlike many modern religionists, who seek to find excuses for sin and to explain away its seriousness, most of the writers of the Bible had a keen awareness of its heinousness, culpability and tragedy. They looked upon it as no less than a condition of dreadful estrangement from God, the sole source of well being. They knew that apart from God, man is a lost sinner, unable to save himself or find true happiness.[19]

The implications of sin for Orthodox Christian Ethics are many.[20] The first has to do with the understanding in Orthodox Christian Ethics of sin on the one hand as the breaking of the relationship between the human being and God and on the other as the rebellious violation of the divine commandments. Ethics will also deal with the questions of responsibility and guilt, especially as these relate to original sin and committed sin. Connected to responsibility and guilt, there are the ethical aspects of shame arising from the committing of sin, which is seen as a function of the conscience.

The Christian experience of the event and condition of sin has led to a multitude of attempts to define it. In the Old Testament the Hebrew word *hattat* and the Septuagint word ἁμαρτία carry the same connotation of missing the mark. Other Hebrew words for sin indicate "straying from the right path," "distortion," "rebellion" as well as "evil-doing." In the New Testament the idea of the non-fulfillment of the will of God is the bedrock of the idea of sin. "Thy will be done on earth" is a characteristic phrase.[21] Other images of sin have been used by both Scriptures and the Fathers of the Church. The Fourth Gospel characterizes it as darkness and death as does Eastern Christian liturgical piety. Clement of Alexandria saw it as a perverse form of irrationality.[22] Chrysostom saw it as ingratitude and insult,[23] an idea picked up later by Anselm and emphasized in a feudal society which was in a particular position to appreciate it thus defined.[24] Other expressions with which the Christian experience has sought to define sin are transgression, disobedience, unlawful act, failure, a defective act, impiety, a debt or trespass, an injustice and inequity.[25]

However, in spite of the plethora of adjectival descriptions nearly all of these can be reduced and have been so reduced in the mainstream of Christian thinking to two fundamental approaches. The one is relational in character and the other legal. On the one hand are those expressions or concepts which see sin essentially as the breaking of the appropriate relationship between man and God, and also between man and his fellow man. On the other hand, there are those expressions which lend themselves readily to the understanding that the essential nature of sin is the disobedience of the law of God. That the Roman legal tradition of the West found the understanding of sin as violation of the law of God more appealing does not surprise us. Further, there is much biblical and patristic support for the idea. On the other hand the Eastern patristic tradition tended to see the character of sin in the fact that man was not sharing in and responding to the action, activity, and energy of God on his behalf. Irenaeus writes for instance that "the glory of God is a living man; and the life of man consists in beholding God."[26] But "separation from God is (spiritual) death" in the words of one of St. Irenaeus' commentators.[27] An Eastern Christian theologian, Constantine Callinicos, writing in 1909, expressed the idea characteristically in the following words:

> If religion is defined and is the innermost bond of man with God, and if sin is nothing other than the opposing force which seeks to destroy that bond with satanic passion and to snatch the child from the arms of its Creator, then Christianity . . . must needs present itself in no other light than as any enemy of this opposing power and as a restorer of the broken bond.[28]

It is not necessary to document the legal understanding of sin which became common practice not only in Roman Catholic catechetical instruction, but also in the Protestant sectarian and perfectionist traditions. It should be noted, however, that there is always the reciprocal danger and the temptation of allowing the one to be swallowed up by the other. If it is true that in the past in western Christian traditions the idea of "sin as disobedience to law" was dominant, the present corrective re-emphasis of the idea of sin as the break of the relationship between God and man and between man and his fellow man seems to be moving toward the other pole. No one has done this more powerfully in recent times than Joseph Fletcher. His definition of love as the only intrinsic good,[29] his exclusion of law as a norm,[30] his understanding of justice merely as love distributed,[31] and his admitted relativism[32] are the collapse of the one pole of the traditional understanding of sin into the other. It is thus possible in his situationist ethic to pronounce, in certain cases, right and good, those acts which by a scriptural and patristic standard would be characterized as sinful. In contrast, it would appear more faithful to the tradition of faith that the two affirmations (sin as broken relationship and sin as disobedience to God's law and will) be affirmed side by side. The first attests to the experience of sin in the Christian community as a personal separation from the source of light and life and strength and power. As separation from God it is meonic, it is the absence of reality. As we have seen, St. John of Damascus says in this connection, "evil, then, is nothing else than the absence of the good, just as darkness is the absence of light."[33] Yet, if the breaking of the relationship permits Christians to see sin as meonic, as not having the characteristic of true reality, the view of sin as disobedience to the will and law of God points to the empirically real content of sin experienced as rebelliousness, passion, hatred and positive evil acts of destruction. To collapse the law aspect of sin into the relational aspect of sin as Fletcher does is to lose the Christian experience of the concrete power of sin. It is this same danger which is attendant to all meonic concepts of evil. That is why the Eastern church has always felt the need for correctives in dealing with this issue.[34] On the other hand to collapse the relational aspect of sin into the law aspect of sin is to depersonalize and make rigidly formalistic a living human experience. The answer, then, from an Orthodox perspective, is to do neither. To keep a place for sin as the violation of God's commandment and will, while keeping alive the sense of sin as a separation from the source of life and the breaking of a relationship is the course dictated by the Orthodox tradition. It is not necessary to maintain an absolute one to one parity between the two. Certainly the relational aspect of our understanding of sin especially as a denial of God's love and the denial of love as the primary root of human evil can be maintained without denying the character of sin as concrete disobedience to the law of God. Maximos the Confessor, the 7th century vigorous opponent of Monotheleticism seems to have put his finger on the issue when he wrote:

> Just as it is the characteristic of disobedience to sin, so it is the characteristic of obedience to act virtuously. And just as disobedience is accompanied by the violation of the commandment and separation from the giver of the command, so it is that obedience consists of the fulfillment of commandments and unity with the giver of the command. Thus, he who keeps, through obedience, the command has done the right and has kept unsundered the loving unity between himself and the giver of the command.[35]

The act of sinning implies responsibility for the act. Because of this, the violation of the commandment or the breaking of the relationship with God has consequences upon the sinner and his standing as a member of the Church. In the first case, the violation of commandments leads to guilt, implying personal responsibility. This is most clearly seen in the penetential system of the Church. John Erickson has noted that

> The penetential system of the early Church patterned as it was, on the paradigmatic sin of apostasy, presupposes what might be called the *objective nature of sin*. Sin is not just a disposition, an inclination, a psychological state. Rather, the sinner, operating in full knowledge, makes a deliberate, conscious choice, and completes this movement of the will with an act that manifestly excludes him from the body of the faithful and identifies him with the works of the Evil One. [36]

This description of the early Church's penitential discipline which focused on the deed-the violation of a commandment—was subsequently balanced in the monastic tradition—which tended to focus the issue precisely on the inner disposition. Thus, St. Basil "regretted that his predecessors were so pre-occupied with grave sins that they neglected others which they deemed less serious: wrath, avarice and the like . . ."[37] These and other dispositional sins came to the forefront in the Byzantine confessional practice. Spiritual growth and development were emphasized with inevitable concern for the inner life. Here, sin is precisely thought to be in large part "a disposition, an inclination, a psychological state." Thus the Council of Trullo, using the medical analogy regarding repentance focused on the dipositions of the sinner:

> Therefore he who professes the science of spiritual medicine first of all should consider the disposition of him who has sinned, and to see whether he tends to health or, on the contrary, provokes his disease by his own behavior . . . .[38]

In both cases, however, the presupposition of penitential discipline is responsibility for the act (disobedience to the commandment) or the continued cultivation and submission to the inappropriate disposition (passion). Thus, without question, the Greek Fathers "as teachers of the Church and educators of the Christian people, most assuredly speak regarding the ethical responsibility of the person in the commission of sin. They repeatedly emphasize the obligation of mankind to unceasingly struggle against sin, and constantly lift up the possibility of victory."[39] In the canons and in preaching, the Greek Fathers never minimized this personal responsibility. Thus, Cyril of Alexandria can write "The devil is able to suggest, but he has no power to force himself against our choosing," concluding that "it is by choice that we sin."[40] And St. Basil also comments: "the source and root of sin is our self-determination *(autexousion)*. This side of the picture is most powerfully stated by one of the Neptic Fathers, Mark the Hermit, who in the treatise, *Concerning Holy Baptism* writes:

It is necessary to understand that we are made to act by sin through our own cause. Therefore it is up to us who listen to and learn of the commands of the spirit, to walk according to the flesh or according to the spirit . . . for the doing of these things or the not doing of them is ours. Consequently, neither is it Satan, nor is it the sin of Adam, but we ourselves who are to blame.[41]

John Karavidopoulos has, however, indicated that this patristic focus on personal responsibility is not one-sided. In his work *Sin According to Saint Paul,* he notes the equally well-documented patristic theological tradition which sees sin as a condition of distortion, defectiveness, sickness and wounding and the death of human existence. This condition of incomplete, inauthentic and corrupt existence is precisely the definition of original sin in the Greek Fathers. Prof. Karavidopoulos dramatically summarizes the Patristic position:

> Original sin, according to the theology of the Fathers of the East, had as an immediate consequence a "sickness," the wounding, that is, and the weakening of human nature, so that there was created an unnatural and sickly condition within the world characterized by corruption, sin and death. The paradisial harmony in humanity between reason and feelings was basically shaken in such a fashion that together with the damnation of the materialistic side of life, humanity fell under the tyrannical lordship of desires and was made a prisoner of sin and the devil. Communion with God, the source of life, was interrupted, with death as the unavoidable consequence.

One of the consequences of this condition of sin affects the issue of guilt and responsibility. Karavidopoulos continues:

> Man finds this sickly and unnatural (*para physin*) condition as pre-existing. He is caught in a complex web, and the threads which sin and the devil have woven about him, have made him captive, totally incapable of freeing himself and escaping by his own powers. The expression and verification of this condition are the concrete sins of human beings, which feed and foster this condition of sin so that it continues to exist, new sins constantly sprout from it . . .[42]

Freedom of choice on the one hand, seems to speak of full human responsibility. Original sin—as perceived by the Greek Fathers—in seemingly contradictory fashion speaks of a pre-existing condition of sin which binds human beings in an inescapable network of sin. Such a condition would seem to demand a view of human responsibility which would see man as a victim of sin, to be pitied perhaps, but not to be blamed and condemned as guilty.

What appears to be the problem is that the Greek Fathers, and Eastern Orthodox Christianity with them, affirm both views simultaneously. We

81

are free, and therefore responsible; we are concurrently under the dominion of sin, the devil and death in a condition over which we have no control, and therefore, it would appear, may not be adjudged as guilty or responsible. The Greek Fathers, however, and Orthodoxy with them, deny neither, nor do they collapse the one into the other. "The Eastern patristic tradition," Jaroslav Pelikan has noted, "was able to look seriously at the fact of human death and corruptibility without lapsing into the determinism that is always lurking in Augustinian anthropology."[43]

How is this done? Essentially the answer to this question requires the serious acceptance of that thread of New Testament teaching of Christ as victor over death, sin and the devil in His Incarnation, teaching, earthly life, His suffering, death on the Cross, and most importantly, His resurrection.

Commenting on the atonement emphasis of the Greek Fathers, and especially Irenaeus, Gustaf Aulén summarizes succinctly this teaching.

> The work of Christ is *first and foremost* a victory over the powers which hold mankind in bondage: sin, death, and the devil. These may be said to be in a measure personified, but in any case they are objective powers; and the victory of Christ creates a new situation, bringing their rule to an end, and setting men free from their dominion.[44]

This work of ending the rule of death, sin, evil over mankind *has been accomplished* by Christ on a cosmic level. The personal appropriation of it continues in the Church as a result of the work of the Holy Spirit, *to which each person must consent and with which each person must willingly cooperate*. This is the doctrine of "Synergy" which gives to us a solution to the dilemma. The power of death, sin and evil is broken. But it is not expelled from human life as if by magic. This would be a "reverse determinism," which would force us into goodness. Its *determining* power is shattered. But its *influencing* power remains. The devil still tempts. The flesh still "leans toward evil," the spirit still revels in its pride and selfishness.

It is here where the patristic doctrines of synergy and *"autexousion"* (self-determination) come to their own, as we shall see further on in this study (see below, chapter 5). Suffice here to note that the influencing power of death, sin and the devil (evil) need the cooperation of human choice, in large part, to have effect. That is why, as noted above, our responsibility remains, even though there are powers of evil and sin with which we must contend. Thus, in general when we sin, it is we who are responsible: "Neither is it Satan, nor is it the sin of Adam, but we ourselves who are to blame," as Mark the Hermit noted.

The nature of the responsibility, however, is significant. It is not that of an autonomous and independent, ethical agent. Our choice consists of aligning ourselves to God, of becoming in St. Paul's words "servants" and "slaves" of the Lord (δοῦλοι Κυρίου) and opening our lives to the enabling of God's Holy Spirit. The sinning is the result of our choice to abandon our self to the influencing power of the devil, sin and death. Virtue, obedience, life are the consequence of our choice to open up our lives to the influence, presence and communion with the Holy Trinity. However, that choice is ours. Thus we may conclude with the Greek Fathers, that there is an influencing power of sin which pervades our moral existence. It is real and significant and truly *a power,* pervasive and insidious, which undermines authentic human existence. Yet, together with the Fathers, we equally affirm human responsibility in the choice of that to which we will conform our lives and more importantly, the choice of with whom we relate and with whom we live in communion.

The Eastern Orthodox doctrine of synergy weighs the balance on the side of self-determination and moral responsibility. Consequentlyn it emphasizes the responsibility of the sinner when sin is committed. Yet, here a caution needs to be strongly emphasized. The Greek Fathers almost never speak of guilt (ἐνοχή) either on an individual basis or in a cosmic sense as related to the doctrine of original sin. Rather, there is a sense of responsibility for one's actions which arises out of the violation of one's status as a member of the community, the *ecclesia.* Thus, in the patristic literature the word εὐθύνη (responsibility) nearly always is used in a setting of public judgment, with meanings such as "rendering of account," "public examination," "showing of proof," "accusation," "conviction."[45]

It is no surprise, then, that responsibility for sin is not perceived as something suppressed within the *psyche,* as in Western psychiatric theory, but rather an act which places the sinner in public (ecclesial) disapproval and for which the sinner experiences shame. Justin Martyr's comment is indicative of this attitude. Christ's words, he opines, "have in themselves something of dreadful majesty, and are enough to put to shame those that turn out of the right way, while rest most delightful comes to those who carry them out in practice."[46] The New Testament expresses the same viewpoint. "And now, little children, abide in Him, so that when He appears we may have confidence and not shrink from Him in shame at His coming."[47] This clearly relational context of shame in I John is completed with the clearly ethical context of the first twenty verses of Ephesians 5, where it is noted . . ." try to learn what is pleasing to the Lord. Take no part in the unfruitful works of darkness, but instead, expose them. For it is a shame even to speak of the things they do in secret."[48]

Perhaps of all the Fathers, St. John Chrysostom most fully understood the significance of shame for sin. First, he clearly discerned between shame appropriate to the virtuous life and misplaced shame. For example, in commenting on St. Paul's denial of any shame for being jailed for Christ's sake, Chrysostom makes the distinction: "that we should be bound for Christ is no shame, but for fear of bonds to betray anything that is Christ's, this is shame."[49] This refers to shame subsequent to sin. Chrysostom sees shame for committed sins as part of the "given" of our created reality, that is, what we will refer to in chapters to follow in this book as "Human Moral Capacities." The saint notes:

There is, indeed, even in the shameless a small portion of shame. For God hath sown in our nature the seeds of shame; for since fear was insufficient to bring us to a right tone, He hath also prepared many other ways for avoiding sin.[50]

Given, however, the Patristic view which always looks forward to growth in the fulfillment of the divine image in human life, shame is not to be perceived as only condemnatory, whose major purpose is to convict the sinner of guilt. Rather, the emphasis should be put on shame as a motive to avoid sin to do good.[51]

This approach, which acknowledges responsibility for acts done, but does not focus on guilt, is not to be perceived as taking sin lightly, however. There is a sense of responsibility for sin in the liturgical life of Eastern Orthodoxy which is deliberately distinguished from guilt. In some of the prayers of absolution there is reference to "sins, both voluntary and involuntary (ἁμαρτήματα ἑκούσιά τε καί ἀκούσια)." "Involuntary sin" is a paradoxical phrase. Generally speaking, as we have seen, choice, decision, and exercise of the *autexousion* are an integral part of the understanding of sin. Strictly speaking, there can be no guilt if the act takes place without the exercise of the will. Yet, the Church acknowledges, as well, sins which we have not willed, and for which it cannot be said that we are guilty, strictly speaking. Involuntary sins refer to our personal involvement in circumstances and events which are evil, which have caused evil results, yet which we have neither willed, chosen or desired. For example, a careful, law-abiding motorist may become involved in "involuntary sin," if his auto strikes a child darting onto the street. Supposing no malice, carelessness, violation of motor vehicle laws, etc., the unhappy combination of circumstances which has involved him in this accident in the strict sense must leave him without guilt. Yet he is not without responsibility. He may be adjudged formally innocent, and rightly so. Yet he has been involved in a frightening, tragic and damaging accident. The sense of evil is real. As is the sense of responsibility arising out of the motorist's involvement in the accident. Accepting this involuntary involvement in this situation, pastoral sensitivity demands a category of "involuntary sin" for which it offers prayers of absolution.

Therapy for Sin: Repentance, Forgiveness, Reparation

Sin, then, is destruction of the proper relationship with God; a violation of divine commands; a disorientation of fitting and proper relations with our fellows and an unnatural state of inner dispositions; the personal and social embodiment of *meonic* existence and a characteristic of a less-than-human existence both personally and corporately.

If there is to be growth in the fulfillment of our human destiny to achieve Theosis, then sin must be overcome. It is the cornerstone of Christian faith that God Himself undertook the task of freeing humanity from the burden of sin through the saving work of His Son, Jesus Christ. Through the Incarnation, the teaching, example, direction, healing, suffering, death, resurrection and ascension of Jesus Christ the power of sin, death and evil have been vanquished and overcome for the whole of humanity.

From one perspective, the Church is the incorporation, in the life of persons and the community of believers, of the victory of Jesus Christ over sin. Thus, the sacramental life, beginning with Baptism is a process, means and celebration for the expulsion of sin from our life and increased communion with God in whose image we are to grow.

In Eastern Orthodox Christianity this victory over sin—not as a merely pronounced or "forensic" victory—is in fact, a transfiguration and transformation of life. However, it is not automatic. It does not occur magically. On the personal level, the beginning, middle and end of the process is imbued with the experience of repentance.

Repentance is a return of our spirit to its true self, a regrouping of one's self, a restoration of our spiritual existence.[52] Because this conversion of our life of necessity cannot be forced, but must be freely chosen, it is a moral act, a decision, a choice, a willed act. It is "a continuous effort of our will, seeking to keep us continually facing in God's direction." The task of repentance is synergistic. God's grace constantly prompts, invites challenges and calls for the turning of the human heart from sin to God. But the human spirit must choose to respond.

Since we are constantly under the continuing attacks of the passions, one repentance is not adequate. "We must be constantly and continuously returning to God" in repentance. Thus, repentance is a constant and perpetual stance of those who truly wish to overcome sin and grow in the image and likeness of God.

> Repentance (in Greek *"metanoia"*) literally means a "change of thought," a "transformation of mind." To say, "I repent" means that I change my way of thinking. It means that I change the thoughts and opinions which I have had until now in my mind and which I expressed in my daily life with sinful deeds and words. Repentance means that I regret every sin which I have done. I reject and condemn them and I make a sincere decision not to do them again. Rather, I will have my opinions, my thoughts, my words and my actions and my whole life turned in God's direction.[53]

Repentance is self initiated under the constant prompting of the Spirit. It opposes an attitude of pharisaical self-satisfaction. It does not need to be accused of sin by others, but it is ready to hear the criticisms of others, examining those criticisms to ascertain their validity. It is far from the spirit of pride and self-satisfaction which can only be based in ignorance of self and of our human purpose, for "the person who is ignorant of himself is not aware of the tremendous need which he has to step out of his old condition and to turn once again to God." Thus, St. John of the Ladder writes:

We will not be condemned at the end of our lives because we did not perform miracles. Nor because we failed to theologize. Neither will we be condemned because we have failed to achieve the divine vision. But because of one reason only: that we did not repent continuously.[54]

There are several important expressions of this continuous experience of repentance. One, emphasized in the monastic tradition of the East is the gift of tears.[55] Another is the sacrament of Holy Confession. Here we must caution that a routine, perfunctory and formalistic attendance at this sacrament is not what is meant. Rather, what needs to be emphasized is that true, sincere and a fully adequate confession is the result only of genuine repentance. It is in the Sacrament of Holy Confession that the Christian expresses his or her repentance in a concrete and specific manner, in which the Christian receives assurance of forgiveness of sins and guidance for growth in the divine image. There is a long history of scholarly and polemical effort to discredit this Sacrament as an authentic expression of the Christian teaching.[56] Yet, the empowering words of the apostolic absolution of sins found in Matthew 16:19, Matthew 18:18 and John 20:23 seem to have been rapidly followed in Church practice with the formal confession of sins before bishops and later, priests. Evidence from Ignatius of Antioch,[57] Tertullian,[58] Origen,[59] Cyprian,[60] as well as many other early writers support both its antiquity and authenticity.[61] Whatever the case, the fact is that the Sacrament of Reconciliation has been a continuing factor in the spiritual life of the Church and the locus for forgiveness of sins in its life.

However, the forgiving action of the Holy Spirit appears not to be limited to the Sacrament of Holy Confession for it also includes the Christian life as a whole. "The Spirit blows where it will."[61] The Church has always seen forgiveness as available to the faithful within the total framework of the Church's life. For the early Church, prayer, fasting, and most important, almsgiving as expressions of repentance and remorse were thought as effective means of forgiveness of sins. Almsgiving seems to be one of the criteria for entrance into the Kingdom in Jesus' teaching.[63]

Almsgiving, as an important aspect of Christian life rapidly increased in importance so that Augustine's position can be summarized as follows:

At the heart of penance is alsmgiving. The greatest form of almsgiving is forgiveness of others who have wronged one. For to forgive a man who seeks pardon is itself a giving of alms and accordingly, our Lord's saying 'Give alms, and behold all things are clean to you' applies to every useful act of mercy.[64]

The sacraments present themselves, also, as arenas of forgiveness and reconciliation. The Eucharist is not only presented as offering forgiveness with the repetition of the words of institution ("this is my blood of the covenant, which is poured out for many for the forgiveness of sins")[65] but the whole liturgical action is the making real of the Kingdom of God, a Kingdom of forgiveness and reconciliation.[66] The frequent appeals for mercy and forgiveness in all forms of the Eucharist, so readily subsumed in the simple formula, "Lord have mercy" show clearly that the Eucharist is also a locus of forgiveness as a work of the Holy Spirit. The words of institution of the Sacrament of Holy Unction express the same point: "Is any among you sick? Let him call for the Presbyters of the Church and let them pray over him anointing him with oil in the name of the Lord; and the prayer of faith will save the sick man, and the Lord will raise him up; and if he has committed sins he will be forgiven."[67] A survey of the liturgical expressions of all the other Sacraments in the practice of the Church shows the same anticipation of forgiveness.

In addition, common worship carries the same pre-supposition of appeal for and expectation of forgiveness. In the rich and varied tradition of the Eastern Orthodox Church it is to be found everywhere, from the Churching of a mother and her baby on the fortieth day after birth, through the blessings of inanimate objects, to prayers for healing, to the funeral service itself. This is perhaps nowhere more profoundly registered than in the Orthodox doxology. Rationally one would expect a doxology to be an act of the pure adoration of God. Yet of its twenty distinct stanzas (not counting the exact repetitions) nine stanzas are appeals for mercy or for forgiveness of sins or for aid to keep from sinning.[68] Finally, it ought to be pointed out that a large portion of Church discipline, i.e., Canon law, functions on the presupposition that it operates within the whole framework of the forgiveness of sins and the reconciliation of the sinner to the body of Christ.[69]

Thus there are two poles where the Holy Spirit makes the present dimension of forgiveness real: concretely and specifically in the Sacrament of Holy Confession and in a more diffused manner in the whole Christian life. The temptation here is to collapse the one into the other. The tendency of theological definition in the history of Christian thought seems to have sought to downgrade the general Christian experience of forgiveness while insisting on the absolute exclusiveness of the Sacrament of Holy Confession for forgiveness of sins. For example the Council of Trent promulgated a *Catechism for Parish Priests* in which "the high Roman Catholic view of the authority of the priest is affirmed. The words 'I absolve thee' signify that remission of sins is effected by the administration of this Sacrament. How thankful should sinners be that God has bestowed on priests this power! Penance restores us to the grace of God. There is no hope for remission by any other means."[70]

Christos Androutsos, the well-known professor of Orthodox Dogmatics was able to argue that ". . . the general opinion that one is able to achieve direct forgiveness from God without need of confession to the Spiritual Father is considered by the Orthodox as impious and foolish."[71] In both cases the experience of the life of the Church as a community of reconciliation is subsumed to the specific sacramental tradition.

On the other hand, the denial of the Sacrament of Holy Confession in Protestantism generally has meant that forgiveness of sins has become a highly subjective experience. In sectarian expressions it has become the drive for the creation of a strict, unbending, rigorous, charity-less, literalist and legalistic understanding of Christianity, a fact delineated by Ernst Troeltsch so clearly in his *Social Teachings of the Christian Churches*.[72] In mainline Protestantism it seems rapidly leading to a secularization of much of the reconciling function of the Church. The alliance of psychology with religion in some of its practitioners leads to a deterioration of the element of gracious forgiveness and the relativising of the reconciling, forgiving and redemptive function of the Church.[73]

The errors on both sides can be avoided if the Sacrament is seen as the focus for the sharpest expression of forgiveness and as a necessary aspect of the living of the Christian life in the Spirit, while the Christian life as a whole both in its corporate and personal dimension is perceived to be the more diffused realization of one of the ever-present activities of the Holy Spirit in the lives of the faithful.

The salient characteristic of the Sacrament of Holy Confession consists of the oral expression of repentance for sins committed to a priest and the reception of forgiveness from God pronounced orally by the priest.

Why is it necessary for the confession to be oral? There are several reasons we could point to. The psychological need for expression of repentance to make it real and fulfill its essential nature is an insight supported by much contemporary psychological theory. One theologian put it categorically several years ago in the following words: ". . . one might say that where there is no desire for confession it is the result and manifestation of the absence of true penitence."[74] But further, the aspect of growth requires that the person repenting also receive guidance, comfort, advice, suggestions for correction and direction. Without oral confession such would not be possible. Even in the light of non-directional counseling such oral confession is a requirement. This will have serious bearing on the nature of imposed penances, a topic we will return to shortly. Further, oral confession in the earliest history of the sacrament was an act done before the whole body of the Church. Despite the drawbacks of such situations, it points to the need for the penitent to be reconciled to the body of the faithful, the Church. Confession to the priest as a representative of the Church not only gives assurance of forgiveness in a concrete way, it also assures the repentant person of his continued membership and solidarity in the Body of Christ.[75]

This identity of the Church with the penitent and the penitent with the Church is graphically illustrated in the oldest extant complete service in the East of the Sacrament of Penance, that of Patriarch of Constantinople, John the Faster, who lived during the latter half of the sixth century. In this service the Father Confessor and the penitent pray together at the beginning of the service. Both kneel together three times. The Father Confessor is then instructed to ask questions of the penitent with kindness and gentleness and if possible to embrace him and to place the hands of the penitent upon his own head, especially if he sees him suffering and overtaken by unbearable sorrow and shame and in a humble and most peaceful voice he is to say to the penitent 'How are things with you my lord brother or sister' . . . and he proceeds with the questions. Oral confession makes the presence of the Church and membership in it a channel and instrumentation of the experience of forgiveness.[76]

What of the content of the confession itself? Since the repentance of the penitent is the *sine qua non* of the act, the details of the confessed sins are not the primary criterion. Enough should be said, however, so that the spiritual father is capable of understanding the condition of the penitent, but there is no need to have every detail, every instance, every aspect of the sin ferreted out. The 102nd Canon of the 5/6th Ecumenical Council in Trullo very wisely compares the work of the Father Confessor with that of the physician, whose task it is to find out enough about the penitent so to heal him, maintaining the middle road between simple generalities and too detailed specifics for, as it says, ''the sickness of sin is not simple but varied and multiformed.''[77]

What is the nature of the absolution offered? The absolution restores the relationship between God and man, it empowers the penitent to continue to grow in the image and likeness of God; that is, it does not remove the history and the fact of the sin, it removes the effects and consequences of the sin. St. Athanasios says, ''He who repents ceases from sinning, but he still has the marks of the wounds.''[78] The penitent becomes a new creature again which makes possible his obedience to the will of God and his growth in the divine image. It is the pronouncement of the Father Confessor which actualizes this: ''Whose sins ye forgive, they are forgiven, whose sins ye retain, they are retained.'' Yet, the pronouncement of that forgiveness ought to point to the philanthropy and mercy of God, rather than the power of forgiveness granted to God's agent. ''Behold,'' the priest says to the penitent, ''through the will of the philanthropic God, who wishes the salvation of all, having come in repentance and having confessed all, you are released from your previous evil works,'' is a characteristic prayer of the service of Patriarch John the Faster mentioned above.

Finally, what is the nature of any penances which the Father Confessor may choose to require of the forgiven penitent? On the one hand they cannot be acts of atonement or satisfaction, so to speak, for the sins committed since the purpose of the Sacrament is to mediate the forgiving grace of God, to restore the relationship, to provide new freedom of growth. Rather, the penances may serve two purposes. The first is to impress upon the penitant the reality of the forgiveness. This is solely remedial and medicinal and not vindictive and punitive (for) ''The Blood of Jesus . . . cleanses us from all sin''[79] . . . ''nor is there any condemnation to them which are in Christ Jesus.''[80]

Such penances need not be imposed if the Father Confessor deems it unnecessary, for they are not an essential aspect of the sacrament of Holy Confession. The second purpose of the imposition of penances relates to the penitent's need for guidance, assistance and direction. Penances should be imposed on the basis of the specific condition and needs for the improvement and growth of the penitent. They should be designed and

89

imposed with the specific intent of helping him or her to grow in the Spirit into the image and likeness of God.

It is in this light that reparation or restitution may be required of the penitent. When the sins committed have caused harm or injury or unjust treatment of another, genuine repentance will require not only the future amendment of life, but will also cause the desire to repair the harm done, or to minimize the consequences or to make restitution. Not only is such an attitude a requirement of simple justice, the spirit of genuine repentance will demand it. When it is possible that restitution be made directly, the Father Confessor should direct the penitent to this course of action. In circumstances where this cannot be done, it is the responsibility of the Father Confessor to direct the penitent to some other act of repair of injuries caused. In no case, of course, should these acts be seen as "purchasing" forgiveness but rather only as a kind of almsgiving expressing repentance and simple justice. Without this intent, and its reasonable implementation, repentance must certainly be considered defective.

Moral Optimism and Pessimism

As a conclusion to our discussion of evil, the question arises regarding the relative relationship of good and evil in the world. Is human life and existence "basically good" or is life a "vale of tears" in which the evil far outweighs the good? What is the appropriate stance? Moral optimism or moral pessimism?

There are three basic approaches to this question from a philosophical point of view. The first is that of complete moral optimism (aisiodoxia). This view does not hold that everything is perfect, thus denying the existence of evil. Rather, it holds that the world as it is, is the "best possible world." If Plato's idealism is carefully examined, the physical world is seen as necessarily imperfect because of its relationship with matter; yet, if the world is to exist materially, then it cannot be any better than it is. Improvement *means* de-materialization of the world. Thus, the world cannot be any better than it is; it is "the best possible world." A more modern philosopher has also held this position. For Leibnitz, of all possible worlds, this world as it is, alone could exist. Leibnitz reasoned in his famous "Trilemma" on the basis of a belief in a perfect and all-powerful God that if the world was not the best, then God did not know how, or did not want to or was not able to make it as good as it could be. Since we cannot accept that God did not know how to make the world as good as it could be (God is all-knowing and all-wise), nor can we accept that God did not want to make the best possible world (God is all-good), nor that He was unable to make the world as good as it could possibly be (God is all-powerful), we must conclude that the world as God made it is "the best possible."

This view is countered by a cosmic moral pessimism which sees this world and the life in it in the worst of terms—it is "the worst possible." Some have done this on the basis of empirical observation. Looking at history and life as it exists in fact, they have concluded that, indeed the world and life in it are full of many evils and few good things; pain, sickness, suffering, desires, greed, hatred, vanity, pride, the "right of the mighty," injustice, poverty, robbery, murder, wars and death. Several schools of thought, both philosophical and religious have elevated this observation to a generalized view of life. Much of contemporary existentialism, for instance, sees all of life as in fact meaningless, purposeless and as completely alienated from the individual. This basic stance is met with a call to a courageous effort "to be" inspite of the reality of the situation. This view has entered into much of the literature, theater and films of our times. One student of this viewpoint has summarized this stance as follows:

1. Chance and absurdity rule human actions. What the philosophers call "reality" is really chaos. There are no real causes, only twitches and spasms, ludicrous and grinding.

2. There are no accepted norms—of feeling or conduct—to which a man may appeal. There is no general standard for thought or for action to which one may refer unfailingly.

3. To live is to be at odds—with environment, with others, with oneself—and so always to be somehow an alien, a misfit. Others aren't aids and comforts, but others are the enemy.

4. The characteristic of life, of personal existence, is ambiguity. Human motives are forever mixed; irony and contradiction prevail. No thought or action is ever pure. Blameless purity is an impossibility, but pure pusillanimity is probably also ruled out. Free and yet a slave, actor yet acted upon; everything is mixed. And one who is completely neutralized is in danger of becoming a neuter.

5. A man can't know much. Limitation and relativism, tininess and partiality are the major makers of our manhood. [81]

This view of great pessimism about life and the world reflects—though for different reasons—an earlier philosophical view propounded by Schopenhauer and an even more ancient view as embodied in the Hindu religion. In the Vedas, the most ancient literature of the Indian subcontinent, the doctrine of reincarnation is taught. Life is seen as a dreary and burdensome succession of reincarnations, each dependent upon the preceding incarnation for its quality and character. That is existence. Salvation from this "eternal wheel of suffering" is to escape existence, to achieve "non-being" to enter into a stable state of unconscious non-existence known as Nirvana. The world is evil; the human goal is to escape it; to escape it is to cease to exist. In Greek this view is known as *"apaisiodoxia."*

Standing between these two extremes is the position which might be characterized as "ameliorism" *(beltiognosia)* which holds that morally speaking this is not either the "best" not the "worst" of all possible worlds. It recognizes the imperfection of the present, yet seeks actively to improve conditions. This is the most dominant view in the modern world. Under the impetus given to it first by Capitalism and subsequently by Communism, the view that human resource and ingenuity can eliminate evil and substitute it with good informs much of our contemporary thinking. The nineteenth century views of "Progress, ever onward and upward" and the Marxist trust in the inevitable laws of economic development expressed themselves in a trust and dependence upon technology. Science and Technology were considered (together with their handmaiden, Education) as the key forces by which the process of improvement and development were to bring a new eon to humankind. This stance still prevails, albeit in a chastened and less enthusiastic form since the advent of nuclear weaponry and the ecological crisis. What might have been called a "modified optimism" in the past has become a "modified pessimism" now. The need to control technological development has become apparent; that progress can destroy as well as heal, that technology is not an unmitigated good, that science can be used for good and for evil, that development in one sector often causes undesirable consequences in other parts of the life-system are all common-places to modern man. Yet, the basic stance has not yet changed. Secularist society still sees the evils that surround us and has confidence that the "right" knowledge, applied in the "right" manner and in the "right" places will correct those evils. Only now, we are much more cognizant of the dangers to the ecosystem (pollution) and to civilization itself (nuclear warfare). Modern secular man is now less a moderate optimist and more a moderate pessimist than he was before. But he still remains an ameliorist.

In Christianity, many different views, reflecting the above basic three stances have been articulated. In the ancient Church heresies such as Pelagianism have emphasized the natural goodness of man and the world, holding that man in essence is capable of self-salvation. Augustine, on the other hand seems to have emphasized the tremendous and overpowering strength of sin and evil, relying almost totally on Divine Grace for its correction. This view was sharpened and emphasized in the subsequent Reformation doctrine of "total depravity" and salvation through "faith alone." The Reformation responded to a strong emphasis in medieval Roman Catholicism which emphasized "works." Augustine and the early Protestants were certainly "moral pessimists." Pelagius, and depending on what one emphasizes in Roman Catholic doctrine and practice, might well be characterized as "moral optimists."

Orthodoxy, too, has had its varying emphases. One need not read long in the monastic writings to obtain a definite "pessimistic" bias about mankind. Yet, the triumphal character of Orthodox worship, which is interpreted as a presence and foretaste of the Kingdom of God here on earth seems "quite optimistic." However, these are only partial expressions of the whole teaching of the Orthodox Church of Christ. As we have noted, the world was created "very good" by God as was humanity. Evil and sin entered the world through the self-determining choice of rational creatures. For the Christian, the redemptive work of Christ is decisive and it provides sure hope. The Kingdom of God has already begun and yet it is not completed nor fulfilled as yet. The empirical existence of evil is affirmed. Yet, its ultimate neutralizing is expected as a firm reality. The Christian view is neither a facile optimism nor a general pessimism. "If because of one man's trespass (Adam), death reigned through that one man, much more will those who receive the abundance of grace and the free gift of righteousness leads to acquittal and life for all men."[82] Orthodox Christianity underestimates neither the power and reality of evil, nor the victory over evil and sin and death which was accomplished in Jesus Christ. Consequently in its basic outlook, Christianity comes close to moral ameliorism. This is confirmed in the Orthodox doctrines of the image and the likeness, *askesis,* growth toward Theosis and sanctification. Yet, there is a basic difference when Orthodox ameliorism is related to secular ameliorism. For the latter is based totally on human ability and activity. The former places its trust and hope in the living God. "For to this end we always pray for you, that our God may make you worthy of his call, and may fulfill every good resolve and work of faith by His power so that the name of our Lord Jesus Christ may be glorified in you, and you in him, according to the grace of our God and the Lord Jesus Christ."[83] Our hope and confidence is based on "His power" and not our own.

It is also important to note that this Orthodox ameliorism refers primarily to the possibility and potential we have for moral and spiritual development—not upon the empirical and historical situation which is dependent upon numerous circumstances and conditions. Different ages, external circumstances and conditions improve or lessen this optimism which we have about the future development on the historical plane. Times during which society is receptive to the Christian gospel make us more confident and optimistic. On the contrary, times such as our own which seem intent upon substituting essentially pagan values for those of Christianity make us less optimistic.

Further, the Orthodox Church finds it easier to be optimistic about personal and primary group morality than about society as a whole. It is much easier (though still difficult) to permit God's grace to transform the personal life of the believer and to touch the common life of the faithful in the Church and as members of a family unit than to welcome the grace of God into the activities of the state, the factory, the bank and the stockmarket. There is a sense in which Christians work for the amelioration of conditions in a system which in its unredeemed and distorted condition has been and will be "in the power of the evil one"[84] until the coming of Christ again when it will be said: "Then I saw a new heaven and a new earth; for the first heaven and the first earth had passed away, and the sea was no more . . . and I heard a great voice from the throne saying 'Behold, the dwelling of God is with men. He will dwell with thee, and they shall be His people, and God Himself shall be with them; He will wipe away every tear from their eyes, and death shall be no more, neither shall there be mourning nor crying nor pain anymore, for the former things have passed away'.''[85]

It is this eschatological expectation which, in the end, keeps Christians optimistic and confident in the face of much human evil, pride and injustice. It is the fact that much of the cosmos is still under the sway of the Devil which keeps Christians realistically free from facile optimism. Thus Demetropoulos can properly summarize:

> . . . According to Christian teaching, God created the world as "very good" and potentially excellent, that is, having within itself the perfect capability of achieving the excellent purpose with which the Creator endowed it. The appearance of evil, caused by the fall of a portion of the angels and of man, which evil is distinguished as metaphysical, physical and moral evil, does not invalidate the Divine purposes. The Good, rather, in its struggle with that evil caused ultimately by the wrong use of freedom by rational beings, will in the end be victorious. At that time evil will disappear. Thus, the element of optimism in Christian thought does not consist of the view that God created the most perfect of worlds possible, but rather in the expectation, which Christianity holds as a sure conviction, that the world, in spite of all the evils in it, as it moves along toward its appointed end, will one day arrive, as God intended it, to full perfection, that is, the realization of the Kingdom of God. In the Kingdom, man, as a child of God and a co-heir of Christ, will reign together with Him forever in the vision of God, not as is the case now "through a glass darkly," but "face to face."[86]

Thus to conclude, Orthodox Christianity does have a bias toward moral ameliorism which is dependent both upon divine grace and human cooperation with it, but an ameliorism which is tempered by a serious consideration of the power and influence of sin.

1 Romans 12:2.

2 1 John 2:15.

3 1 John 2:17 KJV.

4 Edgar Sheffield Brightman, *A Philosophy of Religion,* Chapters 8, 9, 10.

5 *The Oxford Dictionary of the Christian Church,* New York: Prentice Hall, Inc., 1940, pp. 848, 854.

6 *Hexaemeron,* Homily 2.

7 MPG 25, 16A.

8 MPG 94, 973A, 927A.

9 *University Notes, op. cit.,* p. 71.

10 *Oratio catechetica,* 26.

11 *Chapters on Physics, Ethics and Practical Issues,* section 44. *Philokalia,* op. cit., vol. 4, pp. 149-150.

12 St. Augustine, *The City of God,* Bk. 12, Ch. 6.

13 *On Perfection,* P.G. 46. 285 A-D.

14 Romans 8:18-23.

15 *Orthodox Christian Ethics, op. cit.,* p. 48.

16 2 Thessalonians 2:8.

17 St. John of Damascus, *Exposition of the Orthodox Faith,* Bk. II, Ch. 4.

18 Gustaf Aülen, *Christus Victor,* New York: Macmillan, 1951.

19 S. J. De Vries, "Sin, Sinners" *The Interpretor's Dictionary of the Bible,* New York: Abingdon Press, 1962, Vol. R-Z, p. 361.

20 Portions of this section are slightly revised forms of an article of mine "A Theology of the Sacrament of Holy Confession," *The Greek Orthodox Theological Review,* Volume XIX, No. 2, Autumn, 1974, pp. 177-201.

21 J. J. Von Allmen, ed., *A Companion to the Bible,* New York, 1958, pp. 405-410 and Panagiotes Demetropoulos, "Amartia," *Threskevtike kai Ethike Encyclopaideia, op. cit.,* pp. 250-255.

22 *Paidagogos,* Ante-Nicene Fathers, II, 1.210.

23 *Homilies on Matthew,* LXL, 1. in *Ante-Nicene Fathers,* X, 376-377.

24 See Etienne Gilson, *Reason and Revelation in the Middle Ages,* New York, 1938.

25 Constantine Callinicos, *E Amartia Kata tin Christianiken Antilepsin,* 2nd ed., Athens, 1958, p. 31.

26 *Against Heresies,* Bk. IV, XX, 7, see also Bk. IV, XX, 5 and Bk. V, XX, 5 and B., V. XII, 2. *Ante-Nicene Fathers,* II, 49, 538.

27 John Romanides, *To Propatorikon Amartema,* Athens, 1956, pp. 118-119.

28 Callinicos, *op. cit.,* p. 16.

29 Joseph Fletcher, *Situation Ethics: The New Morality,* Philadelphia: Fortress Press, 1966.

30 *Ibid.,* p. 69.

31 *Ibid.,* p. 87.

32 *Ibid.,* pp. 40-56.

33 *Exact Exposition of the Orthodox Faith,* PG, XCIV, 973A.

34 See Vasilios Antioniades' quite vigorous critique of meonic concepts in his *Eucheiridion Kata Christon Ethikes,* Constantinople: Fazilet Press, 1972, I. 190-93.

35 Maximos the Confessor, "Peri Theologias, Deutera Hekatontas," *Philokalia ton Neptikon Pateron,* Athens, 1960, II, 70.

36 Penitential Dicsipline in the Orthodox Canonical Tradition," *St. Vladimir's Theological Quarterly,* Vol. 21, No. 4, 1977, p. 195.

37 *Ibid.,* p. 199.

38 Canon 102.

39 Ioannis Karavidopoulos, *E Amartia Kata ton Apostolon Pavlon.* Thessaloniki, 1968, p. 139.

40 *Catechesis* 4, 21 PG 33, 480, 481, 494.

41 PG 65, 1000, 1012.

42 *Ibid.,* p. 132.

43 "Puti Russkago Bogoslavia," in *The Heritage of the Early Church: Essays in Honor of the Very Reverend George Vasilievich Florovsky.* Ed. by David Neiman and Margaret Schatkin, Rome: Pont. Institutum Studiorum Orientalium, 1973, p. 13.

44 Gustaf Aülen, *Christus Victor: An Historical Study of the Three Main Types of the Idea of the Atonement,* Tr. by A. G. Hebert, London: S.P. C. K., 1965, p. 20. (Emphasis mine.)

45 See Lampe, *A Patristic Greek Lexicon,* relevant entries.

46 *Dialogue with Trypho:* 8.2.

47 1 John 2:28.

48 v.12.

95

⁴⁹ *Homilies on Philippians*, III, V. 20. *Nicene and Post-Nicene Fathers*, First Series, *op. cit.*, Vol. XIII, p. 195.

⁵⁰ *Op cit.*, p. 201.

⁵¹ *Op. cit.*, p. 224.

⁵² Christoforos Stavropoulos, *Partakers of Divine Nature*, tr. by Stanley S. Harakas, Minneapolis: Light and Life Publishing Co., 1976. This section on Repentance is based on pp. 50-55 of the above work.

⁵³ *Ibid.*, p. 51.

⁵⁴ *Ladder*, 7, 73. P. G. 88, 816D.

⁵⁵ See Kardamakis, *op. cit.*, pp. 53-55.

⁵⁶ What follows is a modified text from a portion of my article "A Theology of Holy Confession," *The Greek Orthodox Theological Review*, Vol. XIX, No. 2, 1974, pp. 188 ff.

⁵⁷ *Epistle to the Philadelphians*, VIII, 1.

⁵⁸ *De Paenitentia*, Chapter 9 and *De Pudicitia*, Chapter 18.

⁵⁹ *2nd Homily on Leviticus: Homily XVIII on Luke*, and *Homily V, 3 on Leviticus*.

⁶⁰ *De Lapsis*, 16 and 29 and Epistles IX, 1: XI, 2.

⁶¹ Epiphanios Theodoropoulos in "Sacrament of Repentance," *Threskeutike kai Ethike Encyclopaideia*, Vol. VIII (1959-66).

⁶² John 3:8.

⁶³ Matthew 25:35-46 and Matthew 6:2-4. See also Cecil John Cadoux, *The Early Church and the World*, Edinburgh, 1955, pp. 198-99, 285 ff.

⁶⁴ Emerson, *The Dynamics of Forgiveness*, Philadelphia: Westminster Press, 1964, p. 123.

⁶⁵ Matthew 26:28.

⁶⁶ Alexander Schmemann, *Introduction to Liturgical Theology*, Trans. by Ashleigh E. Moorhouse, London: The Faith Press, 1966; see also, Emerson, op. cit., pp. 94-95.

⁶⁷ James 5:15.

⁶⁸ *Iera Synopsis kai Akolouthia ton Pathon*, Athens, 1966, pp. 10, 11, stanzas: 5, 6, 9, 11, 13, 16, 17, 19, 28.

⁶⁹ *Ibid.*, pp. 99-100.

⁷⁰ Mc Neill, *A History of the Cure of Souls*, New York: Harper & Bros., 1951, p. 289.

⁷¹ *Dogmatike tis Orthodoxou Anatolikes Ekklesias*, 2nd ed., Athens: 1956, p. 387.

⁷² Ernst Troetsch, *Social Teachings of the Christian Churches*, op. cit., Vol. II, Chapter III, 4.

⁷³ This is my main criticism of Emerson's work, which is an heroic attempt to keep the Church in the process of forgiveness and reconciliation. Yet the weak ecclesiology underlying the book opens the door to understandings of forgiveness and "wholeness" which in the end deny the necessity of divine forgiveness and see it as a simple psychological process. See Chapter 2, and especially the conclusion.

⁷⁴ Constantine Dyoyouniotes, *Ta Mysteria tes Anatolikes Orthodoxou Ekklesias ex epopseos Orthodoxou*, Athens, 1912, p. 133. Quoted in Gavin, *Some Aspects*, p. 361.

⁷⁵ Canon 28 of Nikephoros the Confessor takes this into consideration when it cautions confessors not to prohibit Church attendance as penance to those who have sinned secretly, so that others may not "lord over them."

⁷⁶ Found in P.G. 88, 1890-1901 and Moremus, *De Disciplione in Administratione Sacrament: Poenitentiae*, Antwerp, 1982, pp. 77-117.

⁷⁷ Canon 102, in Hamilkar Alivizatos, *Oi Ieroi Kanones*, 2nd ed., Athens: 1949f, pp. 116-17.

⁷⁸ *Epistle to Serapion*, 4, 13, PG, XXVL, 656.

⁷⁹ 1st John 1:7.

⁸⁰ Romans 8:1. See also Frank Gavin, *op. cit.*, pp. 367-368.

⁸¹ Ihab Hassan, *Radical Innocence*, Princeton: Princeton University Press, 1961, pp. 116-118.

⁸² Romans 5:5: 17-18.

⁸³ 2 Thessalonians 1:11-12.

⁸⁴ 1 John 5:19.

⁸⁵ Revelation 21:1-4.

⁸⁶ 1 Cor. 13:12, *op. cit.*, p. 55.

Chapter Five

HUMAN MORAL CAPACITIES

"In the beginning God made the human race with the power of thought and of choosing the truth and doing right."
(Justin Martyr, First Apology, *Chapt. XXVIII.)*

We now turn our attention to the moral capacities which are normal to human beings and human societies as a whole. The view which sees ethical categories and moral discrimination in human beings as completely learned or conditioned by society is considered false by Orthodox Christian ethical teaching. That which contradicts it at heart is the anthropological teaching of Eastern Christianity which perceives us as created in God's image, part of which is the capacity to distinguish between good and evil. It is part of the human *donatum* that we think, act and judge in ethical categories. This capacity is so commonplace that we take it for granted, yet, as we have seen, ethical language has a quality and character all its own, unlike our usual descriptive approaches to the world about us. The imperative "ought" arises out of our inner being in a unique fashion. It might seem that this is the most which can be said about our inner moral capabilities—that to think, judge and act in moral categories is in fact a uniquely human phenomenon based upon our creation by God in His own image. Yet, in the writings of modern Greek Orthodox ethicians, efforts have been made to analyze this primary ethical *donatum* so that it may be more fully understood. To my knowledge, these views are not specifically based on patristic sources, yet they are within the framework of patristic thinking and teaching, because they are efforts by theologians standing within the patristic tradition to respond to new challenges, questions and formulations arising out of psychological theories which have been developed in recent years. Using both the traditional faith of the Church, especially its anthropology, certain distinctions and concepts have been developed to take into consideration the genesis and formation of human ethical capacities especially important in the light of modern psychological theories.

Thus for Orthodox Christian Ethics, human beings are not born as *Tabula rasa.* From an ethical point of view we have an ethical *donatum* which has important dimensions for our ethical thought. There is a certain ethical content to our humanity for which careful claims may be made. For, as we shall see, the inborn human ethical capacities of which we speak below are understood neither minimally (as if they have no significant practical importance), nor maximally (as if they have an exclusive determining power of their own). The traditional Protestant perspective was minimalist at best, while the traditional Roman Catholic position was very strong on this point. Contrarily, the dynamic character of all Eastern Orthodox theology, and specifically its anthropology, is present in its analysis of our human ethical capacities, which is presented under the headings of "the ethical drive," "the ethical sense," "moral freedom," "the conscience," and "the moral law." The first four of these will be dealt with in this chapter. The final one, because of its theological importance will be dealt with in a subsequent chapter.

Human Capacities in General

Perhaps the most lucid of all the Greek Orthodox writers on this topic is Vasileios Antoniades of the Patriarchal Theological School of Halki (Constantinople), who subscribes to a psychology which we would today describe in terms such as "wholistic" or "organic" or "contextual" (not to be confused with situation or contextual ethics). He makes no absolute claims for environmental influences upon human development, nor does he accept the opposite extreme which sees the moral and ethical aspects of our being as independent realities fully present and determined in our psyche upon birth as some creationist views of man hold.

Antoniades thus writes: "the unique character of our feelings and conceptions has as its cause the unique nature of our human psyche, which has the ability and capacity, when aroused by external stimuli, to respond toward them with an analogous inner condition particular to it."[1] As an example of this general statement regarding our human capacities, Antoniades finds an analogy in a seed. As seed has the potential of the mature plant within it, its capacities are already within it. The seed of the orange tree and the seed of the apple tree have all the genetic information within them to produce their appropriate fruit. No amount of normal external conditions can make the apple seed bear oranges or the orange tree bear apples. But neither seed can produce its respective tree and fruit without the presence *also* of certain external conditions. Kept in a packet, untouched by water, earth, sunlight and appropriate nutrients, the seeds will never achieve their potential. But given the right external conditions appropriate to their inner unique and special nature, the potentialities locked within the seed are released and actualized. The right amount of light, water, temperature and nutrients will cause the seed to fulfill its potential. And inasmuch as the seed has an inherent capacity to become an orange tree, it will so become. Inasmuch as the apple seed has the inherent capacity to become an apple tree, it will become one. But no amount of external conditions can make an apple tree produce—of itself—oranges. What the seed produces is determined by its inherent capacity.

Antoniades moves the argument along by noting certain qualities and phenomena of human life in general, which indicate certain incipient human capacities. Inasmuch as human beings create works of art, human capacities for art (appreciation of beauty, harmony of line, color, form and space) are conceived to exist. Ethically "inasmuch as man produces ethical phenomena, he is properly considered an ethical being, endowed with inner abilities, which have need of external conditions and circumstances for their development and perfection . . ."[2]

Together with other writers, such as Chrestos Androutsos and John Papadopoulos, Antoniades probes deeper into this "inner ethical capacity" and distinguishes two aspects of it, the Ethical Drive and the Ethical Sense. These are two aspects of the basic ethical *donatum* of our human nature which produce three important expressions and activities which may be characterized as primitive ethical capacities: freedom, moral law and conscience.

The Ethical Drive

There appear to be two bedrock sources of our ethical life in the human personality. These two sources have been characterized by modern Greek Orthodox writers on ethics as the "Ethical Drive" *(Ethike Orme)* and the "Ethical Sense" *(Ethike Aesthesis)*. Antoniades has, perhaps, the clearest exposition. He defines the Ethical Drive as:

> . . . a kind of need and inclination of the soul toward the good and just, or, more accurately an undefined desire and attraction for those things required by ethical life and moral well-being, much like our other drives and inclinations. It is expressed in an automatic fashion at an early age concretely seeking or avoiding what is appropriate or inappropriate to the ethical life. Later, however, it ingeniously (using both reason and feeling) defines and articulates the appropriate ethical behavior . . .[3]

Antoniades thus identifies a certain inborn capacity of human beings to see events, actions, situations and conditions in ethical categories. This inborn ability is often taken for granted. We simply accept the phenomenon of ethical distinction without reflection. Yet, as we have seen, ethical language deals with a totally unique type of human experience, as compared with our usual descriptive forms of communication. The universal tendency to perceive events in the ethical categories of good and bad, right and wrong, just and unjust, etc., is what is described by the term "ethical drive."

However, one of the terms in Antoniades' definition needs some additional attention. It is the term "automatic." By it, he appears to mean that it is an activity which is non-reflective. The Ethical Drive expresses itself without any mediating rational or cognitive activity. Just as the eye blinks when an object approaches it, human beings react in ethical categories to particular external events. That this of necessity should take place is neither obvious or explainable in other non-ethical terms. However, Antoniades holds that this "automatic" character of ethical judgment is very elementary and is soon augmented by other factors.

The automatic character of this activity retreats little by little with age and the development of intellectual ability. The maturing mind appears as though it replaces the ethical drive, but in fact it does not disappear, and oftentimes its automatic (unreflective) character reappears.[4]

Some of the examples which he gives are the feeling of responsibility parents have for their children, the sense of appreciation and gratitude appropriate to one's benefactor, the shame one feels before others whom we have harmed or misused, etc. Such responses are not just the result of socialization which are taught to us, but rather they are based on a fundamental structure of the human psyche, for the

> soul is thus created and is of such nature, so that it responds with analogous dispositions and conditions to the dispositions and conditions in others.[5]

This view is not based on any particular school of psychology, though it clearly would reject a psychological view which assumed nothing particularly distinctive in the psychic make-up of human beings. The Ethical Drive is thus seen as a characteristic of human beings to view their experiences and life-events in ethical categories. Thus he writes,

> The human soul, in obedience to its own nature automatically desires and seeks out that which is in accord with it and rejects and avoids that which is out of harmony with it.[6]

The Ethical Sense

If the Ethical Drive is understood to be the tendency of our human nature to view external events, as well as internal experiences in ethical categories in a sort of "automatic" fashion, the "Ethical Sense" (*Ethike Aesthesis*) is the movement within our psyche to proceed to the evaluation of the expressions of the Ethical Drive. Thus, Antoniades writes

> Man is found to have in natural relation to the Ethical Drive a certain sense or ethical sensitivity, as a kind of an inner sense organ, which functions as a critical ability to discern points of difference and to discern that which is good and pleasing and perfect.[7]

This inborn ability at first, in infancy, is thought to function in a non-reflective fashion, but quickly becomes conscious and little by little, develops in relationship to the other human capacities. This basic human ethical *donatum* is to be understood not as a psychological theory, but as a development of the Orthodox Christian doctrine of the creation of the human being by God. The "Ethical Drive" and the "Ethical Sense" are to be understood as aspects of the Image of God in human nature. Part of the original gift of God to His creature, man, was a sensitivity toward the ethical dimension of life. Certainly, this did not exhaust the meaning of the Image of God in man. Modern Orthodox theologians, however, seeking to understand the meaning of the Image in more current terms and with reference to secular (psychological) approaches to man, have devised these two descriptive categories to refer to the uniquely ethical dimension of the Image of God in man. This is seen more clearly in the three expressions of this *donatum* which have basic importance to both our humanity in general and to our ethical lives in particular: that is, freedom, moral law and conscience.

Ethical Freedom or Self-Determination

It is a unanimous patristic position that God's Image in man of necessity includes freedom, or as the Fathers of the Church prefer to call it, "self-determination" (αὐτεξούσιον). Thus St. Gregory of Nyssa says "if the rational and intellectual nature puts off its self-determination, then it also loses its rational grace." It is primarily the *autexousion*[8] which lifts up the human being to the status of ethical personhood, which is distinguished "from other beings, such as plants and animals," which "are not able to act by choice in any way." And if man was denied it, he would not be worthy "of reward or praise" for then he would not freely "do the good of himself." Consequently, virtue cannot "take place out of necessity" but by "free decision" only.[9] The close connection of the creation of man and human freedom with the ethical abilities and potential of man is found in many patristic passages. Suffice it for now to quote Justin Martyr.

> In the beginning He made the human race with the power of thought and of choosing the truth and doing right *(dynamenon airesthai t'alethe kai ev prattein),* so that all men are without excuse before God; for they have been born rational and contemplative.

We understand the human capacity for freedom as a basic human ethical capacity in the framework of the Orthodox Christian understanding of man, that is, the doctrinal teachings concerning Anthropology.

The first observation which has to be made is that even the basic ethical capacity for freedom is not to be understood as functioning autonomously separate from divine grace. Supported by the ongoing providence and care of God our whole life and all the expressions of it are intimately related to the divine energies. Alone, man's freedom is incapable of fully realizing human purpose. Man's freedom is in need of divine grace to realize the image and likeness of God and to achieve Theosis. Thus, John Karmiris writes:

> Precisely for the attainment of this perfection and immortality and likeness and divinization of man, in the patristic understanding, the Greek Fathers especially exhalt human freedom, binding it harmoniously with divine grace. Without the cooperation of both, the ethical perfection and salvation of man becomes impossible . . . Without the "cooperation and aid of God" we are incapable of desiring or doing the good.[10]

101

The second observation relating human freedom to the anthropological teachings of the Church is that our freedom, as we empirically experience it, is influenced by sin. Sin plays a role in our understanding of the exercise of our *autexousion* as well as the limitations imposed upon it as a consequence of the condition of original sin.

> Man had received from the Creator "the self-determining drive" *(autexousion ormin)* most appropriate to rational nature . . . which naturally exercised self-determination enabling it to move back and forth between the two in order to choose good or evil.[11]

> Consequently in the self-determining capacity *(autexousion)* of the first human being there already existed the potential for sin.[12]

On the one hand, this meant that the proper use of freedom would have led to the ethical development and perfection of man and the development of the "image" into the achievement of the divine "likeness," by which humanity would have overcome corruption and would have achieved incorruptibility. On the other hand, from the improper use of freedom would come the fall of humanity from communion with God. The description of the Fall, among other things is also an interpretation of the empirical reality which we human beings experience at present. Original Sin points to human pride and self-will which is present in all of us and which is the chief expression of the wrong use of our free will. The doctrine of Original Sin profoundly points to a willfully rejected appropriate relationship with God and the choice of an inappropriate relationship with God. That is, instead of the human acknowledging the Divine as the source of his own being, upon whom man is dependent in order to achieve his own perfection, in disobedience and rebellious use of his freedom, man continues to choose wrongly. The chief aspect of sin is that it leads man mistakenly to choose to act in isolation from that which is the source of his true and authentic being and selfhood—God. This is true experientially. It is also expressed as an event in the Genesis description of the first human couple. Freedom, or the gift of the *autexousion* made it possible. The doctrine of Original Sin describes the consequences of its improper use.

> The consequences of Original Sin were, on the one hand, the disabling and the dimming of the divine image in man, but not its total erasure and disappearance. On the other hand, it was the loss of all the adornment making up the gifts of man's original righteousness together with the "likeness." It further meant the severance of the inner and direct relationship (communion) of humanity with God and our fall "from the grace of the image of God,"[13] the weakening and distortion of the spiritual, volitional and emotional capabilities of man, as well as the total spiritual and physical corruption and weakness of human nature; and finally it meant death both physical and spiritual, as well as eternal, which was permitted and tolerated by God so that evil might not be without end.[14]

Thus the exercise of our *autexousion* in the choice of evil, rather than good, has led to a weakening of that self-determination itself, though not its total elimination.

Thirdly, we must note that in our present state, our ability of self-determination is seen by Orthodox anthropology as weakened and somewhat distorted. If it were true that even in the first created state, our *autexousion* had need of divine grace to assist it so as to achieve the good, this holds true even more so in our present state. Though we are able to choose rightly sometimes, by ourselves, we cannot fully choose the good and reject what is evil without the energies of God, especially as the good has been revealed and made available to us in the person and work of Jesus Christ. Thus, though unredeemed man is found to have some of the power of self-determination, it is only in Christ and His redemption that the *autexousion* is slowly restored to its fullness. This two-fold truth is expressed well by Patriarch Dositheos of Jerusalem in his *Confession of Faith*.

> That man is naturally able to do the good is suggested by the Lord in saying that the gentiles love those who love them, and is taught most clearly by Paul specifically when he says that the gentiles who do not have the law, do by nature what the law requires. From which,, this also is clear: it is impossible that whatever good man does to be sin, for the good is incapable of being evil. But taking place only by nature, and remaining carnal, it does not make the one who does them spiritual, nor does it contribute by itself, without faith, to salvation . . . nor, however does it lead to condemnation, for neither is it acceptable that the good, as such, should be the cause of evil. But in those who have been reborn, when the good is activated under and by grace, it makes the person who does it perfect and worthy of salvation.[15]

The freedom to choose remains, but it is not adequate, of itself to achieve salvation. It needs grace, the active relationship of God with man, to achieve salvation.

We thus are called to choose to enter the proper relationship of man with God, and to accept the active relationship of God with us. *Autexousion* and grace remain both intertwined and necessary. Vladimir Lossky, among others, articulates this truth.

> The deification or *theosis* of the creature will be realized in its fullness only in the age to come, after the resurrection of the dead. This deifying union has, nevertheless, to be fulfilled ever more and more even in this present life, through the transformation of our corruptible and depraved nature and by its adaptation to eternal life. If God has given us in the Church all the objective conditions, all the means we need for the attainment of this end, we, on our side, must produce the necessary subjective conditions: for it is in this synergy, in this cooperation of man with God, that the union is fulfilled.[16]

The Eastern Orthodox tradition never separates these two elements: grace and human freedom are manifested simultaneously and cannot be conceived apart from each other. St. Gregory of Nyssa describes very clearly the reciprocal bond that makes of grace and free will two poles of one and the same reality: "as the grace of God cannot descend upon souls which flee from their salvation, so the power of human virtue is not of itself sufficient to raise to perfection souls which have no share in grace . . . the righteousness of works and the grace of the Spirit coming together to the same place *(proelthousai eis tauton),* fill the soul in which they are united with the life of the blessed."[17] Thus grace is not a reward for the merit of the human will, as Pelagianism would have it; but no more is it the cause of the 'meritorious acts' of our free will. For it is not a question of merits but of cooperation, of a synergy of the two wills, divine and human, a harmony in which grace bears ever more and more fruit, and is appropriated—acquired—by the human person. Grace is a presence of God within us which demands constant effort on our part; these efforts, however, in no way determine grace, nor does grace act upon our liberty as if it were external or foreign to it. This doctrine, faithful to the apophatic spirit of the Eastern tradition, expresses the mystery of the coincidence of grace and human freedom in good works, without recourse to positive and rational terms.

> Eastern tradition has always asserted simultaneity in the synergy of divine grace and freedom. As St. Macarius of Egypt says, "The will of man is an essential condition, for without it God does nothing."[18] In the nineteenth century Bishop Theophanes, a great Russian ascetic writer, asserted that "The Holy Ghost, acting within us, accomplishes with us our salvation," but he says as the same time that "being assisted by grace, man accomplishes the work of his salvation."[19]

Our self-determination, our *autexousion,* is a given of our being as creatures of God. It is a part of the selfhood given to us as human beings. It is not destroyed by sin, neither is it overcome and minimized by divine grace. But the fact that it has little significance separated from divine grace also points to the fact that it is not absolute and totally independent either. The *autexousion* is always related to the whole disposition of the person.

Thus, the New Testament, in speaking of our fallen condition, St. Paul speaks of powers existing over us, and more concretely, of our will being subject to the powers of sin. St. Paul thus expresses the problem in *Romans:*

> We know that the law is spiritual; but I am carnal, sold under sin. I do not understand my own actions. For I do not do what I want, but I do the very thing I hate. Now if I do what I do not want, I agree that the law is good. So then it is no longer I that do it, but sin which dwells within me. For I know nothing good dwells within me, that is, my flesh. I can will what is right, but I cannot do it. For I do not do the good I want, but the evil I do

not want is what I do. Now if I do what I do not want, it is no longer I that do it, but sin which dwells within me . . . I see in my members another law at war with the law of my mind and making me captive to the law of sin which dwells in my members.[20]

The captivity of our *autexousion* to evil, to sin which dwells within, i.e., to "the world," indicates that the role of the *autexousion* must be understood not as some absolute power of human beings to control and to determine, but as an ability to decide concerning a multiplicity of influences in our lives.

The exercise of our *autexousion* is at the first instance a choice of what shall determine us. The self makes choices as to which sort of influences will be accepted and permitted to exercise influence upon the present and future direction of the self's life.[21]

Basically, we have one of two choices of fundamental character to make. We must choose either to subject ourselves to God or to the world (e.g., "the flesh," evil, sin, the devil, pride, self, etc.). Thus Lossky explicates the basic Orthodox position.

> The beginning of the spiritual life is conversion *(epistrophe),* an attitude of the will turning towards God and renouncing the world; e.g., "The World" has here a particular ascetical connotation. "The world is said by speculative examination to be the extension of a common name to distinct passions," says St. Isaac the Syrian. For this great ascetic and mystic, the "passions are part of the usual current of the world. Where they have ceased, there the world's current has ceased . . ."[22] "The World" signifies here a dispersion, the soul's wandering outside itself, a treason against its real nature . . . Renunciation of the world is thus a re-entering of the soul into itself, a concentration, a reintegration of the spiritual being in its return to communion with God. This conversion is a free act, just as sin also is a voluntary separation from God; and conversion in this sense may be defined as a constant effort of the will turned towards God.[23]

This return to one's true nature is, in fact, a turning to God in whose image we have been created. The *autexousion,* then, is the power, both in the first instance and subsequently, to choose to whom we will be subject. St. Paul dramatically describes this state of affairs by speaking to the Christians of Rome in terms of their choice as to whom they will be slaves.

> Do not yield your members to sin as instruments of wickedness, but yield yourselves to God . . . Do you not know that if you yield yourselves to anyone as obedient slaves, you are slaves of the one you obey, either of sin which leads to death, or of obedience, which leads to righteousness . . . When you were slaves of sin, you were free in regard to righteousness . . . But now that you have been set free from sin and have become slaves

of God, the return you get is sanctification and its end, eternal life.[24]

More succinctly the idea is expressed elsewhere in Scripture, also. "For freedom Christ has set us free; stand fast therefore and do not submit again to the yoke of slavery"[25] and "Live as free men, yet without using your freedom as a pretext for evil; but live as servants *(douloi,* slaves) of God.[26] A contemporary philosopher has stated this understanding of the *autexousion* in more secular terms: "If there be such a thing as free choice it would appear to consist in man being able to choose which of his outside circumstances will determine his conduct." Bishop Gerasimos of the Greek Archdiocese of North and South America is reported to have aptly stated this truth when he said "Freedom consists of being able to choose who your master will be."

Perceptions of Conscience

Conscience has not always been viewed or described in a uniform manner.[27] Non-rational concepts of the conscience tend to see the conscience as an invisible, mysterious power or presence, watching over the enforcement of what is right and condemning evil thoughts and actions. Socrates' *Daimon* is an example of this view. Sometimes, the Christian concept of the Guardian Angel has also been used to embody the conscience. More frequently, Christians speak of the conscience as the "voice of God" at work in the soul of each person.

In Scholastic theological ethical discourse, a distinction is made between "synderesis" and "conscience." Synderesis is identified as the recognition of the authority or claim of the moral law in general. Conscience is understood as acknowledging the duty to perform concrete acts of moral obedience. This, combined with an examination of the facts of the circumstances, a logical deduction from moral principles, and the application of the principles to concrete and specific cases, is the practice of casuistry—an act of the conscience.

Other views of the conscience may be characterized as intuitionist. These theories view the conscience as an "innate faculty of moral judgment" and some, who hold this view see the conscience as capable of determining what is right in each instance. Demetropoulos' definition of the conscience tends to belong to this family of views. He defines: "The Conscience is called the inborn ability of the practical reason to express correct judgments on the morality of persons, regarding the harmony or disharmony of their intentions and acts in regard to the moral law."[28]

Empirical theories of the conscience, based primarily on psychological learning theories explain conscience as acquired knowledge and attitudes. In Freudian psychology, conscience is the functioning "Super Ego" by which society imposes its will upon the individual. Behaviorism sees conscience as the result of a punishment-reward conditioning process in which the person learns to avoid certain kinds of prohibited actions and to perform certain other kinds of encouraged actions, sensing blame for the first and praise for the second.

The non-rational views trend to hold that conscience involves more than the individual and emphasize the imperative character of the experience of conscience. The Scholastic view emphasizes the fact that the conscience seems most powerful when it deals with concrete and specific actions and decisions. Intuitionist theories emphasize the seriousness with which the conscience is taken in seeking to guide action or reflect on it. Conscience and the things it deals with are never passing issues—they always are of first-order importance, having direct and determining effect on our personal self-image and identity. Empirical theories point to the fact that conscience is and can be formed, that it is not a mere mechanical psychological function.

The Facts of Conscience

The facts of conscience seem to include the following elements. First, that there is, generally speaking a universal human experience of the sense of obligation which seems to carry with it both an undeniable character, as well as an unexplainable dimension. Secondly, it is quite clear that the functioning of the human conscience is in large part a factor which permits the existence of human society. Much of social control and organization is dependent upon this human tendency to internalize and live by the rules of life as they are required in society. The third fact of conscience, however, points to the opposite characteristic of conscience, its frequent independence from society. Conscience often leads persons to reject and oppose social norms, to stand up against them and to seek to change them. Thus, there is a certain autonomous character to the conscience, which is not totally subdued to the pressures of society, the so-called super-ego. A fourth factor is the intimate connection of the functioning conscience with the religious dimensions and perspectives of life. The conscience is strengthened and seems to take on more force and authority over life as it is perceived to be associated with belief in God, for instance. If a person holds that what the conscience requires or condemns is in fact required or condemned by God, the matter takes on a more serious dimension and tends to elicit a more serious response as compared to the merely private perception of moral duty or responsibility. The nature and functioning of conscience is one of the great problems of ethical theory as it seeks to take into consideration all of these facts and others as well. No understanding of the conscience should be permitted to be a simplistic absolutizing of any of these dimensions of the phenomenon of conscience.

Scriptural and Patristic Views on Conscience

Christian Ethics takes into consideration the scriptural and patristic perceptions of conscience. The scriptural view of conscience appears to have little direct contact with contemporary psychological or sociological interpretations of conscience, such as that of Freudianism, Intuitionism or Behaviorism.

> The conscience bears with it contemporaneously an ethical and religious character . . . The conscience is presented in the Bible

clearly as one of the major subjective aspects of the religious and ethical life. Thus, in the 1st Epistle to Timothy, St. Paul writes: "the aim of our charge is love that issues from a pure heart and a good conscience and sincere faith."[29]

Both Old and New Testaments provide reference to the conscience. The description of the sin of Adam and Eve is very instructive. The action of the couple who "hid themselves from the presence of the Lord God among the trees of the garden" points to one of the dimensions of a functioning conscience, the unique and significant sense of guilt and shame. In such a case of guilt, there is also a sense of separation from the source of good, God Himself: "I was afraid, because I was naked, and I hid myself." This story also points to the tendency of the guilty conscience to seek to escape blame by making excuses and to justify one's actions, something which would be unnecessary if there was no sense of obligation to do good and avoid evil. Adam blames Eve: "The woman, . . . she gave me fruit of the tree, and I ate." And Eve blames the devil: "The serpent beguiled me, and I ate."[30] An example of a guilty conscience in the New Testament is the behavior of Judas Iscariot. In both examples, another feature of the guilty conscience is seen, i.e., the acceptance of punishment or retribution for an evil deed done. In the words of one of the Deuterocanonical books, "Wickedness is a cowardly thing, condemned by its own testimony; distressed by conscience, it has always anticipated the difficulties."[31]

On the other hand conscience may also justify one's actions, even in the face of much public criticism to the contrary. The conscience is the main agent in helping persons maintain their sense of moral integrity in the face of criticism and condemnation. Job responds to the condemnation of Baldad, one of his friends: "Far be it for me to acknowledge you to be right; for till I die, I will not give up mine innocence. And for asserting my righteousness I make no apology; for I am not conscious to myself of having done amiss."[32] Even the example of Jesus before the High Priest points to this powerful and empowering aspect of conscience. After He had been struck by one of the officers of the High Priest, "Jesus answered him 'If I have spoken wrongly bear witness to the wrongs but if I have spoken rightly, why do you strike me?"[33] St. Paul also appeals to his conscience to justify his ministry against those who would condemn him. Thus he writes, "For our boast is this, the testimony of our conscience that we have behaved in the world, and still more toward you, with holiness and godly sincerity, not by earthly wisdom, but by the grace of God."[34]

That conscience can both condemn and justify is witnessed to also by St. Paul. He indicates that often the functioning of conscience is not so clear cut, and that there is a frequent sense of conflict and struggle in the experience of the conscience. Thus, in speaking of the Gentiles who do not have the Mosaic Law, but do have a natural comprehension of right and wrong, he says that "they show that what the law requires is written on their hearts, while their conscience also bears witness and their conflicting thoughts accuse or perhaps excuse them."[35]

The patristic tradition elevates the conscience to an important part of the moral and spiritual life. The conscience is seen as a part of the created endowment of the human person. "In creating the human being, God placed within an impartial and just court, that is, the reckoning of the conscience in each person."[36] Abbas Dorotheos says, "When God created man, He placed within him something divine-like, as a sort of intense reasoning . . . which enlightens the mind and shows him the difference between good and evil. This is called the conscience . . ."[37] The conscience in patristic thought is given an important and critical place in the practice of the moral life, as well. It is not just a *donatum*. Thus Clement of Alexandria writes that "the conscience is an excellent means for exact choosing of the good or avoiding (evil); the correct life is its foundation."[38] St. John Chrysostom has high regard for the conscience. With a strong vote of confidence in the sufficiency of the conscience, he writes, "In the conscience we have an adequate teacher, and one ought not to deny oneself the help which comes from it."[39] Equally strong support for the adequacy of the conscience as a guide for the moral life is given by Leontios of Neapolis who says, "The conscience is an able and capable teacher which counsels obedience to every good thing and avoidance of evil things."[40] In addition, the Fathers point to the judging and decision-making character of the conscience. Chrysostom thus instructs us: "open the doors of your conscience and look at the judge seated within your mind."[41] As St. Paul indicated in Romans, the conscience condemns us for evil which we do. This emphasis on the function of conscience to raise up our sense of having violated our moral responsibility is also found in the patristic writings. "The Master . . . created man placing within an unceasing accusor, the conscience."[42]

Both scripture and the Fathers speak of "good" and "bad" consciences. Thus, in the New Testament the conscience is characterized as "good" *(agathe, kale)*, pure *(kathara)*, divine, and clear *(aproskoptos)*.[43] Chrysostom points to the source of the good conscience: "the good conscience comes from a life and acts which are good."[44] "Nothing rejoices us from within as a good *(chreston)* conscience" he says elsewhere.[45] On the other hand there is also a "bad" conscience which in the New Testament, may be called "evil" *(ponera)*, weak *(asthenes)*, idolatrous, seared *(kekavteriasmene)*, corrupted *(memiantai . . . nous kai e syneidisis)*.[46] Origen speaks of conscience "corrupted by sin."[47] One "should not defile *(molynein)* one's conscience by unlawful gain."[48] To have such an evil conscience is "truly fearsome, for then the conscience is consumed by fire," nor is one even "able to sleep, and through it to be freed from the agony of an evil *(poneron)* conscience."[49] An evil conscience is "skilled in defense . . . and is no longer able to accuse."[50]

Source, Nature and Functioning of Conscience

This evidence points to an understanding of conscience which combines the various views which we noted at the beginning of the chapter. In the first instance, the conscience is considered as a "given" of our human constitution. Theologically speaking, it is part of the "image and likeness" of our creation. Modern Orthodox writers tend to see it as one of the immediate consequences or outgrowths of our basic human moral capacities, the Ethical Drive, the Ethical Sense and the *autexousion*. The inborn capacity and the human penchant to interpret events in ethical categories, to in fact make ethical evaluations and to sense personal responsibility for our behavior is the foundation of the experience of and universal functioning of conscience. Both Androutsos and Demetropoulos accept the view consequently that the conscience is an expression of the whole psychological functioning of the person and not as an isolated faculty. Thus, emotions, will and intellect all share in the experience of conscience. The sense of pleasure, peace and happiness which comes to us when we have "done our duty" and which comes from an approving conscience is one aspect of the sharing of our emotions in the functioning of our conscience. The pain, anxiety, guilt, and agony of a "bad conscience" also evinces the involvement of the emotions.

The *autexousion* is equally involved. The conscience both orders us to behave in a particular way or judges us as responsible for the ways in which we have acted. This implies we either are able to obey its dictates or were free to choose how to act in the past. When the conscience debates courses of action, the implication is that they are all open to us and subject to our volition.

In addition, the intellectual involvement in the exercise of conscience is also quite clear. Alternative possibilities are weighed, balanced rationally against each other. Motives and intentions are analyzed. Consequences and circumstances evaluated and cosidered both in deciding what is right and in judging what has been done.

Yet that which pulls them all together and permits us to speak not of numerous psychological functions, but of the unique experience of conscience is the profound sense of serious moral obligation and personal responsibility with which the conscience is identified. This imperative character of the conscience is its distinguishing characteristic. And it is in this sense that it is properly referred to as the "voice of God." As we shall soon see, this phrase cannot properly be applied to the conscience if we are primarily referring to the content of the conscience. It is as we focus on the demanding pressure of the conscience upon our being, the profound sense of obligation that the understanding of the conscience as the voice of God makes sense.

The fact that there can be "good" and "bad" conscience indicates that the conscience does not function in some mechanical or automatic fashion. Unlike our heartbeat or our metabolism, the conscience needs to be developed, formed, enriched and sharpened. Which, of course, also means that it can remain stunted, it can be weakened, it can become distorted. Consequently, what we call the "content" of the conscience not only can be, but properly must be cultivated and educated. In this sense the psychological theories of Freudianism and Behaviorism are correct. A

110

large part of moral education is just this—educating, exercising, cultivating and informing the conscience. This process takes place both unconsciously and deliberately. The experience of family life, of the whole acculturation process, the sharing in culture in group mores, etc. all serve to provide content to the conscience. However, explicit teaching of a religious and moral nature, as well as self-discipline serve to educate, sharpen and hone the conscience to greater sensitivity. The examination of conscience, for instance, as part of development of the spiritual life is an essential element. Thus St. Basil instructs:

> When the day has passed . . . and before falling asleep, it is appropriate for each to examine his conscience with his own heart.[51]

And St. John Chrysostom instructs: "when you have entered into yourself and have reviewed those things which you have done wrongly, strictly demand to clarify your (moral) responsibility for them."[52] Whatever else this indicates, it also points to the fact that the content of the conscience is subject to change, evaluation, judgment and development. The commonly used description of the conscience as the "voice of God" when it is meant as literally, i.e., that God always speaks to each person telling him or her what is right or wrong, thus, cannot be accepted. If that were the case, then there could never be differing ethical perceptions of the same moral situation.[53]

This understanding of the conscience, taking into account both its inborn, as well as its developmental character is in full harmony with the Eastern Christian doctrine of man. The gifts of God which constituted man were by and large retained even after the Fall. The conscience, indicating the practical discernment of right and wrong as well as the experience of the sense of responsibility issuing in the experience of moral guilt or peace, is an integral part of the constitutive human make-up. Yet, Orthodox Christian theological anthropology also recognizes the difference between the gifts and their fulfillment. As we have seen, divinely given human freedom implies that the fulfillment of the basic human *donatum* is dependent on the proper exercise of that freedom. This in turn clearly means that the conscience is subject both to development (through the right use of freedom, including self-discipline, education, choice of environment, etc.).

It is, thus, in two senses that a conscience may be determined to be "good" or "bad." When an active conscience evaluates past acts and is pleased and content that the behavior was proper it may be called "good" or conversely, when the active conscience condemns evil acts and is disturbed by them, it may be called "bad." In both cases, however, the conscience is functioning, sensitive, awake and active. The second sense in which the conscience may be called "good" or "bad" is on the basis of its functioning role in the whole life of the person. If it is active, as described above, it is a "good" conscience in that it is contributing to the spiritual and moral growth of the person, leading to his of her fulfillment and perfection as God's image and likeness. In order to achieve *Theosis,* a strong, sensitive, active conscience is necessary. In this second sense, a "bad" conscience is one which is not contributing to that growth toward *Theosis.* It may be weak, insensitive and inactive. In that case, it is a spiritual and moral requirement for growth in the image and likeness of God that the "bad" conscience be rectified, enriched, sensitized and strengthened.

Occasionally, a person's conscience may become so insensitive that it appears to have ceased to exist. A criminal may give such an impression. "Appeals to conscience" appear to have no effect and the conscience seems to be totally insensitive. This condition is sometimes referred to as a "hardened conscience." In Greek the phrase used is *"peporomene syneidesis."* The root word used here is *"poroo"* which means "to petrify, to turn into stone," and metaphorically, "to harden, to make callous." This emphasizes the insensitive conscience which becomes so because of misused freedom, improper formation, education or environment. However, we would hold that the conscience never completely dies. The sixth century ascetical writer, Abbas Dorotheos graphically describes the condition.

> When our conscience says to us, "do this now" and we ignore it; when it again tells us to do it and we don't do it, and when we persist in placing it under foot, we in fact bury it. Consequently it is no longer able to speak to us with any boldness . . . Thus we reach the condition in which we have no sensitivity for the things our conscience says, so that it appears to us that we almost do not have a conscience any more. However, there is no person without a conscience.[54]

The conscience may become deformed and hardened, weakened and inactive because of the environment, experience or an enslaved *autexousion.* But because it is part of the very gift of humanity which comes from God, it cannot completely disappear.

This situation is rare. Rarer still is the hyperactive conscience. This is tied closely to the practice of extreme casuistry, which applies ethical norms in an overly meticulous and detailed fashion. It is also closely tied to a strongly legalistic understanding of Christian ethics. A consequence of an overly "deontic" view of ethics,[55] it tends to emphasize the importance of specific and concrete acts as opposed to the emphasis of ethics as *"aretaic"* which tends to concentrate on the whole of the ethical personality including motive, intent, character and virtue. It has appeared primarily in Western Christianity and has been characterized as "scrupulosity." James N. Lapsley defines it as follows:

> Scrupulosity is a term used in Catholic moral theology to denote the over-use of the confessional for the confession of trivial and diminutive sins. Though absolution is eagerly sought, it is never fully satisfying to the scrupulous person, in this sense of

"over-scrupulous," who fears he may have forgotten something, and who will soon return to confess many of the same offenses.

Though Protestants who do not have formal confession do not use the term, the phenomenon is present in the over-zealous church worker who ssemingly cannot find enough to do in the Church and also frequently seeks the pastor to pour out his troubles and get his advice, which is seldom taken.[56]

Scrupulosity, then is as inappropriate as a "hardened conscience" and perhaps it is true that both are more in the nature of psychological illnesses than moral sins.

However, in most of us it would appear that the cultivation and development of the conscience is a requirement for our spiritual and moral growth. It is toward this end that one of the chief virtues discussed by the ascetic Fathers of the Eastern Church points. This virtue is known as *"diakrisis." Diakrisis,* in this sense, is spiritual and ethical discernment. Thus in the book of Hebrews it says "solid (spiritual) food is for the mature, for those who have their faculties trained by practice to distinguish *(pros diakrisin)* good from evil."[57] Nilos of Ancyra an ascetic writer of the fifth century in a work entitled "Concerning the Eight Spirits of Evil" *(Peri ton Okto Pneumaton tis Ponerias)* characteristically writes: "The source, and root and head and bond of every virtue is discernment *(diakrisis).*[58] It is probably correct that discernment is not limited to the ethical sphere of life, nor that it is purely an act or virtue of the conscience. Yet the diagnostic quality of discernment is central to conscience. Thus Peter of Damascus writes:

In all things we need discernment *(diakrisis)* so that we can constantly judge our every pursuit in life. For *diakrisis* is a light which reveals to the person who has it, the time, the undertaking, the pursuit, the strength, the knowledge, the age, the power, the weakness, the motive, the willingness, the contrition, the habit, the ignorance, the physical strength and inclination of the body, both health and suffering, the manner, the place, the behavior, the education, the faith, the mood, the purpose, the course of life, the permissiveness, the science, the natural knowledge, the effort, the watchfulness, the hesitancy and other such things. In addition, the things of nature, the use, the quantity, the forms, the purpose of God . . . *Diakrisis* clarifies all of these things, and not only these but also the purpose of the patristic teachings, for it is not just the thing that is done which we seek, but why it is done . . . He who cultivates the mind is able to contemplate, to pray, to theologize and to achieve every virtue.[59]

The Centrality of Conscience

We have not given a definition of the conscience, as is customary. Perhaps it is now clear why this would not be very helpful. A definition such as that of Demetropoulos, mentioned above, or that of Frangos ("the ethical conscience appears as an inner witness and judgment, by which, through a sort of 'voice of God,' the human being distinguishes between good and evil, is thrust toward the first and disuaded from the latter, and, finally, in accordance to his acts is accused or comforted, spiritually")[60] is not fully adequate because it does not point to its centrality in the ethical life.

In doctrinal discussions concerning the saving work of Jesus Christ it is customary to distinguish between the "objective" work of salvation as realized in Christ as Prophet, King and High Priest and the "subjective" appropriation of that salvation in the soul and spirit of the faithful. Something similar takes place in the specifically ethical sphere of life. We have seen that the only absolute good is God Himself. The truths of His revelation both in creation and revelation are, so to speak, external to us until there is a personal meeting, an inner experience which brings the objective good into direct, intimate responsible, felt and personal relationship to ourselves. For want of a better name or description of the locus where this takes place regarding the ethical dimensions of the Christian life, we call it conscience. Conscience is the means by which the human being appropriates the good into and for his or her life. It is the meeting place of the good and the realization of that good in the specific, concrete, living existence of the person, the community and society in general.

There is, then, an affinity between this emphasis on the centrality of the conscience for the appropriation and realization of the good in our personal existence and what Kant called the autonomy of the ethical life. The objective good must become personalized, internalized and practically realized in the person. This is implied in the patristic doctrines of purity and true freedom. A moral imperative appears not to have fully valid claim upon a person unless he or she does in fact accept it for him or herself, even though it be "objectively" correct. This convinces because we feel that the good cannot be heteronomous, that is, external to the moral agent. As we have seen, the genius of the Eastern Orthodox position is to affirm that the human good is intimately related with the divine objective good because humanity is not only created in the image of God (the only absolute good) but also destined to become—ought to become—"like God" thereby achieving and realizing true and full humanity, i.e. *Theosis*.

The conscience is the agent for what we have called *the-anthroponomy*. As it functions, the conscience works in three different and distinguishable spheres. The moral life, approached as a total phenomenon can be described as dealing with a) being good, b) deciding for the good, and c) doing the good.

"Being" refers to character and virtue as a mode of existence. It is the formation of certain dispositions, traits, habits and qualities which form a stable pattern or style of life. It is to this sphere of the ethical life that we refer when we say that a person is "saintly," "fairminded," "Christ-like," "a good person." A cultivated, developed conscience both

114

functions out of such a state of being and contributes to its ongoing growth, development and enrichment. It is to this sphere of ethical life that we will turn our attention to in Chapter Eight on the topic "Being Moral: Conformed to the Image of God."

Conscience, however, also, clearly functions as a judge discerning the right and wrong courses of action. It does this both in advance of an action, during it, and after it, as well. It is before an action that the conscience most frequently functions in a decision making capacity. It seeks to determine, in difficult and complicated moral situations, the right course of action. In the process, it takes into account the facts of the situation, motives, intentions, immediate consequences, ultimate goals and values, etc. As Peter of Damascus noted "In all things we need discernment so that we can constantly judge our every pursuit in life." Its conclusion is to commend an action or to dissuade one from an action. It concludes with the prescription "This course of action is right: do it!" or, "This course of action is wrong: avoid it!" In traditional ethical terminology this is called a "Preceding Conscience" *(Proegoumene syneidesis)*. In addition the conscience often functions after an act, judging it as to its moral quality.

Here, praise and blame are primarily operative. Thus we judge personalities in history, our contemporaries, as well as our own already performed acts. We have already commented on the "good" or "evil" conscience according to which the conscience feels praise, commendation, inner peace and satisfaction at having done what is right; or, blame, condemnation, guilt and discomfort for having done evil. The traditional description of this judgement which takes place after the act is called "Subsequent Conscience" *(Epomene syneidesis)*. Sometimes the two are mixed together both prescribing and judging as well as praising and blaming as the act is in process. This has been described as "Concurrent Conscience" *(synodevousa syneidesis)*. A more careful account of both decision-making and judgment making will be made in Chapter Nine, "Ethical Decision Making."

The third sphere in which the conscience acts as the agency for the appropriation and realization of the good by the person, is the doing of the good. How are we moved to do the good in fact? We have seen Demetropoulos' criticism of philosophical ethics, i.e. that it tends to be abstract and theoretical and without application. In contrast, he pointed to religious ethics, and specifically Christian ethics, emphasizing its empowering capability to move to action. This will be the subject of our concern in Chapter Ten, "The Politeia of Theosis: Living The Image and Likeness of God."

However, before proceeding to these three spheres of concern, we must deal with two other dimensions of the ethical life, closely related to the conscience. In a sense, the conscience may be understood as a process or ability to discern, to distinguish, to evaluate and to judge without however, having a fundamental standard of what is in fact good and in fact evil. Those who hold that the content of the conscience is wholly learned would then be correct. However, this is not the case. Eastern Christianity has affirmed that part of the "given" of our humanity, the "image of God" in all of us is also a basic perception and understanding of what is good and what is evil in content. The name usually applied to the specific inborn moral content of our nature, is natural law. It is because natural law is perceived to be equally a created "given" of our nature, that it must be discussed in close conjunction with conscience. Both, in modern Greek Orthodox Ethics, are understood to be outgrowths of the basic human moral endowments of the Ethical Drive, the Ethical Sense and the *Autexousion*. We turn our attention to this dimension of the moral life in Chapter Six, "The Natural Moral Law."

This is followed by an effort to understand the content of ethics in its specifically Christian content. The Christian conscience is not limited to the precepts of the natural moral law. A new dimension is provided by the teaching of Jesus Christ and the new dispensation begun in Him. Thus, Chapter Seven will deal with the "Evangelical Ethic."

[1] Vasileios Antoniades, *Encheiridion Kata Christon Ethikes*, Constantinople: Fazilet Press, 193, Vol. 1, pp. 55-6.

[2] *Ibid.*, p. 57. For a parallel discussion on human nature as a developing potentiality, see Gregory of Nyssa, *On The Making of Man*, XXVIX, 3-6.

[3] *Ibid.*, p. 59.

[4] *Ibid.*, p. 59.

[5] *Ibid.*, p. 60.

[6] *Ibid.*, p. 60.

[7] *Ibid.*, p. 63.

[8] In this work the Greek term, αὐτεξούσιον, well translated as "self-determination" or "the self-determining power" is transliterated as "autexousion" so as to retain its distinctive patristic flavor and character.

[9] Gregory of Nyssa, *M. Catechesis*, 31 as quoted in P. Trembelas, *Dogmatike Tes Orthodoxou Catholikes Ekklesias*, Athens: "ZOE," 1959, Vol. I, 489-490.

[10] Ioannis Karmiris, *Synopsis tes Dogmatikes Didaskalias tes Orthodoxou Katholikes Ekklesias*, Athens, 1957, p. 32-33. Quoting John of Damsacus, *Ekdosis Orthodoxou Pisteos* II, 30.

[11] St. Basil, *Oti Ouk Estin Aitios Ton Kakon O Theos*, 6.

[12] Karmires, *op. cit.*, 1957, pp. 33-34.

[13] Athanasius *Peri tes Enanthropiseos tou Logou*, 7.

[14] Karmiris, *op. cit.*, p. 35.

[15] Oros 14. See Karmiris' *Ta Dogmatika Kai Symbolika Mnemeia tes Orthodoxou Katholikes Ekklesias*, Athens, 1953. Vol. II, pp. 756-767.

[16] Vladimir Lossky, *The Mystical Theology of the Eastern Church*, London: James Clarke & Co., Ltd., 1957, pp. 196-199.

[17] *Peri Tou Kata Theon Skopou*, P.G. XLVI, 289C.

[18] *Spiritual Homilies*, XXXVII, 10, P.G. XXXIV, 757A.

[19] *Letters on the Spiritual Life*, pub. Mt. Athos, pp. 19, 65, 67, 83 (in Russian). Vladimir Lossky, *The Mystical Theology of the Eastern Church*, London: James Clarke & Co., Ltd., 1957, pp. 196-199.

[20] Romans 7:14-20, 22.

[21] Stanley Hauerwas, *Character and the Christian Life: A Study in Theological Ethics*, San Antonio: Trinity University Press, 1975, Chapter 1.

[22] Isaac of Nineveh, *Mystic Treatises*, trans. A. J. Wensinck, p. 13.

[23] *Op. cit.*, pp. 199-200.

[24] Romans 6:12-23.

[25] Galatians 5:1.

[26] 1 Peter 2:16.

[27] Much of this chapter was previously published in the *Greek Orthodox Theological Review*, Vol. 23, June, 1978, pp. 131-144.

[28] *Op. cit.*, p. 58.

[29] 1 Timothy 1:5. Constantine Frangos, *Threskeutike kai Ethike Encyclopedia*, Vol. 11, p. 558-559.

[30] Genesis 3:8-14.

[31] Wisdom of Solomon 17:11.

[32] Job 27:5. *The Septuigint Bible*, Indian Hills, Colo.: Falcon's Wing Press, 1954.

[33] John 18:23.

[34] 1 Corinthians 1:12.

[35] Romans 2:15.

[36] Chrysostom, *Exposition of the Psalms* 14 7:9.

[37] *Doctrinae Diversae* 3.1.

[38] *Stromata* 1.1.

[39] *Homily of Genesis* 54.1.

[40] *The Life of Symeon Sali*, 2.

[41] *Homily on 2nd Corinthians* 9:3.

[42] Chrysostom, *Homily on Genesis* 17.1.

[43] Acts 23:1.

[44] *Homily 1 on 2nd Corinthians*, 4:13.

[45] *Contra Eos Qui Subintroductas*, 11.

[46] Hebrews 10:21, 1 Corinthians 8:7, 1 Timothy 4:2, Titus 1:15.

[47] *Homily on Jeremiah*, 6:2.

[48] Hippolytos, *Refutation of All Heresies* 9:23.

[49] Chrysostom, *On the Statues* 5:3; *Homily of Romans* 12,7.

[50] Nilos of Ancyra, *Peristeria*, 12,8.

[51] *Ascetica* 1,5.

[52] *Homily on Romans*, 5,6.

[53] Numbers 23:19, Romans 3:4.

[54] *Doctrinae Diversae* 3.1.

[55] See Frankena, *Ethics*, 2nd Ed., Prentice Hall, Inc. Englewood Cliffs, N.J., 1973, pp. 12-60.

[56] In John Maquarrie, *Dictionary of Christian Ethics*, Philadelphia: The Westminster Press, 1967, p. 313.

[57] Hebrews 5:14.

[58] Migne PG 79, 1468B.

[59] *Philokalia, op. cit.*, Vol. 3, pp. 66-67.

[60] *Threskeutike kai Ethike Encyclopedia, op. cit.*, Vol. 11, p. 562.

117

Chapter Six

THE NATURAL MORAL LAW

"God gave us the prophets for every law and even before them, He gave the unwritten natural law, which is the examiner of those things which ought to be done." (Gregory of Nazianzos, Orations 24,27)

St. John Chrysostom comments that "We were given two teachers from the beginning, nature and the conscience, theirs being an impartial voice which teaches human beings in silence."[1] In addition to the conscience there is a second expression of the Ethical Drive and the Ethical Sense, which is known as the "Inborn Moral Law," or the "Natural Moral Law" *(Emphytos Ethikos Nomos, Physikos Ethikos Nomos).* The natural moral law provides elementary content to the conscience in its process of judging and evaluation. It is considered to be part of the "given" of our creation and consequently a part of the Divine Image within us. As a "given" of our human nature, it is less an ability, capacity or function (as is the conscience), and more a specific and definable inborn comprehension of behavior which is fitting and/or not fitting to our human condition. As we have seen in a previous chapter, the history and thinking and teaching on the natural moral law is long, varied and subject to much criticism. In this chapter, we hope to clarify the place of the natural moral law in Orthodox Christian Ethics, and to provide a basic understanding of its content. In addition, we will seek to determine the place of rules and commandments in Orthodox Christian Ethics.

Natural Law - Distinctions and Definitions

Generally speaking, law may be described as a stable and permanent order according to which the same action and the same phenomenon always expresses itself in the same fashion, given the same circumstances. This understanding of law points directly to what is often called "The Law of Nature" or "Scientific Law." Scientific law is a specific formulation of an observed recurrence, order, relationship, or interaction of natural phenomena. It is a generalization based on the observation of repeated events. Thus, the Law of Gravity deals with the attraction of physical bodies, at once describing the phenomenon and providing us with a generalization which takes into account the "stable and permanent order" and the "circumstances" under which it functions. For our purposes, the important fact to note about Scientific Law is the element of necessity. Where we have a description—given the same circumstances—of what always does take place, in which the consequences of the given conditions are perceived to be without exception and necessary, we speak of a "Law of Nature" or of Scientific Law. Thus, given the condition normally present on earth, the law which describes the attraction of bodies, accurately describes how gravity functions. This description of necessary relationships is Scientific Law.

A second form of law, sharply distinguished from Scientific Law, is called Moral Law. The distinguishing characteristic of moral law is freedom of choice. The moral law may describe facts, e.g., "If everyone went about murdering each other, it would destroy society." Yet, more accurately, the moral law is prescriptive in character. It orders us to behave in certain ways, defining the actions which are prohibited or enjoined. The crucial difference is that we are free either to obey or disobey. Unlike material bodies subject to the law of gravity (meaning that they are subject to necessity), rational beings (angels and human beings) have the choice whether to obey or violate the moral law. In addition, there is another important factor of the natural moral law. It is the sense of obligatoriness, the experience of moral demand which it places upon us. Any kind of rule or law carries with it a requirement or demand that it be obeyed. If it does not have this dimension, it cannot properly be referred to as a law. Thus, the moral law shares in common with positive (enacted) and scientific law the sense of obligatoriness, while it differs from scientific law in that it includes the element of freedom which—in spite of the demand for obedience—permits us to choose whether to obey or disobey. A third point, which should be obvious, but is often overlooked, is that the natural moral law takes the form of rules or quite specific principles of conduct. The natural moral law does not in itself point to consequences, nor does it point to ultimate goals for human existence.

It has been customary to distinguish between the natural, or unwritten moral law, on the one hand, and the positive or written moral law, on the other. The natural, or unwritten moral law is perceived to be a panhuman, inborn perception of certain types of behavior which ought not to occur. It is held that these perceptions are fundamentally unconditioned by the specifics of varying cultures. As we have previously noted, the natural moral law is perceived to be rational, independent of positive laws and customs, universal and unchanging. In the context of the distinctions made in this chapter, it is not limited to the special revelation acknowledged by Orthodox Christianity, as found in Scripture and in Holy Tradition.

Thus, Cyril of Alexandria refers to "three laws, the natural, and the Mosaic and the evangelical"[2] and Theodoretos, in his commentary on Psalm 18:1 writes: "There are three kinds of divine law . . . the first is without letters, given to human beings through creation and nature . . . the other . . . through Moses in writing . . . and the third . . . the law of grace."[3]

In patristic thought these are closely tied together. The natural moral law, the Old Testament moral law, and the ethical teaching of the New Testament are not sharply divided, but rather, point to different dimensions

119

of the same reality. St. Maximos the Confessor perhaps overstates the truth somewhat when he refers to two laws, the natural and the written, "neither of which has more or less than the other."[4] But the point is made.

Thus, the Eastern Orthodox Church accepts and teaches the reality of a natural moral law which is found in human beings, through which the fundamental rules and laws of human moral and social life are acknowledged. This law has its source in the will of God, who created humanity in His own image and after His own likeness, and which may be discerned through experience and reason.[5] St. John Chrysostom describes the Church's teaching in his usual direct fashion:

> In creating man at the beginning, God placed within him a natural law. And what is this natural law? He structured our conscience and made it so that our knowledge of good acts and those which are not so, was self-learned *(autodidakton)*.[6]

Natural Law and the New Testament

The source of this teaching on the natural moral law is the same as that of all Eastern Orthodox teachings, that is, Divine Revelation as found in Holy Scripture and in Holy Tradition. In actual practice, the sources for Eastern Orthodox teaching on the natural moral law are found primarily in Saint Paul and in the writings of the Fathers of the Church of the first five centuries of the Christian era.

Many students of the New Testament have questioned whether the passage in Romans 2:14-15 does indeed point to a natural law teaching. Certain protestant scholars discount its value as a biblical support for the teaching. Thus, it is important to examine with care the context of this passage, to see not only what is being said in Romans 2:14-15, but also the necessity of a natural law concept for the wholeness and integrity of Paul's teaching at this point. A further question deals with St. Paul's use of natural law teaching in relationship to the current philosophical, especially Stoic, teachings of his time. Did Paul use a convenient popular philosophical teaching just to prove a point? Or was his natural law teaching an essential part of the Christian Gospel, a doctrine which would have been taught even if there were no Stoic or other philosophical teaching on natural law? Thus, we ask, what is the New Testament teaching on natural law?[7]

Our first and major concern is the well-known passage of St. Paul in Romans 2:14-15:

> When Gentiles who have not the law do by nature what the law requires, they are a law to themselves, even though they do not have the law. They show that what the law requires is written on their hearts while their conscience also bears witness and their conflicting thoughts accuse or perhaps excuse them . . .

We will approach this New Testament teaching concerning the natural law by using a dialogue method to raise up the highlights of the train of thought leading to and following this passage. In this way we will be able to arrive, perhaps, at a clear and definite understanding of Paul's meaning in the above passage. Subsequently, we will make certain conclusions pertinent to our subject, hoping thus to indicate and define St. Paul's beliefs concerning natural law. We will conclude this section by attempting to ascertain the relationship between this New Testament teaching and the Stoic concept of natural law.

The great theme of St. Paul's epistle to the Romans, which covers the first and larger portion of the epistle is the absolute need of faith for justification before God (1:18-11:36). The first important point which he seeks to establish is that all persons, regardless of their present religious identification (whether, that is, they are Jew or Gentile) are *in need* of justification through Jesus Christ. He begins speaking of all men in general.

His first sentence roars out the wrath and condemnation of God upon the wickedness of man: *"Apokalyptatai gar orge Theou."*[8] All are guilty; they cannot plead lack of knowledge *(dioti)* "what can be known about God is plain because God has shown it to them."[9]

First, through Creation. The nature of the world makes clearly visible, God's power and divinity.[10] And as a result of this knowledge of God, the wicked are without any excuse.

How does the failure to know God make them morally guilty?

Because in spite of their knowledge of God they did not act on that knowledge by glorifying God and thanking Him. Rather, they turned away from this knowledge of God and with their darkened minds "followed senseless reasonings and willingly were drawn into the darkness of unbelief."[11] The result of this rejection of the natural knowledge of God was that "God gave them up," that is, "did not push them, but rather made them naked of His assistance."[12] This led to idolatry, unnatural acts, a mind incapable of fulfilling its role *(adokimon noun)* and general moral decay.[13] The lack of an excuse for this act of rejection of God by man, secondly, is heightened by the fact that they "know" *(epignontes)* that God has decreed punishment for those that do such things.[14] For, God will "render to every person according to their works."[15] To the good He gives eternal life. To those who are disobedient to the truth and obedience to evil, there will come His "wrath and fury."[16]

At this point in the discussion, after speaking generally of mankind as a whole which has been disobedient instead of obedient to God, he particularizes by specifying that the rule of reward to the good and punishment of the evil rests equally upon the Jew and the Gentile, "for God shows no partiality."[17]

There is a difference, however, between the Jew and the Gentile. The Jew has received the written law, the Mosaic Decalogue, which has clearly placed him in a position of responsibility before God. Clearly, "all who have sinned under the (written) law will be judged by (that) law."[18]

But what of the Gentile? He has no written law. He is ignorant of that revealed law of Moses. Is he also going to be judged by that written law?

121

By no means. "All that have sinned without the law, will also perish without the law."[19] Therefore the Gentile is not free from moral responsibility and he is subject to judgment even though he has never heard of the written law of God.

Is this not unjust?

No, says Saint Paul, because hearing or knowing of this written law is not what makes a person righteous; but rather, doing what it says justifies a man before God.

But how can a person do what the law says if he has never heard of the written law of God?[20]

The Gentile may fulfill the law of God even though he does not know of it in its written form if he does "by nature *(physei)* what the law requires." For the Gentiles, the law is not external, but rather within them *(eautois eisi nomos)*.[21]

But how are we sure that the law of God, to which the Gentiles are subject is something which they truly know and sense and towards which they feel responsible?

These Gentiles show that they know that they are responsible before this law. The same function that the written law serves for the Jew, is served by the law written in their hearts. They are aware of its influence and demands upon them "when their conscience gives witness to them concerning each act, and their internal thoughts amongst themselves condemn or occasionally justify them."[22] The Gentile therefore is subject to God's judgment, not only because he has a natural knowledge of God, but because within himself he has a law which is natural to him *(physei)* and a part of his makeup *(eautois eisi nomos)* to which his conscience constantly witnesses.

Thus if the Gentile does not fulfill that law (as he has not) he is just as guilty as the Jew who also has a law, though written, and who also has not fulfilled it.[23] "Both Jews and Greeks are under the power of sin."[24]

How, then, can we become righteous, if under the law, be it natural or revealed, all are guilty and neither Gentile nor Jew is able to fulfill the demands of the law?

As long as all are subject to the law alone, none can fully be righteous. "But now the righteousness of God has been manifested apart from the law . . . since all have sinned and fall short of the glory of God, they are justified by his grace as a gift, through the redemption which is in Christ Jesus."[25]

Does this redemption by Jesus Christ now abrogate the law?

No, ". . . the law is holy, and the commandment is holy, just and good."[26] But the weakness engendered by sin keeps man from fulfilling its holy and good precepts.[27] Man still knows what these precepts of the law are, for as St. Paul confesses "I delight in the law of God, in my innermost self" *(ton eso anthropon)*.[28]

Why can't the law be fulfilled if it is known?

Because the power of sin and the flesh and "evil lies close at hand."[29] "I of myself serve the law of God with my mind, but with my flesh I serve the law of sin."[30]

Does the redemption by Christ help us not only know, but also fulfill the law?

Yes, the redemption in Christ helps us in our weakness "in order that the just requirement of the law might be fulfilled in us, who walk not according to the flesh, but according to the Spirit."[31]

In analyzing this teaching we first note that St. Paul's use of natural law concepts is seen not as an attempt to argue philosophically for the position, but rather as a necessary aspect of a larger, more inclusive teaching. In his purpose to establish the need of redemption and justification for *all* men, the natural law concept is brought to bear on the issue in order to show that the Gentiles have a law to which they are morally responsible, just as the Jews have the Mosaic Law to which they are responsible. There being very little required to show this regarding the Jew, he must, however, show to which law the Gentile is subject since the Gentile does not have the revealed, written law. This he does by indicating that there is a law "written in his heart," a "law of the mind;" according to which he does "by nature what the law requires;" that his "conscience bears witness" to this law and that in this sense the Gentiles are "a law unto themselves." Because they have this knowledge of the law of nature, they stand guilty of disobedience to it, just as the Jew is guilty of disobedience to the written mosaic law.

Since this is the thrust of his argument in Rom. 1-3, it seems that any interpretation given to Rom. 2:14-15 which does not give a place to natural knowledge of the moral law in man will not fit into the course of the argument used by St. Paul.

We thus conclude, in as objective a manner as possible to us, that St. Paul teaches, even though it be in passing, that which is commonly referred to as a "Natural Law Doctrine."

Obviously, St. Paul does not see this in terms of unruffled, detached and isolated function of the human mind. Sin has taken its toll. The mind was "darkened" and man does not see with absolute purity the commandments of natural law; and further, few are able to fulfill its commandments because of the "law of sin" in their members. They knew, but could not fulfill. Therefore, redemption by Christ was needed "in order that the just requirement of the law might be fulfilled." The implications of this Pauline teaching on natural law are the following.

1. That the natural law is universal, for it is in all persons.

2. That the natural law in human beings gives true knowledge of the moral law, just as the Mosaic Law gives moral knowledge to the Jew. Because of this, later writers were easily able to identify the content of natural law with the core of the Mosaic Law, the Decalogue.

3. That people have the ability to fulfill this law, but that ability has been seriously hampered by the "law of sin," the consequence of sin. This came about by a willful rejection of the knowledge of God. This ability must necessarily be

123

considered an actual ability of fallen man and not merely one "in principle" because otherwise St. Paul's argument predicating willful disobedience and therefore real guilt would have no validity.

4. Conscience is the sign or indication, however, that even in fallen man, the knowledge of natural moral law is not destroyed, and that it still exists as a part of our humanity.

5. Natural law is, therefore, part of the natural endowment of all persons, it is the "law of (the) mind," from which the positing of the natural law in reason can be reasonably deduced.

6. This knowledge is not a theoretical knowledge; it has a binding character. Persons are responsible to it, and know that disobedience to it is subject to punishment. New Testament scholar Vasilios Ioannides concludes:

> Therefore, the real opinion of the Apostle is, that the Gentiles, even before the coming of the Savior had from God certain means, by which they were able to know God and to live a moral life. But in spite of these means, they fell into idolatry and into a continuously progressing moral decay, which made even more necessary the need for salvation from above. Exactly because they did not live in accordance to the demands of the innate moral law and of conscience, they were guilty before God. However, it was because of these very ethical powers that the Gospel was able to find responsive chords in the souls of the Gentiles and as a result, be spread more easily among them.[32]

These, however, are not the only passages which in the New Testament give indication of natural law concepts. Paul's as well as Peter's teaching that the civil ruler is a servant of God for the good,[33] Jesus' statement that the authority of the civil ruler is God-given,[34] the Apostolic dictum that "it is better to obey God than to obey man"[35] and Jesus' teaching in the form of the negative question "and why do you not judge for yourselves what is right"[36] all support the concepts usually associated with a natural law position. It must, though, be admitted, that there is neither a sustained exposition of a natural law position, nor is it anywhere in the Scriptures the main thrust of any argument.

We now raise the question regarding the relationship of the New Testament teaching on natural law and Stoic concepts. Here we meet a most wide-ranging array of opinions. None of the investigators of this problem, with its admittedly scanty evidence, seems to accept unequivocally that Paul conscientiously and knowingly adopted a Stoic concept for use in Rom. 2:14-15. However, there is still a range of opinion. There are those who seem to feel that the idea came to Paul from the then current philosophically permeated culture. For instance, R. M.

Wenley in his *Stoicism and Its Influences,* says "St. Paul's Tarsan associations so exposed him to Stoicism and to the mystery religions, that it is impossible to assess their influence even yet."[37] Nock, in specific reference to the passage under discussion, judges that Paul's use in Romans of the idea of the conscience and the belief that the Gentiles had the law written in their hearts "looks like elementary Stoicism."[38] But he does not preclude the possibility of Paul's source being biblical also; "a recollection of Jer. XXXI, 33." Carl Clemen, in his valuable *Primitive Christianity and its Non-Jewish Sources,*[39] seems to accept that these concepts come ultimately from Stoic philosophy, quoting Norden's *Kunstprosa* in support. Referring to the natural law teaching in Romans, he says "this very idea passed into general consciousness through agency of the Stoa."[40] The aspect of the theories relative to the relationship of Stoicism to Paul's teaching on natural law represented by these and other authors[41] is that Paul, more or less, adopted current widespread Stoic concepts, consciously or unconsciously and used them without fundamental change.

Others, though recognizing the similarities, point out the differences and new emphases in Paul's thought. Though not touching on the question of the sources of Pauline thought, Ernst Troeltsch goes to some length indicating the substantial differences between Stoic and Pauline thought. After noting the analogies and tracing them through the institutions of the family, slavery, charity and peace, he also notes the differences: Stoic pantheism and Christian theism, Stoic appeals to aristocratic attitudes and Christianity's lower class appeal, Stoic restriction to the present world order and the spiritual revolution engendered by "Kingdom" ideas in Christianity are lifted up for scrutiny.[42]

Carlyle, though considering the source of St. Paul's natural law teaching a mute question and accepting that the Pauline teaching is "fundamentally the same conception" as that of the Stoics, feels that Paul has made a significant "translation" of that concept in his presentation.[43]

The next position seeks to draw Paul further away from Greek sources. Those who hold this position do not in reality doubt the common character of the teaching, but rather question whether this is any thing more than a surface conformity. Zepos does not deny the connection (συνάφεια) of the two teachings, but he does feel that St. Paul's use of natural law concepts is a necessary consequence of his "theological theories."[44] Holzner refers to the idea that Paul ranged wide over the Hebrew and Hellenic ideas with which he was familiar and "with a certain naivete, takes up whatever serves him to express with clarity his ideas which shook the world."[45]

Bonhoffer, in his book *Epiktet und das Neue Testament* concludes that those who believe that there is an internal dependence of Paul's thought upon popular Greek philosophy have failed to prove their point, with special reference to the theology of Bultmann. Similar doubts are expressed by Grandmaison concerning the use by St. Paul of technical Stoic terms.[46] This position finds a very clear exponent in the person of

Kyriazis. He seeks to show that the foundations of these two positions are fundamentally different, and that the natural law teaching would have been part of the Christian message, regardless of the position of the Stoa. In summary he writes:

> Until a short while ago this (Stoic) influence was considered a fact. However, recent investigation, founded on important facts, has shown that any essential influence must be denied, and that, simply, the doors must be left open for discussion concerning the possibility of common external form and verbal formulation. The Stoic and Christian teaching concerning natural moral law has an essentially different basis and an essentially different content. That is, while in the Stoa, God and divine law are not separated basically from nature, in Paul God is the creator and governor of it. No road can lead to the Christian doctrine now under discussion for the natural law concepts of the Stoa, in which strong elements of monism and pantheism predominate. There is no doubt that even without the Stoa there would have been formed a teaching regarding natural moral law. The general lines of such a teaching are included already in seed (σπερματικῶς) in Christian revelation and especially in the dogmas of the creation of man (in the image and after the likeness) and redemption.[47]

It now remains to us to formulate our own conclusions on this matter. The key, it seems, to this problem is found by approaching the problem internally, from the rationale of Paul's argument. As we have seen, Paul needs a natural law doctrine in order to show that all men are guilty before God, and that all men, both Jew and Gentile, are in need of salvation. This is why he must make use of this doctrine. Kyriazis' statement that "even without the Stoa there would have been formed a teaching regarding natural moral law," though hypothetical in nature, does seem correct. Certainly, Paul did not feel obligated to the Stoic or any other philosophical system for the rest of his teaching.

But the fact is, that such ideas *were* current at that time and part of the matter-of-fact concepts in circulation, not only in the Gentile world but probably also in Jewish Palestinian culture. Paul certainly does not struggle to prove his point on natural law. He seems to take for granted that his readers know and accept as truth the natural law concept. Thus we can, without compromising the integrity of the Pauline revelation, agree with Lightfoot in his judgment on the parallels between the Stoics and Paul, that: "Information failing it is the part of caution to trace them to common sources in the whole circle of ideas, emotions and desires of Hellenistic culture then in rapid change."[48]

Even if it be accepted that the idea itself came to Paul in his early training through Stoic influence, we must emphasize that Paul chose and rejected what he desired from this "whole circle of ideas." What Siotis says about the manner of external influence upon the Jews of the Diaspora seems to hold true here also. "These influences took place by choice of the Jews themselves and always by adapting them to fit into their own religion."[49] Even if it could be proven beyond a doubt that Paul, in an outright manner, adopted the Stoic concept of natural law, the choice of this doctrine and the rejection of other basic and fundamental Stoic positions still gives to Paul the initiative. In such a case, he chose to use what he agreed with and rejected what he did not agree with. To paraphrase the statement quoted above, "these influences (if it be accepted that there were such influences) took place by choice of Paul himself, who adapted them to fit his own religious convictions."

Regardless, however, of the above possibilities, that which seems clear to us is that natural law beliefs of themselves, seem to make up an essential aspect of Paul's argument in Romans, and also appear here and there in other parts of the New Testament, as seen above.

Natural Moral Law and the Fathers

Evidence has already been presented that indicates the interest of the Fathers of the Church in natural law. It is generally accepted that the Fathers of the West, especially Augustine, and the Eastern Fathers of the fourth and fifth centuries taught a form of natural law morality. What has not been generally recognized is that the Ante-Nicene Fathers also taught a form of natural law morality.[50] Part of the reason which has caused this oversight is the fact that the early patristic view of natural law never received the theoretical development which the doctrine of natural law received in the West. The strong legal tradition mediated through Augustine and Thomas of Aquinas and the canonists of the Christian West elicited a development never realized in the East. The main theoretical reason for this is found in Patristic theology itself. While natural law has a place in the theological fabric of the East, the doctrines of creation, anthropology, grace and soteriology in Orthodoxy simply do not permit or call for an understanding of the natural moral law in any fashion distinct or autonomous from the whole understanding of revealed truth. The West, on the other hand, has tended to sharply distinguish between nature and grace, natural knowledge and revelation, natural law and evangelical ethics. The East's relatively high regard for the created cosmos, the capacities of fallen man, the salvation and theosis of the body *and* the soul, tend to keep natural law thinking closely related and integrally tied to the full Christian experience. Not only this, but the rather restricted definition of the content of the natural law, as we shall see below, insures its limited, yet significant place in Eastern Christian ethics.

We will survey some of the early patristic writers as well as a few of the later Fathers to firmly establish their acceptance and teaching on the natural law. Among the Apologists, *Athenagoras* writes "(God) made man of an immortal soul and a body, and furnished him with an understanding and an innate law for the preservation and safeguard of the things given by Him as suitable to an intelligent existence and a rational life."[51] However, it is perhaps true to say that the father of natural law patristic thought is

Justin Martyr. Theorizing as a Christian, he sought to explain in an acceptable Christian manner the fact of the moral and spiritual endowment of the non-Christian philosopher. He recognizes that in some cases both Christians, on the one hand, and pagan poets and philosophers, on the other, teach the same truths.[52] Justin's explanation of this phenomenon of a co-incidence of teaching takes place in the form of the doctrine of the "spermatic logos" or "spermatic word." The first element in this doctrine is the conviction that men are rational.

> God has created the human race from the beginning able to choose the truth and able to do the good so that before God all men are "without excuse" for they have been born rational and contemplative.[53]

With this emphasis on a common human God-given rationality, he emphasizes that "in all persons, there appear to be seeds of truth *(spermata aletheias)*. The existence of these "seeds" is explained by the doctrine of Christ as the pre-existent "Logos" (word, reason, rationality). The "logos" is reason. Christ is the "logos." Man's reason is Christ in man. The wisdom of the pre-Christian world is thus to be attributed to the Logos, the reason in all men:

> For whatever either law-givers or philosophers uttered well, they elaborated by finding and contemplating some part of the Word (Logos). But since they did not know the whole of the Word, which is Christ, they often contradicted each other.[54]

This view naturally leads to a natural law position. Justin says, "it is in the nature of human beings to know good and evil."[55] The clearest statement with which we will and our treatment of Justin is found in his *Dialogue With Trypho:*

> God sets before every race of mankind, that which is always and universally just, as well as all righteousness; and every race knows that adultery, and fornication and homicide and such like, are sinful; and though they all commit such practices, yet they do not escape from the knowledge that they act unrighteously whenever they do so, with the exception of those who are possessed with an unclean spirit, and who have been debased by education, by wicked customs and by sinful institutions, and who have lost, or rather, quenched and put under, their natural ideas. For we may see that such persons are unwilling to submit to the same things which they inflict upon others, and reproach each other with hostile consciences for the acts which they perpetrate.[56]

Another early Father is *Irenaeos*. His major struggles were with Gnostic heretics who used platonic and neo-platonic concepts to blur the distinction between the Creator and the creation. Irenaeos sharply distinguished between God the Creator and the creation, emphasizing the doctrine of creation *ex nihilo*. He also opposed Gnostic views which posited the existence of pure or ideal "eternal worlds" in imitation of which God created this concrete world. For Irenaeos, God created the world freely by His own will and design, unconstrained by any metaphysical pattern, reality, design or ideal. "He is the Former, He the Builder, He the Discoverer, He the Creator, He the Lord of All; and there is no one beside Him or above Him . . . There is only one God, the Creator—He who is above every Principality, and Power, and Dominion and Virtue."[57]

One of the things which the Creator has done, is to implant in human beings a perception of the moral law. In creating man, God gave him naturally, the knowledge of good and evil. Such knowledge consists of believing in God, obeying Him and keeping His commandments—"this is the life of man." To disobey God and not heed His commandments—"this is death." Since God, therefore "gave (to man) such mental power, man knows both the good of obedience and the evil of disobedience, that the eye of the mind, receiving experience of both, may with judgment make choice of better things."[58]

Another early Christian writer is *Clement of Alexandria*. Clement's purpose is to develop a Christian philosophy which will include what Greek philosophy has to offer, but also show its inadequacy. As in Justin, the vehicle for this is the doctrine of the Logos which touches on nearly all which he has to say on our topic. The Logos has a three-fold meaning: a) the incarnate Word of God, b) the mind which guides the world, and c) reason, found in all rational beings, which is the natural moral law. Thus, "according to Clement, that which is objectively the Son of God, the establisher of the natural law, subjectively is—for men—their innate reason and at the same time the natural law inscribed within them."[59]

For Clement, the Logos is the creator of human beings and the instructor of humanity:

the holy God Jesus, the logos ruling over all humanity, the very philanthropic God, is the Instructor.[60]

Man was created in the image of God, in the image of the Logos,[61] by nature not different or strange to the world,[62] but yet "a superior living being by nature."[63] He was created for virtue "not as having it at birth, but as capable of gaining it."[64] Though virtue must be acquired, the knowledge of right and wrong is given to man through the natural law. God gave the "rule of right" to man alone in the world. "Whether, then he speaks of the law given at birth, or of that given afterwards, whatever the case, it is from God; the law of nature and the law which is learned, are one."[65]

Origen also gives some attention to the question of natural law, seeing it as a law given by God to man. This law, however, is subject to development in each person. "The 'law written in our hearts' and the 'things of the law which the pagans do by nature' is none other than the common concepts *(koinas ennoias)* written in our mind *(hegemonikon)*."[66]

In passing, we might also note that Origen contributes to our understanding of the natural law "by differentiating the natural law from conscience by noting that the first is a rational power of the soul for discovery of the content of the law which the second is a spiritual power which serves as a guide to the moral life, praising the good and condemning evil."[67] In criticizing those who called positive enacted law "the king of all," Origen counters, saying "we Christians, who have come to the law by which nature is the "King of all," which is the very same as the law of God, attempt to live according to it, having bid a long farewell to laws which are not laws."[68] And elsewhere, even more clearly, he says:

> . . . there are then, generally two laws presented to us, the one being the law of nature, of which God is the legislator, and the other being the written law of the cities.[69]

For Origen, part of the "image of God" in mankind is "the ability for right action *(dikaiopraktein),* and when vigorous, the general capability of performing every good thing." This belongs to him "according to the image of God."[70]

Tertullian discusses the natural law in conjunction with his teaching about the Mosaic Law. Thus, he writes

> In short, before the Law of Moses, written in stone tablets, I contend that there was a law unwritten, which was habitually understood naturally, and by the fathers of the race habitually kept.[71]

He also speaks of the "rule of nature which we share with mankind in general,"[72] and he teaches that "everything which is against nature deserves to be branded as monstrous among men."[73] To the pagans asking for a law of God, he responds,

> Demanding then a law of God, you have that common one prevailing over all the world engraven on the natural tables to which the Apostle is wont to appeal.[74]

And in the same place, he speaks of "natural law and law-revealing nature."[75]

St. Methodios, writing in the early fourth century treats the natural law in reference to man's condition of sin and in reference to his theodicy. In the discourse *On the Resurrection* we read this passage:

> There are two kinds of thoughts in us: the one arises from the lust which lies in the body, which, as I have said, comes from the craft of the Evil Spirit; the other kind comes from the law *(nomon),* which is in accordance with the commandment *(entolen)* which was implanted in us as a natural law *(on emphyton elabomen ehein kai physikon nomon)* stirring up our thoughts to good."[76]

Thus, in the sweep of the Ante-Nicene period we discover a firm and continuing recognition of the natural moral law. It remains to mention briefly some later Fathers so as to establish conclusively the existence of a patristic position holding to the existence of a natural moral law. Thus, *Eusebius* teaches that "the creator of all provided for every soul a natural law as an aid and ally to it concerning the things which ought to be done.[77] *St. Athanasios* emphasizes the natural law idea in connection with the creation of man in God's image, holding even that some of the "righteous ancients" were "justified in the natural law."[78] *Gregory of Nazianzos* says that "(God) gave us the prophets for every law and even before them, He gave the unwritten natural law, which is the examiner of those things which ought to be done.[79] *St. Basil the Great* also teaches the truth of the natural moral law. In his *Hexaemeron* he argues that the general order and harmony existing in creation is a prototype for the ordering of human life. He holds that the social order of human society is an expression of the natural moral law.[80] He teaches that "within us there are virtues by nature to which the soul conforms itself, not through the teaching of men, but out of nature itself, in which it exists."[81] As we have already seen above, Cyril of Alexandria, Theodoretos, St. Maximos the Confessor and others also teach concerning the natural moral law. But perhaps it is *St. John Chrysostom,* of all the Eastern Christian Fathers, who elaborated most on the natural law. Though he did not contribute new understandings, he did express more clearly than any other Eastern Father the teaching of the Church on the question of natural law, the *nomos physeos* or law of nature, as he preferred to call it. The law of nature, for Chrysostom, is a true law and any positive law opposed to it is not worthy of obedience as false. The law of nature is general, eternal and immortal. Special revelation is not needed to understand its precepts; it is known naturally. The law of nature is identified with the natural logos or reason. It is the moral teacher of mankind. "God placed in man the inborn law *(emphyton nomon),* to serve as does the captain over a ship, or the charioteer over the horse."[82]

The Content of the Natural Law

As we have seen in Chapter Three the most serious criticism of all natural law theories is the fact that they seem to have difficulties in determining the actual content of the natural law. A contemporary example is the claim by the Roman Catholic Church that birth control is wrong because it is opposed to the natural law. This claim is refuted by others who simply do not recognize the issue of birth control as being an issue of natural law.

If a natural law theory is to be acceptable, it is necessary to articulate the content of the natural law concretely. Only if this is done does it at once deserve credibility and does it then have practical applicability. As a first and basic statement of content, we might again note the view that the natural moral law is perceived as an outgrowth of the Moral Drive and the Moral Sense. As we also noted before, the source of the ethical ought is based in the inborn claim which all persons have for "equal treatment." We have seen this as a basic element of the whole ethical experience. It also lies at the heart of the natural law. This basic idea may be presented in many ways. It simply may be an appeal to equity, fairplay or justice, understood as "receiving and giving each person his due." Thus Tertullian writes

> For whence was Noah "found righteous," if in his case the righteousness of a natural law had not preceded? Whence was Abraham accounted "a friend of God" if not on the ground of equity and righteousness (in the observance) of a natural law?[83]

St. Basil also writes, "Righteousness, of the kind which is within, is equal distribution *(e tou isou dianome)*.[84] St. Gregory of Nazianzos says, "Justice is the distributive practice *(exin aponemetikin)* of giving equally and according to the worth of each."[85] This fundamental element of law, the claim to justice or equal treatment is a basic element to the content of all law, including the natural law.

However, the concept of equity may also take the form of the so-called "silver" or "golden rule." This rule seeks to particularize and place more clearly in a social context the mutual claims of persons for equal and fair treatment. Thus St. Basil asks "Do you know what good you should do to your neighbor? That which you would will to be done to you by another. Do you know what it is that would be evil? That which you would not want to suffer from another."[86] The first of the two is the "Golden Rule": Do to others as you would have them do to you." The second, or "Silver Rule" is put negatively: "Don't do to others that which you do not want them to do to you."

A further point which must be noted is the social character of these injunctions. At its heart the natural moral law speaks to basic social relationships. The natural moral law is perceived by the Fathers as an expression of the basic conditions permitting and protecting the existence of human society. Thus, St. John Chrysostom, in his *Sermons on the Statues* characterizes the natural moral commandments as "necessities which hold together our lives."[87] In summarizing the patristic position regarding the basic social character of the natural moral law, Kyriazis states:

> The task of the natural law is to establish surely the foundational rules which make up the necessary basis of social life. Because of this is it characterized as a necessity for life and consequently it is said by some Fathers that without it the world would have long ago been destroyed.[88]

The patristic position then points to the content of the natural moral law as quite basic, fundamental and universally applicable to human social (societal) life. The content of the natural moral law is to be identified with the essential rules of conduct which insure the continued existence of any social group. In the mind of the Fathers, these requirements can be specified and particularized.

Thus, various Fathers attribute certain kinds of rules, especially negative rules, to the content of the natural law. Theodoretos, for instance, notes that Cain was taught by nature "that murder was against the moral law."[89] He also speaks of the natural law of Marriage.[90] However, on the whole, the patristic tradition identifies in large part, the content of the natural law with the Ten Commandments. Irenaeos sees the natural law as given by God to all persons. This permanent law is identified with the Decalogue.

> Preparing man for this life, the Lord Himself did speak in His own person to all alike the words of the Decalogue: and therefore in like manner, do they remain permanently with us, receiving by means of His advent in the flesh extension and increase, but not abrogation.[91]

In addition, Irenaeos is careful to distinguish the moral law of the Decalogue from the ceremonial law of the Old Testament, as well as from the laws given on account of the sin which occurred with the making of the Golden Calf.[92]

Clement of Alexandria notes "whether then he speaks of the law given at birth, or that given afterwards, whatever the case, it is from God; the law of nature and the law which is learned are one" as noted previously.[93] Origen relates the natural law to the commandments of scripture as well:

> It must be said of those who ought to draw the just judgment of God, that the condemnation of sinners would be excluded if all did not have, according to common understanding, a healthy concept concerning morality. Therefore, it is not extra-ordinary that the same God should have sown in the souls of all men those same things which he taught through the prophets . . .[94]

Though the Decalogue is not referred to specifically in these passages, it is clear that in both Clement and Origen, this could not refer to the unique message of the Old Testament regarding the chosen people, the references to the Messiah, etc. The identification of the content of natural and revealed law would, of necessity, have the natural law as its lowest common denominator.

This connection between natural law and the Decalogue was more clearly indicated by Tertullian in the passage noted in the previous section in which he identifies the natural moral law which was "habitually understood naturally" and the Law of Moses "written on stone tablets." Justin Martyr, also makes a similar comparison in the passage noted previously[95] in which he particularizes his reference to the natural law by referring to adultery and whoremongering *(porneia)* and homicide "and such like." It is true that Justin does not identify the natural moral law with the Decalogue in so many words. Yet as the above reference indicates, he does identify it with what are concretely injunctions of the Decalogue.[96]

Chrysostom, as usual, is the most detailed and specific.

We have no need to learn that fornication is an evil thing, that chastity is a good thing, but we know this from the first, the Lawgiver, when He afterwards gave laws, and said "Thou shalt not kill," did not add, "since murder is an evil thing," but simply said, "Thou shalt not kill;" for He merely prohibited the sin, without teaching. How was it then when He said, "Thou shalt not kill," that He did not add, "because murder is a wicked thing?" The reason was, that conscience had taught this beforehand; and He speaks thus, as to those who know and understand the point. Wherefore, when He speaks to us of another commandment, not known to us by the dictate of conscience, He not only prohibits, but adds the reason. When, for instance, He gave commandment respecting the Sabbath; "On the seventh day thou shalt do no work;" He subjoined also the reason for this cessation. What was this? "Because on the seventh day God rested from all His works which He had begun to make." And again; "Because thou wert a servant in the land of Egypt." For what purpose then I ask did He add a reason respecting the Sabbath, but did no such thing in regard to murder? Because this commandment was not one of the leading ones. It was not one of those which were accurately defined of our conscience, but a kind of partial and temporary one; and for this resaon it was abolished afterwards. But *those which are necessary and uphold our life,* are the following: "Thou shalt not kill; Thou shalt not commit adultery; Thou shalt not steal." On this account then He adds no reason in this case, nor enters into any instruction on the matter, but is content with the bare prohibition.[97]

Though the teaching is nowhere stated with precision and exactitude, we are still able to agree with Kyriazis who summarizes this teaching, noting that the basic content of the natural law is equated with the Decalogue. It follows that the three kinds of law noted by the Fathers, the natural, the mosaic and the evangelical have a common core. This moral law refers to the relations of persons toward each other and particularly in the social life (with special, but not exclusive reference to the fourth through the tenth commandments).[98] In a slightly different perspective the Apostolic Constitutions articulate the same truth serving to conclude this paragraph: (God) gave a law as an aid to the natural one *(eis boetheian tou physikou),* pure, saving, holy . . . complete in ten words."[99]

If we approach the prescriptions of the Decalogue with this frame of reference, their basic and quite elementary character is laid bare. The ties of family are clearly pre-supposed by "honor your father and mother!" the essential right to life is protected by "You shall do no murder;" the marital bond is made firm by "You shall not commit adultery;" property is protected by "You shall not steal" and "you shall not covet;" normal trustworthiness for the conduct of human relations is upheld by "You shall not bear false witness." Even the need for any society to have a source for its values and its group orientation and its criteria of right and wrong is indicated by the commandments "You shall have no gods before me;" "You shall make no graven image," and "You shall not take God's name in vain." The need for physical rest and relaxation from work as well as the need to honor the sources of a community's value structure is found in the commandment "Remember the Sabbath day to keep it holy. Six days you shall labor, and do all your work; but the seventh day . . . you shall not do any work."[100]

The basic and elementary character of the Decalogue (and consequently of the natural law of which it is an excellent expression) is shown even more clearly by asking if any society could long stand if its negative proscriptions were made into positive injunctions. Were we to make as requirements of behavior maxims such as those which follow, the consequences would be disastrous:

"Despise your gods or all things valuable in your society"
"Speak of your gods or whatever is the source of value in your
    society vainly and with disrespect"
"Never rest"
"Dishonor your family and parents"
"Murder people"
"Commit adultery"
"Steal from others"
"Tell lies and deceive others"
"Be jealous of others and seek to make them lose what they
    have"

Such "rules of conduct," it is clear, would quickly destroy any society in which they were consistently practiced for any period of time. For example, if all persons lied to each other including promises, appointments, check balances, contracts, etc. it would soon be impossible to maintain any pattern of order in a given society. Normal social, political, economic, educational, recreational and all cooperative activity would dissolve in chaos.

Thus, the patristic understanding of the natural law sees it as a very elemental moral law which articulates the absolutely necessary modes of behavior for the maintenance of the human community. The Fathers see the Decalogue as an excellent expression of the natural moral law, which of course has its particular form because of "the unique context in which it is found—the Old Testament." Yet, for this identification of the content of the natural law to be valid, it must also be shown that this kind of moral understanding is widely accepted and recognized. It is not the place here to make a detailed study of pan-human ethics. However, a study of the ethical teachings of world religions, that is, those having written scriptures, shows conclusively that at the basic level of ethical relationships of which we speak, none of the world religions teach in opposition to that which is found in the Decalogue, especially, commandments four to ten. None teach dishonor of parents, murder, adultery, theft, deceit and lying and jealousy and greed as morally approved. Of course, some emphasize some commands over others. For example, Confucianism has a very high evaluation of filial respect and honor. It is also true that each has additional emphases, beyond the basic moral affirmations of the natural law, which make the ethical teachings of the various world religions distinct and unique. From a patristic viewpoint, however, the doctrine of the creation of humanity in God's image, the teaching of the ''spermatic word'' and the reality of a natural moral law, are affirmed empirically and in fact.

The Natural Law and Rules in Ethics

This understanding of the natural moral law leads us to certain additional and important affirmations.

The first is that the natural moral law is *limited* to certain basic and elementary ethical affirmations. As we have seen, it refers to those relationships which effect the fundamental social conditions for existence. It is a common practice of Christian teachers and catechists (not to mention moral theologians) to interpret the Decalogue as a statement of the whole Christian ethic. This is a mistake. The Decalogue and the natural law which it represents cannot bear the weight, in themselves, of the revealed truth of God on moral matters. A very careful examination of the Commandments, distinguishing between what they do say and what they do not say, is instructive. The commandment says, ''you shall not commit adultery;'' it does not say, ''you shall not commit fornication.'' The patristic understanding of the natural moral law however, is vindicated by this distinction. No society could long stand which had as a moral command ''commit adultery'' because it would destroy the most fundamental building block of any society, the family, however it might be conceived. To make ''commit adultery'' an ethical requirement would be tantamount to saying ''destroy the family and the whole society upon which it is built.'' But, fornication is another matter. The Christian ethic condemns it. It is perceived as an improper exercise of sexuality. Yet, so long as fornication is not an attack on the structure of the family as an institution, it in fact can take place much more widely without having the impact of adultery on a society. Of course, if it becomes so wide spread that it does threaten the existence of the institution of marriage and family it would deserve condemnation from the point of view of the maintenance of the social character of human existence. But the point is that the Decalogue speaks of adultery and not fornication. In like manner, it speaks of murder, but not war or hatred or vindictiveness. It prohibits stealing; it does not speak of the active pursuit of justice. It condemns bearing false witness; it does not speak of telling the whole truth, etc. What this means is, that in fact, the natural moral law points to a relatively *low level morality*. One might say it is a sort of common denominator ethic.

This fact points to a second affirmation. The natural moral law is useful to Christian ethics as it seeks to speak to some *moral issues in a pluralistic society*. The Christian could note that since the natural moral law, the written law of the Old Testament and the evangelical ethic all have this common core, there is no need for Christians to concern themselves with the natural law since they have a higher, more complex ethic in the gospel. This would perhaps be a practical truth in a homogeneous Orthodox Christian society. It obviously is not a practical affirmation in a pluralistic society and world. The "low level morality" of the natural moral law is a very important means for Orthodox Christian ethics to relate to such a society as citizens especially in participatory democracies. Thus, it is not acceptable to argue against a public policy of abortion on demand with the argument that abortion on demand violates the Orthodox Christian ethic of the value of personhood which is based on the Orthodox doctrine of the Holy Trinity. This would be perceived as a sectarian approach to a public issue, and therefore unacceptable. But, by approaching the issue of abortion on demand as a question based on the natural moral law and as a case of "you shall do no murder" we can participate in the public debate in an acceptable manner.

This also cautions us about the limits of the appeal to the natural moral law from an Orthodox perspective. For example, by no stretch of the imagination can Orthodox Christian Ethics base its views on bioethical issues exclusively on the natural moral law. Issues such as birth control, genetic engineering, vasectomy, human experimentation, artificial insemination, organ transplants and other such issues are too complicated and involved to be reduced to exclusive natural law treatment.

The third very important issue which this treatment of the natural law leads to is the question of the place of *law and rules* in Eastern Orthodox ethics. It is a current commonplace to emphasize the central place of the interpersonal, "human" encounter in ethics. As we have seen, this is characteristic of the "situational ethics" approach. It also is characteristic of those who strive to eliminate "Western legalism" and the "juridical mentality of Western Christianity" from Eastern Orthodoxy.

Perhaps the most outspoken upholder of this view is Chrestos Yiannaras. He correctly points to the Orthodox Christian source of life in God; that the individual person finds his or her ontological reality in the fundamental interpersonal relationship of the Holy Trinity. He points to the fact that it is quite possible to negate that truth by objectifying the meaning of the existential meeting of the divine and the human in the process of Theosis into "objective" rules, laws, requirements; i.e. into a false law. In a powerful statement in his *The Freedom of Ethos (E Eleutheria tou Ethous),* he writes:

> The consequence is for us to define persons with ontic attributes (objectified impersonal properties) of individual nature, that is to confuse nature with the person, to understand persons atomistically as individuals. Thus the person is understood as a natural, individualistic self-consciousness and as a psychological "ego," which stands thoroughly distinct from the differentiated, independent, individual natures of others, thus creating relationships of rights and duties. This is the path which leads to

137

the individualization of ethos and to the concept of Ethics as individual *(atomistikon)* responsibility or individual *(atomistikon)* accomplishment. Ethics ceases to be concerned with human reality, that is, with what the human being truly *is*. Rather, it is conceptualized within the objective dimensions of social relations and becomes an external—and finally legalistic—necessity. The suppression or the ignorance of the truth of the person in systematic theology has, as an inevitable consequence, led to the creation of a conventional, legalistic Ethic. The human ethical problem is no longer real, i.e. a problem of faithfulness to the authenticity of human existence, to the truth of personal existentiality *(hyparktikotes)*. It is no longer a problem of *salvation,* but rather a pseudoproblem of conventional objective duties. When in Christian Theology ontic (i.e. objective, impersonal, individualistic) categories displace ontological (i.e. personal, existential, interpersonal, divine-human categories), then in the practical life of the Church the problem of salvation is confused by the objective dimensions of a new "Law." [101]

Yannaras' emphasis on the "personal" and "ontological" is authentic Eastern Orthodox theology, as we have seen. The question is whether it is equally authentic Eastern Orthodox Ethics to understand any and all objective statements of right and wrong, good and bad, as incompatible with the "ontological" theology of the Church.

Certainly the issue cannot be dismissed lightly, for the tradition of the Church, in its historical reality, while affirming the first does not deny the second. The most cursory survey of the tradition discovers a use of and important place for rules, commandments and laws. Jesus frequently speaks of the "commandments of God" [102] and refers to the Decalogue's injunctions. St. Paul says "the commandment is holy, just and good" [103] but even more significantly, frequently gives commandments, rules, laws and directives to the Christian communities to which he writes. For example in Romans alone, the following instructions are given:

"Let love be genuine; hate what is evil;" [104]

"Contribute to the needs of the Saints, practice hospitality;" [105]

"Live in harmony with one another; do not be haughty, but associate with the lowly, never be conceited;" [106]

"Live peaceably with all;" [107]

"Beloved, never avenge yourselves, but leave it to the wrath of God;" [108]

"If your enemy is hungry, feed him;" [109]

"Let every person be subject to the governing authorities." [110]

All these are commandments and rules, that is, concrete, "objective" imperatives.

We have seen the insurmountable evidence of the patristic teaching regarding natural law. The Fathers also speak of commandments which are

138

to be obeyed. Even the *Philokalia* which gathers together some of the most spiritual writers of the patristic corpus refers frequently to the need to be obedient to rules, commandments and laws. Suffice it to note just a few authors of the *Philokalia:*

Kallistos and Ignatios Xanthopoulos write a sub-section in their larger work with the title "That he who would live according to God must obey all of the commandments . . ."[111] St. Gregory Palamas, in a short study of the Decalogue discusses each of the commandments. In his conclusion, he writes: "Thus by keeping them (the commandments) with all of your strength and by living in them, you will place in your soul the treasure of piety and you will please God, and you will be treated well by God and those who live according to God, and you will inherit every eternal good thing."[112] St. Symeon the Theologian, speaking of the manner by which the soul is united to God, writes: ". . . The shining of grace is not established in us before the commandments are obeyed and the virtues acquired."[113] In addition the whole canon law, and the respect shown for it points to an important place for rules in the Eastern Orthodox Church.

Thus we face a dilemma, the Tradition of Eastern Christianity seems to emphasize, on the one hand, an open, free personal, "ontological" understanding of the Christian life which is highlighted by the doctrines of the Holy Trinity, man's creation as the image and likeness of God, and the human destiny to enter into divine communion and to achieve Theosis. Yet, on the other hand, it speaks of obedience to commandments, rules, laws, injunctions, and canons, in a quite "objective" fashion. Does this mean that there is a basic ethical inconsistency in Eastern Orthodox Ethics? Must we accept the one and reject the other as incompatible?

The solution to the problem of rules and commandments within the ethical teaching of the Church is provided for us by St. Maximos the Confessor. For St. Maximos, the commandments and rules are embodiments of the meaning of true humanity and theosis. The rules are not external codes, imposed from without upon mankind in an alien fashion. The rules and commandments of God are articulations of the fitting and appropriate modes of behavior for the human person in the realization of his or her destiny to be in full communion with the Trinity and to achieve the fullness of humanity, Theosis. In Yannaras' terms, the commandments are statements of the modes of behavior appropriate to our ontological reality. The commandments and the relationship with God are two aspects of the same reality. Thus St. Maximos writes,

> The Divine Logos of God the Father is completely indivisible and is naturally totally within His Word (Logos). Now he who receives a divine command and does it, receives the Logos of God residing in it; and he who receives the Logos through the commandments has received naturally through Him and together with Him, the Spirit . . . Thus, he who receives and fulfills the commandment, has mystically received the Holy Trinity.[114]

139

"He who receives and fulfills the commandments has mystically received the Holy Trinity!" This is the positive affirmation of the place of rules and commandments in the ethical life. A negative formulation of the same truth is made in the same work by St. Maximos the Confessor.

> As long as I am imperfect and disobedient, not obeying God in the fulfillment of His commandments, I cannot become perfect in knowledge and in mind; not only this, but in addition Christ Himself appears to me as imperfect and disordered. I diminish Him and maim Him by not growing together with Him spiritually, as a member in part of the body of Christ.[115]

Thus, rules and commandments are properly seen as expressions of the type of behavior which is appropriate to the life which leads to the fulfillment of our divine/human destiny. Thus, the command "Beloved, never avenge yourselves" is a shorthand way of saying that persons who are growing in Christ, who are recipients of divine forgiveness and who are on the road toward Theosis in the Holy Trinity, violate and tear down that ontological human reality if they become overcome with the desire for revenge and/or act on it. The commandments make sense for us only within the larger framework of the whole Christian life. Obedience to God's commandments is the mode of behavior appropriate to those persons united with Him. And oppositely, at its heart "sin is not really the violation of a law—the violation of a law is sinful when it reflects the breaking down of the relationship of unity, which ought to exist between man and God."[116] Thus, the Eastern Church is spared from legalism, even though it has a high regard for commandments. The practice of "Economia" respects the law and the commandments, but permits a certain flexibility of application without abrogating the law or setting up precedents. All this is done in the name of the same reality; the fitting and appropriate mode of behavior for those in "ontological" relationship with God.

It is true that we can fall into legalism. But this occurs only when we forget the whole divine drama in which we find ourselves. We make the commandments and rules of God—His will—legalistic, "ontic," objectified devices when we see them as separate from the whole economy of deification. The commandments of God, in fact, have to do with the purpose, intent and over-all direction of the Christian life and not with a mere concern for conformity to external standards. In the words of St. Gregory of Sinai,

> The commandments require neither laxness nor overstrictness, but rather a will whose purpose it is to seek out God and to do what is pleasing to God. Otherwise, the effort is in vain, and in the words of Scripture "does not make straight the ways of the Lord." For it is the purpose of every act which is significant . . . Without a sincere heart it is impossible to properly fulfill the way of the commandments and act guiltlessly.[117]

This final reference to "purpose" and "sincere heart" points to another dimension of the Christian life. If Creation (through natural law) points to rules and commandments, Redemption in Christ points to another dimension of the ethical life, in addition fo the first. We now turn to that new dimension: "The Evangelical Ethic."[118]

[1] St. John Chrysostom, *Homily on Anna*, 1, 3.

[2] *Old Testament Commentaries*, Migne PG, 77, 1253B.

[3] Commentary on Psalm 1:7. Migne P.G. 80, 873.

[4] *Peri Diaphoron Aporion Aghiou Dionysiou kai Gregoriou*, MPG 91, 112BC.

[5] See my article, "The Natural Law Teaching of the Eastern Orthodox Church," *Greek Orthodox Theological Review*, Vol. IX, No. 2, 1963-64, pp. 215 ff. and Martin E. Marty and Dean G. Peerman, *New Theology No. 2*, New York: Macmillan, 1965, pp. 122-133.

[6] *On the Statues*, 12, 3.

[7] The balance of this section is taken in large part from my dissertation, *The Natural Law Teaching in the Ante-Nicene Fathers and in Modern Greek Orthodox Theology*, 1964, pp. 20-36.

[8] Romans 1:18.

[9] Romans 1:19.

[10] Romans 1:20.

[11] Commentary by Theodoritos on Romans 1:21, quoted by Panagiotes Trembelas, *Ypomnema eis tas Epistolas tes Kaines Diathekes. (Commentary on the Epistles of the New Testament.)* 2nd Ed. Athens: Zoe Publications, 1956, Vol. I, p. 42.

[12] Chrysostom, quoted by Trembelas, *ibid.*, p. 43.

[13] Romans 1:24-31.

[14] Romans 1:31.

[15] Romans 2:6.

[16] Romans 2:7-8.

[17] Romans 2:9-11.

[18] Romans 2:12b.

[19] Rom. 2:12a.

[20] Rom. 2:13.

[21] Rom. 2:14.

[22] Paraphrase of Rom. 2:15 by Trembelas, *op. cit.*, p. 54.

[23] Rom. 2:17-29.

[24] Rom. 3:19.

[25] Rom. 3:21, 23-24.

[26] Rom. 7:12.

[27] Rom. 7:14.

[28] Rom. 7:22.

[29] Rom. 7:21.

[30] Rom. 7:25.

[31] Rom. 8:4.

[32] Vasilios C. Ioannides, *Ho Apostolos Pavlos ke oi Stoikoi Philosophoi (The Apostle Paul and the Stoic Philosophers)* 2nd. ed., Athens: Ekthesis Christianikou Bibliou, pp. 107-108.

[33] Rom. 13:1 and I Peter 2:13.

[34] John 19-11.

[35] Acts 5:29.

[36] Luke 12:15.

[37] R. M. Wenley, *Stocisim and Its Influences,* New York: Longman's, Green and Co., 1927, p. 115.

[38] Arthur Darby Nock, *St. Paul,* New York: Harper & Bros., 1938, p. 239.

[39] Carl Clemens, *Primitive Christianity and its Non-Jewish Sources,* tr. by Robert G. Nisbit, Edinburgh: T & T Clark, 1912, p. 59.

[40] Quoted by Clemens, *ibid.,* p. 59.

[41] Cf. Edward Westermarck, *Christianity and Morals,* New York: Macmillan Co., 1939, pp. 106-107; Heinrich Rommen, *The Natural Law,* tr. by Thomas R. Hanley, St. Louis: B. Herder Book Co., 1955, p. 35.

[42] Ernst Troeltsch, *The Social Teaching of the Christian Churches,* tr. by Olive Wyon, New York: Macmillan Co., 1931, Vol. I, pp. 65-68.

[43] A. J. Carlyle, *History of Medieval Political Theory in the West,* New York: Barnes & Noble, 1950, Vol. I, pt. 3, chap. viii.

[44] Panagiotes J. Zepos, "O Pavlos os Ergates tou Dikaion," ("Paul as a Worker for Justice"), *Aktines,* Volume 14, June, 1951), p. 260.

[45] Joseph Holzner, *Pavlos,* (Paul) Greek trans. by Jerome Kotsonis (3rd ed., Athens: Damascos, 1953), p. 21.

[46] Referred to in Holzner, *ibid.,* p. 486. Bohnoffer, p. 176; Grandmaison, *Jesus Christ,* I, 24.

[47] K. B. Kyriazis, *ibid.,* Pt. 1, Vol. 1, pp. 54-55. See also Herbert Spiegelberg, *Gesetz and Sittengesetz,* p. 295. Theodore Zahn, *Der Brief des Paulus an die Romer durchgeschen von Friedrick Hank* (in "Kommentar sum Neuen Testament," no. 6), s. 124, referred to by Kyriazis, *ibid.* See also Markos Siotes, *Istoria kai Apokalypsis (History and Revelation)* Thessalonika, Stougianakis, 1953, Sec. 28, pp. 51-56.

[48] J. B. Lightfoot, *St. Paul's Epistle to the Phillipians,* London: Macmillan & Co., Ltd., 1875), p. 301.

[49] Markos Siotes, *ibid.*

[50] Rommen, Heinrich, *The Natural Law,* St. Louis: The B. Herder Book Co., 1955, and Felix Fluckinger, *Geschichte des Naturrechts,* Vol. I, Zurich: Evengelischer Verlag, 1954.

[51] Athenagoras, *On the Resurrection of the Dead,* XIII.

[52] *First Apology,* 20:3.

[53] *Ibid.,* 28:3.

[54] *Second Apology,* 10:2, 3.

[55] *Ibid.,* 14, 2.

[56] *Dialogue with Trypho* 93:1-2.

[57] *Against Heresies,* Book II, Chapt. xxx, 9.

[58] *Ibid.,* Book IV, Chapt. xxxix, 1.

[59] K. B. Kyriazis, *To Physikon kai to Kanonikon Dikaion ex Epopseos Orthodoxou (Natural and Canon Law From the Orthodox Perspective),* Athens: Apostolike Diakonia Press, 1957, Vol. 1, p. 69.

[60] *Exhortation,* IV.

[61] *Ibid.,* X.

[62] *Stromata,* 4, xxvi.

[63] *Instructor,* 3, vii.

[64] *Stromata,* 6, xi, also xii.

[65] *Stromata,* 2, xxix.

[66] *Commentary on Romans* 7,7.

[67] Stanley S. Harakas, "The Natural Law Teaching of the Eastern Orthodox Church," *op. cit.,* p. 218.

[68] *Contra Celsus,* V, 40.

[69] *Contra Celsus,* V, 37.

[70] *Commentary of Genesis, Bibliotheke Ellenon Pateron,* Vol. 15, p. 133.

[71] *Adv. Judaeas,* II, ii.

[72] *De Corona,* VIII.

[73] *Ibid.,* V.

[74] *Ibid.,* VI.

[75] See also, *Adv. Marcionem,* II, v.

[76] *Logos* II, vi. See also *Logos* II, vii.

[77] *Preparation for the Gospel,* 6, 6.

[78] *The Incarnation Against Apollinarios* 2, 9.

[79] *Orationes* 14, 27.

[80] *Hexaemeron,* 29, 193.

[81] *Ibid.,* 29, 196.

[82] *To Those Who Are Scandalized,* 8. MPG 52, 479.

[83] *Adv. Judaeas,* II, ii.

[84] *Homily on the Introduction to the Proverbs*, 8.

[85] *Logos on the Beatitudes*, 4.

[86] *Homily on the Hexaemeron*, 29, 196.

[87] *Sermons of the Statues*, 12, 3.

[88] Kyriazis, *op. cit.*, Vol. I, p. 103.

[89] *Questions on Genesis*, No. 57.

[90] *Questions on 2nd Kings*, No. 7.

[91] *Against Heresies*, Book IV, Chapt. xvi, 4.

[92] *Ibid.*, IV, xv, 1.

[93] See also *Stromata*, 2, xxix and 7, ii.

[94] *Contra Celsus*, I, 4.

[95] *Dialogue With Trypho*, 93.

[96] For another view see Theodore Stylianopoulos, *Justin Martyr and the Mosaic Law*, Missoula, Montana: Scholars Press, 1975, p. 59.

[97] *The Statues*, XII, 9. (Emphasis mine.)

[98] Kyriazis, *ibid.*, Vol. I, pp. 104-107.

[99] 6, 19, 2.

[100] Exodus, 20:1-17.

[101] *Op. cit.*, p. 25.

[102] Matthew 15:3, 6; 22:36-39; Mark 7:809; 12:30-31; John 10:18; 12:19.

[103] Rom. 7:12.

[104] Rom. 12:9.

[105] Rom. 12:13.

[106] Rom. 12:16.

[107] Rom. 12:18.

[108] Rom. 12:19.

[109] Rom. 12:20.

[110] Rom. 13:1.

[111] *Concerning Those Who Would Live the Hesychastic Life*, in *Philokalia*, Vol. 4, pp. 201-202.

[112] *The Decalogue of the Law According to Christ*, in *Philokalia*, Vol. 4, 116-122.

[113] *Chapters Practical and Theological*, 77 in *Philokalia*, Vol. 3, p. 251.

[114] *Concerning Theology, Second Hekatontas*, 71 in *Philokalia*, Vol. 2, pp. 82-83.

[115] *Ibid.*, 30, in *Philokalia*, Vol. 2, p. 75.

[116] Stanley S. Harakas, "The Orthodox Christian Approach to the 'New Morality'," *Greek Orthodox Theological Review*, Vol. XV, No. 1, Spring, 1970, p. 136.

[117] *Chapters Most Useful*, 14-15, in *Philokalia*, Vol. 4, p. 33.

[118] Portions of this chapter were published in the *Proceedings of the American Society for Christian Ethics* 1974, edited by Max Stackhouse; also in the *Journal for Jurisprudence*, Spring, 1979.

Chapter Seven

THE EVANGELICAL ETHIC

"Having purified your souls by your obedience to the truth for sincere love of the brethren, love one another earnestly from the heart."

(1 Peter 1:22.)

As we have seen, our conscience has need of a certain content to do its ethical work. In the process of forming character, making decisions and implementing them in a total style of life (our *politeia,* in patristic terms), there is need to have concrete and definable standards of what is in fact right or wrong, appropriate or inappropriate, fitting or unfitting, subject to praise or blame, what is righteous or what is unrighteous, what is virtuous or what is sinful, what is good or what is evil.

We have discerned in the previous chapter a basic elementary content to the moral life in the natural moral law, whose very broad and general requirements provide a basis for human social living. It stands between tolerable social existence and social chaos. It provides a norm of behavior, a content for ethics, a standard for public law and morality which is necessary for all peoples, societies, cultures and nations. It is basic, elementary and low level.

In fact, it fails to account for the sorts of behavior which we have come to admire most. We do not consider it particularly virtuous for a person *not* to be a thief or *not* to be a murderer, or *not* to be an adulterer, etc. The Ancient Greeks spoke of four cardinal virtues; prudence, justice, temperance and courage (or fortitude). These are not part of the natural law as understood in the Eastern Christian Tradition. They in fact arise out of a particular concept and understanding of humanity. This view of humanity, which emphasizes the "rational man" produced certain evaluations of what a person ought to do or what a person ought to be like in the light of that vision or image of what human beings truly are. In another perspective, the determination of the ultimate meaning of the good by various philosophical schools has resulted in each of them establishing norms of behavior for mankind. Thus, if man is truly man in his seeking after pleasure and his avoidance of pain, then , it is argued by hedonists, he is subject to the norm "seek pleasure and avoid pain."

For Christian Ethics, God is the good and man's destiny and relationship with God is the vision which provides the motif for the normative content of the ethical life. Put in other terms, the "Christian story" provides a wholistic view of what life is all about. That story of humanity's present state, its ultimate destiny, its authentic existence, provides certain norms and standards of behavior. Precisely because Christianity claims that its message describes the total human situation accurately, its ethic is applicable to all of mankind. While the natural moral law speaks to all of mankind in its most elementary moral existence, the Evangelical Ethic speaks to its greatest potential and its total fulfillment.

That is why we must first speak of the context of the Evangelical Ethic and then speak of the content of the Evangelical Ethic. We will follow this with a deeper look at Christian love, and conclude with some comments on certain issues related to the Evangelical Ethic.

The Context of the Evangelical Ethic

The ethic appropriate to human beings, that is, the norms which direct us will be based on our understanding of what the human situation is in relation to God Who is the good. Our previous treatment of the good tended to have a static, metaphysical, objective character to it. However, it would be a total distortion of the Christian message to leave it there. The "Christian story" leads, rather, to an open, vital and dynamic Evangelical Ethic. This ethic, while including the natural moral law and the perspectives of the ethics of philosophy, in fact transcends both of them and transforms them into something quite new.

The story of man and God which forms the context for the Evangelical Ethic has been told in Scriptures and in Holy Tradition, in brief and in length. As a story of salvation, it may be summarized as follows.

God created humanity in His image and likeness to be in communion with Him. Free to respond to this opportunity for a fulfilling relationship with God, mankind breaks that bond, isolating itself from the Triune God. The consequences of this break of relationship with God, the source of our existence as human beings, is a loss of the potential to become fully human and a distortion of our remaining capacities. As long as we are separate from God, we are in an imperfect condition, a state of sin. Alone, we are unable to redeem ourselves. We are incapable of restoration to wholeness; we cannot forgive ourselves, we cannot re-establish relationships with the source of our being, God.

Freely and without constraint, God moves to restore the life-giving relationship to mankind. First, through His Chosen People, the Jews, by revealing Himself and His will to them through Moses, the Prophets and the whole history of this people. He reveals truth about Himself, about our fallen state, about His expectations regarding human behavior, about the future full restoration of the relationships of humanity and God on the basis of His own initiative.

Finally, the second person of the Triune God, the Son, takes on human nature, becoming incarnate, and He accomplishes the restoration of persons and humanity as a whole to their appropriate relationship to God. Jesus Christ teaches the truth about God and man. He gives direction for living this new life and He makes this new mode of existence a possibility through His death on the Cross and His resurrection. He saves all of mankind from the condition of sin, providing the potential to all persons to be restored to wholeness.

With His Ascension, the Holy Spirit, the third person of the Triune God, enters the life of mankind to accomplish, fulfill and realize the potential now made possible by the work of the incarnate Son. Choice *for* God and what He has done for humanity is now demanded of each person. Once that choice is made, we are introduced into the totally new life of the Kingdom of God. In the Sacraments we are presented with the life of the Kingdom and share in it. Concurrently, as persons, we grow in grace and virtue, accomplishing the likeness of God in our lives, but only with the constant presence of the Holy Spirit. This growth in the life of the Kingdom is both a gift (grace) and an accomplishment (freedom). We grow toward Theosis as persons and towards the realization of the Kingdom as a community of His body.

We grow, but we never *fully* achieve. We experience the Kingdom in worship and in love, but we do not do so fully. The fullness of sanctification and the realization of the Kingdom await in the future, when Christ will return to judge the living and the dead and to establish God's Kingdom in its fullness.

This is a poor attempt to sketch out the "world view" of the Christian faith. A much more beautiful and inspiring description of the "Christian story" in a liturgical setting is the great prayer of the Anaphora in the Divine Liturgy of St. Basil. This and many other such "summary statements" of the Christian truth, including that written above are partial expressions of the mystery of the divine economy, each emphasizing some aspects of that truth at the expense of others.

For Orthodox Christian Ethics, this "world view" has many implications. We have seen many of these implications in the theoretical topics which we have discussed to this point. We will see many other implications of the Orthodox Christian Faith for the questions of Orthodox Christian Ethics as we proceed.

However, one of the central ethical implications arising from the Orthodox Christian understanding of the Triune God, Creation, Humanity's creation in the image and likeness of God, the person and work of Jesus Christ, the continuation of that work for the redemption of mankind, the sacramental life, including the eucharistic manifestation of the Church, and the eschatological teaching, is growth toward Theosis.

For Christian Ethics, that new condition which comes into being after Baptism and Chrismation and which continues to exist until death or until the Eschaton is the period of growth and development in the God-like life toward "Theosis." Oftentimes, this growth is not specifically identified as ethical. It may take upon itself many different manifestations and it may be characterized in many different terms and with various expressions. Thus, we are called upon to "grow in Christ," to "live in the Spirit," "to live sacramentally," and to "manifest the mind of Christ." These and many other similar expressions refer to a God-supported re-orientation of our lives. They focus on the personal experience of the Christian with the living God. When, however, this same reality is viewed less from the perspective of God's energies outpoured upon us, and more from that smaller portion of our own active response to that loving grace, then we move into the sphere of ethical living. Growth however, is characteristic of that aspect of the Christian life. Ethics is particularly involved when some effort, some free choice, some struggle against evil and against temptation is required for that Christian growth to take place.

Because Orthodoxy does not know of the mere imputation, forensically, of justification and salvation, but understands the actual saving work of Jesus Christ as communicated in the Church as a real event and an empirical experience, we are called to change, to develop, to grow, to mature, to be transformed and transfigured so that our lives reflect the divine life as much as is humanly possible for created beings such as ourselves. St. Paul articulated this so powerfully in the Epistle to the Ephesians. Thus, the goal of Christians (and, by extension, the goal of all human beings whether they are aware of it or not) is to

> attain to the unity of the faith and the knowledge of the Son of God, to mature manhood, to the measure of the stature of Christ . . . Speaking the truth in love, we are to grow up every way into Him who is the head, into Christ, from whom the whole body, joined and knit together by every joint with which it is supplied, when each part is working properly, makes bodily growth and upbuilds itself in love.[1]

That this growth has mainly ethical dimensions is made clear by the fact that this passage is followed by a thorough ethical exhortation. We are "no longer to live as the Gentiles do (darkened in their minds, callous, licentious, greedy, unclean),"[2] but we are to change our very nature. "Put off your old nature which belongs to your former manner of life and is corrupt through deceitful lusts and be renewed in spirit of your minds and put on the new nature, created after the likeness of God in true righteousness and holiness."[3] In large part, growth into our "new nature" is ethical in character—"true righteousness and holiness." Thus, St. Gregory of Nyssa writes characteristically:

> Though it may not be possible completely to attain the ultimate and sovereign good, it is most desirable for those who are wise to have at least a share in it. We should then make every effort not to fall short utterly of the perfection that is possible for us, and try to come as close to it and possess as much of it as possible. For it may be that human perfection consists precisely in this constant growth in the good.[4]

The same patristic author, in another work, in the context of speaking about the mutability of our human nature, indicates that its "finest aspect

. . . is the possibility of growth in good," noting that "this capacity for improvement transforms the soul, as it changes, more and more into the divine." He speaks, subsequently, in "ought" (ethical) terms.

> One ought not then to be distressed when one considers this tendency in our nature (our changeableness); rather let us change in such a way that we may constantly evolve toward what is better, being "transformed from glory to glory" (2 Cor. 3:18), and thus always improving and ever becoming more perfect by daily growth, and never arriving at any limit of perfection. For that perfection consists in our never stopping in our growth in good, never circumscribing our perfection by any limitation.[5]

The pattern of growth gives to Ethics as understood in Eastern Orthodox Christianity a dynamic, developmental character, while at the same time, keeping the truly good person from pride and smugness. In another frame of reference, that of obedience to divine commandments, Jesus makes the same point to His disciples: "When you have done all that is commanded you, say 'we are unworthy servants; we have only done what was our duty'."[6]

Thus, growth gives the dynamic dimension to Orthodox Christian Ethics; eschatology explains its limitation, yet at the same time gives it hope and power; the Kingdom gives it its sense of communality in the Church, rescuing it from individualism; Theosis gives it its content and its telos; the image and likeness give it its beginning and foundation; and the Triune God determines it forever as both objective and inter-personal, at once. This is the context of the Evangelical Ethic.

The Content of the Evangelical Ethic

The Christian Ethic then is to be found and described primarily within the context outlined above. Its content, however, still needs to be determined more specifically. Just as the Decalogue is an excellent expression of the natural moral law, it is generally accepted in the Church that the Sermon on the Mount is the expression *par excellence* of the Evangelical Ethic.

The relationship between the law and the new Evangelical Ethic is not one of displacement, but of fulfillment. In the Sermon on the Mount, we read "Think not that I have come to abolish the law and the prophets; I have come not to abolish them, but to fulfill them."[7] In part, that fulfillment consists in pointing to the inner attitudes, dispositions, motives and intentions which inform our external behavior. The Sermon on the Mount, especially as recorded in Matthew 5 and 6, focuses on the new mode of existence which characterizes those who have been reedemed in Christ, who have entered the Kingdom, who share its promises, its forgiveness, and its growth in perfection and towards Theosis. It is at once a description and an imperative for the way of life appropriate to those who are in communion with God.

Yet, the Sermon on the Mount is subject to many interpretations. In Christianity, it has oftentimes been understood as a noble, yet impossible

148

expression of the highest moral idealism. Others have seen it as an amplification of the Golden Rule or the commandment of love for neighbor. Theologians, also, have tended to emphasize one or another aspect. Thus Ritschel saw it as an exposition of generalized moral principles. Rauschenbusch saw in it the basis of the "Social Gospel." Its demanding and radical character has prompted varying responses. For some it is a literal, legal demand; for others it is applicable only to a certain group of people as a monastic or a sectarian ideal. Some, such as Albert Schweitzer, saw it as an out-dated, short-term ethic for the period between the proclamation of the coming Kingdom and the imminent return of Christ which never came. Others, such as Bultmann and Giannaras see it primarily as an internalized radical ethic which sets one apart from conventional behavior. Others such as Martin Luther, perceived it as an impossible demand which has as its purpose to drive people to recognize their sinfulness.[8]

However, in the long history of the Eastern Orthodox Church, the key interpretation of the Sermon on the Mount was that of St. John Chrysostom. "It was upon him that the medieval interpretation of the Sermon on the Mount was based, both in the East and in the West."[9] For the Church, "the Sermon on the Mount was believed in as the ideal program of the Christian life."[10] In the early patristic corpus[11] injunctions from the Sermon on the Mount are presented as rules for living. In addition, Chrysostom also points to the fact that the Sermon on the Mount emphasizes the inner dispositions as well as the external acts. It all begins with humility in which the life of the Kingdom comes to us as a gift and not as a right. This gift, however, demands an important and clear-cut response on our part both in our inner dispositions and our external behavior. Difficult as they may appear, Chrysostom points to the need for Christians not to compromise, but to struggle to conform their inner and outer living to the new life in Christ as exemplified in the Sermon on the Mount. It calls the Christian not "to the measure of empirical, ordinary humanity, but to the measure of a new type of human being, who is like Christ . . . What is clear from the Sermon are the characteristics of the ethos of a journey of eschatological character."[12] Agourides holds that the Sermon on the Mount is not directed to some special class of persons (monks, gnostics, the "perfected," etc.) "but to all who have entered the new life in Christ."[13] He holds that the radical character of the Sermon is found in its Christological center as that affects all of humanity.

> Behind all of the teachings and demands of the Sermon on the
> Mount, that which is presupposed is the presence of Him, and
> the appearance of a new possibility for mankind and the world.
> Without Him, what meaning do all of the other particulars have?
> . . . The teaching of the Sermon assuredly refers to the new
> righteousness, to the new demand of God upon human beings.
> But this new righteousness, this new absolute and ultimate
> demand of God upon man is incomprehensible, if it is seen as

unrelated to that newness which entered into history in the person of Jesus Christ. [14]

This absolute, new requirement does not lead to hopelessness and mere conviction of sin. Without question "the Sermon on the Mount does reveal our ethical nakedness . . . (But) the whole Sermon gives a picture of man which is, in truth, divine-like. The Sermon does reveal our ethical poverty. But it does this with the conviction that we are able to journey toward perfection, toward an ethos which is the ethos of God." [15] In response to the crucial question whether the Sermon on the Mount is a set of rules or whether it is in fact an expression of an existential, eschatological frame of reference, Agourides avoids both extremes. In the first case, the Sermon would present the Evangelical Ethic as a "new law," a rigid and demanding code of the most radical nature. The second sees it primarily as an "ethic of the mentality of the whole man" as he lives within the new order created by the eschatological vision. The Christian is thus freed—in this interpretation—from rules, laws, prescriptions and proscriptions. He is perceived as living out his Christian life in pure existential relationship with God and man.

The legalism of the first view is easily countered by the whole spirit of the Gospel. The second view needs more attention. Is the Evangelical Ethic in fact "a way of life in the eschaton" only? Agourides rejects this view. He notes that "the justified fear of a casuistic ethic, of a legalistic religion, often leads to the other extreme, to the danger of an ethical indefiniteness and hesitation before concrete situations." [16] The eschaton can be overemphasized at the expense of the historical and the daily life. Man himself can be overemphasized as an "existential being" at the cost of the human journey within life both as a person with a history and a future. A journey which takes place in relationship with other concrete persons—who have their own histories and futures—and who travel the same road which he or she does. He concludes the expression of his view with the words of W. D. Davies,

> Can we not conceive that radicalism and legislation coincided sometimes in his ministry? Can we not trace the mark of the Sage in him as well as the Eschatological? [17]

Agourides thus sees the Sermon on the Mount within the traditional ecclesiastical tradition as a program for living, as the constitutional document of the Kingdom of Heaven, as the new law of Christ. In this he is joined by nearly all modern Greek Orthodox writers on the subject, i.e. Nicholas Damalas, [18] Komnenos, [19] Panagiotes Trembelas, [20] Andreas Papageorgakopoulos, [21] as well as Markos Siotes in his yet incompleted series of articles in the periodical *"Epistasia."*

This "program for living" is neither Faith, Grace, Eschatological Hope or Existential Ethos alone on the one hand, nor is it Ethical Commands and New Law alone, on the other hand.

> The Gospel is not only a gift, it is also a demand. An interpretation of the Sermon on the Mount is erroneous if it takes

150

place with the assumption of the antithesis of Law and Gospel, requirement and grace. The Sermon on the Mount is, it is true, not a program for the political or social reformation of the world. But neither can it be limited to the sphere of the inner personal life, nor can it be considered as a mere reflection of the awesome need which we have for redemption. A correct interpretation of the Sermon on the Mount, must, under the light of Christological truth, maintain a balance between promise and demand, between the disturbing power of its commands and the encouraging power of its promises.[22]

Thus, the Evangelical Ethic certainly includes rules, commandments and laws. It includes the Decalogue and the ethical injunctions of the Old Testament. Jesus, St. Paul and the other sacred writers of the New Testament clearly give commands for Christians to follow, which, as we have seen, prescribe behavior which is appropriate to a life of growth in the Kingdom and, conversely, proscribe behavior which is not in fact fitting to the growth toward Theosis.[23] These and many other commands, rules and laws are part of the Christian Ethic. They clearly refer to external behavior and clearly are given in the expectation of obedience.

Yet, as we have seen, it would be quite inaccurate to point to these as the sum total of the Christian Ethic. There is a dimension of the Christian Ethic which is more than rules, commandments and laws. It comes out clearly in Jesus' condemnation of the Pharisees and scribes for their hypocrisy. Jesus demands more than mere external conformity to rules, regulations and laws. The well known "Chapter of Judgment" (Matthew 23) roundly condemns the hypocrisy of these religious leaders. Their commandments are not condemned, however: "practice and observe whatever they tell you,"[24] the Master instructs. But their overt behavior is condemned. They speak and teach, but they do not do what they teach. Further, their sense of values is distorted; they do not know what is of more importance and what is of lesser importance.

> Woe to you scribes and Pharisees, hypocrites! for you tithe mint and dill and cummin and have neglected the weightier matters of the law, justice and mercy and faith; these you ought to have done, without neglecting the others.[25]

But the most reprehensible is the disharmony between their external acts and appearances and their inner dispositions. Jesus puts the priorities in proper order:

> Woe to you, scribes and Pharisees, hypocrites! for you cleanse the outside of the cup and of the plate, but inside they are full of extortion and rapacity. You blind Pharisee! first cleanse the inside of the cup and of the plate, that the outside also may be clean.[26]

Outside, they are like whitewashed tombs which appear attractive to the eye, but within there are rotting corpses. "So you also outwardly appear

151

righteous to men, but within you are full of hypocrisy and iniquity."[27] This contrast between external behavior and inner dispositions is a key, though not exclusive, element of the Evangelical Ethic and more specifically of the Sermon on the Mount. By focusing on the need for these two to be in harmony, external behavior is given even more significance: it is not adequate to merely "go through the motions of good behavior." A truly good act and a truly good person will act out of an inner disposition which is in harmony with the external act or style of life. Conversely, good motives will express themselves by and large in external deeds and in a lifetime "politeia" which conforms with the spirit and the letter of the law. However, for the Evangelical Ethic, the inner disposition is primary and most significant. Jesus' ethic weighs on the side of formal (motive) ethics rather than on consequence ethics, without, of course, abrogating the need for conformity to His commands.

We can obtain a clearer view of the nature of the inner attitude appropriate to the new life in Christ by a more careful examination of the Sermon on the Mount. The Sermon itself begins with the Beatitudes. Jesus blesses the "poor in spirit," "those that mourn," the "meek," those "who hunger and thirst for righteousness," the "merciful," the "pure in heart," the "peacemakers," those who are "persecuted for righteousness' sake." The Beatitudes direct themselves to inner attitudes and dispositions. Chrysostom interprets "poor in spirit" as "the humble and contrite in mind" adding "He blesses them first, who by choice, humble and contract themselves."[28] Those who mourn are specified by the Holy Father as in fact not those who mourn at the death of a loved one ("how can one call those 'blessed'?"), but those who "do so for sins."[29] Meekness is blessed with the promise of reward in this life as well as the next. Hungering and thirsting after righteousness is interpreted as the attitude toward righteousness which "with all desire we may pursue."[30] The "merciful" is clearly both an attitude and a mode of behavior. Chrysostom holds that this speaks "not of those only who show mercy in the giving of money, but those likewise who are merciful in their actions." The "pure in heart" are understood as those "who have attained unto all virtue" or "those who live in temperance."[31] "Peacemakers" refers both to "our own inner strife and hatred" but also "that we should set at one, others who are at strife."[32] Those "persecuted for righteousness' sake" are blessed because of their concern for

> virtue's sake, and given to others, and for godliness: it being ever His wont to call by the name "righteousness" the whole practical wisdom of the soul.[33]

Here we have a description and at once an injunction appropriate to the person whose "politeia" of life is fitting and appropriate to life in the Kingdom and to personal growth toward Theosis. It calls for a person who is humble and open to the grace of God; whose attitude and mode of operation is not one of violence, but one of gentleness and meekness; who has a strong desire that whatever is good and right may prevail; who deals

152

with mercy and understanding with himself and with others; who avoids duplicity and who is a person of virtue both within and without; who seeks to avoid strife and hatred in his or her life and to establish and maintain peaceful relations elsewhere; here is described a person who has such a deep conviction of what is right and good, that he or she is willing even to suffer persecution because of it. The inner focus of this "personality description" is evident. It does not, obviously, exclude external behavior; rather, it is intimately related to it. But the emphasis is on the kind of person distinguished by a certain set of inner motives. What emerges is a Christ-like figure of gentleness, combined with moral and spiritual seriousness; a combination of tenderness and strength, a person of virtuous integrity whose relationship with others is redeeming and reconciling.

That this is not a purely personal or individualistic experience is seen in Matthew 5:13-16 where the "Blessed ones" are characterized as "preservers" (salt) and as "lights" for the world, and as "cities set on hills." The "Blessed ones" exist for the welfare of others. The ethical implications of both the Beatitudes and this passage are clear. The gentle and ethically rigorous person is an example for all of society and serves, even more significantly, as its preserver and its "light." Concern for personal life and concern for the welfare of society are intertwined. Personal spiritual integrity feeds social well-being. Social health supports personal morality. True humanity demands a mutual, inter-related emphasis on both.

As the Matthean account of the Sermon on the Mount proceeds, it then focuses on certain specific dimensions of the moral law, giving to each of the commandments selected a new emphasis focusing on the inner disposition appropriate to a member of the Kingdom. There is no antinomianism here. The moral law is both respected and obedience to it is taught. However, Jesus' teaching fulfills those commandments (5:17-20). Not only is murder prohibited, the anger which provokes it is condemned (5:21-22a). Insults are not appropriate to those growing in God's image, but reconciliation goes beyond just avoiding conflict. It demands a willingness of spirit to overcome strife and it demands acts which initiate the opportunities for reconciliation (5:22b-25). Adultery and fornication are wrong, but lust, which is the inner disposition leading to them needs to be plucked out of the true human being's character (5:27-31). Lying and falsehood are condemned, but deceit which seeks to cover up the truth is at its heart; it is to be replaced by direct and simple honesty (5:33-37). Revengeful action is not appropriate behavior for the child of God on the road to perfection and its impulse is to be reversed. The mentality of returning evil for evil is not God-like. The deification of life means acting as God does, by returning good for evil (5:38-42). That same deification of human life means more than mere returning love for love. It presents us with a divine ethos which goes so far as to love those who do us harm. This is divine perfection in human life (5:43-48).

More religiously speaking, the practices of the religious life must also have the same harmony between external behavior and inner disposition.

153

Charity must be given for the benefit of the recipient, not the benefit of the giver. The motive for the giving of alms ought to be concern for the needy, not self-aggrandizement (6:1-4). Prayer must be for the sake of communion with God, not for show (6:5-6) and it should be direct, sincere and honest (6:7-13). Forgiveness of others should be offered generously, just as God forgives generously (6:12, 14-15). Fasting, too, should have inner motives directed to personal spiritual growth and not to external praise or observation (6:16-18).

The next section of the Sermon speaks about ultimate loyalty. The truly human person does not place his or her ultimate loyalty in money or material things (6:19-24) or, for that matter, anything other than God Himself (6:25-33). His Kingdom must be of first priority for the person who seeks to be fully human (6:33). This trust in God leads to further instructions and descriptions regarding the person growing into the perfection of the Kingdom. Such a person is not to be anxious about the problems of this life (6:34-35). Such a person ought not to condemn other people, but should be sensitive to his/her own faults and shortcomings (7:1-7). This person does, however, discern evil wherever it exists (7:6), treats people justly, equitably and fairly (7:7-13), tries hard to conform his/her life to what is right (7:13-14), guards him/her self from evil influences (7:15-20).

The Sermon ends with a warning that overt behavior is important—it is not enough just to talk religion or goodness, not enough even to have good motives or intentions, not enough just to call upon God. In the last analysis "evil-doers" find themselves condemned and he or she who "does" what Jesus teaches will stand in the end (7:21-27).

What comes out of this analysis is that the Evangelical Ethic is concerned with both external actions and their *appropriate* inner dispositions. The integrity of the inner and outer *data* is important. It is a rigorous, demanding ethic which speaks to both specific deed and general character. In part, it is in conformity to the customary ethical standards of the natural law and mosaic legislation. In part, it transcends that ethic, especially as it commands love as the appropriate course of action to those who would be like God.

The Sermon on the Mount is not an exhaustive description of the new ethical life in Christ. It indicates some aspects of this new "politeia." Elsewhere the New Testament fills out this image. For instance, in the Epistle to the Galatians, the "fruit of the Spirit" is described. These fruits are clearly perceived to be gifts from God. Yet, at the same time these "gifts" are also virtues which can be chosen, cultivated and developed in the Christian character.

> But the fruit of the Spirit is love, joy, peace, patience, kindness, goodness, faithfulness, gentleness, self-control: against such there is no law. And those who belong to Christ Jesus have crucified the flesh with its passions and desires.[34]

The inner dispositions dominate in this description. They clearly arise out of the ecclesial and eschatological experience of the new life in the

154

Spirit ("those who belong to Christ Jesus. . ."). Yet, they also become imperatives for ethical growth. The transition from the description and celebration of the new "politeia" to the ethical mode for living the new life takes place a few lines later in the same epistle:

> Do not be deceived: God is not mocked, for whatever a man sows, that he will also reap *(lex talionis).* For he who sows to his own flesh will from the flesh reap corruption; but he who sows to the Spirit will from the Spirit reap eternal life (consequences). And let us not grow weary in well-doing (proscription), for in due season we shall reap, if we do not lose heart. So then, as we have opportunity, let us do good to all men, and especially to those who are of the household of faith (prescription).[35]

The same gifts of the Spirit are given as ethical injunctions in another epistle of the New Testament. In Colossians, these virtues of the Christian life are, in contradistinction to Galatians, seen as prescriptions for behavior to which Christians are called to conform themselves because they are appropriate to the whole economy of the saving work of God. Thus, we are enjoined to "put on then, as God's chosen ones, holy and beloved, compassion, kindness, lowliness, meekness, and patience, forbearing one another . . . forgiving each other."[36] We are to do it because "the Lord has forgiven you," because "you were called in the one body,"[37] because "whatever you do, in word or in deed, do everything in the name of the Lord Jesus."[38]

The ethical injunctions in the Gospel focus on the inner motives and dispositions. However, they are inextricably bound up with the experience of the redemption given by the Father, through the Son, in the Holy Spirit. That new life is both a given as well as something to be achieved. Its essence is personal, free, authentic, faithful, sincere involvement in the new life of the Kingdom and can be described as growth toward perfection and Theosis. Much of the essence of the Christian life is conformity to ethical rules. Much of it, however, fulfills those commandments by conforming not only our external behavior, but also our inner disposition to the new life in Christ. It also transfigures those rules with an ethical seriousness which becomes radical in character, transcending both rules and dispositions. Just as the natural moral law embodies the basic ethical *donatum* of all human social life, and just as the Sermon on the Mount points to the new style of life of the redeemed community—the Church—so the Commandment of Love points to the radical dimension of the "ethos of God" which is appropriate to true human living. Thus, the content of the Evangelical Ethic cannot be fully comprehended without special attention to Christian Love.

Christian Love

It is interesting to note that though love is mentioned in the Sermon on the Mount, it is not the exclusive Christian virtue, which many, primarily Protestant, ethicists make it to be. Yet, its supreme position among the Christian virtues and within the "politeia" of the new life is witnessed to by the New Testament and the whole patristic corpus. The well-known 13th Chapter of 1 Corinthians is rivaled only by the words of 1 John in marking love as the pre-eminent virtue of the Christian life-style. Yet what is so universally recognized as supreme in the Christian "politeia" is quite often misunderstood and used for conflicting purposes. "Love" is a much mis-used word. We will first look at some of its varied uses. Secondly, we will try to understand the meaning of Christian love by analyzing it as carefully as we can. Next, we will turn our attention to its dimensions and we will conclude this section with some words about love's application.

The Varied Uses of Love

A little time spent with an ear and an eye open to catch the uses of the term "Love" makes us immediately aware of the fact that people talk about love in many different ways. A sampling of such uses of the term "love" showing the tremendous variety and multiplicity of meanings for this term is listed below.

—In Gilbert and Sullivan's play *Iolanthe,* one of the characters says "It's love, it's love that makes the world go 'round!''

—At a local sweet shop, one teenager says to another ". . . don't you just *love* his hair?''

—We read from a page of William Faulkner's novel *Light in August,* "Perhaps they were right in putting love in books . . . Perhaps it could not live anywhere else.''

—In 19th century India, the Englishman Rudyard Kipling thinks of home, remembers a loving mother and writes

"If I were hanged on the highest hill Mother o' mine,
O mother o' mine!

I know whose love would follow me still, Mother o' mine, O mother o' mine!''

—In the Old Testament, King Saul's son meets David, the man who is destined to become his father's successor on the Throne of Israel and we read: "It came to pass that when (David) made an end of speaking unto Saul, that the soul of Jonathan was knit with the soul of David, and Jonathan loved him as his own soul.''

—There is a parked car on a dark road. A boy and a girl are petting. The radio is playing a current song "Hey baby, I'm in love with you . . .'' only to be interrupted by a commercial: "Love is groovy, love is clothes nice and clean with COLD POWER.''

—A woman dreams of her beloved and rises to write these lines found in the *Sonnet* of Elizabeth Barrett Browning:

How do I love thee? Let me count the ways.
I love thee to the depth and breadth and height
My soul can reach . . . .
. . . .

I love thee freely, as men strive for Right:
I love thee purely, as they turn from Praise
I love thee with the passion put to use
In my old griefs, and with my childhood's faith.
I love thee with a love I seemed to lose
With my lost saints, —I love thee with the breath,
Smiles, tears, of all my life! —and, if God choose,
I shall but love thee better after death.

—In Hitler's Germany, the daggers of Hitler's elite S.S. Officers, bright and shining, bear the phrase "For the love of Fatherland and Fuehrer."

—In the midst of a small gathering of persecuted Christians in the first century, the aged Apostle John speaks:
    "Love not the world, neither the things in the world. If
    any man love the world, the love of the Father is not in
    him."

—A mountain. Jesus sits on a promontory and speaks to the people gathered to hear Him:
    You have heard that it was said, "Thou shalt love thy
    neighbor and hate thine enemy, but I say unto you,
    love your enemies . . ."

It does not take much to see why people are confused about the meaning of "love." What *are* Christians talking about when they use that word? Like "motherhood" most people are for "love." But when we utter the word, what exactly is meant? Can the same thing be the subject of all of these situations? Is love in a popular song the same thing as "loving" the color of a boy's hair? Are they the same as a mother's love, the love of Jonathan and David, the passion of romance, the love of parents, patriotism, love of the "world" and love of the Father? What do all of these things have to do with Jesus' "love for enemies?" The confusion has led philosopher Dagobert Runes to conclude that "the word 'love' belongs in that small group of general terms which is used more frequently to disguise an intent or thought than to divulge it."[39] That conclusion may or may not be true. But that there is much imprecision in the use of the word, is a fact nearly everyone would agree. As we have seen in the third chapter, theologians are no less at variance about their understanding of love. Ethicists have made various efforts to capture the essence of Christian love. Certainly, it is a necessary task if we are to come to a more complete understanding of the Evangelical Ethic. To this task we now turn.

The Meaning and Source of Love.

One of the reasons that we are confused about the meaning of love is a linguistic one. The English language uses the word in so many ways so as to cover so many situations that it presents us with the confusing array of applications which we have described. If we turn to the Greek language however, we have a different picture. There we have a series of words, all translated into English by the word "love," yet which have clearly distinguished and specific meanings. The first of these is the word "eros." "Eros" has many connotations. It is most often understood as sexual love. Thus, "erotic love" usually refers to physical sexual relationships. More broadly, the term "eros" refers to "desiring" to "selfish wants" and to "passionate desire." At its broadest, "eros" is the fulfillment of self.

Another Greek word for love is "storgē." At its basis, "storgē" is parental love. It carries with it a sense of tenderness, exhibited by parents for little children as well as a desire to protect and enhance the lives of their progeny. This Greek word for love is taken from the root verb "stergo" which means to be attracted to something. The other side of "storgē" is filial piety, the dependence, respect, attraction and devotion of children for their parents. Both, however, are characterized by an attraction based on the relationship which exists between them; the parent because he/she has given birth to the child, and the child because it has its life from the parent.

"Philia" is a third Greek word. We sometimes refer to it as love of friends. Most often, however, we say we "like" our friends. Philia is friendship. At heart, unlike the strong passionate character of "eros" and the biological attraction of "storgē," "philia" is based on mutual advantage. Friendships exist when each partner in the friendship gains something from the relationship. Thus, each partner in the relationship of friendship must also give something. This mutual exchange of benefits according to which both or all of the friends profit maintains the experience of friendship. When one of the "friends" begins to feel that he or she is being exploited, then friendship ceases and the relationship breaks up.

The Greeks also used the word "agape" but only rarely. When it was used, it tended to mean "to treat with affection, to receive with outward signs of love, to be fond of."[40] Homer uses the word only once. In the Tragedies, it is used occasionally in the sense of showing affection to the dead. In Plato it is used both of persons and of things and mostly with the idea of desire. Thus, modern Greeks who say "agapo pagoto" (I love ice cream) use the term in its classic sense. In its classical use it was often used in the place of "phileo," "erao," and "stergo," much as it is used today. Yet, that very fact indicates a certain lack of specificity of meaning for "agape."

It was Christianity which gave "agape" specific and concrete meaning of a totally new character. The Christian understanding of love begins with the Christian understanding of God. The Scriptures teach that God is love,[41] and that love comes from God.[42] How are we to understand this teaching? What can such a statement mean when we know that we are incapable of comprehending the essence of God? Is it a mere tautological statement which, in fact, provides us with little or no content? Certainly, we must first acknowledge, that as it is with all things regarding God, we always stand before a mystery. We will be able to say some things about "agape," perhaps even enough to be sufficient for our needs in ethics. Yet, without a doubt, we will not be able to penetrate the full mystery of "agape."

If we understand the scriptural teaching as focusing primarily on the being of God, the teaching that "God is love" most obviously refers to the Triune character of the divine nature. Whatever "God is love" may mean in the "hidden cloud" of the divine essence—a reality we may seek to penetrate with impunity at the risk of sounding mundane or even ridiculous—it is the Holy Trinity which has been revealed to us and which provides us with our first concrete understanding of "agape." In more than any other book of the Bible, the Gospel of John speaks of divine love. We get a glimpse at the relationship of love in the Holy Trinity from some of the passages in that Gospel. Thus, Jesus teaches His disciples "I do as the Father has commanded me, so that the world may know that I love the Father." (14:31) In His great prayer before His death, in which He prayed for His disciples, He says, "thou, Father, art in me, and I in thee" (17:21), "thou hast loved me" (17:23), "behold my glory which thou has given me in thy love for me before the foundation of the world" (17:25) and He prays "that the love with which you have loved me may be in them (His disciples) (17:26). Agape is at the heart of reality, because agape characterizes the relationship of the persons of the Holy Trinity. We know little as to how to characterize that relationship of the three divine persons of the one divine essence. From the passages above, we can at least penetrate the mystery of love in Trinity by pointing to the indications of interpenetrability, interpersonal relation, mutual giving, and permanency of the relationship of love among the persons of the Holy Trinity. What is most important, though, is the verification that the persons of the Holy Trinity relate to each other in love. Yet, love does not exhaust the relationship of the unity and trinity of God. It is greater and more profound and more mysterious and higher than that. Vladimir Lossky writes,

> To say: "God is love," "the divine Persons are united by mutual love," is to think of a common manifestation, the "love-energy" possessed by the three hypostases, for the union of the Three is higher even than love.[43]

It is because of this, that we gain a fuller understanding of "agape" not from an effort to penetrate the meaning of the love of the Three Persons of the Godhead, but rather from the love of God toward His creation. It is in this relationship—one of the chief "energies" of God by which He manifests Himself—that we obtain a basic understanding of His "agape." "God is love" may also be understood in terms of His relationship to others, to His creation. This relationship appears most clearly in the life and work of Jesus Christ. If we are to understand the meaning of "agape" we will do well by starting from a passage in the 1st Epistle of John: "herein is love, not that we loved God, but that He loved us."[44] This passage is the key. If we really want to know what love is about, we are going to have to turn our attention to God. We are going to have to ask how God has dealt with us. How has agape-love as it exists in God been expressed toward us? 1 John again informs us:

> Herein was the love of God manifested in us, that God has sent his only begotten Son into the world that we might live through him.[45]

Certainly, God has shown His love to mankind in many ways: through His creation, through His selection of the Chosen People, through the raising up of prophets, through punishment, forgiveness, reconciliation of those same people, through the giving of intelligence and the natural moral law to the Nations, through His continuing providence and care. Yet, in Jesus Christ the love of God became fully manifest. The greatest act of love was to give to mankind the means to become once again what mankind was originally designed to be. And this was accomplished by His Son. The Son of God was incarnated, He taught, He performed miracles, He died an unjust yet willingly accepted death, He was resurrected, thus being victorious over death and sin and evil, He sent the Holy Spirit to establish His Church. And all of this took place as a result of an outpouring of agape for the world. Its motive was love.

> For God so loved the world that he gave his only begotten Son, that whoever believes in Him should not perish but have eternal life. For God sent the Son into the world, not to condemn the world, but that the world might be saved through Him.[46]

In order to get to the heart of this expression of agape-love by God for the world, we must ask a rather strange question. What did God get out of this act for Himself? To ask the question is to answer it. Anyone who is familiar with Christ's character as it is presented to us in the scriptures knows that Christ, as the Son of God, had no need of anything from us, nor any desire for Himself of anything. What He did, as we have seen, He did "that *we* might live through Him," that *we* "not perish, but have eternal life," for "He sent His Son to be an offering for *our* sins." The conclusion comes easily and clearly. Whatever Christ did, He did it for *our* welfare, *our* good, *our* advantage. His work restored the possibility to all of humanity to become truly human once again, to achieve our human destiny, to be deified, to arrive at Theosis!

This means that in its most elemental form, agape is self-less, that is, it is *not* self-concerned, but other-concerned. God's energies in Christ were and are not extended outwardly toward His creatures out of some *divine* need, nor is His agape an essential demand of *His own* nature which He must obey for *His own* sake. It is a free, unconstrained outpouring of divine concern for the welfare of His creatures. Agape is uninterested in what rewards will accrue to the one who loves. Agape is concerned only with the other. Its concern is directed to what is the true good and welfare of the other. It seeks to benefit the other in his or her own requirements and needs, as a child of God, as the image and likeness of God, as a being whose potential is Theosis. Some people have summarized this understanding of agape as "disinterested benevolence." I prefer to modify this phrase and use the term "selfless benevolence." It is a handy term. As we have noted "selfless" means lack of a selfish motive. What is done, is done for the benefit of the other, not for one's own sake or benefit. It is clear that we are first of all speaking of an inner disposition. Two acts may be the same externally and overtly. However, the motive which brings them into being may vary. The same act may be done "selflessly" or it may be done with self-serving purposes. It thus becomes easier to understand the famous passage in 1 Corinthians which speaks of many good-appearing overt acts which are considered as "nothing" because they are done without love.

> If I speak in the tongues of men and of angels, but have not love, I am a noisy gong or a clanging cymbal. And if I have prophetic powers, and understand all mysteries and all knowledge, and if I have all faith so as to remove mountains, but have not love, I am nothing. If I give away all I have, and if I deliver my body to be burned, but have not love, I gain nothing.[47]

Certainly as overt acts, speaking about God and salvation, teaching the truth to others, doing great works in God's name, great charity, abandoning all things for the faith and even martyrdom are acts which Christians have praised as good and fitting to the life in the Kingdom. But St. Paul points to the one essential thing: that these not be done for our own benefit, but that they be done for the benefit of others. All these objectively good things lose their value if the motive for doing them is not "selfless."

The motive we call "selflessness" has a positive side. Love is not merely a passive lack of caring for our own interests. It has a positive dimension; it is to be "benevolent." The Latin roots of this word are "bene" and "volo." "Bene" means good. "Volo" means "to will," a term also related to the Greek word "boulesis," meaning "to will." To be benevolent means to "will the good," especially for another.

Thus agape-love, reflecting the love of God for mankind and for all of His creation, seeks to accomplish what is of benefit and what is the welfare of the other without seeking to gain or profit anything for one's own self. It is true, however, that when we act with "selfless benevolence," that is, when we love a person for their benefit and not for our own, the consequences of our love may, in fact, be to our gain also. That is not the issue. The issue is that for love to be genuine, we must act on motives and intentions which seek to realize what is good for the other, and not with an eye for our own benefit and interests.

Something which shakes our usual understanding of love, arises then, as a consequence of *this* understanding of agape. Agape, at its most elementary level, is not an emotion or a feeling. It is a direction of attitude and concern which has to do with our willing, rather than with our emotions and feelings. It is, to put it differently, not necessary to *like* a person in order to *love* him or her. While it is almost irrational to command other people's feelings, one *can* appeal to the will so that persons may carefully examine their motives and intentions in acting. Even of God, it is said:

> When we characterize God's goodness, mercy, and generally, His love, we must not understand these as a kind of emotional disposition, as the feelings and sympathies of a passionless and immutable God, but as an undistorted energy, coming from Him . . .[48]

The most striking support of this elementary understanding of agape is the command that we love our enemies, as we have seen in the Sermon on the Mount. An enemy is one who does or threatens harm to us. If love means that I should have pleasant feelings about someone who does harm to me, it would have all of the characteristics of a pathological psychosis or neurosis. To have warm, kind, happy feelings about someone who is your enemy is a contradiction in terms. To command that people be emotionally attached, to like, to have good feelings and emotions in relationship to an enemy is to ask the psychologically impossible, *so long as the person is an enemy*. (Below, we will see that the command to love the enemy is calculated to change the other person from the stance of being an enemy, that is, one who desires your harm to a new, loving stance.) But it is not possible to *like* your enemy, to have affection for him. Much less possible is it to *command* that we like our enemies and have affection for them as enemies. What *can* be commanded is that we make every effort not to return evil for evil, and in addition, that we will what is good for them. We may not be able to *like* our enemy; but it is within our ability to be benevolent to our enemy: to seek his or her good without trying to get anything out of it for our own advantage. It is of course difficult. But it is not an impossible commandment because it appeals not to our feelings but to our will, to our choosing ability, to our *autexousion*.

This understanding of agape is elementary, basic and, in fact, incomplete. Yet, it provides the proper orientation to agape as we seek to understand it in the whole Christian context. However, someone with apparent justice may object that this understanding of agape is nothing other than the philosophical position of altruism. Altruism is the philosophical theory of ethics which enjoins "conduct aimed at the good of other persons."[49] How then is agape different? The substance of the teaching does not differ, at least on this basic level. But altruism can give no reason *why* I should look after someone else's good, without concerning myself about my own. If pressed, the altruistic moral philosopher will conclude that one should be altruistic because ultimately, it is to our own benefit. Thus, it is no longer the equivalent of agape; it is trading favors.

162

On the other hand, Christian agape is totally related with how God is, and how God deals with us. Since God is the good, it is significant that "God is love." Further, God created the world out of love; He sustains the world out of love; and, He has redeemed the world out of love. We do not love, for the purpose of getting something back. Our motive is simply one of response to what God has done. As the Bible says, "Beloved, if God so loved us, we also ought to love one another."[50] Put more prosaically, we could say, "Since God has looked out for our welfare, the least we can do is to look out for the welfare of our fellows, whether we like them or not!" More profoundly, Agape is response in relationship with Him who has dealt lovingly with us. Because we have been loved, we love. Further, since God is love, and since our true nature is to be like God, we are truly ourselves when we love. It is not a benefit which we seek; acting with selfless benevolence is a large part of what it means to be human.

If agape as selfless benevolence is a first and basic element and aspect, it is certainly not limited to such dispassionate relationships. Jesus' compassion, His gentleness, His pain, yes, even His anger was closely tied to His concern for the welfare of others. The sense of well-being, of happiness, of joy, of unity and mutuality which so often colors our understanding of agape is not inappropriate. A welfare office may disinterestedly (unselfishly) distribute checks—at least on appearances. But it is not an act of agape. In the first instance it is done out of coercion engendered by the force of the law. Further, the law has probably been passed for prudential reasons (it is to the advantage of the state to issue welfare checks). In addition, it is a mechanical process, not primarily a relationship of persons. Alone, "selfless benevolence" has a coldness to it which is not appropriate to the relationship of the Triune reality, to the concern of God for His chosen people, to the love of Christ for people, to the Christian relationship of brotherhood and unity in the Kingdom. Agape comes from a free act, willed to bring benefit to another, but which also carries with it—normally—real concern, interest, compassion, fellow-feeling, identity, unity, warmth, attachment, happiness and joy.

It may be true that love for enemy is only capable on the first level. But certainly, Christian agape directed toward those in need, those who suffer, those in danger can be an act of feeling and warmth, but not for the sake of self, but for the sake of the other. The combination of disinterested concern for the neighbor and the unity of feeling which can and does arise out of this selfless benevolent relationship which brings people to a sense of unity among themselves and with God is the heart of Christian love. Christian love does not require that I like those whom I love. But dealing with people with Christian love leads to the situation in which we both like them and they like us. Agape is fulfilled when our whole inner world conforms itself to the disposition of caring for the welfare of others, acting on the basis of that disposition and experiencing the inter-personal unity which it produces.

In this context, agape becomes the chief virtue and the source of all of the other virtues. We can understand more about agape and its practice if

163

we turn our attention to the dimensions of love, that is, those to whom we direct our love.

The Dimensions of Love

We are given to understand the three-fold objects of our love by the commandment given by Jesus when asked by a Pharisee "Teacher, what is the great commandment in the law?" Jesus' response is classic:

> You shall love the Lord your God with all your heart, and with all your soul, and with all your mind. This is the great and first commandment. And a second is like it. You shall love your neighbor as yourself.[51]

The commandment, as we have already noted, emphasizes the divine aspect of love. It places it first. Love for neighbor and for self are subsequent. In practice, we cannot love our neighbor unless we have experienced God's love first and responded to it. Yet, in terms of understanding, it is easier to reverse the order and begin with the self as an object of love, proceeding to love for neighbor and then to love for God.

You shall love your neighbor *as yourself.*" We have said that agape is concern for the welfare of the other and that it is not concerned with ourselves. Thus, it would seem impossible then to love ourselves! If concern for the other is basic to the concept of love, how is it possible for scripture to speak of love of one's own self? This dilemma is easily overcome when we recognize that we are able to distinguish between a sickly and egotistical and narcissitic regard for ourselves, characterized by selfishness and self-indulgence on the one hand, and a mature and understandable concern for our real welfare. Thus, St. Paul can note, in another context ". . . no man ever hates his own flesh, but nourishes and cherishes it."[52] Agape for one's self, in a sense, puts the self at a distance and asks, what is *really* good for me? Agape sees the self in the light of the whole divine economy of salvation and growth in the image and likeness of God toward Theosis. And then, agape *does* what is in fact good for the self. This is the kind of love for self of which Jesus speaks. Such love for self, however, is not easily accomplished. The spiritual tradition of Eastern Orthodoxy knows well the danger of self-deception. It is all too easy to convince ourselves that our desires for what is not fitting are our true good. As St. Mark, the Ascetic says, "If, according to Scripture everything, involuntary has its cause in voluntary actions, nothing is as great an enemy to man, as he is for himself."[52] That is why a continuous vigilence is needed. However, love for self, if properly monitored and properly understood, is necessary for true growth. A healthy, measured, mature regard for our own best welfare in the light of what is truly good for us and in our largest best interest, is what is being spoken of here. If we can accept this, it means two things: that we can and do love ourselves in a perfectly acceptable way, and that this perception of our own welfare can be exercised on behalf of others. Thus we come to the other half of that commandment.

164

"You shall *love your neighbor* as yourself." As we have seen, love for neighbor means basically and fundamentally my concern for what is good for him or her. I love my fellow human being when I act in order to contribute to *his or her* welfare, to *his or her* good, to *his or her* need, without trying to get something out of it for myself. It is a disinterested act. When selfless benevolence is coupled with tender-feeling, compassion, respect, warmth and human regard, it is the kind of agape-love which is best exemplified in the relationship of Jesus toward others. Jesus' tenderness is seen in His love for children. For example, "Permit the little children to come to me, for such is the Kingdom of Heaven."[53] It is seen when He met the funeral procession at the city of Nain led by the widow who had lost her only son. "And when the Lord saw her, he had compassion on her, and said to her, 'Do not weep.' It is seen when he wept at the tomb of his friend, Lazarus. It is seen when he was anxious over Jerusalem.

O Jerusalem, Jerusalem, that killeth the prophets and stoneth them that are sent unto her! How often would I have gathered thy children together, even as a hen gathereth her chickens under her wings . . . (Matthew 23:37).

When the disposition for selfless benevolence is combined with warm, human, tender feeling for the person I am seeking to assist or benefit (without seeking anything for myself in the process), I am loving in a Christian way. Thus, St. Maximos the Confessor instructs "The work of love is the heartfelt doing good to the neighbor."[54]

But, who specifically is this neighbor, this other? St. Maximos again informs us.

Perfect love does not discriminate regarding the one human nature, dividing people into different categories. Rather, love always looks at the oneness of humanity and loves all persons equally. Love considers those who are good as friends. Those who are evil, it loves as enemies, doing good to them and acting in patience and with forbearance in the face of what they do, not considering as most important the evil which they do. Rather, love suffers on their behalf so that in due time, if possible, one might turn the enemy into a friend. And if he is not able to manage that, he does not abandon his own motives, rather, he who loves continues to display towards all persons the fruits of love.[55]

Thus, the neighbor is any human being who in one way or another can be helped by our concern for his or her welfare. Obviously, we are not capable of responding fully to all persons everywhere and under all conditions. Yet, as much as is in our hand to do so, we are to love our neighbor.

This affirmation, especially as it has been raised in the preceding passage from St. Maximos, leads to the commandment of love for our enemy. Jesus' words are still revolutionary:

You have heard that it was said, "You shall love your neighbor and hate your enemy." But I say to you, Love your enemies and pray for those who persecute you . . . For if you love those who love you, what reward have you? Do not even the tax collectors do the same?[56]

What Jesus means for us to do is not merely to feel friendly to those who harm us and are our enemies. His teaching is much more radical than that.

You have heard that it was said, "An eye for an eye and a tooth for a tooth." But I say to you, Do not resist one who is evil. But if any one strikes you on the right cheek, turn to him the other also . . .[57]

Repay no one evil for evil.[58]

Do not return evil for evil or reviling for reviling: but on the contrary bless . . .[59]

In the common mind of men, such advice is seen as foolishness. Others, who would not want to use that term, consider it impractical. Yet, in fact, Jesus was not instructing us to do something which was in fact either foolish or impractical. In fact, He was speaking most profoundly and most practically. Jesus knew that hatred begets hatred. It is the elementary *lex talionis*. Harm inflicted on a person tends to demand that it be repaid, given back and recompensed. That mode of operation thus creates a vicious circle of hate and evil doing. "Vendettas" and "retaliation" justify many kinds of evil committed by persons against each other. The evil is justified in this manner, and it tends to escalate. Jesus knew that when the *lex talionis* guided our behavior there was only the possibility for more and more evil to take place. The only way to stop the vicious circle of "evil for evil" is to seek to reverse the procedure. Instead of returning evil for evil, one is to take the next positive step—return good for evil. By doing that, the vicious circle of "evil for evil" may be broken. Thus, He teaches "Love your enemies, do good to those who hate you . . ." (Luke 6:27). St. Maximos the Confessor clearly points to the practicality of these injunctions. God asks this of us

so that first *you* remain without anger and undisturbed and without hurt, and secondly so that your enemy be instructed by your patient endurance of evil, so that in the end the Good God can lead you both to love.[60]

Love for enemy, and all that it implies, is the only way the vicious circle of hate can be broken. It must first be stopped (return not evil for evil). Then, it may be reversed (return good for evil). It is true that love for enemy may not succeed. But *if* enmity, hatred, evil-doing are ever going to be reversed and substituted, then something like "love for enemy" will have to take place. And fortunately, the *lex talionis,* also can contribute to this reversal. Just as evil tends to beget evil, so good tends to

166

beget good. When the vicious circle of evil is reversed, it becomes a benevolent circle of mutual love!

"Love for neighbor" informs all of our human loves, eros, storgē and philia. It extends itself to individual and public well-doing and to social concern which seeks to modify the consequences of evil (philanthropy) and to correct the systemic causes of evil upon the lives of people (social action). But at its heart is the basic understanding of love as selfless benevolence.

"You shall *love the Lord your God.*" That is the first and chief commandment, the source of all other kinds of love. Yet, what is it that we can do for God? What need does He have that we can seek to fulfill? Certainly, God needs nothing. There is nothing which we can do "benevolently" and "selflessly" for God. But, at least, agape-love means concern and interest in another. The Otherness of God, however, is unique. He is at once, the transcendent, totally Uncreated One, who is radically different than His creation. But at the same time, He is the loving God who has created us in His image and in His likeness. What does it mean, then to love God with our whole heart and soul and mind?

As we have seen above, we love because God first loved us. Our love for God is a response to what He has done for us. He has brought us into being, He maintains our existence, He has redeemed us in His Son, He sanctifies us and leads us toward Theosis by His Holy Spirit. The love for the Father, the love for the Son and the love in the Holy Spirit are all our responses to what God has done—in love—to us. St. Paul, articulated this understanding of love for God most graphically in his Epistle to the Romans.

> If God is for us, who is against us? He who did not spare his own Son but gave him up for us all, will he not also give us all things with him? . . . Who shall separate us from the love of Christ? Shall tribulation, or distress, or persecution, or famine or nakedness, or peril, or sword? . . . No, in all these things we are more than conquerors through him who loved us. For I am sure that neither death, nor life, nor angels, nor principalities, nor things present, nor things to come, nor powers, nor height, nor depth, nor anything else in all creation, will be able to separate us from the love of God in Christ Jesus our Lord.[61]

This emphasis on the bond between the believer and God is important for our understanding of love for God, as we shall see immediately below. Our loving response to God is complex, and it cannot be reduced to one single factor. It is first of all a simple recognition and appreciation of what God is and what He has done. That acknowledgement of His love for us expresses itself in many ways: worship, obedience to His commandments, love for neighbor. More concretely, love for God develops in us "a filial devotion to God and His will" and "a trust in the divine goodness of God."[62] To love God means to acknowledge His love for us, to be devoted to Him, to trust in Him and to express that acknowledgement, devotion and trust in our actions. This relationship of love, in order to be genuine must also be supreme. Jesus taught, "He who loves father and mother more than me is not worthy of me."[63] That is why we are called to love God with our whole being.

But one more dimension of the love for God must be highlighted here. It harkens back to the passage in Romans 8, quoted above. Love for God means more than acknowledgement, devotion, trust and the appropriate expression of that love in worship, in sacrifice, in obedience to His will, in love for the neighbor. It points to something even more profound: to the lack of separation between God and the soul which loves God. It points to the desire of the human soul to be united with God. Thus, the Fathers consistently speak of a state of mind which is a "happy and grateful remembrance of God,"[64] and further, of an unfulfillable divine love (eros) and passion for God. *(Eros theios kai pothos tou theiou akorestos).* In mystical theology, as it has been formulated in the Eastern Church, the highest expression of love for God is this ever unsatisfied desire for God and the search for full human completion in the love for God. Such an "eros" is seen as the ultimate goal of the Christian life as regards the personal relationship of the individual with God. In the *Philokalia* we read many such descriptions. In a section called "Concerning the Good, the Ecstatic Love (Eros), and Divine Beauty," Kallistos and Ignatios Xanthopoulos write:

> This whole kind of desire, and this heartfelt and ecstatic love (eros) and this total feeling toward the supremely beautiful beauty man sees as most blessed. When it is reached, the Fathers describe it as the highest experience . . .[65]

Thus, in a sense, we have gone full circle. What began at first as mere "selfless benevolence" and then found human feeling, achieves the most powerful personal (erotic—but *divine* erotic) fulfillment. These aspects of love are not contradictory, they are mutually fulfilling, each leading to the other. Of course, love is still a mystery which no one will be able to capture in words or thought or rational schemata. But as a part of the Evangelical Ethic, we have attempted to clarify it and to give it a concreteness which will prove useful to our work in Christian Ethics. Whether we speak of agape or eros, in the last analysis, there is no essential difference for they speak of the one reality of relationship of God for man, of man for God and the mode of behavior appropriate to human beings who are growing in the divine image.

The Application of Love

We have noted above that love expresses itself in various ways. One of the most important is obedience to the will of God. It is a tendency both inside and outside the Church to emphasize the existential dimension of love, its free expression, its openness and its sincerity. As far as this goes, it is correct to make that emphasis. However, the implication made by this emphasis, is that the basic rules, canons and commandments are thereby invalidated. The freedom of the new ethos in Christ tends to be perceived as anomianism—the absence of moral direction and rule. This misunderstanding appeared early in the Church and became a cardinal feature of certain Gnostic sects. However, it is interesting to note that the Scriptures closely relate agape with obedience to the commandments of God. Thus "For this is the love of God, that we keep his commandments."[66] Jesus, Himself taught "If a man love me, he will keep my word,"[67] and "He that hath my commandments, and keepeth them, he it is that loveth me . . ."[68]

Even more concretely, St. Paul identifies the Decalogue with the command to love the neighbor:

> Owe no one anything, except to love one another; for he who loves his neighbor has fulfilled the law. The commandments, "You shall not commit adultery, You shall not kill, You shall not steal, You shall not covet," and any other commandment, are summed up in one sentence, "You shall love your neighbor as yourself." Love does no wrong to a neighbor; therefore love is the fulfilling of the law.[69]

The relationship of Christian freedom to commandments and to the practice of love by Christians is also clarified by St. Paul, this time in the Epistle to the Galatians where he writes,

> You were called to freedom, brethren; only do not use your freedom as an opportunity for the flesh, but through love be servants of one another. For the whole law is fulfilled in one word, "You shall love your neighbor as yourself."[70]

In Christ, we are free from the fear and condemnation which the ancient understanding of the law caused. The commandments, as we have seen, both of the natural moral law and of the new Evangelical Ethic as expressed in the Sermon on the Mount, indicate the kind of behavior appropriate to the life of the Kingdom. The commandments provide a sketch of the kinds of behavior most likely to be in conformity with growth in the image and the likeness of God. The teaching on love, and the emphasis of the Sermon on the Mount on the purity of the inner dispositions and their identity with the external actions, point to inner motives, intentions, attitudes and goals.

What we thus see, is an ethical style of life which is a single fabric with love as its highest ethical expression, but which includes the totality of that life in its journey toward Theosis. Thus, in the writings of the Fathers of the Church, love is seen "as a many-sided prism of virtues, which in the first instance, presupposes obedience to the divine will, far from the fear of punishment or reward, but for the sake of love and it alone."[71] It is in this patristic spirit that St. Maximos the Confessor writes:

> He who loves God is not able but to love every person as himself . . .[72]

169

He who does not love the neighbor does not obey God's commandment. And he who disobeys the commandment, is not able to love God.[73]

Thus, the whole complex of the good life, the virtuous life, the life of the Kingdom is caught up in the love for God which makes possible the love for man, which is expressed in conformity with the commandments of God. St. Clement, writing in the first centuries of the history of the Church, put it in a nut-shell in his Epistle to the Corinthians: "Apart from love, nothing is pleasing to God."[74]

Growing in Love

However, the practice of agape, both as inner disposition and as overt action, is a complex experience for persons. More than any other aspect of the Christian life, agape-love is subject to development, fulfillment, growth toward the full communion with God, the achievement of Theosis in personal existence and the realization of the Kingdom on the corporate human level. The theology of the Holy Trinity as a communion of persons in love, an "agapaic community" stands as the ultimate pattern of true human existence. But, the implementation of agape-love moves from one level of growth to another, from "glory to glory."

The reason that agape-love is never empirically achieved in its fullness and divine completeness at the beginning of our growth toward Theosis, both as persons and as persons in community, is that our very condition of separatedness from God, our distorted image, in short our sinfulness, by its very essence, precludes our full and experiential communion with the God who *is* love. Thus, we grow toward love, achieving one "glory" after another in our process of spiritual maturation.

To genuinely love at any level requires from us the sacrifice of our own will and our own self's desires. To love, as we have indicated above—as God has loved us—is to seek another's benefit rather than our own. To say this without acknowledging how revolutionary and how difficult this is to actually *do,* is misleading to say the least. For the egotistical and self-centered sinful individual, who is fully bound-up in his or her own interests, welfare and concerns to "come out" of him or herself, to be able to stand (if only for a short moment) outside of his or her own desires, appetites and advantage requires a revolutionary reorientation. What makes it possible is our commitment to Him who first loved us. Yet even then the practice of genuine agape-love is a costly and difficult thing. Especially, when at first, we do it without understanding and only as obedience to the commandment. In such a state, love calls out from us an attitude of sacrifice. When such a person steps out of him or herself as God stepped into the created world with his Incarnation, there is always a cross. To love in these circumstances is to suffer. To sacrifice one's ego for the sake of another and to first do this consciously and willfully is a costly and painful experience, and it is glory. Perhaps such is the first "glory" which leads us from "glory to glory" toward the full realization of agape-love.

170

Somewhere in the progression of these "glories" we come to point of concerning ourselves for the welfare of another not as obedience to the command, but because, in spite of our ego, we *want* to love, even though it is costly to us. The suffering and deprivation are no longer seen as sacrifice, even though they continue to be felt. This is a glory. It is a progression in our perception and experience of love—a growth toward the fulfillment of the image of God in us.

Further along in the path of growth, agape-love begins to flower and our ego-concerns begin to recede. As the needs of others impinge on our lives we begin to react with concern for the other's needs more freely, not seeing them as impositions upon us demanding sacrifice, but as God-presented occasions to express God's loving care to those in need. It is a glory when we reach that plateau.

But the mountains of love have even higher peaks. No longer is the occasion for agape-love seen either as demanding sacrifice and suffering, no longer is the occasion for agape-love merely a response to the claim to others. It becomes a new glory in us when sensitively and carefully we begin seeking out the hurt and pain of others, when we become sensitive in an active way. For agape-love has now become an out-reaching, incarnationally motivated, God-like glory. If we continue to grow, it soon becomes a privilege to love, a glory for which we now feel gratitude and thanksgiving to God for having given us the opportunity to love. Somewhere on the highest of the mountain tops a glory is achieved when our union with God is so complete that the self stands in worshipful awe before the divine glory and we lose all thought of ourselves—being one with the Triune God. In that sacred community, knowing that we are loved and loving in eros-communion with Him in whose image our being exists, we express agape-love for others as overflowing vessels of the love which is in God. Having become gods by grace, the love of God pours freely, effortlessly, divinely as part of our very being. In that glory, agape-love has transfigured our being and made over our whole being into itself and we love because we can do nothing else. We love freely and without constraint—we are in truth *eleutheroi,* truly free to be our genuine selves.

We travel the road of Theosis in love—realizing the growing toward God and the divine likeness in us from the glory of one manifestation of agape-love to another until the mystery of love in its fullest expression becomes hidden behind a cloud of glory which cannot in any way be known, described or communicated—but only experienced.

Some Issues Concerning the Evangelical Ethic

What has been described in this and the preceding chapter constitutes the core of the content of the Christian Ethic. The natural moral law as summarized in the Decalogue; the emphasis on personal, ontological dimension of divine-human existence; the consequent importance of inner dispositions and their conformity with overt behavior; the primacy of love as both an inner disposition and a mode of action; all these lead to a style of living, a "politeia" which is appropriate to the person or group of

171

persons (Church) and to a society which is in harmony with the fundamental human purpose which is to realize our full humanity as the image and likeness of God.

However, there are some problems regarding this approach which need to be addressed. The first problem which we face is the constant temptation to reductionism. Reduction of the Christian Ethic to any one of its components distorts it and falsifies it. Equally destructive is the over-emphasis of one of these dimensions of the Christian Ethic to the point where, though the other aspects be acknowledged, they lose practical importance. Thus, Geisler's approach is to exclusively equate love with obedience to divine commands. Fletcher's is to take the opposite course and identify it almost exclusively with a disposition of some vague "good feeling." Yannaras focuses on the inter-personal relationship and the ontological existence of the ethical agent. Traditional scholastic ethics turned love into an agent of the Natural moral law. Pietism, a sort of romantic Christianity, concerns itself primarily with inner dispositions, with "being" rather than "doing." All of these are distortions. In large part they fail to capture the wholeness of the Christian Ethic because they are reductionist in character. In looking for the one and only dimension, they miss the truth that the Christian Ethic is a complex whole, with many dimensions. It is not sufficient to identify, its "most important" element. It, without the other aspects, becomes a distortion in itself.

Thus, we can without too much reservation identify Agape-love as the key and center of the Christian Ethic. Yet, agape-love must be seen as framed by the ontological reality implied in the doctrines of image and likeness/Theosis, by commandments, both natural and revealed, and by the requirement for the conformity of inner dispositions with external appropriate ethical behavior. What emerges is not a strictly rational ethic, but an ethos, a style of life, a "politeia," or what Modern Greek ethics calls a "B(v)ioma" i.e., a mode of living. There is an element of indefinibility in this wholistic approach, a certain lack of rational precision. The acknowledgement of the claim of all of these aspects upon us as persons developing character, making decisions and acting morally, provides for a certain complexity which is never reducible to a formula or a recipe for living. Because the freedom of the new life in Christ is more than a rhetorical device, but rather, because it is the consequence of the redemption in Christ which makes the Christian Ethic possible in the first instance, there are no ethical absolutes in the strict sense of the word. The only ethical absolute is God. Thus, a certain amount of fluidity, resiliency, and flexibility is both necessary and desired. There is, in a sense, a mystery to the ethical dimension of the Christian life. We shall probably never be able to capture the perfect balance of its parts in this life. In the Kingdom to come, we may be able to see, in this matter, as in others, "face to face." But until then we must admit to "looking through a glass, darkly."

If, however, it is true that we do not have, in Christian Ethics, any absolute other than God Himself, we do have what might be called

"Relative Absolutes." By this rather paradoxical term is meant that there are certain ethical norms which, relative to our human condition, serve as stable, firm, trustworthy foundations for our ethical life. The key, again, is that we human beings derive our nature from the immutable God. Thus, love is part of what it means to be human. Thus, justice and the rules and commandments which seek to embody it, are part of what it means to be human. Thus, integrity of inner dispositions and the behavior appropriate to our condition as persons and societies growing in the divine image, are part of what it means to be human. These things do not change significantly. They stand as constant, clear, relatively absolute categorizations of the behavior appropriate to human beings. What is good and what is bad are not "one thing in Athens and another in Jerusalem." Good and bad are not today "one thing in New York and another in Paris." Yet, our "absolute" is relative, also. It is relative to the human situation as it finds itself in this world. at a particular age and time. This means that there is a certain amount of flexibility of application, a certain need to take into consideration all of the circumstances. Such an understanding makes Christian Ethics an open and free discipline. Yet, all of this is done within a certain prescribed framework. A greater good may demand that a lesser good be violated. But the lesser good is violated precisely for the sake of the greater good. And yet, most often, the lesser good may be needed by the greater good for its own fulfillment. Thus, for example, some justify fornication for the sake of experience leading to a more successful married life. But, we are entitled to question such logic. The foundation of married life is not sexual experience, it is mutual faith and devotion, in as much as it depends on the couple. What Orthodox Ethics holds is that all of the facets of the Evangelical Ethic, e.g. law-commandments, ontological relationship, integrity of disposition and ethical acts, Christ-like ethos are inter-related and inter-penetrate one another. All form a complex whole. What is essential can be distinguished from what is peripheral or culturally conditioned. The Christian Ethic is basically firm, clear and specific in its requirements. Its injunctions are "Relative Absolutes" for human living.

Yet, this perspective on Christian Ethics as supplying us with "Relative Absolutes" for our lives does not lead to formalism and to legalism in Orthodox Christian Ethics. This is not a theoretical statement; it is a description of the facts. Perhaps the key reason for this is that Christian Ethics, from the Orthodox Christian point of view is directly and intimately related to the whole Christian economy. Ethics does not have the autonomy in Eastern Christian thought and life that it has in the West. Ethics speaks of a dimension of a larger whole, the Christian life. Because of this ethical concerns interpenetrate all of the other aspects of Orthodox Christian theology and life. It is experientially related to faith, doctrine, worship, piety, sacramental life. Though some thinkers on Ethics can and do make a sharp distinction between Ethics and Religion, for the Orthodox, such a distinction is wholly artificial and improper. It would in fact be a distortion of both.[75]

Though we will deal with these factors below, it is necessary at this point to indicate how the "Relative Absolutes" of Orthodox Christian Ethics are tempered by the whole ethos of the Church so that they do not become legalistic in character. Some of these factors are the following: the doctrine of Economia, the doctrine of voluntary and involuntary sin, and the doctrine of growth.

The well-known doctrine of "Economy," as it is expressed in Orthodox Canon law also has its application in Ethics. "Economia" permits the abrogation of a law or rule when it is perceived that its enforcement will cause harm or will prevent a greater good from being achieved, without such abrogation causing a precedent to be established. What may appear as an arbitrary decision not to apply the rule, may, in fact, speak directly to that which is appropriate and fitting to the Christian ethos. The fact that the law is seen to be controlled by the larger ethos of the Christian life keeps it from becoming an end to itself. The fact that Economia never sets precedents, permits the continuing respect for the place which the law and which rules have within the larger framework of the Orthodox Christian Ethic. In both cases, we see the "Relative Absolute" of the Christian Ethic rsecued from legalism and rigidity.[76]

Another aspect of Orthodox Christian thinking and practice which both respects the "Relative Absolute" character of the Orthodox Christian Ethics, yet which concurrently allows a humane relationship to it is the doctrine of voluntary and involuntary sin. Voluntary sin is generally understood and perceived as an easily comprehended term. A sin, which has been voluntarily chosen and voluntarily acted upon carries with it a just sense of guilt and moral responsibility. Kant's dictum "the only evil thing is an evil will" finds some response in all of us. When we will to do evil and do it, it is clear that we bear responsibility for it. Thus, the practice of the sacrament of Holy Confession, calling for us to repent of our sins, is generally acknowledged as appropriate and fitting. If we have violated God's law, we are guilty and we ought to acknowledge it. However, in the Orthodox tradition, there is also the concept of "involuntary sin." This refers to wrong or evil acts or events in which we are involved, but which we have not willed, nor for which we can be held morally responsible. An example of such a situation is when we are involved in an automobile accident in which persons are killed or injured, but through no clearly evident fault of our own. Let us suppose that we were not speeding or violating and traffic laws; we were seeking to drive safely; we were attentive to our task; we have maintained our automobile well. Yet some fortuitous event occurs and people are maimed and killed. In all honesty, we did not will this evil to happen, we cannot attribute any previous decisions or acts which caused the accident (use of alcohol or drugs, etc.). Yet, we were in fact the agents of the evil. It is *our* car which has killed and maimed; the auto which *we* were driving. Strictly speaking, there is no guilt, no moral responsibility. However, we still feel a certain sense of guilt, we irrationally feel responsible, even though we know we did nothing voluntarily to cause it. The doctrine of involuntary sin speaks to

174

such a situation. By calling the situation a "sin," it acknowledges that evil has occurred. It is an evil thing for innocent people to be maimed or killed. By calling it "involuntary" it both acknowledges the formal lack of responsibility, while at the same time accepting the involvement in the accident. More importantly, the feelings of guilt are both acknowledged and forgiven. All the sacramental services of penance include prayers of absolution which include the phrase "and forgive the sins of thy servant, both voluntary and involuntary." This doctrine, like that of the practice of Economia introduces a dimension to ethical thinking and experience which provides a legitimate release from "the Relative Absolutes" of the Christian Ethic.

Both of the above are examples—though it be rather formal ones—of the Orthodox tendency to introduce philanthropic, merciful, patient, accommodating dimensions into the statements which purport to describe the ethos appropriate to the life of a person or of a community which is committed to the life in God. There is "akribeia" or "exactitude" in the application of the ethical code and ethical requirements. That which dictates "exactitude" is the well-being of the soul and of the spiritual situation in which the soul finds itself. It is the same criterion which may lead to "Economia" or the declaration of "involuntary sin" or "philanthropia." There is no incongruity in this. For the "akribeia" of the law or rule or command exists for the very same purpose—spiritual well-being and growth. Thus, in most cases, the "exactitude" of the Decalogue will be upheld. But, occasionally, in specific situations, elasticity, in the form of "philanthropia" or "mercy" may be indicated. That which distinguishes this course of action from mere violation or "bending" of the rule, is the goal which is being sought—moral or spiritual growth. Usually, we are much too involved to make such decisions ourselves. We are better off with the wise and objective counsel of a Father Confessor, a spiritual counselor or a trusted friend. When the rules are relaxed to satisfy our own passions, for the sake of personal advantage or pleasure, we can be quite sure that it is not a case of proper "philanthropia" but of self-indulgence and sin.

Further, the "Relative Absolute" of the Orthodox Christian Ethic is protected from rigid formalism and legalism by the Orthodox teaching about growth, to which we referred above. Growth in the Christian life requires different modes of behavior at different times. Thus, spiritually, it may be a good to be strived for—and when accomplished, to be praised—for a person at an early stage of the Christian life, not to act out feelings of revenge. For such a person, this is good. But growth in the Christian life will lead this person to another good—to tranform the feelings of revenge so that he/she does not return hatred for hatred. Further Christian growth will lead to the returning of good for evil. At each stage of growth all of these actions are "good" for they are pointed in the same direction. Growth in the image and likeness of God from an ethical perspective (and it certainly is more than just ethical) provides us with this realistic and flexible dimension; a dimension which keeps the "Relative Absolute" of the Christian ethic from being rigid and formalistic.

Finally, the "Relative Absolute" of the Orthodox Christian Ethic is given a totally new aspect when it is seen as embodied in the life and ethos of our Savior Jesus Christ. Below, we will have much more to say about the "imitation of Christ" in the Orthodox Ethic. However, it suffices to point out here that the concrete embodiment of Theosis and the experiential expression of what "image and likeness" means in human terms, is Jesus Christ. Ethical terms, judgments, values, concepts, yes, even our "Relative Absolute" of the Christian Ethic are linguistic and rational abstractions of aspects of that one true life which in fact and in truth was perfectly human and perfectly divine. Though Ethics must as of necessity objectify the truth of which it speaks, it must always be remembered and kept before us that our main focus is a way of life, an experience of being which is epitomized in the living person of the Son of God become human—Jesus Christ.

Thus, as we seek to articulate the specifics of the "Relative Absolutes" of Orthodox Christian Ethics, we will never allow to escape from us the fact that we are not primarily interested in principles, rules, judgments, etc. What interests us is the realization of our full humanity, the achievement of the image and likeness, the experience of true and unhindered living community with God and our fellows. This experiential reality which the Orthodox call Theosis, may be described in part by our "Relative Absolutes" but it is only in life itself that they take on meaning. The Evangelical Ethic is not a set of principles, rules, judgments and evaluations. It is a life-style, an ethos, a "politeia." The "Relative Absolutes" are useful and necessary. But they should never be confused with the life itself. They are helpful as tools to help live that life, to guide it and direct it, but they are not substitutes for living it.

Our task now is to move on to clarify how our conscience serves to: a) form our being, b) aid us in making ethical decisions, and c) act ethically. This we will seek to do in the final three chapters of this volume.

---

[1] Epistle to the Ephesians, 4:13, 15-16.

[2] *Ibid.,* v. 17-19.

[3] *Ibid.,* v. 22-24.

[4] *The Life of Moses,* PMG 44, 300B-301C, tr. in Jean Danielou and Herbert Musurillo, *From Glory to Glory,* New York: Scribners, 1961, p. 81.

⁵ *On Perfection,* MPG 46; 225A-D. In *From Glory to Glory,* pp. 83-84.

⁶ Luke 17:10.

⁷ Matthew, 5:17.

⁸ Richard Davis, in *Baker's Dictionary of Christian Ethics,* p. 616.

⁹ Agourides, "The Sermon on the Mount," *Deltion Biblikon Meleton,* Vol. 2, 7, p. 195.

¹⁰ *Ibid.*

¹¹ 1 Clement 13:1-2, 2 Clement 5:2-3; Barnabas 5:8-9, Aristides 15:4-12.

¹² *Ibid.,* p. 198.

¹³ *Ibid.,* pp. 198-200.

¹⁴ *Ibid.,* p. 203.

¹⁵ *Ibid.,* pp. 204-205.

¹⁶ *Ibid.,* p. 207.

¹⁷ W. D. Davies, *The Setting for the Sermon on the Mount,* Cambridge, England: University Press, 1966, p. 434.

¹⁸ *Ermeneia eis tin Kainin Diathekin,* Vol. 2, Athens, 1892.

¹⁹ *Ermeneia eis tin Epi Tou Orous Omilian tou Kyriou,* Constantinople: 1911.

²⁰ *Ypomnema eis to Kata Matthaion Evangelion,* Athens: "Zoe" Publications, 1951.

²¹ *E Epi tou Orous Omilia tou Kyrios,* Athens: 1960.

²² *Ibid.,* p. 210.

²³ E. G. Matthew 5:17-18, 22:36 ff., 23:23; Luke 15:26 ff; Romans 3;19, 3:31, 7:12-16; Galatians 5:19-21; Ephesians 4:28-29, 5:3-5, 6:1, 4, 5; Colossians 3:18-25, 4:1, 5, etc.

²⁴ V. 3.

²⁵ V. 23.

²⁶ V. 25-26.

²⁷ V. 28.

²⁸ *Homily XV on Matthew,* tr. in *The Nicene and Post-Nicene Fathers.* First Series, Vol. X, p. 92.

²⁹ *Ibid.,* p. 93.

³⁰ *Ibid.,* p. 94.

³¹ *Ibid.,* p. 94.

³² *Ibid.*

³³ *Ibid.,* p. 95.

³⁴ Galatians 5:22-24.

³⁵ Galatians 6:7-10.

³⁶ Colossians 3:12-13.

³⁷ V. 13, v. 15.

³⁸ V. 17.

³⁹ *Treasury of Thought,* p. 229.

⁴⁰ Liddell-Scott, *A Greek-English Lexicon,* New York: Harper and Brothers, 1883.

⁴¹ 1 John 4:8.

⁴² 1 John 4:7.

⁴³ Lossky, *The Mystical Theology of the Eastern Church, op. cit.,* p. 81.

⁴⁴ John 4:10.

⁴⁵ 1 John 4:9.

⁴⁶ John 3:16-17.

⁴⁷ 1 Corinthians 13:1-3.

⁴⁸ Trembelas, *Dogmatike tes Orthodoxou Katholikes Ekklesias, ibid.,* Vol. 1, p. 222.

⁴⁹ John Macquarrie, ed. *Dictionary of Christian Ethics, ibid.,* p. 9.

⁵⁰ 1 John 4:11.

⁵¹ Matthew 22:37-39.

⁵² Ephesians 5:29.

⁵³ Matthew 19:14.

⁵⁴ *Chapters Concerning Love,* 1st Hekatontas, 40.

⁵⁵ *Ibid.,* 41.

⁵⁶ Matthew 5:44, 46.

⁵⁷ Matthew 5:38-39.

⁵⁸ Romans 12:17.

⁵⁹ 1 Peter 3:9.

[60] *Ibid.*, 62.

[61] Romans 8:31, 32, 35, 37-39.

[62] Antoniades, *op. cit.*, Vol. 2, paragraph 86, pp. 236-239.

[63] Matthew 10:37.

[64] *Antoniades,* ibid.

[65] Vol. 4, 278, 84.

[66] 1 John 5:3.

[67] John 14:23.

[68] John 14:21.

[69] Romans 13:8-10.

[70] Galatians 5:13-14.

[71] Spyridon Abouris, *Threskeutike kai Ethike Encyclopaidia,* Vol. 1, p. 131b.

[72] *Philokalia,* Vol. 1, 13.

[73] *Ibid.,* 16.

[74] Corinthians 49:5.

[75] For a contemporary Protestant treatment which supports this view see James M. Gustafson, *Theology and Christian Ethics,* Philadelphia: United Church Press, 1974.

[76] For additional information regarding "Economia" see F. Thomson, "Economy: An Examination of the Various Theories of Economy Held Within the Orthodox Church," *Journal of Theological Studies,* Vol. 16, 1965, pp. 368-420.

178

Chapter Eight

BEING MORAL: CONFORMED TO THE IMAGE OF GOD

"On this day of the Resurrection , shine brightly, O you Peoples; it is Pascha, the Pascha of the Lord. For Christ our God has brought us over from death to life, and from earth to heaven. Let us sing the victory song." (Katavasia *from the Canon of Easter)*

The new life given to the Christian by the saving work of Jesus Christ is a "passover" from one kind of existence to another. The images are many. Life in Christ means that we are "a new creation."[1] We have been transferred from the sphere of darkness to the sphere of light: "Once you were in darkness, but now you are light in the Lord."[2] We are no longer servants of the Devil, but we are servants of Jesus Christ:[3] "No servant can serve two masters."[4] Our Baptism separates us from the body of sin and makes us members of the one body of Christ.[5] There is a former condition, an old nature which has now been replaced by a new nature: "You have put off the old nature with its practices, and have put on the new nature, which is being renewed in knowledge after the image of its creator."[6] We are no longer homeless and exiled, but we belong to God's household: "You are no longer strangers and sojourners, but you are fellow citizens with the saints and members of the household of God."[7]

Thus, we have a new "being;" we *are* something as a result of our response to God's saving work. This "being" may be examined from the ethical, as well as from many other perspectives. Ethically speaking, "being" refers to a person's mode of existence, to character and virtue. "Being" is the complex of dispositions, traits, habits and qualities which together make up a stable pattern or style of life. When we have "being" before us, we speak and think in terms of the over-all ethos and style of life of a person. Thus, we speak of persons who are "saintly," "fair-minded," "diligent," "Christ-like," "dependable," etc. While acts and deeds tend to be characterized by terms such as "right" and "wrong," "Being" tends to be characterized by terms such as "good" and "evil." It is more precise to say "He acted rightly in that case" than to say "He did good in that case." It is more precise to say "He is a man of good character" than to say "His character is right." Of course, in daily conversation, these distinctions tend to blur. However, most people do distinguish between deeds and the general character of persons. Thus we may comment that a person has "acted out of character" when a particular deed is not in conformity with his customary pattern and style of life. In this chapter, we will discuss 1) Character, 2) Virtues and Virtue, 3) Rights and Duties, 4) the Imitation of Christ and 5) Christian Formation and Radical Christian Demands.

Character

The English word "character" is a direct transliteration from the Greek noun. Its verb form in Greek is *harasso* which means to engrave, to mark permanently. Therefore, it means a permanent marking of someone or something. In more metaphorical terms, character identifies and uniquely marks a thing or person. For example, if we speak of a willow tree as having a "stately character" we are giving a description of the over-all impression we receive from the tree, an impression of its general and permanent quality. A person of "joyful character" is a person who in most of his or her expressions and relationships is happy, open, enthusiastic, smiling, joyful. A "morose character" would be just the opposite: a person who is generally withdrawn, sad, sorrowful, depressed, etc. Thus, in general, Demetropoulos defines character as "the unique manner of each person in thinking, feeling, willing, and acting." More in the direction of character definition in the light of behavioral terms, he defines: "character is the totality of our psychological traits upon which are dependent our feelings as well as the inner inclinations and motives which lead to acts." [8]

Ethically understood, the good character is that character which consistently and predictably is oriented toward doing what is right and avoiding what is bad. A good character is so formed, so that both dispositions and overt behavior create an ethos and a customary way of behavior which generally conform to the ethical good in feeling, choosing and acting. The emphasis of character is stability and dependability.

It is easy to see how this ethical category has its application in Christian Ethics, especially in relation to the doctrines of the image and likeness of God, growth and Theosis. Certain aspects of the Christian life, developed early in the Christian life, provide the groundwork for further ethical growth. The Christian faith understands the self—and the self in relation to God and the children of God—as involved in the whole economy of Divine creation, redemption and sanctification. This leads to certain ethical stances which are fitting and appropriate to a Christian character. Such would be a dependence of trustworthiness, a concern for the good, an abhorance of evil, basic honesty, a spiritual orientation to life, etc. These are necessary foundations for spiritual and ethical development. As we grow in the Christ-like life, the kind of character described in the beatitudes comes to the fore. Integrity of dispositions and of actions, together with gentleness and mercifulness provide, in broad strokes, the description of a character which is at once morally strong and serious, but also sensitive and gentle. The progression of development, as outlined in works such as the *Climax* of St. John of the Ladder, is also a description of the sort of character which is appropriate to the Christian.

Character does not just happen. It is formed and molded by many influences. Some of those influences may be called personal and others environmental. Certain highly influential personal traits which tend to influence character development may be identified under the headings of sex and psychology. A person's character is influenced by his or her maleness or femaleness. It used to be said that "the active virtues, such as initiative, courage, persistence and devotion to ideas are manly, while the female virtues are attentiveness, patience and devotion to persons."[9] Though we are now aware that categorical statements such as those do not, in fact, capture the whole range of possible appropriate modes of behavior for either men or women, it is equally mistaken to assume that our maleness or femaleness does not in fact help form our characters. Masculinity and femininity are in part biological and in part cultural. There is hardly a culture anywhere in which little boys and little girls are not taught "appropriate roles" for their sex. It is both disturbing and illusory to assume an attitude which holds to a "unisex" perspective. In fact, our sex and our sex roles do influence our character development highly. This has nothing to say to the question of equality, personal worth and spiritual maturity. It does affirm the uniqueness of femininity and masculinity.

People's character is also influenced highly by their personal psychology. In earlier days character types were distinguished as sanguine, choleric, melancholic and phlegmatic; that is, enthusiastic, bad-tempered, sorrowful and unemotional. Since then, many efforts have been made to show both various personality types and their influence upon character development. A standard text in the field of personality theory, describes in its table of contents, a whole series of theories which seek to provide an adequate description of the personal psychology of individuals. The following are listed: Freud's Psychoanalytic Theory, Jung's Analytic Theory, Social Psychological Theories: Adler, Fromm, Horney and Sullivan, Murray's Personology, Lewin's Field Theory, Allport's Psychology of the Individual, Organismic Theory, Sheldon's Constitutional Psychology, Factor Theories, Stimulus-Response Theory, Roger's Self Theory, Murphy's Biosocial Theory, etc. What is significant for us, is that character in specific persons is in part influenced by their psychological predispositions.

Character is also influenced by the general level of intelligence. Other factors could also be determined. What is evident is that character is developed in all of us under the influence of certain "natural" aspects of our being which we carry with us and within us.

However, our environment also has a great role in character development. It is said that even geography influences people's character. A mountain people may tend to be more self-reliant, independent, uncommunicative and suspicious than a people who live on plains, who may be more gregarious, cooperative and sharing, simply because of the differing influences of geography on their life style. More commonly, family, school, social customs and practices, society as a whole and the whole spiritual, cultural and ethical atmosphere in which a person lives, tend to form a person's character.

Religiously and ethically speaking, one of the most important aspects of the work of the Church is to provide an environment which is conducive to the development of Christian character, not only among children, but for the whole *pleroma* of the Church. The community of Christian love, the worship experience, spiritual counseling, preaching, study, mutual support of Christians, and the caring community, which are factors of the total experience of being a member of the Church, certainly provide a host of influences in a stable environment which contribute to the character development of every member of the Church, whether active or non-active.

However, although these influences are important and must be taken into account by the teaching and forming Church, the Orthodox would continue to emphasize the determinative influence of each person's own self-determining will. The *autexousion,* and our status as self-determining beings point to the fact that, not only are we able to direct our character development, but that we are also required to develop and form our Christian character. In large part, the formation of "Christian Character" is the result of our own self-determination and our willing acceptance of guidance and moral direction. Ethically, that means we—in part—choose our character. In so much as we do that, we act ethically. Our free, self-determination of the kind of persons we are to be keeps character as a part of the ethical enterprise, even though, as we have seen, much of character is subject to powerful influences from both within and without.

When character is measured in accordance to some standard or goal or ideal, then we are able to evaluate it. For the Christian, the Evangelical Ethic is the standard. A person who generally lived in harmony with its content would be evaluated as a person of "saintly" or "perfect" character. Persons who are within its general orbit are characterized as having "good," "fine" or "Christian" characters. Those whose characters evince much distance between the Evangelical Ethic and the reality of their lives, might be called "weak" or "undeveloped" or "sinful." Occasionally, we meet persons whose character is so hardened in evil practices and in sinful styles of life, that they seem to be devoid of contact and embodiment of the Evangelical Ethic. Such "hardened" consciences and characters are called *peporomenai* in Greek.

More specifically, the Church uses various concrete means to help in the formation of Character. The first of these is education (*agoge*). The earlier that Christian education is begun, the more effective it is considered to be. Thus, the place of religious practices, conversation, visual images, etc. in the home and family life is considered very important. Formal education in the Church is also thought to be important, as well as the informal education which takes place in worship, community (parish) life, peer group experiences (youth groups), etc. Church school and conferences, camps and retreats all contribute toward the formation of character. This educational role of the Church is one of its most important functions and which deserves much attention and responsible concern by the hierarchy, the local clergy and lay leadership. The fact that it is (or at least appears) not to be effective as we would wish is no excuse for abandoning it. Rather, continuing effort and resources should be directed toward improving the materials and methods used, as well as the quality and preparation of the teachers.

Another traditional method of character development used in the Church is spiritual development or *askesis*. Askesis is the submission of one's self to a program of spiritual exercise. In its most general form, it is the voluntary and willing acceptance of the Church's requirements and spiritual direction regarding fasting, prayer, and works of charity (alms-giving). More specifically, it takes place in conjunction with the practice of Holy Confession, under the guidance of an experienced Father Confessor. *Askesis* has two foci, both of which contribute to character development. The first of these foci is called *gymnastike* which is the cultivation, through various spiritual practices with the purpose of development of positive traits and aspects of the Christian character, of the virtues. The other focus is the effort to avoid sins and failings. This negative aspect of *askesis* is called *enkrateia* or temperance which "helps us to cut the growths of sins, and the useless weeds of the mind that spring up round the vital fruit, till the shoot of faith is perfected and becomes strong." [10] Consequently "our nature . . . needs self-constraint, by which disciplining itself to the need of little, it endeavors to approximate in character to the divine nature." [11]

Attentiveness and spiritual sensitivity (*egregorsis*) is a third character formation practice which the spiritual tradition of the Church counsels. Avoiding both extremes of frivolous lack of interest in one's character development, on the one hand, and extreme austerity, on the other, attentiveness or *egregorsis* seeks to cultivate a perspecuity about things which affect one's character; so that choices, acts and situations may be either selected or avoided in the light of the whole relationship which they have with the total Christian life. This attentiveness is a basis for self-evaluation, a practice counseled, as we have seen, throughout the history of the Church.

Further means which in fact serve to form character, though that is not their first and primary value, come from the exercise of the life of faith. Prayer, scriptural study, the study of the Fathers and the lives of the Saints, as well as conscious participation in worship contribute to character formation. These and many other factors form the Church's means which aid the development of Christian character.

Recently, some non-Orthodox ethical studies have begun emphasizing the place and importance of character in ethics. In a chapter entitled "Sanctification and the Ethics of Character," Stanley Hauerwas comes close to the relationship of character and theosis in the Orthodox tradition. Basing most of his discussion on the views of important Protestant writers and theologians (Calvin, Wesley and Jonathan Edwards) he relates character development and sanctification very closely.

The ethics of character is concerned with the self's duration, growth, and unity. The moral good cannot be limited to the self's external conformity to moral rules or ideals; goodness is a way of being that which brings unity to the variety of our activities. One theological rubric that has been associated with these concerns is the doctrine of sanctification.[12]

He concludes his study of the relationship of character and sanctification with the "striking idea . . . that sanctification involves the determination of a man's 'person,' his most basic being. It is not a shallow or surface change of a man's way of life, but rather it affects a man at the very heart of his existence. It is the determination that gives a singleness to his being." The conformity of this view with the "image and Theosis" anthropology at the basis of Eastern Orthodox Christian ethics is evident. Sanctification is not forensic, it is not just the conviction of sin. It is the real formation of the person into the divine image. Secondly, Hauerwas concludes that "this determination or qualification of man's being cannot be reduced to any one disposition or act, but rather it represents a general orientation of our own being." Hence, the Orthodox unwillingness to accept any form of ethical reductionism, which would point to some "one and only" virtue, e.g. self-denial or agapism. The good is God, and mankind's ethical destiny is to become divine, with all that implies. He further concludes that "this shaping of our life involves both a man's innermost dispositions and beliefs as well as his outward behavior, his most general dispositions as well as his most concrete and particular acts." This wholistic approach to the Evangelical Ethic is also characteristic of the Eastern Orthodox understanding of the Evangelical Ethic and fits most appropriately to Eastern Orthodox views of theological anthropology. When talking about growth, in relation to sanctification and character, Hauerwas has some difficulty in understanding growth and the progress it implies. He holds

> To have one's character formed in Christ is to always have one's life directed toward fuller realization of that formation. Thus to have Christian character is to really be changed and directed by Christ, but not in a way that Christ becomes a possession in which I can feel secure, but rather it is to be subject to a restlessness that knows no end in this life. The Christian's character is nonetheless a real orientation in the sense that limits have been placed on what we do and do not do; or perhaps better the possibilities of what we can do have been extended.[13]

That growth is something much more concrete than this, yet still encompassing of the openness described above, is evident from the concreteness of the "image and Theosis" doctrines. That there is adequate specificity to the goal to which we are to grow in the formation of Christian (true human) character has not only been indicated in the preceding two chapters, but will be further specified in the sections which follow. Yet, Hauerwas is right when he indicates a certain openness and freedom which also characterize growth of character. Orthodox Christian Ethics, however, would be able to be more concrete in the description of the Christian character because of its "image-Theosis" anthropology.

Virtues and Virtue

One traditional way of specifying the content of Christian (true human) character is to speak of virtues and virtue. As we have seen, when we speak of character, we speak of the whole make-up of a person, especially insofar as the "being" of the person is seen as consistent and constant, that it has a certain strength and staying power (strength of character, we say) and that it has a certain integrity of self-determination in which both the inner and outer factors are in harmony. If the whole of the character is moved by choice and voluntarily toward the realization of the image and likeness of God, this is done as a general exercise of self-determination and as the effort to conform to the divine image in particulars. As a general exercise of self-determination, it might be expressed in phrases such as these:

"I am a Christian"
"I am an obedient servant of God"
"Christ is being formed in me"
"My goal is to achieve Theosis"
"I wish to be perfect, as my Father in Heaven is perfect"

However, as a concrete effort to conform to the divine image in the particulars of our behavior, it has become both customary and useful to speak about virtues and virtue.

The Greek word for virtue is "aretē." The Latin word, from which the English is directly derived, is "virtus." Both are instructive regarding the meaning of the word in ethical use. The root of "aretē" is "ar" which in turn is the root of the verb "ararisko" which means "to join, to fit together." Its basic meaning is to "be appropriate to something." Ethically, it means that which is appropriate and fitting to the ethical activity of human beings. The Latin helps us see more specifically, what the object of that appropriateness is, for "virtus" comes from "vir" which means man or manliness. "Virtus" carries with it the connotation of manly strength. Virtue is the habitual and firm orientation of the will and of the whole character to act in specific and concrete ways which are appropriate to those who are in the process of growth in the image of God and Theosis. Virtues as the plural of virtue, are the specific stable and habitual modes of action appropriate to the specific circumstances and situations addressed by a person growing in the image and likeness of God. *Virtue* emphasizes the strength of character which leads to appropriate behavior; *virtues* emphasize the particular modes of action appropriate to the Christian character.

The Ancient Greek philosophers sought to delineate specific and concrete virtues. In large part, the concrete and specific virtues are determined by the image held of the truly good person. Since the virtues are, so to speak, constitutive aspects of the whole virtuous character, the

185

most important of them will reflect the main lines of the character which is presented as normative. For the ancients, a good man was a rational man. Thus, for Socrates—inasmuch as he can be separated from Plato—the chief virtue was wisdom (*sophia* or *phronesis*). Other aspects of the ideal human character are revealed by such virtues as temperance (*sophrosyne* or *enkrateian*), courage (*andreian*), justice (*dikaiosyne*) and piety (*eusbeian*). Plato further refined these virtues and tied them systematically to a view of man psychologically understood. To the rational part of man (*to logistikon meros*) he attributed the virtue of wisdom, which was the proper functioning of the intellectual aspect of man. To the spirited, desiring, passionate aspect of human life (*to epithymetikon meros*) he attributed the virtue of courage. To the deciding, willing, choosing, ordering dimension of the human character, he assigned the virtue of self-control. He saw all of these three virtues as the most appropriate functioning of the three parts of the human psychology as he perceived it. When each of the parts acted in a way which best expressed its nature, these three major virtues were being practiced. When the three virtues of wisdom, courage and self-control were practiced in harmony and in proper relationship, i.e., the wisdom guiding self-control with courageous strength and ordered determination, a person achieved justice (*dikaiosyne*), in which all parts functioned properly and appropriately. Thus, justice is the virtue of the virtues for Plato.

Aristotle tended to tone down the intellectual aspect of Plato's theory of virtue, though he did not fail to speak of the intellectual virtues (*synesis, sophia, phronesis*). Among other kinds of virtues, Aristotle also spoke of the familiar ones (*sophrosyne, andreia, dikaiosyne*), but he also emphasized other virtues such as friendship (*philian*), humility (*praoteta*), sense of honor or self-respect (*philotimian*) and a virtue of "grandness of character" which he called *megalopsychian*. These latter virtues point to the fact that Aristotle's view of the good, and consequently of the good person, was colored by a different perspective than the psychology of Plato. For Aristotle, the good for man was happiness (*eudaimonia*). Further, Aristotle, in his discussion of virtues introduced a dimension which pointed to the mode of expression. He introduced the concept of "measure" to the discussion of virtue. Vice, which is the opposite of virtue is found in extremes. Thus, there is to be found in relation to every virtue appropriate to the happy life, a set of two extremes, that which is too much and that which is too little. So, if generosity is a virtue, miserliness is its vice on the side of "too little" and extravagant wastefulness is its vice on the side of "too much." The Stoics, in accordance with their pantheistic views saw virtue and the virtues as expressions of their view that man ought to conform to nature and that nature was at heart rational.

Thus, in large measure, Greek philosophy serves to illustrate the fact that one's view of what it means to be truly good, or, put otherwise, what one perceives to be truly human, will determine which modes of concrete and specific actions will be designated as virtues and which will be

186

designated as vices. Thus, in the philosophy of man which finally came to be developed in Nazi Germany before and during World War II, the ideal of the "Aryan Superman" led to all kinds of behavior abhorrent to the rest of the world, but tolerated and praised and rewarded as virtuous within Nazi Germany. The Nazi "virtues" were our "vices" and the Nazi "vices" (gentleness, forgiveness, kindness, etc.) were our "virtues."

Christian ethics also speaks of virtues and vices. The terms "virtue" and "vice" however, are not Scriptural terms. The Old Testament speaks of many virtues, which are appropriate both to the man of God and to the people of God, but it does not use the term virtue outside of some of the deuterocanonical books which were, significantly, originally written in Greek. The New Testament uses the word only rarely, twice in reference to God.[14] However, the Scriptures, both Old and New Testaments, speak of specific virtues and specific vices which are either fitting and appropriate modes of behavior to the life in Christ, or, ways of being and acting which do not fit the Christian life, respectively. Among the chief virtues, are those which St. Paul mentions in his hymn to agape in the 13th chapter of 1 Corinthians: faith, hope and love. He places agape-love on the highest plane among Christian virtues. The modes of behavior which are most appropriate to the Christian ethos and to the experience of growth in God's image toward Theosis are the Christian virtues. Those courses of action and patterns of functioning which detract from the Christian life are vices. Christian ethicists have often combined uniquely Christian virtues such as "Faith, Hope and Love" with the Ancient Greek philosophical virtues, so as to speak to the whole man. Thus, Scholastic moral theology often spoke of the "Cardinal Virtues" of Justice, Wisdom, Courage, and Temperance, and of the "Theological Virtues" of Faith, Hope and Love.

In fact, the virtues and vices of the Christian teaching are not so rigid and limited in number. However, virtues and vices, are not perceived so much as specific acts and deeds, but rather as concrete modes of being a Christian or failing to be a Christian, so that they tend to describe how people ought to be or ought not to be, rather than to order specific acts to be done or to be avoided. Thus "virtue and vice" are the specifics of character; "good acts and sins" are the specifics of decision making. People *commit* sins, but they *are* of good character or *have* virtues. Both demand an exercise of the *autexousion,* but the former deal with discernable acts, while the latter tend to be more diffuse and include more of the dispositions, the general style and ethos of life, and the general appropriateness to the whole goal of the Christian life.

In spite of the fact that the term "virtue" is not frequently used in the New Testament, we have a number of lists and characterizations of the Christian life in the Scriptures which serve to delimitate the kinds of traits and courses of action which are virtuous from the Christian understanding of human life, as well as the vices inappropriate to the Christian character.

Thus, we have the following from the New Testament, which could be characterized as rather unsystematic presentations of Christian virtues:

Let love be genuine; hate what is evil, hold fast to what is good; love one another with brotherly affection; outdo one another in showing honor. Never flag in zeal, be aglow with the Spirit, serve the Lord. Rejoice in your hope, be patient in tribulation, be constant in prayer. Contribute to the needs of the saints, practice hospitality.

Bless those who persecute you; bless and do not curse them. Rejoice with those who rejoice, weep with those who weep. Live in harmony with one another; do not be haughty, but associate with the lowly; never be conceited. Repay no one evil for evil, but take thought for what is noble in the sight of all. Beloved, never avenge yourselves . . . Do not be overcome by evil, but overcome evil with good. [15]

The virtues in this passage are love, persistence in the good, respect for others, zeal, service, joy, patience, prayerfulness, generosity, hospitality, lack of vindictiveness, returning good for evil, sympathy. The vices spoken of are vindictiveness, revenge, haughtiness, pride, conceit. More specifically, Paul speaks of character traits, including both virtues and vices in some of the following passages:

Do you not know that the unrighteous will not inherit the kingdom of God? Do not be deceived; neither the immoral, nor idolators, nor adulterers, nor homosexuals, nor thieves, nor the greedy, nor drunkards, nor revilers, nor robbers will inherit the kingdom of God. [16]

Be watchful, stand firm in your faith, be courageous, be strong, Let all that you do be done in love. [17]

But we have this treasure in earthen vessels, to show that the transcendent power belongs to God and not to us. We are afflicted in every way, but not crushed; perplexed but not driven to despair; persecuted, but not forsaken; struck down, but not destroyed . . . So we do not lose heart. [18]

Now the works of the flesh are plain; immorality, impurity, licentiousness, idolatry, sorcery, enmity, strife, jealousy, anger, selfishness, dissension, party spirit, envy, drunkenness, carousing and the like. I warn you, as I warned you before, that those who do such things shall not inherit the kingdom of God. But the fruit of the Spirit is love, joy, peace, patience, kindness, goodness, faithfulness, gentleness, self-control . . . If we live by the Spirit, let us also walk by the Spirit. Let us have no self-conceit, no provoking of one another, no envy of one another. [19]

I therefore, a prisoner for the Lord, beg you to lead a life worthy of the calling to which you have been called, with all lowliness and meekness, with patience, forbearing one another in love, eager to maintain the unity of the Spirit in the bond of peace. [20]

Let all bitterness and wrath and anger and clamor and slander be put away from you, with all malice, and be kind to one another, tenderhearted, forgiving one another, as God in Christ forgave you. Therefore be imitators of God as beloved children. And walk in love. But immorality and all impurity or covetousness must not even be named among you, as is fitting among saints. Let no filthiness, nor silly talk, nor levity, which are not fitting; but instead let there be thanksgiving . . . Look carefully then how you walk, not as unwise men but as wise, making the most of the time, because the days are evil. Therefore do not be foolish, but understand what the will of the Lord is. And do not get drunk with wine, for that is debauchery; but be filled with the Spirit, addressing one another in psalms and hymns and spiritual songs . . . Be subject to one another out of reverence for Christ.[21]

These are just a few New Testament passages which point to specific and concrete traits of character which we today would call virtues and vices. There are many others.[22]

That which keeps Christian ethics from making long and exhaustive lists of the kinds of attitudes and behavior which are fitting to the Christian life-style (the virtues) and then, making long and comprehensive lists of all of the modes of behavior and inner dispositions which are destructive of the ethos of the life of growth in the Divine image, is the realization that these are not isolated, clearly distinct and insular experiences, but that they are, in fact, part of the single fabric of the Christian life. Such abstractions would certainly lead to a legalism of works. Each virtue, considered by itself, may be thought of as the appropriate and proper response of the Christian to each given situation. It is appropriate because it fits into the larger pattern of the character appropriate to one who is a member of the Kingdom of God. This implies an emphasis on the unity of the virtues. One Orthodox scholar phrased it as follows:

According to the Fathers, virtue is a unified and unbreakable many-faceted reality. According to St. John Chrysostom, "it is not enough to present a single virtue before the throne of God with boldness, but rather, many are required, of different and multiple form, that is, the totality of virtue.[23]

The fact is that numbers are not the relevant thing, nor is the cultivation of certain specific virtues, at the expense of others a correct approach. Their unity and interpenetration must be constantly kept before us, even as we speak of them as separate and distinct. St. Proclos, 5th century Patriarch of Constantinople emphasizes the unity of virtues in the following passage.

There are many kinds of virtues, but there are three which are special, faith, hope and love, of which faith grants to human beings those things which are above nature . . . Hope is not just a dreamy attitude . . . but rather it is courageously holding on in the present preparing for the future . . . and love is the head of our Christian mystery. Each, however, coexists with the other, for faith is the mirror of love, love is the assurance that there is faith . . . Thus, every Christian who is not enriched with faith and hope and love, is not that which he is called . . .[24]

It is true that the Fathers speak both of what have been otherwise termed the cardinal virtues and the theological virtues. St. John of Damascus calls the former *psychikas aretas* and the so-called theological virtues (among which he includes not only faith, hope and love, but also prayer, humility and others) he sees as outgrowths of those traditional virtues of Greek philosophy.[25] In addition, agape is seen as the chief of the virtues, in a sense, including them all. Thus, Origen writes, "There is one which is the most important of the virtues . . . and that is love for the neighbor."[26] St. John Chrysostom says, "the beginning and end of virtue is love,"[27] and another father says "the particular virtues which are listed, are the accomplishments included in one general virtue, whose name is love."[28] The main thrust of all of these observations is that the virtues are not separate and distinguished modes of being and acting in isolation from one another, with a sort of autonomy of existence, but rather, particularly appropriate Christian modes of response as expressions of the whole character.

Once this point has been affirmed, it becomes useful to speak about the development of the various virtues and the avoidance of particular vices. In the process of spiritual counsel and growth, in the confessional, in pastoral counseling, in character education, etc., it is both correct and helpful to speak of concrete and specific virtues and vices, just as we have seen the New Testament writers do. Thus, a person who has the vice of anger, may be directed to develop the virtue of patience. In the past, lists of virtues and vices have been prepared, sermons have been preached on them, treatises have been written on particular virtues and vices. The important thing to remember is that all virtues are in fact expressions of the kind of attitudes, behavior and mind-sets which are appropriate to the life leading toward Theosis.

There are general virtues and vices which apply to all persons. We have seen some of these listed in the scriptural passages noted above. A patristic equivalent is found in St. John of Damascus' *Peri Areton kai Kakion.* Among the virtues which he notes are "faith, hope, love, prayer, humility, gentleness, long-suffering, forbearance, goodness, lack of proneness to anger, divine knowledge, passionlessness, simplicity, calmness, sincerity, lack of conceit. Virtuous persons are without egotism, generous, guileness, not money-loving, sympathetic, merciful, communicative, fearless, joyous, pietous, reverent, respectful, having discretion, desire for future blessedness, attraction to the kingdom of God, seeking the divine adoption." The vices which St. John of Damascus notes are "forgetfulness, laziness, ignorance, by which the eye of the soul, that is, the mind is darkened, and is overcome by all the passions, which are these: impiety, false teaching, that is all heresy, blasphemy, anger, rage, bitterness, quickness to anger, misanthropy, the remembrance of evils, gossip, condemnation, irrational sorrow, fear, cowardice, argumentativeness, envy, love of praise, pride, hypocrisy, lying, faithlessness, greed, avarice, earthliness, heedlessness, smallness of spirit, ingratitude, complaining, self-centeredness, conceit, sadness, showing off, ambitiousness, crowd-pleasing, treachery, disrespectfulness, insensitivity, flattery, deceptiveness, irony, duplicity . . . pride, the birth-giver of evils and the root of all bad things, the love of money, bad manners and wickedness.'' Both of these lists come from the category of *psychika* or spiritual aspects of the Christian life. St. John of Damascus also includes a second category of virtues and vices which refer to the *somatika* or bodily aspects of the Christian life, including such things as ''evil passions, theft, sacrilege, robbery, murder . . . gluttony, luxury, drunkenness, . . . the passionate misuse of the pleasures of this world.[29]

Such lists serve to help us both conceptualize the content of the life which is in harmony with the life of the Kingdom, as well as to help us determine the behavior which is inappropriate to growth toward Theosis.

Such virtues and vices can be applied to all aspects of everyone's life. However, there are also virtues and vices which are appropriate to specific callings and stations in life. Much patristic literature speaks to the virtues and vices appropriate or inappropriate to monasticism. Thus, St. John of Damascus, in his little work entitled ''Concerning the Eight Spirits of Evil'' writes the following:

> Know this, brother, that there are eight thoughts which fight against the monk, as the Fathers teach. First, is gluttony; second is evil and filthy desire; third is the love of money; fourth is sorrow; fifth is anger; sixth is love of attention; seventh is inactivity, and pride is the eighth.[30]

Obviously, this is applicable to all persons. But the Saint continues in this work on virtues and vices to also list such things as ''fasting, thirst, keeping night-long vigil, standing throughout the night, constant kneeling, never bathing, owning of only one robe, a diet of bread and water, etc.'' Clearly these pertain only to monks. In similar manner, there are special virtues and vices applicable to persons in all kinds of callings. We will speak of some of these in subsequent chapters.

Duties and Rights

As we have seen, when we speak of virtues and vices, we speak primarily of traits of character which express themselves in particular situations and circumstances in stable and generally predictable ways. As we move closer to the exercise of ethical acts, considered as distinct and distinguishable concrete and overt courses of action, we move into the realm of duties and rights. Duties and rights are much more concrete and specific as compared to virtues and vices. Yet, as a short period of reflection will indicate, these two classes of ethical concepts are not fully separable. At their sharpest, however, duties and rights can be specified in a way in which virtues and vices may not. Thus, we might determine that our duty is to be at a certain place at a certain time, to perform a certain deed, because we have made a promise to assist in a Church function. If we consistently do our duty in many circumstances and under many different conditions, we will have developed the virtue of dependableness. Duties and rights are specific: virtues and vices are long-term concrete aspects of our whole character.

In Orthodox Christian Ethics, duties and rights have as their source the basic and common background of all ethical caregories: God as the good, our human *donatum* as image and likeness of God; and our human *telos* of Theosis. Certainly, as we shall see, other factors also play a role in the determination of our duties and rights. Yet, even these other factors are built upon that foundation.

"Duty" is defined in different ways by ethicists. It may simply be thought of as the obligation to conform to the moral standard. In this sense, it would be much like what we have called the Ethical Drive and the Ethical Sense. Another definition of duty is "an act or a course of action that is exacted of one by position, social custom, law, or religion." This definition tends to emphasize the imperative or demanding character of duty. It also sees duty as related to the obligations arising out of our relationships with others, especially in structured and organized situations. This leads to a fundamental understanding of duty. Duty is the claim which others properly make of us and upon our behavior. My duty can always be interpreted in the light of other people's rights. Their rights are claims upon our behavior, which we do not have the right to ignore or violate.

From this perspective, my duties toward God, are in fact those claims on my behavior which God has a right to demand because of the kind of relationship which exists between myself and Him. My duties toward a fellow-human being are based on the rights he or she has as a person in community with others. This comes through most clearly in the reciprocal relations of citizen and country. There is a mutual interchange of rights and duties. The state provides protection, order, economic and social well-being to the citizen. This brings into existence an obligation on the part of the citizen to act in ways which contribute to that common protection, order and well-being. From the other perspective, it is the duty of the state to provide these goods, because it is the right of the citizen to be protected, to live in an orderly society which functions for the common good. Conversely, it is the duty of the citizen to respond to the claim that he or she pay taxes, serve in the defense of the nation, obey the laws, because it is the right of the state to be so served.

In the larger theological context, the ethical relationship of rights and duties fits into the relational character of human existence as exemplified in the doctrines of the Holy Trinity and Theosis. Our creation in the image of God, the Trinity, places us experientially in a relationship of mutuality and inter-personal relationship. This, in the image of the Holy Trinity, is certainly much more than the mutual claims of duties and rights. But it also includes duties and rights. The deeper, more profound dispositions, feelings, virtuous motivations which we have seen in the preceding pages are hardly to be understood as divorced from the simple and elementary justice which gives to each that which is due him.

In the 17th Chapter of the Gospel of John, Jesus speaks of His relationship with the Father in connection with the disciples. While in no sense, exclusive "duty-right language," this chapter gives to us a sense of the mutuality in the relationships of the Holy Trinity which are also, in no sense, exclusively dispositional.

> Father, the hour is come; glorify thy Son, that thy Son may glorify thee: As thou has given him power over all flesh, that he should give eternal life to as many as thou hast given him. I have glorified thee on the earth: I have finished the work which thou gavest me to do. And now, O Father, glorify thou me with thine own self with the glory, which I had with thee before the world was.

Such language is certainly more profound than mere duty-rights language, but in fact it includes elements of a duty-right pattern: I ask you to act in a particular way (glorify me), because I have acted in a particular way (I have glorified thee). The Christian ethos is much more than merely acting on the basis of the claims and rights of others in a dutiful fashion. When ethics is lived exclusively on this level, it is an exchange of favors and claims, a "tit for tat" legalistic morality. Yet, it cannot be said that the Christian may ignore his claims on others (rights) or his responsibility toward others (duties) in response to their claims. One does not have to have particularly noble or high ethical standards such as those taught in the Sermon on the Mount, to recognize one's fundamental duties to pay his bills, to fulfill the assigned responsibilities of his or her job, to protect and care for one's children, etc. Duties and rights have a place, though not the supreme place in Christian ethics.

As Christians, what should be the motives which lead us to fulfillment of our duties and to the claim of our rights? We fulfill our duties from different kinds of motives. Some people, whenever they do their duty, do it out of fear of punishment. Most people fulfill some duties out of fear of the consequences. This is the lowest form of motivation, yet, often in the process of growth and development, it is not only an effective way of achieving conformity to duty, but it also serves an educational purpose. It is better to do one's duty out of fear of punishment, than not to do it at all. Others do their duty always out of the hope of reward. Most of us do our duty sometimes, especially when it is in itself onerous, with an eye to the compensation it will give us.

It is easy to disparage this motive, but we should not be so hasty. When put in the context both of duty and of rights, it becomes not only acceptable, but often a question of justice and fair treatment. "The laborer is worthy of his hire" the scriptures teach. It is an injustice to defraud a person of the just payment of wages, which is reward for effort expended and duties carried out.[31] These economic relations have their parallel in all kinds of human relations. Not, for instance, to acknowledge the contributions of another person to a common effort, that is to reward that effort, is to be ungrateful. Acknowledgement for effort expended is a duty of the recipient; it is at the same time a reward for the person who expends the effort. Objectively, then, it is a duty to acknowledge and reward the good that others do. Thus, St. Paul writes "Render therefore to all men their dues. Tribute, to whom tribute is due; custom, to whom custom; fear, to whom fear; honor, to whom honor. Owe no man anything, but to love one another."[32] Even as a motive for action, the desire for reward may be acceptable. As we have seen, it is a powerful force in economic life. Much volunteer work takes place on the basis of a desire for reward, no matter how diffused. A person may "believe" in the goals of an organization, and thus commit much time, effort and money to see that the organization's goals are achieved. For instance, many people wish to see pornography limited and restricted because they do not want their children and their community to be overrun with this filth. There is a personal interest, a reward, so to speak, which they seek to achieve as a result of their efforts. The crucial distinction is not that they benefit by their acts, but whether that benefit (the reward, the goal accomplished), is to their *exclusive* benefit. When the reward may also be seen as having social benefit and general well-being, the performance of duties for the sake of reward is not to be considered morally onerous.

Yet, we are able to distinguish a motive which supercedes this level of duty performance. That is the desire to do that which is right, the love of the good. When a person does his or her duty because "it is the right thing to do," because of dedication to duty, without fear and without the calculation of reward, we generally recognize that this is more within the spirit of the Evangelical Ethic. Christ Himself, through the kenotic experience of His incarnation, life, death and resurrection is the example of that motivation. This is the highest and most noble motivation for the doing of our duties. The "faithful servant" who, unwatched and without prodding, does that which is his or her duty is acknowledged as both praiseworthy and mature. The Parable of the Talents[33] shows both sides of the responsibility for the performance of duty. To the Servant who did his duty for its own sake, the Master is reported as saying "Well done, good and faithful servant . . ." But to the other, who buried the talent the Master says "You wicked and slothful servant!" What Saint Paul instructs slaves and servants to do is also instruction as to the appropriate attitude of every Christian in regard to his or her duties:

> Slaves, be obedient to those who are your earthly masters, with fear and trembling, in singleness of heart, as to Christ; not in the way of eye-service, as men-pleasers, but as servants of Christ, doing the will of God from the heart, rendering service with a good will as to the Lord and not to men . . .[34]

The characteristics of "singleness of heart," of persons who function "as servants of Christ," who do the "will of God from the heart" and who render service "with a good will as to the Lord," are appropriate to the idea of performing one's duty (the legitimate claim of others upon one's own behavior) and as an expression of one's relationship to God, without thought of punishment and reward. Love for God, love for the good, the simple desire to conform one's life with that which is right, to hunger and thirst for righteousness to prevail, are all ways of saying that such motivation is most appropriate to the life of Theosis.

Yet, as we have seen, the other motives are not to be totally excluded. There are times when such motives are all that is possible, or even necessary and appropriate. However, the goal to which Christian ethics would aspire, is that persons fulfill their duties out of love for God and for what is right, rather than out of fear or out of desire for reward.

Some ethicists make an effort to indicate various kinds of duties, such as formal duties, positive duties, negative duties, duties of justice and duties of grace, perfect and imperfect duties. Such distinctions do not appear to be very useful or fruitful. These distinctions are, in fact, rather artificial. For, our duties are part of a single fabric of modes of behavior which arise out of the just claims that others have upon our behavior. The chief duty, then, is that we acknowledge the duty to do our duty. The acknowledgement that we are obligated, as persons and as individuals to respond to the claims of others upon our behavior, is central. Rule Fifteen of St. Basil's *Morals* instructs "that it is not right to neglect one's duty, relying on the good works of others." Thus, in spite of the fact that duties are specific and concrete acts which could be better discussed under the heading of "doing the good," we have included the general treatment of duties in the chapter which deals with "being moral" because the disposition of acknowledging the rights of others and responding to them willingly, with alacrity and for the sake of what is good and God-like, is part of our *being* rather than a mere act.

Duty and duties, however, may be analyzed variously. In determining our specific duties, we are helped in recognizing that certain duties are fundamental, such as love for God, while some are derived from them, such as worship as a Christian responsibility. Duties may be positive (requiring that we do something) or negative (requiring that we not do something). Duties may be universal, in the sense that they are applicable in every situation (to love) or relative, that is determined by the specifics of a case. Duties may be individual or social; they may be duties required by justice (usually imposed by law, and usually negative) or elicited by philanthropy (less specific, but no less required).

Duties may be determined by reference, that is, they may be specified in reference to the person to whom they are directed on the basis of the claim which these persons make upon us. It is customary to see this relationship of rights and duties in terms of God, one's self and the neighbor. More specifically, one may ask what one's duty is in reference to spouse, children, parents, fellow church members, employer, employee, civil ruler, private citizen, customer, etc. The New Testament often takes this approach, in which the responsibilities of husbands to wives (an *visa*

195

versa), parents to children and children to parents, masters to slaves and slaves to masters, etc. are articulated. It should not surprise us that most Orthodox ethicists have found this to be a most useful approach. Our moral obligations are more fruitfully discussed and delineated in reference to the object of that obligation. The same method will be used below in this treatment of Orthodox Christian ethics.

Some questions arise in the treatment of our duties which need brief attention. The first issue refers to the relationship between the existence of our duty and our conscious acknowledgement of it. Is my duty in fact dependent upon my acceptance of it as a duty? Of the same order as the voluntary/involuntary sin issue, Orthodox ethicists tend to differ on this issue. For instance, P. Demetropoulos seems to hold that an atheist in fact has no duties toward God because he does not acknowledge the existence of God, and therefore he cannot recognize any duties toward Him. A similar situation would be that of a person who did not believe in private property, who would then have no reason to avoid theft and robbery, since from his point of view, he is entitled to access to everything. It seems that such a view would deny the possibility of any objective moral truth. It seems more satisfactory to affirm that the claims made by others upon us remain, whether we in fact acknowledge them or not. Because we Orthodox see the whole ethical enterprise within the framework of the Orthodox Christian doctrine of man, it is impossible to accept that the atheist is without responsibility to God, or that one can simply choose to ignore the property rights of others. Our duties remain, whether we acknowledge them or not.

Another serious problem is the question of the conflict of duties. The conflict of duties is when two or more duties present themselves concurrently to us, the fulfillment of one requiring the violation of the others. All of us face such situations frequently. A simple solution to this problem, offered by some is that we cannot have more than one duty in any given time and situation. We simply must choose what we must do and refuse to acknowledge the claim of others upon us, as irrelevant. Most of us would find such an attitude hard to accept, since the feeling of conflict of duties is based precisely upon the fact that we acknowledge the legitimacy of the claims of more than one person or situation upon our behavior. Perhaps it is true that in some ultimate sense, we only have one duty, yet, in practice it is not always clear what it is. In part, the resolution of this issue is a question of decision-making. We will speak to this question below in the chapter on the making of ethical decisions. Let it suffice here to note that often we will have to make a choice of duties, recognizing that there will always be, finally, the *one* duty we should fulfill, while at the same time recognizing the validity of the other claims, even though we are not able to fulfill them. More about this in a subsequent chapter.

Can we ever do *more* than our duty? Are there, what traditional Roman Catholic ethics called "works of supererogation?" This tradition distinguished between "precepts" which were seen to be obligatory duties

196

and "counsel" which is a matter of persuasion. Eastern Orthodox have not accepted this kind of distinction. The monk, for instance, who does all that he does because he is called to this special form of the Christian life. He does no more than what *his* Christian calling requires of him. The fastings, vigils, prayers, discipline, etc. of the monastic calling are not duties of supererogation, but requirements of his role or status as a Christian of this particular kind. The same is true of the married Christian. There are duties appropriate to the calling of the marital life. Once entered, *all* of those responsibilities are incumbent upon the married Christian. In fact, the whole idea of "doing more than your duty" is foreign to Orthodoxy, since our understanding of the Christian life has nothing to do with the mentality which restricts the meaning of the Christian life to the mere fulfillment of certain legalistic requirements. The faith which understands the Christian life in terms of Theosis and perfection which is a process of moving from "Glory to Glory," can have no place in it for works of supererogation. Rather, the sense of our imperfection, regardless of how much we manage to do, is more appropriate. The Lord's dictum about His servants is much more in the spirit of Orthodox Christian ethics: ". . . when you have done all that is commanded you, say, 'We are unworthy servants; we have only done what was our duty'."[35]

We, of course, may distinguish duties which are related to the various roles we exercise as members of society, and as members of the Church. All Christians share in a common core of duties and virtues which are appropriate to the Christian who in his or her Baptism has "put on Christ." Yet, in addition, or perhaps we should say "within" the numerous other roles which we have, the Christian ethos demands different specific applications of that ethos. Thus, the duties of a monk and of a parent will differ in some respects. The responsibilities of a bishop are different from those of the parish priest in some respects. A Church Council president has duties which may be distinguished from those of the regular parish member. Even more specifically, a Christian who is a journalist will view his work differently than a journalist who does not know Christ. Some duties will be shared with all journalists. But a Christian journalist will see other responsibilities, unperceived by the non-Christian. It is the task of Christian ethics to delineate some of these responsibilities and specific duties. Yet, each person will also make those determinations in detail for himself. No one could possibly assume the responsibility for determining all of the virtues and duties, vices and sins associated with every possible role in a complex society. The individual conscience must constantly ask, in each given situation, what it is that the good requires of him in terms of his attitudes, dispositions, motives and actions. But all duties, regardless of the details, are part of the one response which is appropriate to persons growing in the image and likeness of God.

We have said very little regarding "rights." They certainly do not play a central place in the whole of Christian ethics. Yet, it would be a mistake to assume that Christian ethos does not recognize rights for each of us. Jesus Himself sought an explanation for having been unjustly struck by the High-Priest's servant. Paul appealed to his rights as a Roman citizen, when his enemies put him in a dangerous situation. Christians too, will claim their rights on many occasions. Your right is another person's duty. Thus, a child has the right to expect that his or her parents will do their duty to house, feed, care for, and protect him or her. Christians have the right to expect that their priests and bishops faithfully execute their duties and responsibilities. Employees have the right to expect to be paid justly for their labor. Employers have the right to expect that their workers will be productive in their work. Christianity does not abrogate this basic relationship of rights and duties. Ethically speaking, a right is the appropriate and moral demand of a person who has fulfilled his duties toward others, that others reciprocally fulfill their duties toward him.

Thus, being ethical, requires a certain level of respect for one's own rights, *vis a vis* those with whom we are in relationship. A certain sensitivity to one's rights is required. However, this ought not to be the focus of one's ethical activity to the exclusion of other aspects of the ethical life. Nevertheless, in the normal course of behavior, there are certain human rights which each person properly expects to be fulfilled by others and which he or she must defend when attacked. There are circumstances which justify, or even require that we sacrifice our rights. As we shall see below, the sacrifice of our rights cannot be a general standard of behavior in every situation. What are our human rights?

Human rights, as we have seen, are the opposite side of human duties. Though ethics places its emphasis on the behavior appropriate to human living in terms of people's duties, rather than their rights, some specificity is also required in speaking of rights. The first thing to note is that rights are as fluid and flexible in determination as their opposite duties. Just as virtues are not distinct, isolated and unrelated, so it is with our rights. Our rights arise from the fact of our image and likeness toward God, our inviolate dignity as creatures of God created with the destiny of achieving perfection. There is an intrinsic human value which arises out of the care and love for the human which comes from God. There is a certain objectivity to whatever is human that demands respect and honor, simply because God has brought mankind into being. In spite of sin, weakness, failing and shortcoming, the image of God in mankind provides each human being with an irreducible dignity which must be respected by others.

> What is man that thou art mindful of him,
> And the son of man that thou dost care for him?
> Yet thou has made him little less than God,
> And dost crown him with glory and honor.
> Thou has given him dominion over the works of thy hands;
> Thou has put all things under his feet.[36]

The respect for what God has created in man is expressed in the rights claimed for him. Though it is impossible to adequately enumerate and isolate every right appropriate to human beings *qua* human being, we can refer to some of the more commonly acknowledged human rights. For the Church, the most basic and important right which all persons have, is the right to life. All other human values, in the course of normal human behavior, are related to the right to life. Another right which the Church acknowledges as basic and essential to our human dignity is the right to freedom, i.e., to self-determination. Without freedom, we lose much of what is unique to our human condition. Another right, generally acknowledged within the Church, is the right of persons to hold property. Property is the extension of human personality. The obverse of the duty not to steal is the right to own property. An extension of the rights of freedom and property, is the right of contract, that is, the right to manage oneself and one's property. A further right, increasingly important in more and more complex societal and economic circumstances is the right to education.

In no case, of course, are these rights limitless and absolute. For one thing, the rights of one individual are restricted by the rights of other individuals. The requirements of social living of necessity create limitations on the rights of all. We do not have to accept a contract theory of society to acknowledge this truth. Yet, in the face of society, which through political, technological and economic means, tends to constantly encroach upon basic human rights, the Church will do well to highlight such rights. Thus, in the face of legalized abortion and lax law enforcement, the Church will emphasize the right of all persons to life itself. In the face of the misuse of political power, or the surgical and/or medicinal attempts at personality manipulation of confined persons, the Church will raise the cry of caution.

Though rights are not at the center of Orthodox Christian ethical concern, they are not to be ignored. They have an important place in the whole fabric of the Christian ethic.

The Imitation of God, Christ and the Saints

Our "being" as Christians is constituted, as we have seen by character, virtues, duties and rights. There is a further aspect of "being" which is identified with what it is that we admire and what we imitate. "Being" is formed by what we aspire to. In this sense, the imitation of God, the imitation of Christ and the imitation of the saints of the Church is an important factor of our formation as ethical personalities.

In Orthodox thinking, there has long been an aversion to thinking about the imitation of God, Christ and the Saints, because it was felt that this was a sort of legalistic, external conformance to certain "religious ideals," incompatible to the genuine spirit of Orthodoxy. This reaction has received significant correction recently, especially in the writings of George Mantzarides of the University of Thessalonica. This is especially true of the imitation of God. Thus, Mantzarides writes:

> It would appear, however, that there is in reality a contradiction
> in principle in the concept of the imitation of God by human

beings. How is it possible for man to imitate God, since God is transcendent and unapproachable, while man is finite and subject to decay?

There is a response, however, to this question. Even though man is finite and weak, he was created in the image and the likeness of God. And even though God is transcendent and unapproachable, he is revealed to the world through His energies, which are the expression of His unapproachable essence. Even though man is not able to know God in His essence, because He always remains transcendent and unapproachable, he is able to know and imitate God's energies. It is precisely to the imitation of the energies of God, that the believer is called to devote himself during the course of his life.[37]

The imitation of God is taught in the New Testament. "Be imitators of God, as beloved children."[38] The imitation of God by the faithful is understood ethically, primarily as imitation of God's love and philanthropy. The first and chief energy of God which we are fully aware of as Christians is God's love for us. Thus, we are called by the Apostle to imitate God "as beloved children." Because we ourselves have been loved by God, we are able to comprehend in part the meaning of love and philanthropy, and are then able to imitate divine love in relation to our fellows. "Having been loved, become an imitator of His goodness" we read in the *Epistle to Diognetos*.[39] The practice of love and philanthropy by weak and powerless man, when rewarded by God, is transformed into true "godly imitation" (*theomimesian*)[40] and grants to him "identity of ethos" (*homoetheian Theou*) with God."[41]

Of course, all Christians understand that the exercise of divine-like love, in imitation of God is not accomplished without the help of God Himself. In the synergy of the Christian life, it is God who takes the lead. Thus the Church counsels us: "and do not wonder that the human being is able to become an imitator of God. He is able to do this because God wills it."[42] The same point is made by St. Basil in his *Morals:* "We should not be like those who are hostile to the Lord's teaching, but imitate God and His saints according to the power given us by Him."[43]

While it is clear that the imitation of God is taught not only in scriptural and patristic precepts, but is also a clear implication of the doctrines of our creation in God's image and likeness and our destiny to achieve Theosis, we comprehend the meaning of the imitation of the divine more sharply when we speak of our imitation of Christ. "The imitation of Christ is the imitation of God, not only because Christ was an imitator of the Father[44] but also because Christ is perfect God and co-substantial with the Father."[45] Saint Paul presents himself as an imitator of Christ,[46] and the Thessalonians are recognized as being imitators both of Christ and of Paul. There is a small discrepancy between the Gospels and the Epistles in this matter. The Gospels never speak of the faithful being imitators of

Christ. Rather, they enjoin that we "follow Christ." However, "the 'following after' and 'learning from' of the Gospels include both the idea of imitation and conclude with it. Those who follow Christ do not follow him only in history, but also in his glory.[47] The disciples of the Christ of history are also the disciples of the Lord of glory, that is, his imitators."[48]

The incarnate and risen Lord provides the Christian, and all persons, for that matter a concrete and living expression of a true and fully human life, precisely because of the intimate and profound relationship existing between the divine and the human in His one person. This reality is what keeps Christ from being a mere "example." His very being is the prototype of the condition of true humanity and the divinization of the human. In addition, Jesus is the expression of divine love and philanthropy itself, the very outpouring of God in love. Further, the life of Christ, as reported to us in the Gospels, reveals not in theory or precept alone, but in living reality the meaning of full and true humanity. "And the Word became flesh and dwelt among us, full of grace and truth; we have beheld his glory."[49] Thus it is that the imitation of Christ is an integral part of what it means to be a true and full human being, a genuine Christian, a person who is on the way to Theosis. Thus, St. Basil could define Christianity itself in terms of the imitation of Christ. ". . . the goal of Christianity is the imitation of Christ according to the measure of His incarnation, insofar as is conformable with the vocation of each individual . . ."[50]

There is a certain boldness, however, in such a demand. How can we weak and frail human beings be bold enough to measure ourselves up to the perfection and completeness of Jesus Christ? Our imitation of God and Christ, as an aspect of our call to achieve Theosis, is "by grace." As we look upon the life of Christ, we are fully aware of our inability to form Christ in ourselves through our own ability. We trust in the grace of God to lead our desires, strengthen our wills and sharpen our understanding so that we may move in the direction of the imitation of Christ. Yet, there is another aspect of this boldness. As the Son of God, Jesus did much that was unique to Him and to His work. As the Redeemer of mankind, His death and resurrection are, in themselves, beyond our imitation. In fact, to presume to undertake those roles might in fact be a denial of Him; a form of irreverent blasphemy. However, there is much in the life of Christ that stands ready for imitation on our part. His love, His patience, mercy, kindness, gentleness, His uncompromising opposition to hypocrisy and evil. His forgiving relationships with repentant sinners, His high moral and spiritual standards. His respect for life. Though perhaps they are beyond our imitation in respect to their perfection and their harmonious synthesis in His divine-human person, these ethical aspects of the life of Christ as He has "dwelt among us" are certainly subject to imitation by us. Thus, there is a sort of ambiguous character to our imitation of Christ. On the one hand, there is an aspect of Christ's life, work and being which we are incapable of imitating. On the other, there is much of His life which challenges and informs the Christian life. St. Gregory of Nyssa supplies us with the appropriate response to this ambiguity:

> as many as we are able, we imitate; however, those things which our nature is incapable of imitating, we both respect and worship. Consequently, all the descriptions which interpret the meaning of Christ to us should shine in the Christian life, some through imitation, and others through worship, if the man of God is to be complete.[51]

For ethics, this imitation of Christ is seen primarily as an orientation of our life and not as a specific imitation of specific deeds and acts of Christ. Walking the *via dolorosa* in a pilgrimage to Jerusalem may have spiritual importance, but it is not primarily an ethical act. Showing mercy to a contemporary in imitation of Christ's acts of mercy, is more in the spirit of the imitation of Christ from an ethical perspective. What is important is not a detailed, literalistic imitation of the life of Christ, but rather, the intent and desire to imitate the goodness and love of Christ "insofar as is conformable with the vocation of each individual," to use the words of St. Basil. Thus, monk, householder, wife, teacher, businessman, student, laborer, clerk, office worker, etc. are all able to imitate Christ in their own situations and vocations. The imitation of Christ is less the copying of certain behavior patterns of the life of Christ, as it is a mental set, a spiritual orientation which directs us to do the things we do as Christ would do them, were He in our place. His love, patience, humility, kindness, moral seriousness, obedience, etc. are prototypes of behavior which we seek to implement and realize in our own situations. "The whole life of Christ is presented as a 'program' of 'direction in virtue,' 'as a rule of piety' and as a 'type' (*typos*) for imitation by the faithful."[52]

Thus, it is clear why we include the imitation of God, Christ and the saints in this section about the "being" of the Christian ethical life. The imitation of God and Christ is more a stance and an orientation of our personalities, than it is a copying in a literal and slavish fashion of specific divine-human acts in the life of Christ as recorded in scriptures. To have the mind-set, and the ethos of the person who seeks to realize in his or her own life the character and ethos of Christ, is primary. When that is the case, the whole orientation of our personality is affected. The "whatness" of our being is defined clearly and determined more sharply. We become *mimetai Christou* as an inner pattern and structure of our life. This speaks to our being as ethical creatures.[53]

Obviously, this does not take place in a vacuum, in an ethical context unrelated from the rest of the Christian life. The ethical imitation of Christ and worship of Christ are intimately related, especially in the realm of our being. The beginning of the Christian life, as expressed in the sacrament of Baptism, identifies us with the life and death of Christ, as well as in the resurrection. In this sense, the whole Christian life, not only its ethical dimensions, is an imitation of Christ.

The martyrs of the ancient Church walked the road to martyrdom having as their prototype Christ, who gave himself up for them and for all mankind and rejoicing that they were imitators of his martyrdom: "permit me to be an imitator of the passion of my God," says Ignatios the Theophoros. But even in the peaceful periods of the Church, the believer is able to become an imitator not only of the life of Christ, but also of his death. It is precisely here, that the deeper meaning of the sacrament of Baptism is found, which initiates into the Church and comprises the stable image and the unique indicator of the life in Christ. This is the meaning of Baptism, to imitate the martyrdom of Christ under Pilate and his endurance of the cross and death. Imitation on the one hand is found in the icons and symbols of these sacred things, on the other it is the expression of our religious faith in dangerous situations, when the times demand it."[54]

The sharing and imitating of the passion of Christ is part of our understanding of Baptism as well as of the Eucharist. It is an aspect of our total life in Christ, a dimension of the ecclesiastical reality of our lives as part of the people of God. Thus, the imitation of Christ is based on the fundamental spiritual reality of Christ's saving work, expressed in the life of the Church. The communion of the believer with Christ in faith and sacrament presupposes the ethical imitation of Christ by the believer. That ethical imitation of Christ therefore is more than certain discrete acts. Rather, it is a mood, a certain life-style, and ethos which permeates our motives, intentions and choices. The imitation of Christ is part of our being as persons, having important ethical implications for our lives.

The scriptures also speak of the imitation of the saints. In the book of Hebrews we read, "And we desire each one of you to show the same earnestness in realizing the full assurance of hope until the end, so that you may not be sluggish, but imitators of those who through faith and patience inherit the promises."[55] We read in the lives of the Saints, stories which are presented to us clearly for imitation in our own lives. Often the services of the Church in honor of the saints, usually found in the *Menaion,* call the worshippers to the imitation of the saints. The *Synaxaria* (Lives of the Saints) do the same thing. The imitation of the saints, however, is not absolute in any sense. The theology of the icon, in which the saints are represented, provides the correct perspective on this matter. Just as the icon is a transparent window which points beyond the saint represented in it, to the spiritual reality which vivifies and supports the saint, that is, to God and Christ, so it is that mention of the saints as objects for our imitation, also points to God and Christ. Mantzarides notes:

The saints are members of the body of Christ. For this reason the imitation of the saints is the imitation of Christ. Without the communion of the saints, it is essentially impossible not only to imitate Christ, but also to properly conform to the doctrines of the Church. The dogmas of the Church as expressions of the experiences of the lives of her saints, presuppose the maintenance of communion with them and the imitation of their lives within the Church. Through reference to the saints and the imitation of their lives in the Church, our communion with Christ is made real."[56]

But it should be clear that the Saint whom we imitate and who leads us thus to Christ, is no barrier, but rather a facilitator in seeking to imitate God. He is one who has himself imitated Christ and serves to show us that it can be done as well as how it can be done. Thus, St. Paul says, "Be imitators of me, as I am of Christ."[57] Thus, in speaking of the imitation of the saints,

> this should not be understood as a prideful expression. Rather, it is kenotic. The saint as the imitator of Christ does not project himself. He in fact causes himself to disappear, so that Christ within Him might be revealed. He empties out the space of his individuality and transforms it into a place which reveals Christ. Thus, the imitation of Christ becomes concurrently a sermon about him.[58]

The myriads of saints in the life of the Church represent to us many varied and specific aspects of the full Christian life. Unlike Christ, none is perfect in all fullness. Many provide us with examples of concrete and specific virtues and modes of behavior which we can learn from and imitate in our own lives. We thus speak of the "patience of Job," the courage of St. John Chrysostom, the discipline of St. Basil, the self-sacrifice of St. Anthony, etc. Thus, St. Maximos the Confessor himself speaks of "the saintly athletes of the Savior." Of them he says,

> Let us imitate their unending road, their burning enthusiasm, the forbearance of self-control, the sanctity of pure living, the generosity of patience, the endurance of long suffering, the pity of sympathy, the calmness of gentleness, the excitedness of zeal, the sincerity of love, the superiority of humility, the simplicity of poverty, the courage, the goodness, the clemency.[59]

Of course, our imitation of the saints will be selective and will reflect the status of life in which we find ourselves. The married for instance, will not seek to imitate the rigorous life of the hermit in all of its dimensions. This would be an inappropriate imitation of the life of the saints. It would betray a poor understanding of the Christian life in general, not recognizing that there are both general duties incumbent upon all Christians, as well as duties appropriate to our concrete status and position, that is, to our roles in life.

Thus, we see that the Christian is an imitator of God, of Christ, of the saints, but not so much a slavish copier of concrete details, but rather an imitator of the whole orientation of life. The imitation of God and Christ is an aspect of what it means to restore the image of God in our lives and to move toward Theosis. The ethical virtues which characterize that growth and development make that growth more than mystical experience, sacramental participation, doctrinal affirmation and faith commitment. The imitation of Christ and God and the Saints, brings the life of the true human being to *praxis*. It is part of the realization of our whole being. Clement of Alexandria seems to have captured this truth when he wrote:

> He is the Gnostic (the true Christian), who is after the image and likeness of God, who imitates God as far as possible, deficient in none of the things which contribute to the likeness as far as compatible, practicing self-restraint and endurance, living righteously, reigning over the passions, bestowing of what he has as far as possible, and doing good both by word and deed. "He is the greatest," it is said, "in the kingdom who shall do and teach;" imitating God in conferring like benefits. [60]

Christian Formation and Radical Christian Demands

A serious problem for Christian ethics which has much to do with the Christian requirement of "being moral" and of being "conformed to the image of God" deals with the conflict which seems to appear when the slow, developing, generalized approach to the development of Christian character and the formation of "moral being" is contrasted with what appear to be the more radical and "heroic" demands of the Gospel.

We have spent much of this chapter seeking to sketch out the meaning of "being moral" from the Orthodox Christian perspective. As we have seen, it deals with our general disposition, our character, virtues and vices, generally focusing on the on-going, stable, predictable dimensions of the Christian life. This concern with the "being" of our lives is oftentimes contrasted to the rigorous demands which are also found in the same scriptures and patristic writings. In one sense, this is a contrast between an exaggerated emphasis on "being" and "action," as the two poles of the conflict.

Yet, even the most balanced and careful reader of scripture and the patristic corpus must notice the tension between the two modes of ethical operation.

Jesus and the Apostles often either presented or dealt with such tensions. In the history of the Church several efforts have been made to both understand and deal with the issue. We will briefly turn to these aspects of our topic. Jesus' rigorous demands are well known. There is a certain scandal to their apparent exclusivity.

> Whoever denies me before men, I also will deny before my Father who is in heaven. Do not think that I have come to bring peace, but a sword. For I have come to set a man against his father, and a daughter against her mother, and a daughter-in-law against her mother-in-law; and a man's foes will be those of his own household. He who loves father or mother more than me is not worthy of me; and he who loves son or daughter more than me is not worthy of me. [61]

The distinction between the daily routine of living, of development and growth and the uniqueness of the demand of Christ is sharpened in passages such as these: "He who loves his life shall lose it, and he who hates his life in this world will keep it for eternal life. If any one serves me, he must follow me; and where I am there shall my servant be also . . ."[62] A parallel, yet even more demanding passage is found in Mark 8: 34-38:

> And he called to him the multitude with his disciples, and said to them, "If any man would come after me, let him deny himself and take up his cross and follow me. For whoever would save his life will lose it; and whoever loses his life for my sake and the gospel's will save it. For what does it profit a man, to gain the whole world and forfeit his life? For what can a man give in return for his life? For whoever is ashamed of me and of my words in this adulterous and sinful generation, of him will the Son of man also be ashamed, when he comes in the glory of his Father with the holy angels."[63]

If the injunctions of the Sermon on the Mount tend to be viewed, not as descriptions of "being and character," but rather, as concrete and specific injunctions of conduct, then, this heroic and demanding aspect of the Christian ethics becomes even more sharp. In the Sermon on the Mount, the rigorousness of the law is not abolished, it is perfected;[64] one is not ever to become angry,[65] a lascivious glance demands that the offending eye be "plucked out,"[66] a sinning hand is to be "cut off,"[67] and so on. One of the most striking passages is in the Gospel according to Luke:

> Therefore he said to his disciples, "Therefore I tell you, do not be anxious about your life, what you shall eat, nor about your body, what you shall put on. For life is more than food, and the body more than clothing
> . . . .
> . . . Do not seek what you are to eat and what you are to drink, nor be of anxious mind. For all the nations of the world would seek these things; and your Father knows that you need them. Instead, seek his kingdom, and these things shall be yours as well.[68]

This exclusive focus of spiritual things, in contrast to the things of the world, goes hand in hand, with the teaching of non-resistance to evil. It becomes even more demanding when not only is the inquiring rich young ruler told to sell what he has, give the proceeds to the poor, and thus to follow the Christ,[69] but all disciples receive a similar injunction:

> Fear not, little flock, for it is your Father's good pleasure to give you the kingdom. Sell your possessions, and give alms; provide yourselves with purses that do not grow old, with a treasure in the heavens that does not fail, where no thief approaches and no moth destroys. For where your treasure is, there will your heart be also.[70]

Thus, the absolute and radical allegiance which is required of the follower of Jesus seems to demand that he not care for bodily health, physical well-being, financial condition, self-protection, or the self as a person. Those who tend to understand these injunctions as specific and direct commands to action, do so under a spirit of urgency and the pressure of time. The parable of the Bridegroom[71] demands a certain loose and ready response, without ties and bonds which make up part of a steady and developing routine "Let your loins be girded and your lamps burning, and be like men who are waiting for their master to come home from the marriage feast, so that they may open to him at once when he comes and knocks . . ."[72]

That urgency runs counter to the patience required to build up a Christian character, to develop virtues, and to slowly and painfully root out sinful habits and tendencies, replacing them with virtues appropriate to the Christian life. Some have attempted to explain away the apparent conflict by referring it exclusively to the eschatological expectations of the Scriptures. Thus, St. Paul's injunctions dealing with marriage seem to be an attempt to bridge the expectation of Christ's return with the supposition that certain stable patterns of behavior are necessary for the well-being of society and the good name of Christians in it.[73] Yet, Jesus' teaching seems less dependent upon the Parousia and more upon the particular nature and circumstances of individual character. After speaking about divorce, Jesus' disciples are recorded as saying that since divorce is so difficult to gain, "it is not expedient to marry." And Jesus is recorded as responding, "Not all men can receive this precept, (Greek, *logon*), but only those to whom it is given. For there are eunuchs who have been so from birth, and there are eunuchs who have been made eunuchs by men, and there are eunuchs for the sake of the kingdom of heaven. He who is able to receive this, let him receive it."[74] The virgin state as a choice, quickly takes on a special and unique role in the life of the Church, even in the New Testament. Paul wishes all could be virgins, like himself,[75] and in the book of Revelation the unique place of the virgin in the Kingdom is articulated: "These are they which were not defiled with women; for they are virgins. These are they which follow the Lamb whither-soever he goeth. These were redeemed from among men, being the first fruits unto God and the Lamb."[76]

In the history of the Church, there are many examples of a rigorous, literal, demanding response to these injunctions. In reference to property, the famous story of St. Anthony selling all which he had was imitated by countless others. The non-resistance of the early Christian martyrs was imitated by Sts. Boris and Gleb, acting as Orthodox pacifists, and myriads of Orthodox Christians have chosen to stay celibate as Paul did, and felt themselves able to make the radical decision to become eunuchs for the sake of the Kingdom. Others have made great self-sacrifices for others, even to the point of giving up their lives for others. "Greater love has no man than this, that a man lay down his life for his friends."[77]

Historically, some ethical systems have tended to separate ordinary morality from exceptional morality, by distinguishing them in terms of quality. Thus, property ownership, concern for economic issues, entrance into marriage, the duties of parenting and householding, etc. were seen as of a lower order of the Christian life in general and of Christian ethics, more specifically. The ethical rules governing these, as we have seen were called precepts, which all were to fulfill. A second, supernatural order of virtues however, transcended the common aspects of the first mode of Christian living. Certain Christians followed what were called "counsels," which were interpreted as a rigorous and heroic fulfillment of the whole moral teaching of the Church in total strictness. Since this superior level of Christian living seemed to demand poverty, virginity, non-violence in its fullest meaning, absolute obedience to Christ, and a life totally devoted to prayer, such a life could not be practiced in the world of real political, social, economic responsibilities. This led not only to the establishment of monasticism, but also to its elevation as the embodiment of the heroic and rigorous Christian life, in contrast to the more pedestrian and common Christian life lived in the world.

It would be false to the spirit of Eastern Orthodox Christianity to overlook the tremendous meaning of monasticism for the life of the Church. It would be a denial of the very genius of Orthodox Christianity to count the tremendous achievements of the desert and the monastery for nought. Anyone who would ignore, denigrate or overlook the meaning and significance of the monk and the celibate priest and bishop in Orthodoxy would do violence to the ethos and truth of Orthodox Christianity. But to affirm that is not the same as to accept a two-leveled ethic; a lower, pedestrian ethic for those who aren't monks and a higher, supernatural ethic for those who are. It is the genius of Orthodox Christian ethics to see that there are many ways and styles of the Christian life, all of which share in the common, yet lofty ethic of Christ, yet each of which is expressed in differing ways. Every style of Christian life requires a stable "being" embodied in the development of character, respect for moral commandments, development of virtues, etc. The Christian householder, businessman, civil leader, husband, wife, child and employee, as well as the Christian celibate, anchorite, coenobetic or idiorrythmic monk, archimandrite, Bishop, Metropolitan or Patriarch all share in the need to develop the general character appropriate to the image and likeness of God in all persons, as well as the virtues and duties appropriate to their specific calling. The heroic aspect of the Christian ethic is not limited to certain classes of Christians. The rigorousness of the Christian life comes to the fore in the midst of the life of "being," development of character, and growth in the image of God and toward "Theosis." The parents who sacrifice of themselves to feed, clothe, house and educate their children, are denying themselves no less than the monk who takes the vow of poverty. They differ in the means and the method, but ethically they are both making a heroic denial of the materialistic dimension of life. It is not often that Christians, monastic or lay, are called to give up their lives for another, or for the faith, or for God. Yet is is no less a virtue, no less heroic if it is done by an ordinary Christian. Faithfulness to the sanctity of the marriage bond may require just as much moral energy as faithfulness to a vow of celibacy; it may even require more, for the vissitudes of marriage, family life, children, etc. may strain the Christian more than the quiet of the monastery.

The "heroic" element of the Gospel ethic is real. Its demands come upon us, however, not every day, but abruptly in concrete and unique situations. We can never know fully in advance when we will be called upon to deny ourselves, to function in a role of non-resistance, to sacrifice money, time and talent for others, to bear with great patience injustice, mistreatment, to impose upon ourselves sexual restraint or abstinence, to submit our own interests to the general good, and yes, even to give up our lives. Orthodox ethics sees the development of our "being" as the one sure way of preparing our selves for the rigorousness of the Gospel demands. Thus, there is an interpenetration of these two dimensions of the Christian life, not a sharp distinction. Both are aspects of the one Christian reality.

Thus, as we have seen, there is a dimension of the Christian life which can be described as "Being Moral," a mode of existence according to which we become more and more conformed to the image of God, thus moving in the direction of achieving the image and likeness of God in us. It is ths stable, developing ethos of life which characterizes our lives as wholes. Character, virtue, duty, and the imitation of God, Christ and the saints mark it from an ethical perspective. It is clear to see how this dimension of moral being fits appropriately with the anthropological insights of Easter Orthodox theology. Our conscience, in large part, forms our moral being in conformity to the image of God, by drawing on the inherited moral and spiritual tradition of the Church. The stability of the Christian character and the stability of the Christian tradition walk hand in hand. Yet, the conscience also functions on another level: the level of ethical decision-making. It is to this second aspect of 6ur functioning conscience, that we now turn.

[1] 2 Corinthians 5:17; Galatians 6:15.
[2] Ephesians 5:8.
[3] 1 Corinthians 4:1.
[4] Matthew 6:24.
[5] Romans 12:13.

[6] Colossians 3:9b-10.

[7] Ephesians 2:19.

[8] Demetropoulos, *op. cit.*, p. 85.

[9] *Ibid.*, p. 84.

[10] Clement of Alexandria, *Stromata* Book II, xviii.

[11] *Ibid.*

[12] Stanley Hauerwas, *Character and the Christian Life: A Study in Theological Ethics,* San Antonio: Trinity University Press, 1975, p. 179.

[13] *Ibid.*, pp. 201-202, 221.

[14] Philippians 4:8, 1 Peter 2:19, 2 Peter 1:3, 1:5.

[15] Romans 12:9-19a, 21.

[16] 1 Corinthians 6:9-10.

[17] 1 Corinthians 16:13.

[18] 2 Corinthians 7-7, 16.

[19] Galatians 5:19-23a, 25-26.

[20] Ephesians 4:1-3.

[21] Ephesians 4:31-32, 5:51, 3-4, 15-19a, 21.

[22] E.g., 1 Thessalonians 5:12-22, 2 Thessalonians 3:6-15, 1 Timothy 4:11-16, 6:2b-12, 2 Timothy, 2:14-17, 22-25, 3:1-7, Titus 2:1-10, Hebrews 13:1-7, James 5:7-12, 1 Peter 3:13-18, 4:7-19, etc.

[23] *Threskevtike kai Ethike Encyclopaidia, op. cit.,* Vol. 3, p. 107.

[24] Proclos of Constantinople, *Tomos ad Armenios,* 3.

[25] See *Peri Areton kai Kakion,* MPG, v. 95.

[26] *Peri Proseuhes,* II.

[27] *Homilies on Romans,* 23, 2.

[28] Isidoros Pelousiotes, *Epitularum Libri Quinque,* 4, 15.

[29] Migne, 95, 85-88.

[30] Migne, 95, 80.

[31] Matthew 10:10.

[32] Romans 13:7, 8.

[33] Matthew 25:14-30.

[34] Ephesians 6:5-7.

[35] Luke 17:10.

[36] Psalm 8:4-6. For a fuller treatment of rights from an Orthodox Christian perspective, see my contribution in Arlene Swidler, *ed., Human Rights in Religious Perspective*. Philadelphia: Pilgrim Press, 1982, Ch. 2.

[37] *Christian Ethics: University Lectures,* Thessalonike: 1975, p. 131.

[38] Ephesians 5:1.

[39] *Epistle to Diognetos* 8,4.

[40] See Dionysios the Areopagite, *Epistle 8,* PG 3, 1085A.

[41] Ignatios, *Magnesians,* 6, 2, quoted by Mantzarides, *ibid.,* p. 132.

[42] *Epistle to Diognetos* 10, 4.

[43] Rule 27.

[44] Ignatios of Antioch, *To the Philadelphians* 7, 2.

[45] Mantzarides, *ibid.,* p. 133.

[46] 1 Corinthians 11:1.

[47] *Ibid.,* Matthew 16:27; 24:30, John 17:10, 22.

[48] Mantzarides, *op. cit.*

[49] John 1, 14.

[50] *The Long Rules,* 43.

[51] *Concerning Perfection,* PG 46, 256C.

[52] Mantzarides, *op. cit.,* p. 138.

[53] Romans 8:29.

[54] Nicholas Kabasilas, *The Life in Christ,* 2, PG 150, 557C, quoted by Mantzarides, *ibid.,* p. 138-139.

[55] Hebrews 6:12-13.

[56] *Ibid.,* p. 145.

[57] 1 Corinthians 11:1.

[58] Mantzarides, *ibid.,* p. 143.

[59] *Asketikos logos.* PG 90, 956.

[60] *Stromata,* Book II, xix.
[61] Matthew 10:33-38.
[62] John 12:25.
[63] See also Luke 17:33, Matthew 10:39.
[64] Matthew 5:17-20.
[65] Matthew 5:21-22.
[66] Matthew 5:29.
[67] Matthew 5:30.
[68] Luke 12:22-23, 29-31.
[69] Matthew 19:21, Mark 10:21, Luke 12:33.
[70] Luke 12:32-34.
[71] Matthew 25:1 ff.
[72] Luke 12:35-36.
[73] 1 Corinthians 7.
[74] Matthew 19:10-21.
[75] 1 Corinthians 7:1, 7.
[76] 14:4.
[77] John 15:13.

Chapter Nine

ETHICAL DECISION MAKING

"The queen of all virtues is discernment" (diakrisis).
(Sophronios of Jerusalem, Sermo de Nativitate.)

In Chapter Seven we discussed the conscience and determined that the conscience was the meeting place of the objective good which is God, in His energies, and the subjective reality which is our human existence. The conscience, we noted, is the chief agent of the moral life which deals with the character, "being good," ethical decision making and the actual doing of the good. In the preceding chapter we discussed "ethical being." In this chapter the process of decision making will be discussed in detail.

The focus in this chapter is on what has been called by Orthodox ethicists, the "Preceding Conscience" (*Proegoumene Syneidesis*). "The expression of the conscience as preceding is either persuasive or dissuasive; that is, it either persuades and urges the performance of the act under consideration, if it be good, or it dissuades when oppositely it is evil."[1] But before the conscience is able to dissuade or persuade to action "the act is under consideration." A process of judgment must take place and a decision must be reached as to what is in actuality the right thing to do, or whether the contemplated act is good or evil.

The Virtue of *"diakrisis"* or Discernment

How is such a decision reached? There is a general Christian virtue which responds to this question. In the chapter on the conscience reference was made to it at some length. *Diakrisis,* or discernment is critical to the whole moral and spiritual life for it is "the queen of all the virtues" according to Sophronios of Jerusalem,[2] and, as noted above, discernment is the source, and root and head and bond of every virtue.[3]

It is impossible to avoid the implications of Christ's question: "Why do you not judge for yourselves what is right?"[4] For even in the most clear ethical situation, in which there is no ambiguity or conflict, the conscience must acknowledge personally, for the person himself or herself, that a certain proposed action is right or wrong and that he or she is obligated either to do the good or avoid that which is evil.

Yet often the discernment of the right or the wrong course of action is not easy. Many factors complicate the "discernment of the good and the evil."[5] One "must be wise in the discernment of reason."[6] The first glance at an ethical problem often does not reveal all of the ambiguities, conflicts, and problems involved. Appearances tend to deceive us. It is necessary to get to the heart of difficult issues, to discern what is right and what ought to be done and how it should be done rightly. Most properly did Jesus castigate those who condemned him for healing on the Sabbath, but the words apply equally to each of us when we make ethical judgments. "Do not judge by appearances, but judge with right judgment." [7]

The monastic tradition of the Church has long emphasized the need for *"diakrisis."* Monasticism is fully aware of our tendency to deceive ourselves, to follow our own desires and not the will of God. [8]

Thus, St. Isaiah the Anchorite, describes the role of *diakrisis* in the life of the monk.

> We are recipients of the attacks of thoughts both good and evil, and it is said that the master of the passions is pious and god-loving reason. Thus for us monastics it is appropriate to thoughtfully and with sober mind discern and discriminate between the virtues and vices; and which virtues we should cultivate in the presence of the brothers and fathers and which we should do alone; and which is the higher virtue and which is second and third; and which passion is of the spirit and which of the body; and which virtue is of the spirit and which of the body; and from which virtue pride strikes upon our mind; and from which does vanity come; and from where does anger come, and out of what does gluttony arise. [9]

If *diakrisis* is a necessary function of the monastic, it is all the more necessary for those who live in the world. If it is true that "winds and storms and a dizziness of spirits" [10] attack the sheltered monks, what shall Christians living in the world say? The need for *diakrisis,* to make careful judgment about right and wrong is all the more demanding for those who live in the world. The complexities and difficulties of moral choice need to be faced by each Christian. It is not only that the ethos of the Christian life will demand obedience of us, but so will specific commands and rules such as the Holy Canons or injunctions of the Bible. The call of love for God, and love for our fellows, the need to distinguish between principles and consequences, the appropriateness or inappropriateness of acts in the life growing toward Theosis, the requirements for our being part of the body of Christ, the Church, will all influence the determination of what is right or wrong. Further, the significance of our motives and intentions is also part of the decision to be made in any given situation. Thus *"diakrisis* clarifies all of these things . . . for it is not just the thing that is done which we seek, but why it is done," as well. [11]

The need for ethical judgment becomes even more imperative when we live in rapidly changing times, such as those of our own day. As we shall see below, in more stable and ordered periods of time many moral decisions were provided for by traditional responses and practices. Evaluations were made by relatively simple parallel judgments from what was generally accepted by the Church or the society as a whole. However, such simple appeals to "what has always been done" frequently do not suffice any longer. There are many reasons for this. Values often conflict sharply, not only in highly pluralistic societies such as that of the United States, but we have now become in a sense, a "world community." The sure traditions with which we grew up tend to lose their general and universal character when brought into close contact with other styles of life, practices and traditions. Further, circumstances seem to have changed in radical ways. For example, the population explosion of necessity has caused traditional views regarding birth control, abortion, sterilization, etc. to come under question. Not only that, but new and "miraculous" scientific advances create unheard of situations for Christian Ethics to respond to. "Shall We clone a Man?" asks ethicist Paul Ramsey.[12] There is no answer to that question in the patristic corpus. A judgment needs to be made. *Diakrisis* is needed. Yet discernment and moral judgment need to be made according to some criteria. Guidelines for the making of moral judgments do exist in the tradition of the Church. The kinds of factors which need to be taken into consideration can be enumerated and brought before us for inclusion in the process of discerning the right and the wrong. This, in part is a rational procedure which can be described. It is not foreign to the Orthodox Christian mentality to include this procedure within the Christian life. St. Maximos the Confessor, for example, shows its appropriateness.

> He who has achieved the virtues and has become rich in knowledge, and therefore naturally comprehends reality, always thinks and acts according to right reason, never perverting the whole truth. For it is from our irrational use of things that we become immoral rather than virtuous.[13]

To such an ordered and rational consideration of the elements which need to be taken into consideration for proper ethical judgment, we now turn.

The Goal of Moral Judgment

In a scholarly description of St. Basil's doctrine of the image and likeness of God in man, the statement is made that

> The necessary *gnosis* or knowledge wherein the image of God consists is the knowledge of good, the capacity to discern between what is good and what is evil.[14]

Perhaps the most important and inclusive criterion for the making of correct decisions is the realization of the image of God in our persons and the Kingdom of God in society. The Theosis of persons and of society is the ultimate backdrop against which every ethical dilemma is dealt with and every ethical decision made, because they are directly related to God who is the ultimate good. Thus, in a passage in his "Chapters Concerning Theology" St. Maximos the Confessor gives as the criterion of ethics that which joins human life with divine life, that is, the participation of the human in the divine life.

> In accordance with each one's judgment, the balance of each opinion will be the natural rationale that promotes choice as to what is bad or what is good, according to which participation or non-participation in the divine life is naturally produced.[15]

However, this affirmation does not solve all decision making problems. On the one hand, anything which clearly is at odds with whatever is fitting and appropriate to participation in God and to the image of the Kingdom is easily rejected by the Christian. An action which occurs out of hatred, which brings disproportional consequences, which clearly violates all that is represented by the relationship of love for God and humanity appropriate to the divinized life, will in fact cause no problem since it will be rejected out of hand. Thus, the emphasis on the ultimate end, the eschatological *telos* of reality, as perceived by the Church, serves ethical decision making in a negative sense. It is much easier to determine what is *not* fitting and appropriate to Theosis and the Kingdom, than to determine what is. A certain apophaticism is characteristic of the decision making process.

However, even as we seek to make positive determinations about appropriate courses of action, the teleological importance of the doctrines of Theosis and the Kingdom has to remain forever before us. The ultimate goal of any decision which we make should seek to move the situation in which we find ourselves closer to Theosis and the Kingdom.

Yet, just how to determine what that is in specific circumstances and situations is exactly the issue. When it is "obvious" we do not even sense the need to make a decision. The proper course of action simply "appears" and it is merely a question of doing that which we know is right. In many cases, however, "what is right," is subject to varying circumstances. Often our unreflective perception of what "appears" to be the case, is challenged when new facts and new circumstances are brought to our attention. It seems "obvious" that we should always tell the truth. However, when the whereabouts of a person are asked of us by a crazed, armed, madman, a new circumstance is introduced—which may lead us, without guilt, to misdirect the attacker.

What follows is a treatment of the kinds of factors which enter into decision making. It is not a check-list to be rigidly followed, in a step-by-step fashion. Rather, there is need to be sensitive and aware of these dimensions and factors of decision making, with a clear sense of their interplay in the process. Orthodox Christians will keep their decision making in close touch with the on-going consciousness of the Church and see themselves as operating as ethical decision makers within the body of the Church and in communion with it.

Elements of Ethical Judgment

"The Conscience . . . is in constant activity, especially when we reason (*dialegometha*) concerning judgment," wrote a sixth century

Patriarch of Constantinople.[16] And St. John Chrysostom instructs: "Open the doors of your conscience and see the judge seated in your mind."[17] Whether we are aware of it or not, our conscience is constantly active in judging moral issues and in making ethical decisions. What should we take into account as we do so? Some of these factors are the following.

The Right: Law and Rules

Most situations which we are called upon to face are not unique to us. They have been faced from time immemorial and certain responses appropriate to life in general and to the Christ-like life and the Kingdom, in particular, have been articulated over and over again in the history of the Church. In previous chapters we noted that moral laws and rules are not mere arbitrary and capricious impositions upon our will from without. We have understood rules and laws as the distillation of the experience of the Church as to the most appropriate and fitting responses to the moral situations which we commonly face. Ethical rules are the accumulated ethical wisdom of the Church. They serve to save the continuous expenditure of time and energy in deciding anew each situation. A remarkably large portion of ethical behavior consists of consulting the guidance of the Church in the form of its generally accepted ethical rules and canons. These are found in the Scriptures, in the patristic Tradition, in the Canon law of the Church, in the general ethical teaching of the Church, in the teaching authority of the Bishop and even in the liturgical life of the Church.[18] Together they form the Church's long-lasting general perception of God's will which all Christians are called upon to observe. Speaking of the Canons, Bishop John Rine of Helsinki speaks equally validly of all ethical rules. Thus, for example,

> every form of adultery is considered as being in extreme contrast to the characteristic prototype of behavior of the Christian life. . . . The same stance is adopted concerning other deviations from the moral life, which ought to agree with the requirements of the faith. . . . In every case, however, and in accordance to the fundamental principle, wherever the Christian faith is maintained in truth and wholeness, there ought to be created such uniform prototypes of ethical behavior, so that they be in harmony with that faith and are as much as possible, so to speak, visible expressions of that faith.[19]

Ethical rules, then, are attempts to articulate how the faith ought to be "visibly expressed" in our behavior and activities.

It should not surprise us that one of the chief means of ethical decision making is to learn the rules which apply to a given situation and then apply them to the circumstances at hand.

The chief virtue here, then, is obedience to all of God's commandments. Thus St. Basil strictly writes: "Since, then, they cannot be saved who do not their works according to the command of God and since no precept may be safely overlooked . . . let us who are striving to live the devout life . . . make it our common concern and resolve not to allow any precept whatever to elude our vigilence. If the man of God must be perfect . . . it is all-important that he be made perfect through the observance of every commandment . . ."[20]

This approach, which is continuously repeated in the literature of the Church, is not legalism. It is the necessary consequence of an Orthodox ecclesiology which sees the Church as the people of God and the subject of God's self-disclosure and love. God makes known what is fitting and appropriate to the Christian life in the form of laws, rules, the natural law, the evangelical ethic, etc. Further, as we have seen, growth in the image of God toward Theosis implies choices and behavior in experiential conformity with what divine life has revealed itself to be.

However, as we have noted, rules are not always unambiguous. Even when we have the best of intentions, not only do rules oftentimes conflict among themselves, but they also sometimes appear to do violence to other Christian values. "We must everywhere be on guard lest, under pretext of observing one commandment, we break another."[21] We may acknowledge the rightness of a rule, but be prohibited from fulfilling it—even though we wish to do it—by circumstances of time or place. Often a rule may call us to act in a way which brings harm to others, creating a situation of conflict of rules which places the rule's validity in doubt. Sometimes, our conscience leads us to determine that in a given circumstance a rule is in fact wrong. As we all know, rules tend to be questioned more now, both within and outside of the Church.

Consequently there is need to make decisions. However, a sure and safe way to start in any complex situation, is to consult the rules; the traditional, normal, standard, "uniform prototypes of ethical behavior" which the Church has articulated as being in harmony with the faith, and, which are in fact "visible expressions of that faith."

Consequences: Good and Evil Results

When we find ourselves in a situation in which the rules conflict or in which no rules exist, one of the ways of determining what ought to be done and what ought not to be done is to determine which courses of action are in fact open to us and to try to foresee what consequences will arise with their implementation.

Often the choice of the courses open to us is limited by circumstances. Thus, though we are sensitive to what ought to be done in a given case, it may be outside of our ability to do what in fact we know is best. Assessing the real possibilities open to us—including not doing anything—is a necessary prerequisite to determining the consequences. As we have noted before, consequences are the immediate and short-term results of our actions. However, consequences themselves must be judged by their general impact on society and the life of the Church. Thus, a specific question such as responding to a request of scientists that our hospitalized child be included in an experiment—for which there is no standing rule—will require consideration of consequences, both short and

217

long term. What will be the effect on our child? Is there a chance of healing? A risk that the child's condition will worsen? But further, is it likely that participation in the experiment will advance science and thus help others? What if everyone refused to participate in such experiments?

Consequences range from immediate, to short term, to middle term, to long term. Often the short term result and the middle or long term results are together unacceptable. We are thus helped in rejecting some of the possible alternatives. Conversely, the short and long term results may both be positive, e.g. the experiment offers *some* hope for our child in an otherwise hopeless situation, as well as contributing to scientific knowledge.

Frequently, however, the consequences are mixed, not only in the case of immediate and longer terms, but also among themselves in the same term, for there is rarely a single consequence of any of our actions. Christians will need to bring to bear on their consideration of consequences a whole series of Christian values in such cases, e.g. basic ethical values such as respect for life, trust, love, concern for the well-being of the person, value for social order, as well as the well-being of society, the Christian ideals of patience, forebearance, self-sacrifice, etc.

It is quite possible that we will not be able to sort out clearly enough which probable consequences are most desirable, or even be able to calculate with any sense of certitude what the consequences might be. Other aspects of the decision making process may be helpful to us.

Intent: What is to be Accomplished

Decision making, when part of a management process, always includes consideration of goals. Goals are equally important aspects of ethical decision making. The setting of goals for our acts is a powerful force for making our decisions. In ethics, we usually refer to this as identifying what our intent is, in acting in a particular way. By clarifying our intent—e.g. what we actually want to happen as a result of our moral choice—we are helped in making decisions. Thus, in the First Apostolic Council[22] certain intentions are articulated on the question of gentile membership in the Church. These intentions led to the decision, "the Gentiles should hear the word of the Gospel and believe,"[23] "that the rest of men may seek the Lord,"[24] "to lay upon you no greater burden than these necessary things."[25] With intentions such as these, the right decision was made clearer for the Apostles gathered in council. Thus St. Basil councils, "live out your life in accordance with your intentions."[26]

Obviously, intentions or goals may also be posited on a time range—immediate through long term. "I have decided to punish you so that you will learn that stealing is wrong" is an immediate, short term goal decision. It is also narrow and restricted in terms of its object—the child. Goals can be more general: "feeding the hungry, clothing the naked, visiting the sick and imprisoned."[27] Intentions can be even less specific such as seeking to respond to the apostolic injunction present your bodies as a living sacrifice, holy and acceptable to God, which is your spiritual worship. Do not be conformed to this world, but be transformed by the renewal of your mind, that you may prove what is the will of God, what is good and acceptable and perfect.[28]

To intend to do "what is good and acceptable and perfect" and not what is self-serving, selfish and minimal in a given situation will powerfully influence our concrete decisions. On the broadest level, intentions such as to "do good," to "obey God," to "inherit the Kingdom of God," to "edify the Church" will provide less specific direction to our choices, but even so, they will exclude certain options and move us in the direction of other alternatives.

In each case, we should seek to be as clear as possible about both our short and long-range goals. However, goals are not all-sufficient determiners of right and wrong choices. Our decisions must take into consideration other factors as well. Closely related to our intentions are our motives and the means which we use to achieve our goals.

Motives: What Moves us to Action

As we have seen from our discussion of material and formal theories of the good, material ethicists emphasize the results of our actions on the one hand, or the goals which we seek to accomplish, on the other (consequences, intentions). Formal ethics emphasized the exclusive determining influence of motives. Kant's "categorical imperative" is the best known example of exclusive reliance upon motive for ethical decision making. However, Orthodox Ethics sees motive as one of many factors to be considered, and, as we have seen, generally adopts a "combined theory" which gives place to both consequences and motives. "Things should not be measured only by the end, but should be judged as well by the motive of each person" according to Clement of Alexandria.[29] Chrysostom is even stronger concerning the place of motive. "In many cases motives are enough to do great good."[30] In fact, in one place he teaches that "it is not from the results, but from the motives, that the Blessed One will judge us."[31]

This, of course, is a direct outgrowth of the Evangelical Ethic, in which we saw that Jesus put great emphasis on motives. The focus of the Sermon on the Mount, which is a program for life and not a mere idealistic statement nor a legal directive, is on what genuinely moves us to action.

Motives move us to particular acts. They form the emotional impetus for our decisions and behavior. Thus, a decision and the subsequent act may have good consequences. Yet the same act may be done out of good or bad motives. Or, a decision to obey an appropriate rule may take place on the basis of good or bad motives. We are all familiar with cases in which a right act is done with or because of anger. When we seek to make decisions it is necessary to test our options and choices against our motives. We must be suspicious of any decision for action if we discern pride, hatred, jealousy, envy, greed and the like moving us. St. Paul's list of the fruits of the Spirit is a representative description of the motives which are appropriate to good decision-making: "love, joy, peace, patience, kindness, goodness, faithfulness, gentleness, self-control."[32]

Of all the motives, however, which characterize a good act, love is the chief.[33] We are called to be "rooted and grounded in love"[34] and to "walk in love, as Christ has loved us."[35] If our motive in making a decision is the well-being of another without direct concern for our own benefit and in a spirit of caring and concern for him or her, we can trust that powerful forces are at work leading to proper decisions. Yet even good motives, alone, cannot insure right decisions always. There is need as well for a determination of the appropriate means so as to make the correct ethical decision.

Means: Appropriate Methods

Even when our motives are judged to be good and the goals which we wish to achieve with our acts morally correct, the issue of the means used to achieve the goals becomes an important factor of decision-making. We are all aware of the terrible dangers in the maxim "the end justifies the means." It is an all too frequent occurance that persons committed to appropriate ends feel free to use inappropriate means to accomplish those ends. One of the most serious criticisms of Bolshevism was on this basis. It is a frequently heard appeal to principle in revolutionary and war situations. Political leaders often use these arguments. Even the Church has not been free of them.

Yet, the "end justifies the means" is subject to much criticism. Wrong means to achieve right ends are frequently destructive of the ends themselves. For example, to lie, cheat, distort the truth, torture, and abuse people so as to establish some social order conceived to be ideal (Communism in Russia, American Economic Ascendancy, "A Greece of Greek Christians") has an inherent moral unfittingness to it. It is no less the case in personal ethical decison making. The Christian should be careful, in the words of St. Basil, not "to allow sin to enter into his observance of the commandment."[36] The decisions which we make should provide for means which are in harmony, as much as possible, with the telos, the goals, the rules and the motives appropriate to the Christian life. The means chosen should be in harmony with all the other dimensions of the ethical act, so as to give the decision integrity and wholeness. The proper motto should, rather be, "Choose means appropriate to the end." Such means will always be proportionate, neither too great or too small in magnitude, just, effective, fitting and informed.

For means to be informed, it is implied that the choice of means is based on facts. Actually, all moral decision-making must be informed. Blind obedience to rules without sensitivity to other factors of decision making is improper. Equally misguided is failure to give consideration of circumstances and facts which are relevant. It is, for instance, impossible to deal with an issue such as birth-control today without taking into consideration a whole range of facts including human biology, chemical effects of various conception control medications, population statistics and projections, world energy and food resources, etc. Even on the most personal and immediate level of decision making such as participation in medical experimentations, *informed* consent is considered to be essential. Usually, the facts will have greater impact upon the means used, rather than upon the ultimate norms.

Values and Dis-Values

Another way of testing a situation so as to determine a correct course of action is to use a value-approach. Value is a modern term usually referring to aspects of life which are considered to be desirable, praiseworthy, and prized traits or characteristics of behavior. In Christianity, as we have seen above in the treatment of value theory, there are numerous listings of such traits and characteristics. Sometimes called virtues, Christians have learned to recognize many such traits and characteristics which are apprpopriate to the Christian life. Thus behavior which is loving, kind, caring, just, truthful, sincere, and God-like is valued and praiseworthy. Traits such as "wisdom, understanding, counsel, fortitude, knowledge, piety and the fear of the Lord,"[37] are thought of as covetousness, lust, envy, gluttony, anger, sloth—the seven so-called Christian values. Conversely, sins and vices (κακίαι) such as pride, deadly sins—are disvalues. Often it is not easy to name and label a motive, intent, action or combination of them with a name, either positive or negative. We intuit appropriate or inappropriateness in such cases. Being "in touch with our feelings" regarding these is an important diagnostic method, especially in questionable cases. It is never an exclusive method, such as the total reliance upon the classical formalist criterion of the good based on the feelings. Yet, especially in the case of a developed character, it can be of great help in decision making. The conviction that one has made "the right decision" will in large part arise from the sense of its appropriateness to the values endemic to the Christian ethos.

Further, in coming to this decision we are helped by the value approach since it is susceptible to a ranking of approved traits or forms of behavior, or for that matter, of sins and vices, as well. Thus, on the positive side, we speak of a hierarchy of values. Determining the values which apply to a given situation and then ranking them in importance is a helpful method of arriving at decisions in complex situations. This can be done in an explicitly rational fashion, e.g. "what is most important, what value is to be most realized (developed, affirmed, actualized, etc.) . . . What is next in importance? . . . Third? . . . Fourth? . . ." It can be arrived at with a more theological reference: "What is the will of God in this situation? or "What would Jesus do in my place?" There is, of course, a danger of subjectivism in this approach which will need to be countered by reference to other, more objective criteria, yet it can be a helpful approach to making decisions in difficult circumstances.

The Perception of the Situation

The situation and circumstances pertaining to a moral choice are an important part of ethical decision making. It is, of course, an error to make the concrete and specific situation itself the primary feature and determinant of a given ethical decision. This view was propounded in the late sixties in the United States by several ethicists, most prominent of whom was Joseph Fletcher.[38]

For the Orthodox "the situation" has numerous dimensions. It is never adequate to view the situation as *only* the immediate and concrete circumstances, though these cannot be ignored. In the largest sense

> the "situation" is the whole divine economy. The maximization of the Christ-like image—given the basic order and pattern of society—is the real "situation" . . . The eternal situation is the relevant situation.[39]

However in any given circumstance it is possible to perceive numerous "situations" which are seen, so to speak, as inclusive concentric circles. For example, a moral decision involving a husband and wife can be placed within increasingly inclusive "situations." The situation may arise out of the decision on how the part-time earnings of the wife ought to be allocated—are they personal funds which she has a right to spend as she wishes? In this sense the issue is defined as an individual situation. But is not the situation a marital one as well? Just as the wife has claim on the husband's earnings does he have claim on hers? What of the familial situation? What claims of children or aged parents must be recognized as part of the situation? What of the demands of the very institution of marriage and family? Should any decision be taken which weakens it as a fundamental structure of society? Then there is the "situation" which places all marital relationships within the Church and the Kingdom of God and as part of the *askesis* which leads to the fulfillment of the image of God in growth toward Theosis. We will need to keep all of these situations before us as we seek to make decisions.

Further, the situation varies as well in reference to the spiritual state of the ethical agent as well. Thus the Fathers of the Church distinguish among levels of spiritual maturity. Clement of Alexandria, for instance, distinguishes among the *hylikoi* (matter oriented people), *psychikoi* (life oriented people), *pnevmatikoi* (spirit oriented people) who could become *gnostikoi* (or fully enlightened people).[40] Others such as Niketas Stethatos speak of levels of spiritual progress and spiritual age-development. Of interest to ethics is the classification of the latter. "Babes" are those who are just beginning their development and are moved by "the fear of punishment." "Youths" are in the middle of their spiritual and ethical development and who function "looking for rewards." "Mature adults," in Stethatos' view are "perfect" in that they act out of love for God and in union with Him."[41] The level in which one finds himself or herself will in large part help define the nature, issues, constraints and possibilities of the situation for ethical decision making.

222

Thus decision making of necessity will be based on the extent of the situation and the perception it has for us. That is why, as we shall see below, there is always a need for decision making to be informed by others and not be a purely individual process. However, there is some order in the decision making perception of the situation. One way of perceiving this order of decision making is as follows:

> Where there is chaos, or the threat of chaos, moral order must first prevail. Where moral order prevails, it must be transfigured and perfected. Where moral order exemplifies justice, then love in its fullness takes over. Each specific situation does call for its own response, but only on the basis of the evident will of God for the realization of man's destiny.[42]

Perception of the dimension of the situation, as well as the limitations and constraints of our own stage of moral development need to be complemented by a more wholistic approach. That is why decision making is never to be an isolated experience. It must also take place as an ecclesial and corporate experience.

Decision Making as an Ecclesial, Corporate Process

Existential philosophy and existential ethics have given the impression that decision making is an utterly individual process and responsibility. As a theory Existentialism tends to see norms, standards, "others," as inimicable to human "authenticity." One becomes "authentic" in the making and carrying out of decisions for one's self and by one's self "I gotta be me" and "I did it *my* way" are the lines of a popular song reflecting this view. Much of what has been said up to now in this chapter has tended to concur with that view. There is need for a corrective to that view, which at the same time, becomes another aspect of Christian ethical decision making.

For an Orthodox Christian no ethical decision may be taken in isolation from Church. In a sense, this has already been implied by appeal to the Church's approved rules, motives, and values. Yet in the decision making process there must be more than mere reference to scriptures, canons and formal teaching. To do this would be to miss the extremely significant dimension of the corporate character of the Church. This takes many expressions in Orthodox Christianity. In the case of official teaching on ethical matters this requires action by an Ecumenical Synod. Autocephalous Churches through their synods may make ethical determinations, as well. The counsel and teaching of the Bishop of the Diocese has important standing in determining ethical issues. Even the Clergy-Laity Conferences and meetings of particular jurisdictions provide guidance on these matters since, in part, they represent the consciousness of the Church. Further, theologians and ethicists of the Church contribute significantly to the determination of the issues, frequently by addressing new issues, as well as old issues which have new perspectives, from the viewpoint of the Orthodox Christian Ethos. All these, however, are on the level of teaching and decision making in reference to general ethical guidelines and directives.

None of these, however, relieve the conscience of the individual Christian from making ethical decisions in the particular circumstances which he or she faces. But even here, decisions should not be made alone. Alone, we are too subject to self-deception. Caught in the difficulties of an agonizing decision all of us are too capable of distorting the import and significance of the various factors contributing to our decision. For example, both the spiritual tradition of Eastern Orthodoxy and depth psychology affirm the difficulty in gauging our true motives in choosing courses of action. Monastics know that there can be no spiritual growth without the guidance of another—the *Pnevmatikos,* the *Staretz* or the Spiritual Father. The advice of one of the masters of the monastic spiritual life of the fifth century to his spiritual son remains valuable today for all Christians, monastic or not. Thus, Holy Mark the Ascetic advises his spiritual son, Nicholas, to

> make an effort to keep company with, and be with and be under
> the guidance of experienced spiritual fathers. For it is dangerous
> living alone, on one's own, without supervision or with persons
> inexperienced in spiritual warfare . . . for the deviousness and
> treachery of evil is great . . .[43]

When a decision is difficult, there is need for counsel and the consultation of those who are informed and ethically sensitive in the spirit of prayer. "That which is obscure," says St. Basil, "can be more easily discerned by the earnest scrutiny of several persons, since, to be sure, God grants issue to the quest under the guidance and counsel of the Holy Spirit, according to the promise of our Lord Jesus Christ.[44]

In making decisions, we need to have the assistance of other Christians, our Pastors, spiritual Fathers, and the teaching Church. A valuable method in decision making is to bring the issue to the "earnest scrutiny of several persons" of good conscience.

In the specifically ecclesial context, such corporate consideration has often led to the making of decisions which shows a certain creativity and sensitivity to the problem of conflicting rules, values and consequences. Speaking of a conflict situation regarding litigation involving the Christian, St. Basil makes appeal to numerous, apparently conflicting values such as being "unfairly treated," but the "duty not to be quarrelsome" together with the duty "to bear witness against the unjust," appealing as well to "the rules of piety" which forbid entering into litigation, and to concern for "our brother's salvation" before suggesting a solution. He concludes, trying to show that the proposed solution is sensitive to numerous factors, and not just one.

> In this manner we shall save our adversary also, even against his
> will, from evil consequences and we ourselves will not violate
> the commandment of God, being as his ministers, neither

contentious nor avaricious, steadily intent upon manifesting the truth and never overstepping the appointed limits of zeal.[45]

St. Basil's solution was to allow oneself in such cases to be *taken* to court, but not to *initiate* legal action. Such "bending" of rules in dealing with complex issues, in which many values conflict has come to be known as the practice of *Economia*. Most usually understood as a practice of canon law, it is equally at home in ethical decision making. It is clearly a means for dealing with situations in which there is conflict between rules and consequences. The practice of *Economia* seeks neither to ignore the law nor to discount the consequences. When every solution, such as that of St. Basil noted above is exhausted, the Church has found itself able to make decisions, often ethical in character, which give due respect to both the moral commands and the Christian values involved in consequences.

Economia means permitting an exception to a rule whose strict application (*akribeia*) would result in undesirable consequences from a Christian point of view, *without however thus setting a precedent.*[46]

The significant aspect of this discussion here is not only that *Economia* is a form of decision making, but that *Economia* is always an ecclesial action, never a purely personal decision. The Bishop's synod, a Father Confessor, a Pastor in consultation with his Bishop, a Monastic Community, may make a decision *kat' ekonomian,* but properly never an individual Christian alone, especially for him or herself.

The Decision Process

A good character is the best guide to proper ethical decision making. Nurtured, as it is, by life in the faith, with sensitivity to the mind of the Church, with understanding of Scriptures and the Tradition, with prayer, worship, obedience, love and caring, the developed character has decision making capacities which border on the instinctive saintly wisdom and perspecuity. These are the best guarantee of right judgments. Preparation for ethical decision making is to be found in growth and development of the image and likeness of God in each of us through a synergy of human will and the divine energies of the Holy Spirit. Thus, the injunction of St. Paul: "be transformed by the renewal of your mind, that you may prove what is the will of God, what is good and acceptable, and perfect."[47] Good decision making begins with a mind which is renewed according to the divine image.

That mind will often be able to "intuit" and "sense" the right course of action in a given situation. Yet even this is not totally automatic or unreflective. A famous American Supreme Court judge was once asked how he came to his landmark decisions. "I make them all intuitively" was his answer. However, when pressed, he admitted to many long hours of study of the issues, the law, legal precedents, consequences as well as of the social and moral values involved. The decision often "appeared" of itself, but not without that study. Ethical decision making as we have seen, involves many complex factors which contribute to the final, convincing decision of the conscience which bears with it not only the decision of what should be done, but also the sense of moral obligation to do it. It is the process of considering the kinds of factors outlined in this chapter which is called the decision making process.

There is no final, rigid, arbitrary pattern to this process. On the preceding pages of this chapter we have tried to enumerate some of the factors which enter into a conscious ethical decision. Undoubtedly there are other factors as well which have not been touched upon. In conclusion, this chapter suggests a possible pattern for practical decision making.

First and foremost we will seek to keep before us all the time that our ultimate goal is conformity and communion with the Triune God, that all our ethical decisions—in order to be correct—must be in harmony with and contribute to growth for the fulfillment of the image and likeness of God in persons and to the realization of the Kingdom of God. This is the Orthodox Christian way of saying that our ethical decisions must be in accordance to God's will.

When faced with an ethical dilemma, given this general orientation, the next step would be to determine if, in fact, there is a consensus in the life and history of the Church on the matter, in the form of canons, rules, instructions or directives. Oftentimes, the discovery of this articulated accumulated wisdom, experience and consciousness of the Church is enough to resolve the dilemma.

When it is not, a serious effort must be made to discern what "is the will of God, what is good and acceptable and perfect" in the case at hand. We will take into account conflicting rules, rules applicable to analogous situations, our own stage of moral development as well as that of others, possible consequences of alternative courses of actions, whether they be good, bad or mixed. We will ask which goals (intentions) are being sought and seek to evaluate their conformity to the ultimate criteria of Theosis and the Kingdom. We will acknowledge the limitations imposed on us by circumstances, the demands of those who have immediate claims on us, the means required to carry out proposed solutions, the motives which move us in each of the possible directions. We will share these deliberations with trusted friends and spiritual leaders.

All of this will be done in prayer, that we will be guided by God to the best decision. Christians trust in that divine guidance. "He leads the humble in what is right and teaches the humble His way."[48] Always, with the Psalmist, the ethical decision maker will pray "for thy name's sake lead me and guide me."[49] In every difficult ethical decision there will always be some ambiguity and lack of absolute clarity. However, the decision must be made, for even *not* to decide, is a decision taken from particular motives, implying certain intentions and leading to certain consequences. Ethical decision making cannot be avoided. It is an inevitable consequence of our possession of our God-given conscience. In the process, we will not stand alone, even though as free and *autexousioi* creatures of God the decision must remain our own. For our decision making takes place within the context of the Church. We are helped by wise counselors and guides whom we find there and above all by God, who gives His Holy Spirit to guide us into all the truth.[50]

[1] Demetropoulos, *op. cit.*, p. 59.

[2] *Sermo de Nativitate.*

[3] Nilos of Ancyra, *Concerning the Eight Spirits of Evil*, Migne PG 79, 1468B.

[4] Luke 12:57.

[5] Origen, *Commentary on John*, 6:51; Migne 14, 289c.

[6] 1 Clement 48:5.

[7] John 7:24.

[8] See Saint Kassianos the Roman, *To Hegoumenou Leontiou, Philokalia*, Vol. 1, p. 89ff.

[9] "Peri Tereseos tou Noos," *Philokalia*, Vol. I, p. 24, 34.

[10] *Ibid.*

[11] Peter of Damascus, *Philokalia*, Vol. 3, pp. 66-67.

[12] Paul Ramsey, *Fabricated Man*, New Haven: Yale University Press, 1970, Chapter 2.

[13] *Chapters on Love*, First Hekatontas, 92.

[14] George A. Maloney, *Man: The Divine Ikon*, Pecos, N.M.: Dove Publication, 1973, p. 114.

[15] "Chapter on Theology," *Philokalia*, Vol. 2, P. 158-59.

[16] John 4th of Constantinople, *De Poenitentia Continentia et Virginitate*, MGP, 88, 1968D.

[17] *Homily 9:3 in 2nd Corinthians.*

[18] See, for example, S. Harakas, "The Ethical Teaching of the Pentekostarion," (Greek) in *Theologia*, 1968, Vol. 39, part 3, pp. 368-374; and part 4, pp. 586-612.

[19] Rinne, *Unity and Uniformity in the Church* (Greek) Thessalonike, *Epistemonike Epiteris Theologikes Scholes*, Parartema No. 7, 15th Volume, 1971, pp. 147-148.

[20] St. Basil, *The Long Rules — 1*, Preface. Tr. Sister M. Monica Wagner, from the Series *The Fathers of the Church*, St. Paul Editions, 1950, p. 16.

[21] *Ibid.*, Question 9, p. 44.

[22] Acts 15.

[23] V. 7.

[24] V. 17.

[25] V. 28.

[26] Epistle 293, Migne 32:1036A.

[27] Matthew 25:31-46.

[28] Romans 12:1b-2.

[29] *Stromata* 2.6, Migne 8, 961B.

[30] *Homily on John* 55, 3, Migne 59, 23.

[31] *On the Priesthood* 4,6.

[32] Galatians 5:22-23.

[33] 1 Corinthians 13:13.

[34] Ephesians 3:17.

[35] Ephesians 5:2.

[36] *Op. cit.*, Question 29, p. 22.

[37] Isaiah 11:2 (Septuigint).

[38] See Stanley Harakas, "An Orthodox Christian Approach to the New Morality," *Greek Orthodox Theological Review,* Brookline, Mass. Vol. xv, No. 1, Spring, 1970, p. 107ff.

[39] *Ibid.,* p. 129.

[40] Maloney, *Ibid.,* pp. 53-56.

[41] Demetrios Tsamis, *The Perfection of Man According to Niketas Stethatos.* (Greek) Thessalonike: Patriarchal Institute of Patristic Studies, 1971, p. 65ff.

[42] Harakas, *op. cit.,* p. 133.

[43] Mark the Ascetic, *Epistole Pros Nicholaon Monazonta, Philokalia, Ibid.,* Vol. 1, pp. 136-137.

[44] *The Long Rules, ibid.,* Preface, p. 17.

[45] *Ibid.,* question 9, 44-45.

[46] See, for example, Alivizatos, Amilkos, *E Oikonomia,* Athens.

[47] Romans 12:2.

[48] Psalm 25:9.

[49] Psalm 31:3.

[50] John 16:13.

Chapter Ten

THE POLITEIA OF THEOSIS: LIVING THE IMAGE AND LIKENESS OF GOD

"The Spiritual way of life (pnevmatikes politeias odos) *is best traveled by deeds, rather than by words."*
(Isidore Pelousiotes, Epistles, 1, 14)

"Christianity demands both correctness of faith and a wholesome way of life (hygienousan politeian)*."*
(Chrysostom, Homily on John 28, 2)

"Christ was incarnated . . . so as . . . to teach us the virtuous way of life (enareton politeian)*."*
(Cyril of Alexandria, On the Trinity, 28)

Ethicians of various persuasions often consider their task fulfilled when the basic theoretical questions of ethics are treated. Others, of a more prescriptive bent seek to articulate that which ought to be done in specific cases. Few ever deal with how the good is in fact done, or conversely how evil is in fact to be avoided. One of the few Orthodox who do this in Ethics is George Mantzarides of the University of Thessalonike School of Theology. Yet, Orthodox Christian Ethics of necessity must deal with this practical dimension, simply because the study of Christian Ethics has as its end the direct contribution of doing the good and avoiding evil. Ethics which is not directly related to the *Politeia* or ethos of life is mere intellectualism. As such it does have some value; but it also is a far cry from the central theme of Orthodox Christian Ethics, which concerns itself with the real growth in the Image of God, the realization in character, motives, style of life, ethos and *politeia* toward true humanity, towards *Theosis*.

Thus, there is need to attempt to clarify the specifics of how evil is to be avoided and good to be accomplished. In our treatment of conscience, we saw that it is perceived to be the focal point where the objective good and our personal appropriation of the good is accomplished. The avoidance of evil and the actual doing of what is good (right, appropriate, fitting, etc.) is the work of the "Concurrent Conscience" (*Synodevousa Syneidesis*) which combines prescription and evaluation with the strong sense of obligatoriness and direction. Conscience makes the good imperative. It, however, as we have pointed out so frequently before, is not an automatic function of our psyche. There is a sense in which it controls us, in which it directs, determines, guides and influences us. However, our thoughts, will, self-determination, prayer, faith, etc. also influence the strength and power of our conscience. Conscience guides our actions; however, our choices also influence our conscience. Thus, St. Nikodemos of the Holy Mountain advises, showing the interplay:

> Use all means, brother, to keep your conscience pure in thoughts, words and deeds, let it always remain blameless, let it never reproach you and gnaw at you for anything. If you do this, it will gain strength both in your inner and outer actions and, becoming master over all your life, will govern it rightly. A pure conscience will make your life blameless, for then it will be sensitive and strong for good against evil. Conscience is the law, inscribed by God in the hearts of men, to shed light on their path and guide them in righteousness, as the Apostle Paul teaches, calling it "the work of the law written in their hearts" (Romans 2:15). On the basis of this saying, St. Nilus gives the following advice: "In all your works follow the guidance of conscience like a lamp."[1]

Patristic tradition accords the practical and active guiding function to the conscience. Thus, St. John Chrysostom notes that we are in fact "guided by the teacher found in our human nature, the conscience."[2] "For," in the opinion of Clement of Alexandria "the conscience is excellent for the exact choice (of the good) and avoidance (of evil), having as its foundation the sure, correct life."[3] And St. Basil relates the conscience with the actual doing of the good in the following passage:

> Now this is the definition of vice: the wrong use, in violation of the Lord's command, of what has been given us by God for a good purpose. Similarly, the definition of the virtue which God requires of us is: the use with a good conscience of these same gifts in accordance with the Lord's command.[4]

This last passage indicates quite clearly that from the Orthodox Christian perspective, the doing of the good, will of necessity be connected and intimately related to the whole relationship of the person with God, i.e. the divine economy of redemption which restores the potentiality of "likeness," fulfills the "image" and directs the whole of life toward Theosis. There can be no adequate discussion of avoiding evil and doing the good which proceeds from a perception that the moral life is somehow autonomous and divorced from the spiritual and religious realities as expressed in the Orthodox Christian understanding of the good. The moral life is understood as the life and *politeia* in Christ of the new people of God, an aspect of the mystical communion of the faithful with Christ, within the total life of the Church, its faith, worship, ethos and *bioma,* (which may be translated as "life-style"). Though, as we have seen, various levels of moral and ethical life are spermatically shared by all of humanity, its fullness cannot be known except from within that unique divine-human relationship and reality which is the Christian life and experience. Ethics in practice is ontological, effecting the very being of life, in which life is transfigured and transformed and in which the good is personally experienced, lived and realized. It is at once a present experiential reality which draws faithfully on the tradition of life and faith of the human and specifically Christian tradition of the past as well as the expected and hoped-for eschatological fulfillment of all things.[5]

However, even though this is the context of the doing of the good and avoiding of evil, these do not occur in some automatic fashion. Christian experience has noted that only in a most restricted sense is Augustine's dictum "love God and do what you want" true. There is a discipline, a panoply of guidance and direction required so that we may, in fact, avoid evil and do good. Centuries of Christian experience teach that we do not come to the virtuous living of *Theosis* haphazardly and without specific and close attention to the task. "This, at all events, must be recognized that we can observe neither the commandment of the love of God itself nor that referring to our neighbor, nor any other commandment, if our minds keep wandering hither and yon . . . for one's action must be consistent with the aim, inasmuch as rational ends are not reached by irrelevant means . . . so the Christian directs every action, small and great, according to the will of God, performing the action at the same time with care and exactitude, and keeping his thoughts fixed upon the One who gave him the work to do."[6]

Thus, we hold that the actual practice of the good and the conquering of its opposite is not a matter indifferent to Orthodox Christian Ethics, but rather its concrete and specific purpose and goal. We also see that this is a chief responsibility of that seat of our ethical life, the conscience, seen in the whole context of the journey of human life from Baptism to Theosis. This *politeia,* however, implies a certain "care and exactitude" and the employment of "relevant means." This chapter is an attempt to articulate some of these means in a concrete manner. We will first focus on those elements of Orthodox Theology which speak most directly to the practical issue of doing the good. This will be followed by a closer look at some of the elements from the tradition of faith which speak specifically of overcoming sin and evil, on the one hand, and doing the good, on the other. The final section will seek to treat the issue in its social context.

The Theological Background

As has been made manifestly clear, Orthodox Ethics is inseparable from the doctrines of the Orthodox Faith. Many aspects of the faith have been focused upon in this study relating doctrine to ethics: Apophaticism, Divine Energies, Creation and Natural Law, Revelation, Christian Anthropology, the Incarnation of Jesus Christ, the presence of the Holy Spirit, the Church, Tradition, Worship, Sacramental life, and Eschatology to mention only a few. Several, however, speak quite directly to the practical issue of action.

The first, most crucial, and most direct, is the Orthodox doctrine of synergy. In brief, the doctrine of synergy is the response of the Greek Fathers to the question of Grace and human will. The patristic affirmation is that while human beings can do nothing without God, God does nothing, regarding goodness, righteousness and holiness, without human cooperation. The implications of this doctrine for Orthodox Christian ethics are immense, especially for the spiritual discipline involved in the practical avoidance of evil and the practical doing of the good. The doctrine of synergy is more than a statement of mere "cooperation." It should first be noted that synergy is integrally related to the Incarnation and to the purpose of the Incarnation, the Theosis of humanity. Inevitably, in its definition of the Christological dogma of the Church came to finally affirm-by the inner logic of the doctrine—that the Divine-Human reality of Jesus Christ possessed two distinct wills, the divine and the human. Inasmuch as the restoration and transfiguration of our humanity is directly related to the incarnational reality (the patristic "that which is not assumed, cannot be healed"), the Christian life, its ethos, *bioma* and *politeia,* that is, the life which is the subject matter of Orthodox Christian ethics, is consequently formed by these two wills, the divine and the human.

This means that the ethical life is the product and outcome of the divine energies, i.e., grace, together with the exercise of human will. It is customary to focus on the soteriological dimensions of this truth. God has acted in history and especially in Jesus Christ for humanity's salvation. That divine action is the free, unconstrained outpouring of divine concern for the well-being and restoration of mankind to its original divinely given goal, which had been interrupted by human sin. However, Orthodox theology has always rejected all theories of predestination and electionism as well as universalism of *apokatastasis* which implied in one way or another that persons would be saved without their own desire and willing cooperation. Just as the divine and human wills in Jesus Christ are distinct, yet in harmony, so, in the question of human salvation the two wills, the divine and human are necessary and requisite. God's Grace does not force human will. Rather God offers His Grace and human beings are called to freely respond, to accept it and incorporate it into their lives. That choice is, like the divine will, not constrained or forced. It is free, allowing the possibility both of acceptance or rejection.

However, the synergy of the divine and human is not ever considered an equal yoking. Orthodox theological anthropology perceives human will, not only as created but also as fallen. As created, it is never to be classed or perceived as essentially equal to the divine, simply because the created is fully and totally contingent, that is, dependent upon the divine. As fallen, the Orthodox doctrine of the fall perceives the human *donatum* of the "image," including the *autexousion* as weakened, distorted and disoriented. Thus, the incarnational understanding of the relationship of the two wills in the person of Christ is reflected in the doctrine of synergy as well. In Christ, the human will, though full, perfect, undistorted and distinct, freely "follows" and "conforms to" the divine will. The divine will leads, the human will follows, so that in practice there is a divine-human will in which the uncreated God leads, and the created human will finds its filfillment, completion and divinization.

The theology of synergy, however, is not restricted to the soteriological plane. It does not refer only to the great events of salvation in history. It also finds its reflection in the personal experience in the Christian ethos. In the living of the Christian life in its particular and specific expressions the general doctrine of synergy applies. In the practical area of doing the good and avoiding evil, in which there is growth in virtue and character, in which we progressively "put off the old man" and "put on the new" and in which we grow from "glory to glory" towards Theosis, the principle of synergy also holds true. Thus, St. Macarios of Egypt writes:

> Through grace and the divine gift of the Spirit each of us is directed toward salvation; in faith and love, struggle and self-determining choice (*proaireseos autexousiou*), it is possible to be drawn to the perfect measure of virtue, so that each is able to inherit eternal life not only through grace but also in justice. For each of us is worthy of perfect progress neither by divine power alone, nor by the contribution of our own perspiration nor again is the perfect measure of freedom and purity achieved only by our own efforts and power, nor alone by the divine hand from above which joins our own. [7]

Thus, from the Orthodox Christian perspective the doing of the good is never a purely human venture nor an event of pure grace. It is always a cooperative enterprise between God and the human person. Even here the interpersonal dimension of the Holy Trinity finds application. The good is not abstract, objective, impersonal. It is the outgrowth of an interpersonal encounter.

Yet, in the living out of the truly human ethos of the life in Christ there is a precedence. The uprooting of sin and the planting of virtues is a synergistic task in which grace takes the lead and the more important place. In the practical life this has a two-fold application. It means that there is need to begin with an affirmation that we alone are not capable of accomplishing the good. It means that trusting ourselves to do the good with our own powers is prideful mistake. We are, in the first instance, to "rely not on ourselves, but on God."[8] Because of human pride and self-centeredness this often has been presented in the patristic literature in a fashion which, when taken alone, seems to leave little import or value to the human component. "It is impossible for man . . . to fly up on his own wings toward this high and heavenly prize . . ."[9] Thus, the startling and ego-crushing first directive in the book *Unseen Warfare*—"One should never believe in oneself or trust oneself in anything."[10] This is why those who would follow Christ are enjoined to deny themselves first."[11]

The second aspect of this affirmation is that all of what we do right, our virtues and goodness is the result of grace. A very strong statement of this view comes from St. Maximos the Confessor.

> He is truly blessed who understands and correctly knows that every action and theory, virtue and knowledge, victory and wisdom, goodness and truth, God performs in us as though we were organs, ourselves contributing nothing to the totality, with the exception of the inclination to desire the good. All of the achievements of the saints evidently were gifts of God. None of them had anything of his own at all, other than the good which had been measured out to him from God the Master in analogy to the gratitude and love of the recipient. And he obtains only those things which the master presents to him as a gift.[12]

This points to a profound truth in a practical sense which is an outgrowth of the fundamental ethical truth that God *is* the good. Every practical good is from God as well. This hierarchy of the Divine over the human must always be kept uppermost by those who would do the good in a practical, experiential manner. Otherwise the very acts are compromised from the beginning and irreducibly tainted by human pride and selfishness.

Yet, this is not to obliterate or minimize the place of the human will in the doing of the good, reducing it to passivity. It is merely to put things in their proper order within the pattern of synergy. A recent exposition of this fact states the correct relationship powerfully and accurately.

> On the road of ascesis and effort, development and progress, fulfillment and divinization, the human being is not alone. In every effort and every struggle, in every sigh and every exaltation of the person toward growth and perfection hidden within, the grace of God responds. "Grace is mystically given to those baptized in Christ; it acts in analogy to our working of the commandments. And grace never stops secretly aiding us, it being up to us to do the good within the limits of our abilities." The virtues are energies of God, Who places them in the human heart. To human beings belongs the struggle, the battles, the efforts and the perspiration. We are able to say, paradoxicably, that God works and man perspires or that "as we fight against sin, the grace of God fights as well." To us belongs the good disposition, the freedom of the desire for the good, but the accomplishment of it (*katergasia toutou*) is left totally to God.[13]

There is in consequence a paradox which sees that grace is the source of our victory, our growth and our development in the doing of specific good acts, the avoiding of specific evil acts, the development of a virtuous character and the elimination of vices from our character; yet, which also concurrently acknowledges the need for the effort and struggle, the commitment and exercise of will of the human partner. God is stamped on the Christian, thus permitting him to "live well."[14] We can then come to affirm the importance of the human *autexousion,* the exercise of deliberate concrete and specific choice in the particular situation and case. All discussion of "free will," deciding against evil and for the good, fighting passions, developing character, avoiding vice, doing the good and being virtuous as human activities must be perceived not only from within the context of the doctrine of synergy but also with the powerful realization that divine grace is chief and primary. Within *that* context we must exercise our will positively, firmly and specifically against the concrete temptations and evils which we face and for the doing of the good. Only in that context do the following words of St. Athanasios lose a certain tinge of Pelagian over-confidence in human ability:

> When you hear virtue mentioned do not be afraid of it, nor treat it as a foreign word. Really, it is not far from us. No, the thing is within us, and its accomplishment is easy if we have the will.[15]

As we shall see below, we are called upon to exert much effort and to exercise our self-determining power in the doing of the good. Yet it is always within the larger context of divine grace. It is framed about by communion of the human and divine which constitutes our true humanity and is exemplified in the great doctrines of Christian anthropology: image, likeness, Theosis. Biblically, on the one hand "God is at work in you, both to will and to work,"[16] and on the other, we are admonished to "work out (our) own salvation."[17] Thus, Scripture, as well as Holy Tradition, the Church and even our own conscience speak in "ought" terms to us, expecting and awaiting our willed response, as though it were totally up to us and our choice. Yet we respond knowing that it is God who gives the growth, and, indeed, in the deepest sense, that every good deed and act "God performs in us as though we were organs, ourselves contributing nothing to the totality, with the exception of the inclination to desire the good." We do toil, struggle, exercise our will in the doing of the good, to be sure. But the doctrine of synergy does not allow that to lead us to trust in our own capacities conceived autonomously from God. St. Paul summarized the doctrine of synergy well when he wrote, "To this end we toil and strive, because we have our hope set on the living God."[18]

The doctrine of the synergy of grace and the human will has direct reference to the doing of the good, and is perhaps the chief operative doctrine on this area of Christian Ethics. However, none of the doctrinal faith of Orthodox Christianity is without reference to the practical life. We refer to some of these doctrines below.

The place of Christ in the Orthodox Christian ethical life is central. As we have seen in the discussion above of the doctrine of synergy, the Christology of the Church is definitive. Were the Christology not that of Chalcedon, but something other, our perception of practically doing the good would be different. An Arian Christology, in which the divine substitutes for the human (perfect God, but imperfect man) leaves no place for the human will and self-determination. God is total, man is nothing. A Nestorian Christology sharply separates the divine and the human in man.

In this view it would appear that ethics is autonomous. The human acts independently of the divine. Ethical choice is a human act devoid of intimate divine grace and support.

Christ also is the guarantor to Orthodox Christian ethical action of its experiential character as an ethos, a *Bioma,* an interpersonal reality. There is a danger in Orthodoxy to over-spiritualize, a danger to theological and ethical and liturgical monophysiticism, which makes the concrete, historical, physical and bodily aspect of the Christian life unreal. However, the Chalcedonian Christ does not permit that, in fact. Orthodox ethics does not draw its content from some spiritualized abstraction or some mysterious platonic "aion" or theoretical metaphysical principle. Such a view leads inexorably to an ethic of "objective" acts performed in obedience to objective principles. Rather, Christian ethics is grounded in the divine economy of the creation of humanity in Christ, the Son, and the ongoing sanctification of humanity by the Holy Spirit. Christ reveals the relational reality of the good. In Ethics our growth as human beings is patterned in accordance to the divine-human reality of Christ. Christ's saving work restores the "likeness" of God to all human beings, giving to all the potential of the new life reaching toward theosis. In a real sense, the whole ethical endeavor consists of our imitation (*akolouthein* and *mimeisthai*) of Christ and our "internalization of Christ through the sacramental life and His Holy Commandments."[19] Specifically, in reference to the doing of the good, Orthodox Ethics sees Christ actually present in His commands, in the good which is to be done. Christ "is hidden in His own Commands"[20] for "the Logos of God is revealed in practical things and embodied in the commandments."[21] There is an intimate connection between the relationship of the believer with Christ, and the practical ethical life. It was Jesus Himself who said: "You are my friends, if you do what I command you;"[22] "Truly I say to you, as you did it to one of the least of these my brethren, you did it to me . . . As you did it not to one of the least of these, you did it not to me;"[23] "If you love me, you will keep my command."[24]

That our relationship with Christ is in part realized with the doing of the good, is evident. Doing the good, is not, of course, the condition of Christ's saving work for us. That is an act of pure grace. Yet, if the image of God is to be realized in us, if we are to properly and appropriately respond to His saving work and if the life of the Christian is to be divinized, of necessity our relationship with Christ will include the practical doing of the good. This is also true to our relationship with the Holy Spirit. The Holy Spirit empowers us to act. Without the Spirit we cannot appropriate for our personal existence what Christ has accomplished for all of humanity and the cosmos. Nor, without the Spirit can we do what is truly good. We cannot do the good by a one-sided development of the merely created dimension of our being, the incomplete and fallen potentialities of our human nature. Doing the good is never a mere private accomplishment, a rule unto one's self, a self-justification, an autonomous accomplishment.

Separation from the Spirit kills the human in us, leads to the death of man, consists of his perdition (St. Basil, *On the Holy Spirit* 16, PG. 32; 141B; 40, P.G. 32, 114A). Without the Holy Spirit we are denied true personhood, we are not fully human. We are a separate form, an incomplete human being, estranged. . . . Only there where the Holy Spirit is, does a truly living human being exist, a whole, complete and perfect human being.[25]

The Holy Spirit is the empowering of our ethical life. In this sense, the divine side of the doctrine of synergy is particularized. From this perspective of the whole, the ethical life is the gift and fruit of the Holy Spirit. All the fruits of the Holy Spirit described by St. Paul in Galatians 5:22 may be understood ethically as well as spiritually ("love, joy, peace, patience, kindness, goodness, faithfulness, gentleness, self-control"), as virtues of the Christian life. In the same manner St. Paul indicates that moral vices ("immorality, impurity, licentiousness, idolatry, sorcery, enmity, strife, jealousy, anger, selfishness, dissension, party spirit, envy, drunkenness, carousing, and the like"), which he calls "the desires of the flesh," are "against the Spirit and the desires of the Spirit are against the flesh."[26] His conclusion is important for our discussion. The Holy Spirit is intimately related to the ethical life—"If we live by the Spirit, let us also walk by the Spirit."[27]

The Trinitarian focus of Eastern Orthodox doctrine has its ethical dimensions, as well. We have seen that since the Holy Trinity is a community of persons in oneness, Eastern Orthodox Ethics perceives the ethical dimensions of Theosis and the Kingdom as inter-personal realtionship.[28] However, it is equally part of the tradition to see the specific requirements of living the ethical life as intimately related to the Holy Trinity, as well. The "entolai" are vehicles for our human meeting with the Holy Trinity. Communion with the Trinity is not only a religious mystical experience, it is a religious ethical experience as well. In the words of St. Maximos the Confessor, Christ, the Logos of the Father,

mystically coexists within each of His commands. God the Father is totally inseparable. He is naturally within His own Logos. Thus, he who receives a divine commandment and does it, also receives the word of God found in it. And he who receives the Logos through His commands, receives at the same time, through it, the Spirit which naturally is found in it . . . Thus, he who receives a command and fulfills it, has received the Holy Trinity.[29]

Another aspect of Orthodox Theological doctrine which has direct relationship to the doing of the good is the teaching of the Orthodox Church that salvation is ontological and not merely forensic. The traditional Protestant interpretation of the Pauline doctrine of justification tended to overshadow the Pauline doctrine of sanctification so that the impression given was that the Christian was "pronounced" saved by God in Jesus Christ, but that no objective real change occurred. Through its doctrine of image and likeness, and theosis, Eastern Christianity affirms, rather, that the Christian life, in fact, implies, results in, and requires an ontological change in human life. For Orthodoxy

> Salvation is never individualistic; it is never guaranteed by acts of atomistic merit or individualistic virtues. Rather it is the ontological correction of nature, its perfect therapy, the restoration to that which is in accordance to nature (*kata physin*) on the road to perfection in accordance to God. It is the restoration of the communion of Saints in Christ, the grace of perfection and divinization in the image of the Trinity.[30]

This view, then, speaks directly to the doing of the good. The Christian who has been "baptized in Christ" is not merely pronounced righteous, nor is this new life only celebrated and "manifested" in the liturgical and sacramental life. It affects directly our thinking, feeling and doing. The sixth and twelfth chapters of St. Paul's letter to the Romans are profound statements of the ontological character of the Christian life, with special reference to ethics. Baptism means that "we too might walk in newness of life."[31] Our old sinful self is dead, not merely as a pronouncement for "we are no longer enslaved to sin,"[32] but rather "alive to God in Christ Jesus."[33] This expresses itself in an ethos and a *Bioma* which is clearly ethical in character.

> Let not sin therefore reign in your mortal bodies to make you obey their passions. Do not yield your members to sin as instruments of wickedness, but yield yourselves to God as men who have been brought from death to life, and your members to God as instruments of righteousness.[34]

Before Baptism we are slaves to sin and instruments of it. After, we are slaves to God in "obedience, which leads to righteousness."[35] The ethical dimension of the ontological new reality results in our becoming "obedient from the heart to the standard of teaching to which we are committed."[36] The avoiding of evil and the doing of good are aspects of this ontological relationship to which we are called to respond willingly and responsibly. "Do not be conformed to this world, but be transformed by the renewal of your mind, that you may prove what is the will of God, what is good and acceptable and perfect" is the guidance of Romans 12:2. The balance of that chapter is in large part, a series of ethical injunctions and directives summarized in the 9th verse: "hate what is evil, hold fast to what is good" and the 31st verse, "Do not be overcome by evil but overcome evil with good." There is no life in the fullest sense of the word without the doing of the good and conforming life to the divine will. Irenaeos put it as boldly and clearly as possible:

238

It is good to obey God and to believe in Him and keep His commandments, and this is life for man. Not to obey God is evil and this is man's death.[36]

Another aspect of Orthodox doctrine deals with the relationship of knowledge and action, or to use the traditional terms *theoria* and *praxis*. The issue is raised primarily in the context of the mystical and monastic life. Orthodox spiritual writers separate the two only for purposes of discussion and instruction. In fact, however, they are never perceived as standing apart. "Just as soul and body in synthesis make up the human being, so praxis and theoria in combination make for true wisdom" says, representatively, St. Maximos the Confessor.[37] Often this combination of theoria and praxis is cast in mainly mystical and monastic terms, so that theoria is essentially the mystical vision of God and praxis is confined to ascetical practices such as fasting and the avoidance of sleep (*agrypnia*). However, it is never limited to this perspective, though it always includes them. The broader understanding relates knowledge of God and truth to action and specifically ethical action. Thus, "theoretical understandings without praxis die out; and actions, deprived of theoria, wither away," says Neilos the Ascetic.[38]

The doing of the good is of necessity related to knowledge of the good. The relationship is reciprocal. The Fathers of the Church point frequently to the fact that the knowledge of God is never merely intellectual. Rather, it is an outgrowth of the empirical and experiential. Negatively stated this position says, "If we are inattentive to praxis, we will become totally barren of true knowledge (*philosophia*)."[39] The same author refers to St. Basil as an example of one who arrives at truth as "having received through experience, and thus having been taught, he transmitted truth to us."[40]

But the opposite is equally true. We can in truth do the good and avoid evil only with knowledge. Accidental good deeds and unreflective avoidance of evil may have some value. (However, St. John of Damascus denies this possibility in his *Logos Psychopheles).* But from the perspective of motive, intent and conformance to divine will, there is an unexceptional requirement that praxis be informed by theoria. This is especially true in Orthodox Ethics. The conscience requires that our struggle against evil and for the good be enlightened and conscious. There is "neither sure praxis without theoria, nor true theoria without praxis for it is necessary that praxis be thought through (*ellogimon*) and for theoria to be practiced (*emprakton*). This, so that evil might be made powerless and that virtue be powerful . . . He who exemplifies the embodying of knowledge with deeds and who gives soul to his deeds with knowledge has found the exact way to do the work of God (*theourgia*)," is the teaching of St. Maximos the Confessor.[41]

The goal is *praxis lelogismene,* i.e. "a rational, intelligent, thought through act."[42] By this is meant acts which are based on knowledge, understanding, true faith and right doctrine. That is why, in the same context, Maximos the Confessor notes that "God is not honored with mere words, but rather through works of righteousness. They proclaim the divine majesty much more than do words.''[43]

There is a sense in which the two—theoria and praxis—are means to deeper and closer relationship with God, and therefore, to the fulfillment of the human telos, Theosis. To be involved in seeking out the will of God, searching for understanding of the good and for power and strength to do it, is a means in itself toward Theosis. The ethical enterprise, both as thought and action is a constituent part of the struggle toward the realization of the image and likeness, as well as an embodiment of it. St. John of Damascus puts it well when he says that the truly blessed person is the one

> who seeks after virtue and does it and who persistently and seriously seeks to examine what is the virtuous thing. Through this effort he approaches God and mentally comes to be with Him. [43]

However, when this teaching of theoria and praxis is put in the context of the teaching on synergy, another dimension arises. From the side of our willing and doing, knowledge and action interact and contribute to growth toward theosis. There is, however, another important perspective arising from the Orthodox understanding of synergy. Just as the divine will is dominant over the human will in Christology, and just as grace is superior to human will in the Christian life, so it is that theoria and praxis are made possible for us in a transcendent sense by the divine energies. Our doing of good, as well as our knowledge of virtue (praxis and theoria), are not only related to each other, but are, finally, the result of God's grace in our lives. We act. But it is He who acts through us, using us, so to speak as his willing tools. Again we quote Maximos the Confessor,

> God performs in us, as His organs, every praxis and theoria, virtue and knowledge, victory and wisdom, and goodness and truth. We ourselves contribute nothing to the whole other than the disposition of wanting the good. . . . All of these united together, flash the single glory and brightness of God. [44]

Action informs knowledge, knowledge gives value to action: but both are essentially the fruit of grace.

A final aspect of the theological background is the communitarian dimension of doing the good. The individual Christian is a contradiction in terms. [45] We have noted that Orthodox Christian Ethics at heart is relational in character. God, the Divine Trinity, alone is the good. Human experience of the good, especially in the realization of the image of God is constituted by a divine-human sharing and koinonia. There is no objective, impersonal good. The good is interpersonal, because God is Trinity. The good, for humanity, is inter-personal because it is perceived and lived in the divine-human encounter of creation, redemption sanctification and theosis. That is why, from an Eastern Orthodox point of view, a purely rational, deductive ethic, or, on the other hand, a purely empirical inductive ethic are equally unsatisfactory. The proper relationship with God is in one sense the presupposition for the doing of the good. On the other, it is a condition of that right relationship.

> Fulfilling the commandments of God is not a simple completion of the correct stance of man in relationship to Him. The believer keeps the command of God, precisely because he is in direct relationship and communion with Him. Keeping the commands of God, he cultivates and strengthens his koinonia and unity with God. If man ceases keeping God's commandments, he may not say that he maintains a real relationship and communion with Him. Only he who keeps the commandments of God truly loves God and lives in His love (see John 14:21).[46]

There is, however, another dimension of this relational, communitarian dimension of doing the good. As we have seen in the previous chapter, ethical decision making must properly take place within the ecclesial context and never utterly alone; the good is better done and evil is better avoided and overcome in community. This is a long and widely held Christian perspective and viewpoint. It is, at heart, an outgrowth of the belief that there is no salvation outside the Church, that the Church is the mystical body of Christ in which we live and grow toward Theosis. Just as we cannot know God and come into relationship with Him receiving the fruits of redemption, without the Church, in the same manner the fullness of the struggle against evil and the doing of the good is always perceived to be a communal, ecclesial experience. Individualism has never been a dominant theme in Eastern Orthodoxy, though personal responsibility, has.[47]

There is a responsibility we have for others in the avoidance of evil and in the doing of the good. That also means that others have an equal responsibility for us. "Whoever causes one of these little ones who believe in me to sin," Jesus said, is subject to great punishment. And "Woe to the man by whom temptation comes."[48] St Paul adds, "Brethren, if a man is overtaken in any trespass, you who are spiritual should restore him in a spirit of gentleness . . . bear one another's burdens, and so fulfill the law of Christ."[49] "He who says he is in the light and hates his brother is in the darkness still. He who loves his brother abides in the light, and in it there is no cause for stumbling."[50]

The doing of the good is thus to be seen as taking place in the community of others and not as a purely individual affair. Perhaps, among the Fathers, St. Basil saw this most clearly in his struggle to establish his views on coenobetic monasticism as opposed to the solitary monasticism of the anchorites. His words, though uttered in that context reflect a larger and deeper truth about the Christian life, applicable to this very point. "Community life," he holds, "offers more blessings than can be fully and easily enumerated. It is more advantageous than the solitary life for both preserving the goods bestowed on us by God and for warding off the external attacks of the enemy." The individual is restrained from doing evil and supported in the doing of good by the community environment. Further, the solitary life is "fraught with perils" of which "the first and greatest is that of self-satisfaction . . . since the solitary has no one to appraise his conduct . . ." Secondly the solitary person is unable to either "recognize his own deficiencies nor will he discover the advance he may have made in his manner of acting, since he will have removed all practical occasion for the observance of the commandments." Further, the solitary has no way of exercising virtues such as humility, love and every other "good and pleasant thing." St. Basil's conclusion is applicable to the whole Christian life, and its ethical dimension especially:

> So it is an arena for the combat, a good path of progress, continual discipline, and a practicing of the Lord's commandments, when brethren dwell together in community.[51]

Avoiding Evil

In harmony with the apophatic approach of Eastern Orthodox Theology in general, and ethics in particular, it is first necessary to emphasize the need to approach the issue of doing the good negatively. It is a generally accepted approach in Eastern Christian spiritual and moral writings that the avoidance of bad practices and the passions is the first step in growth toward the fulfillment of the divine image in our lives. Thus, St. John of Damascus writes that it is important and necessary for "those who desire to achieve virtue" to know that "they must make great effort to withdraw from evil."[52] The avoidance of evil is a necessary prerequisite for the doing of the good. Much of the Scriptural guidance in moral matters is negative in character. The Decalogue, as noted previously, counsels avoidance of certain kinds of action. In the Psalms we are counseled to "Depart from evil, and do good"[53] and in the New Testament we are urged to "turn away from evil and do right."[54] Much of St. Paul's moral exhortation is toward encouraging his readers to avoid specific vices: "Do not be conformed to this world;" "hate what is evil," "do not be haughty . . . never be conceited," "repay no one evil for evil;" "Beloved, never avenge yourselves;" "Do not be overcome by evil but overcome evil with good;" are such injunctions from just one of St. Paul's chapters.[55]

This emphasis on the rejection of evil is not mere moralism. It is the outgrowth of our baptismal entrance into the life of the Holy Spirit. The themes of the "death of the old man" and the "birth of the new man" in baptism are familiar. St. Paul emphasizes that the death of the "old man" in baptism took place so that "we might no longer be enslaved to sin"[56] with the result we must consider ourselves dead to sin. He says:

> Let not sin therefore reign in your mortal bodies, to make you obey their passions. Do not yield your members to sin as instruments of wickedness, but yield yourselves to God as men who have been brought from death to life.[57]

242

We see here a close connection between the ontological and eschatological side of baptism and its ethical application. Baptism changes things. The power of sin no longer has dominion over us, we are no longer "slaves to sin," "our old self is crucified" and dead. It is accomplished and we must consider ourselves as "dead to sin." Yet that ontological change of status and relationship needs to be actuated and realized by choice and action on our part. St. Paul speaks deontologically, in "ought" terms: "Let not sin therefore reign . . . ;" "Do not yield your members to sin . . . ;" "yield yourselves to God . . ." In baptism we are renewed and yet we must also act to be renewed. In baptism we are no longer enemies of God, but friends and members of His household, the Church. Freed from satan's domination we are united with Christ.

It is no accident however, that satan must be rejected, first. The exorcisms preceding the baptismal service require a conscious, deliberate rejection of evil: "Do you reject satan? . . . and all of his works . . . ?" are ancient words of the Baptismal ritual.

The new condition and relationship following Baptism is both a given and, concurrently something to be realized. In "image and likeness" terms the potential is restored, but we must now consciously fight against evil and do the good. Though we are forgiven, though we no longer belong to satan and now are members of the household of God we have within us "the passions which must be overcome" through the power of God and the exercise of our own self-determining action, i.e. synergistically.

The passions remain empirically and must be uprooted. What is referred to as the "passions" is also at once an ontological description of what we are, as well as a way of acting, a doing of evil. Ontologically, "the passions" is a description of our still disordered condition. Ethically, the passions are specific acts and modes of behavior which are evil. Thus, in Clement of Alexandria's words, "passions are an unnatural (*para physin*) movement of the soul"[58] and Nemesios says "action is called a passion when it is against our true nature."[59] It is possible to distinguish theoretically between passions (*pathe*) and sins (*amartemata*) as does Abbas Dorotheos:

> The passions are one thing, and sins are another. The passions are anger, pride, hatred . . . and other such things. But sins are the actions (*energiai*) of the passions, when one actively does them.[60]

In practice, it is difficult to separate them. For example, jealousy is sinful if it is entertained and cultivated rather than opposed and struggled aganist whether it expresses itself in acts of not. For Christian Ethics dispositions and overt actions are both "movements of the soul." What is meant, then, by "passions" is a deeply imbedded intellectual and volitional assent and love for whatever is in disharmony and disorder with our true nature which is the divine image and likeness. More concretely

> it is an evil and difficult to uproot assent of the mind and will of the heart which finds pleasure in fearful desires and evil

cravings; it is being captured by an unrestricted longing for objects of the senses (*ta aistheta*).[61]

The Fathers all speak of the passions as sources of evil in our lives, though in their evaluation and their ordering and numbering they differ somewhat. One of the typical simpler approaches focuses on three passions, which are then reduced to two root passions. Evagrios finds the three basic passions in the three temptations of Christ: gluttony (*gastrimargia*), greed (*philargyria*) and pride (*philodoxia*). These are followed by all the other passions. Thus "one does not fall into the hands of lust if one does not first fall into gluttony; one does not get shaken by anger, if one does not battle first on behalf of food, money or glory."[62] Of these pride is the "first offspring of the devil." Evagrios then reduces the three to two: desire and anger. The first of which is perceived to be the expression of all the passions of the flesh and the second, the expression of the passions of the spirit. St. John of Damascos[63] more systematically reduces the passions to these same elements. He divides them into passions of the soul and passions of the body. In the first group he numbers passions such as impiety, blasphemy, anger, bitterness, gossip, hypocrisy, ingratitude, insensitivity, flattery, etc., in all, fifty-four specific passions of the soul. Passions of the body are hedonism, drunkenness, fornication, homosexuality, theft, murder, practice of magic, consulting horoscopes, laziness, gambling, etc., in all, thirty-four in number. However, for St. John of Damascos "The roots of all these passions, their first causes, one might say are love of pleasure, love of self and love of money, from which is born every evil."[64] It is forgetfulness, laziness and ignorance which allows them to appear and grow. But, "the first cause of all of these, their most evil mother, is pride (*philautia*) . . ."[65]

In between we may find in the tradition lists of passions and analyses of them of various lengths. For example in a work attributed to St. Anthony, twelve passions of the soul are listed[66] and Evagrios of Pontos counts eight,[67] and Peter of Damascus considers six to be the chief ones "surrounding men."[68]

What is central is the realization that there nests within us, in addition to all the good elements of the divine image, a disordered disharmonious tendency, ever ready to interfere with the life appropriate and fitting to a child of God growing in the divine image and toward Theosis. How do we succumb to the passions? What is the process by which we are overtaken and by which we submit to their power and influence over us? Of course, every person and every situation has its specific and peculiar circumstances. There is no rigid pattern. However, it is useful for our purpose to investigate the process in order to gain insight into how we come to do evil.

One of the descriptions of this process is by Theodore, Bishop of Edessa:

Every agreement of our thoughts with some prohibited desire, that is, hedonistic attraction, is a sin for the monk. At the

244

beginning, our thoughts, through our passions begin to darken our mind; then the soul submits to the attraction, unable to withstand the struggle. This is followed by what is called assent (*synkatathesis*), which is, as has been noted, sin. When it lasts for a period of time it provokes that which is called a passion . . .[69]

In one sense the passions are at the source of our evil deeds. In another, they are the result, the habitual doing of evil. In the first sense, in the classical Greek idea, it is "the instinctive and irrational part of the human soul." In the second it refers to the understanding of passion "as a deeply rooted condition of evil," "the overtaking of the human spirit by moral disease." This is distinguished from sin which is perceived to be a specific and distinct act rather than a habitual ethos. Further,

> evil does not come from the outside to the soul; rather, it is the willing submission of the soul to things or conditions and the exaggerated and inappropriate attachment to them.[70]

In the *Letter to the Monk Nicholas,* Mark the Ascetic describes in detail the inner process by which we come to do evil. Through a lack of care (*ameleian*) and ignorance (*agnoian*) and laziness (*rathymian*), we fail to foresee the consequences and protect ourselves from their realization. The passions which are hidden deeply within us are activated from without. The result is that our minds are corrupted, by allowing our thoughts to assent (*te ton logismon synkatathesei*) to temptation. These external influences (the devil, temptations, objects, food, riches, praise, etc.) secretly attack us and then conquer us, giving rise to a host of vices:

> most evil envy, zealous love of evil, conflict, argument, hatred, bitterness, remembrance of evils, hypocrisy, anger, pride, boasting, favor-giving, self-pleasing, love of money, spiritual torpor (accidie), desires of the flesh, submission to pleasures in imagination, faithlessness, disrespect, cowardice, sorrow, contentiousness, laxity, excessive sleep, conceit, self-justification, self-aggrandisement, boasting, insatiableness, profligacy, greed, and hopelessness, the worst of all.

St. Mark also points to the evil which sneaks in to accompany even the good which we do. For often we do the good not for its own sake but for the praise and honors which it draws from others. The good things we do often have been "intertwined with the other passions, and have mixed good accomplishments with evil and fleshly attitudes, therefore making them unacceptable and unclean."[71]

How are the passions to be fought and overcome?

We note here some of the more general responses to that question. For evil to be avoided and good to be done, there is need for human beings to possess "knowledge and understanding, and the discernment of good and evil, as well as self-determination."[72]

The chief knowledge is to recognize that evil and sin arise from our separation from God. Avoiding evil means, by definition, that we bridge the gap between ourselves and God. This requires a two-fold act on the part of the person who would avoid evil, the commitment to God and the desire to submit to His will on the one hand, and repentance for evil and sin, on the other. We must be converted to God.

Conversion to God means that our will denies the world and takes up a single stance: orientation toward God. What is the world that we should deny it? St. Isaah the Syrian responds: "The World is an inclusive name which is identified with the passions." The world, that is, the passions, make human beings distant from God; they create a situation of brokenness and of scattering. The soul finds itself wandering outside of itself . . . The denial of the world, then, is a return of the soul to its true self. It is a self-gathering, a restoration of our spiritual existence, which turns back to be united with God.[73]

Conversion, as described above is an act of will, "a continuous effort by our will, seeking to keep us continually facing in God's direction."[74] An extension and necessary aspect of this act of continuous conversion is the rejection of our sins and evil deeds. This is called repentance. In fact, it is difficult to separate our turning toward God, the source of all good, and our rejection of evil. Thus St. Maximos the Confessor notes:

He who first does not come to his true self through the rejection of unnatural passions (*para physin pathon*), cannot be raised up to the source of his own being, i.e. God . . .[75]

In one sense, repentance and the rejection of our passions, sins, and evil deeds is the presupposition of the restoration of unity with God. On the other hand, the desire to be with God, what we have described as conversion, leads to repentance. Thus, the Prophet Jeremiah can put improper relationship to God first and its evil results when he presents God as saying . . .

. . . my people are foolish,
they know me not;
they are stupid children,
they have no understanding.
They are skilled in doing evil,
but how to do good they know not.

The relationship however, is reversed in a subsequent passage:

. . . They are all adulterers,
a company of treacherous men.
They bend their tongue like a bow;
falsehood and not truth has
grown strong in the land;
for they proceed from evil to evil,

and they do not know me,
says the Lord.[76]

But just as conversion is an act of will, so also is repentance. We must choose to repent. Repentance, is a state of mind, a constant turning away from evil and sin

> To say "I repent," means that I change the thoughts and opinions which I have had until now in my mind and which I expressed in my daily life with sinful deeds and words. Repentance means that I regret every sin and violation of God's law which I have done. I reject and condemn them and I make a sincere decision not to do them again. Rather, I will have my opinions, my thoughts, my words and my actions and my whole life turned in God's direction.[77]

Conversion to God and repentance for our sins is a complex, but necessary first step for the overcoming of evil in all of its multifarious dimensions. Unless these take place, there can be no overcoming of evil. "For when the ignorance of God exists in the soul, the passions cannot be healed, and remaining there, they poison the spirit, like a long-term ulcer permeating it with evil.[78]

A second step in avoiding evil, is to uproot the causes of evil which find their place in our soul. The causes of evil are myriad. The Scriptures and the Fathers point to many expressions of the sources of the passions, as we have seen above. St. Maximos the Confessor, for example reduces them to "the passions, the demons and to evil motives."[79] Yet, it is a generally accepted affirmation that self-love (*philautia*) seems to sum up the source of most evil which we cause in our lives. Thus, Thallasios says "If you wish to be freed from evil, you must put away the mother of evils, self-love."[80] St. Maximos repeats, "The beginning of all the passions, is self-love."[81] St. Gregory of Sinai thus holds that it is self-love which feeds all the passions.[82] St. Maximos analyzes the effects of self-love:

> As has been said many times, self-love is the cause of all the passionate attitudes for from it are born the three most general desiring dispositions: gluttony, love of money and vain glory. From gluttony, fornication is born. From vain glory comes pride, and all the others follow from these three, such as anger, and depression, and remembrance of evil, and envy, and back-biting (*katalalia*). All these passions bind the mind to material things, and drag it down to the earth . . .[83]

If we are to avoid evil, then there is need above all to recognize that self-love needs to be controlled and watched over with great care. It is powerfully deceptive and there is need for constant vigilance to overcome its ever present influence. It is, at heart, a concern for motive, recognizing that even the best of acts, in conformity to the divine will must also be done from the right motive, as we saw above in the chapter on Ethical Judgment.

247

More practically, evil is overcome by a complex set of activities known under the collective name of *askesis*. Askesis is struggle; it is the various methods used to fight the passions and evil habits, to overcome temptation. Askesis is exercise, practice and training. It is the exercise of will toward growth in the direction of Theosis. Askesis has wide application in the Orthodox Christian life. It has been used to refer to the study of Scripture, to the practice of piety, to the devout life in general, to spiritual discipline such as prayer and fasting, to austere asceticism, and as a technical term referring to the monastic life with special reference to the penitential practice, etc. Here we speak of it as the struggle against sin, evil and the passions. ''When evil persists, askesis needs persistence''[84] says Thallasios. ''Just as one is not able to know exactly the pathological causes of bodily illness without much experience in the medical science, so one cannot properly know the passions of the spirit without much askesis regarding them'' says the Monk Niketas.[85] And St. Symeon the new Theologian argues that the person who involves himself in the practice of *askesis* needs not only to avoid evil actions, but needs also to free himself from evil attitudes and thoughts.[86] Askesis, of course, has a positive aspect, as well, i.e. the cultivation of virtue and as an aid to the doing of the good. Here, we are interested in overcoming evil and sin through askesis.

There is need to understand askesis in the broadest sense possible as it is applied to the Christian life. Thus, one commentator identifies Christianity with askesis. Askesis has as its purpose ''the return of human beings to the fullness of personal life and communion, toward renewal and transfiguration. . . . The whole of Christianity is the life of askesis. The total life of the faithful is a path of ascetic practice in imitation of Christ, the Apostles and all the Saints, a path of painful askesis and repentance within the grace and love of God, so that we can enter into a spiritual life, a life which is governed by God and doxological at its center.''[87]

Some of the elements of askesis which have particular application to the avoidance of evil are the following:

Askesis in the ethical sense, first and above all, requires *attentiveness* and sensitivity to the moral and spiritual significance of our behavior. Awareness of ourselves, our thoughts, speech, motives, purposes, attitudes, choice of means and courses of action, as well as of our actual actions is a basic element of the struggle to overcome evil and sin. Carelessness on this issue, meaning a lack of awareness and sensitivity, inevitably means that we will perceive evil and sin in our lives as a natural and normal condition. There will never be a recognition of it as *para physin,* but only at most, as troublesome and bothersome. ''That which gives birth to evil passions is people's indifference (*ameleia*) and the laxity (*rathymia*).''[88] ''Ameleia'' which is used in patristic writings primarily in a moral sense, is condemned precisely because it deadens our awareness of evil and sin in our lives. The positive side of this often referred to in the ascetical literature of the Church as *watchfulness over the heart (phylake tes kardias)* perceived to be care over what enters into the heart and mind, and by extension, protection and prevention of evil influences entering into our consciousness. St. Basil compares this watchfulness over what enters into our hearts and minds as to a lightning rod which channels evil and sin away from our inner, spiritual well-being. [89]

If self-love is perceived to be the source of most evil and sin in our lives, then it is clear that not thinking highly of ourselves will be a chief means of combatting evil and sin. Thus, in the Beatitudes Jesus describes the true life of the disciples beginning with His description of them as "poor in spirit" (Matthew 5:3) meaning those who are fully aware of their spiritual need and poverty. *Humility* (*tapeinophrosyne*) is not a false demeaning of one's self, a "putting one's self down." It is in fact self-knowledge, a recognition of our creatureliness, our spiritual and moral poverty and the limited value and importance of our accomplishments. St. John Chrysostom observes, it is not humility, for one who is in fact a sinner to consider himself a sinner. Rather, humility is when one sees many great things in himself, but does not imagine himself to be great. [90] It is the opposite of the tendency we have to irrationally place our selves first in self-love. "With this did Christ begin the Beatitudes. Just as one who is about to erect a huge building, lays a foundation, thus He set humility in place, for without it, there is no salvation."[91] Just as humility is the mother of all virtues, [92] the elimination of self-love and egoistic pride is an essential step to overcoming evil.

Askesis, further implies struggle and difficult effort against evil habits and temptations to sin. The technical term for this struggle is *agona*. In askesis, in the words of St. Basil, "we should be able to overcome our former habits whereby we lived as strangers to the precepts of Christ. . . . It is no mean struggle (*agona*) to gain mastery over one's wonted manner of acting, for custom maintained throughout a long period takes on the force of nature."[93] The acceptance of *agona* as a principle of life is essential to the overcoming of evil. Evil does not just disappear because we are baptized or converted, or even because we love God. More specifically, this holds true regarding specific temptations. There is no virtue without temptation; temptations exist to be struggled against. There is no "cheap grace." Evil, sin and temptation must be overcome by a synergy of grace and painful and difficult *agona*.

The focus of much of the *agona* against evil is upon the major causes of evil. In monasticism, with its vows of purity, poverty and obedience, the tendency was to take a negative attitude toward things such as property ownership, food, sexual relations, physical comforts, etc. For example, in enunciating the monastic ideal St. Basil defines:

Perfect renunciation, therefore, consists in not having an affection for this life and keeping before our minds the "answer of death, that we should not trust in ourselves." But a beginning is made by detaching one's self from all external goods: property, vain glory, life in society, useless desires . . .[94]

In practice, however, even such a rigorous ideal could not and was not followed completely. It is instructive that concern for property, for example, could not be totally dispensed with even in a cenobetic community or even on the basis of the monk's personal responsibility for an inheritance.[95]

In the struggle against the causes of evil this leads to a general requirement for *enkrateia* variously defined as temperance, continence or abstinence from those things which introduce us to evil and open a door to the presence of evil in our lives. Often temperance, continence or abstinence, because of the strong monastic influence, tend to be perceived as being primarily a rejection of sex or property, food, or human initiative (chastity, poverty, fasting, obedience). This is, however, a distortion. *Engrateia* is the control and limitation over many aspects of life which easily lead to sin and evil. St. John Chrysostom defines it in its most comprehensive dimensions: "This is *enkrateia;* not to be dragged down (*hyposyresthe*) in any thing by the passions."[96] It is not limited to monastics, nor to any one facet of our human existence. Nor is it properly perceived as rejection of what is created by God as good. A good summary of the correct understanding of *engrateia,* as well as a guide and directive for its practice in the struggle against evil comes from a monastic source, as well.

> *Engrateia* is appropriate to all persons. . . . The temperance we speak of deals not only with food, but is comprehensive, that is, it is the avoidance of everything prohibited. It is the work of *engrateia* to desist from every irrational pleasure and to do nothing against the commands willed by God. *Engrateia* is the maintenance of control (*halinos archon* = literally, "an animal bridle which controls desires for food, or money, or glory, in short, all our desiring drives"). Without it, good behavior and traits cannot be born.[97]

And Clement of Alexandria holds that *engrateia* refers not only to sex, but to all "those other things which our soul desires improperly, not satisfied with what is necessary. It concerns itself with the tongue and ownership and proper use and desiring . . ."[98]

The image of the animal bridle, guiding and directing the passions is to be found in Plato and in the Bible, as well.[99] Early Christian writers use it, in the period preceding the development of monasticism. Thus, Polycarp exhorts, "let us bridle ourselves from every evil[100] and Hermas speaks of bridling evil desire.[101] *Engrateia* is less a series of techniques, than attitude which acknowledges that every good thing (food, property, money, sex, recognition, etc.) is subject to evil distortion, and that continuous control and discipline is to be exercised over them. This practical attitude and approach to the whole of life is a major weapon in the arsenal for use in the battle against evil and sin in the Christian life.

There are, of course, many *specific practices* which the experience of the Church has found to be especially helpful in the struggle against evil and sin in the life of the Christian. Chief among these is the cultivation of a healthy conscience. Since much has been said about this in a preceding chapter, we need not dwell on this here. Suffice it to note the following. The Christian growing in the divine image will constantly be seeking to refine his or her conscience, so as to understand that which is evil and that which is good. Meditation and reflection on scripture and theological and spiritual literature will aid in sensitizing us to dimensions of our behavior, attitudes and motives. However, as noted before, this should never be a solitary endeavor.

Holy Confession is a useful and necessary aid in overcoming sin and evil in our lives. Since Holy Confession is properly not only the pronouncement of absolution but the oral confession of repentance and counseling as well,[102] it allows the Father Confessor an important place in the development of conscience as it seeks to identify and battle against particular sins and evils.

Another aspect of the development of conscience in the struggle against evil is the daily, or frequent examination of conscience. Origen, early in the history of Christianity instructed "Let each of us examine his conscience."[103] Basil instructed monks to do so at night, just before going to bed.[104] And St. John Chrysostom, in his usual graphic manner instructs:

> Turning our attention to our own conscience let us dialogue with
> it concerning words, and things and imaginings. Let us examine
> it on how it has been spent on things that ought to have been
> done and on what has been to our harm. Which word was spent
> evilly on abuse, on foul language, on insults? What garment
> stimulated the eye to lust? What thought led to an act harmful to
> us either through our hands or tongue or eyes?[105]

All of this, of course, has as its purpose the cultivation of our awareness of evil and sin, and to move us to do battle against it, as well as to encourage us to obey the dictates of a well-formed conscience.

A set of powerful aids in this struggle against evil and sin is *fasting* and *prayer*. Fasting, which is a form of *engrateia* or temperance dealing on its face, with food, is much more than that. In the monastic tradition overindulgence in food is perceived to be a source of many passions. ". . . much food and feasting arouse the passions of evil in human beings. Temperance (*engrateia*) of the stomach humbles the passions and saves the soul."[106] This refers to a general care concerning the diet. However fasting is a deliberate exercise of more than discipline over the diet with the purpose of exercising and developing self-control over all the passions. It is essentially "a tool (*ergaleion*), which directs those who so desire to moderation regarding desires (*sophrosynin*),"[107] and which serves to "weaken the desires"[108] so that they may be controlled more readily.

However, fasting from food is extended to a moral application, as well, which completes and rounds out the meaning of fasting as it applies to the struggle against evil. Chrysostom asks, "Do you fast? Show me through your works. . . . If you see a beggar, show mercy; if you see an enemy, be reconciled . . . do not fast only with mouth, but with your eyes and hearing, and with all of the members of your body. . .''[109] And another Father instructs: "Do you want to fast properly? Teach your tongue and your eyes and your hands and your feet to fast.''[110]

Fasting is intimately related to prayer in the struggle against evil. The work of demons is overcome only by prayer and fasting, according to Jesus.[111] It is one of the chief weapons in the struggle against sin and evil—"lead us not into temptation and deliver us from evil" we pray in the Lord's Prayer.[112] The Lord directed his disciples to pray that they might "not enter into temptation.[113] In the monastic tradition prayer is perceived to be one of the major means to do battle with the passions. St. Maximos the Confessor for instance, teaches that certain practices such as fasting, restrict the growth of passions and other practices such as prayer and love for God reduce the passions themselves.[114] Thus, another monastic writer holds that the passions of the soul, that is "the forceful sinful drives of the mind" are "eliminated from the soul . . . through fasting and prayer.''[115]

An aspect of prayer in the struggle against evil, sin and the passions is *worship*. In general, the sacraments are powerful influences contending against evil in our lives.[116] The Eucharist, from the earliest period, was perceived—among other ways—as a means for struggle against evil. Thus, St. Ignatios instructed "make all effort to come together to glorify God in the Eucharist, for when you come together frequently, the powers of satan are put down, and his destructive influence is destroyed in the unity of your faith.''[117] A study of the Liturgies of St. John Chrysostom and of St. Basil, including the inaudible prayers, readily convinces the objective reader that the Eucharist is perceived in part by the Church as a weapon in the arsenal against sin and evil. Below are a list of some of the passages from the Liturgies and the Prayers before and after Holy Communion which indicate the ethical aspects of the Eucharist.

> Sanctify both our souls and bodies, and grant that we may serve thee in uprightness all the days of our life. . . .[118]
>
> . . . Implant in us, likewise, the fear of thy blessed commandments; that trampling down all carnal desires, we may pursue a godly life, both thinking and performing such things as are well pleasing to thee. . . .[119]
>
> . . . Look down upon me, a sinner, and cleanse my soul and my heart from an evil conscience. . . .[120]
>
> That to those who shall partake thereof they (the gifts) may be unto soberness of soul, unto remission of sins, unto the fellowship of thy Holy Spirit, unto the fulfilling of the Kingdom of Heaven and unto boldness toward thee; and not unto judgment and condemnation.[121]
>
> . . . grant that no one of us may partake of that holy Body and Blood of thy Christ unto judgment and condemnation. . . .[122]

. . . all things which are good and profitable unto our souls . . . a good defence before the dread judgment Seat of Christ. . . .[123]

. . . Do Thou, O our God, who acceptest these gifts, purify us from every defilement of flesh and spirit, and teach us to perfect holiness in thy fear.[124]

O Master . . . comfort, bless, sanctify, strengthen, fortify those who have bowed their heads unto thee; withdraw them from every evil work; unite them to every good work. . . .[125]

. . . wherefore I beseech thee, have mercy upon me and forgive my transgressions, whether voluntary or involuntary; whether of word or of deed; whether committed with knowledge or in ignorance. And vouchsafe that I may partake without condemnation of thine all-pure Mysteries, unto the remission of sins, and unto life eternal.[126]

Lo, this hath touched my lips, and shall take away mine iniquities, and shall purge away my sins.[127]

We give thanks unto thee, O Lord, who lovest mankind, Benefactor of our souls and bodies, for that thou hast vouchsafed this day to feed us with thy heavenly and immortal Mysteries. Guide our path aright; establish us all in thy fear; guard our life; make sure our steps. . . .[128]

Do thou, the same Lord of All, grant that the communion of the Holy Body and Blood of thy Christ may be for us unto faith which cannot be put to confusion, unto love unfeigned, unto increase of wisdom, into the healing of soul and body, unto the turning aside of every adversary, unto the fulfillment of thy commandments, unto an acceptable defence at the dread judgment Seat of thy Christ.[129]

I thank thee, O Lord, my God, that thou hast not rejected me, a sinner, but hast deemed me worthy to become a partaker of thy Holy Things. . . . Vouchsafe that they may be efficacious for me also unto the healing of my soul and body, unto the averting of everything contrary thereto . . . unto love unfeigned; unto the fulfilling of wisdom; unto the keeping of thy commandments. . . .[130]

. . . and grant that, with a pure conscience, even unto my uttermost breath, I may worthily partake of thy Holy Things, unto the remission of my sins and unto life eternal. . . .[131]

. . . consume thou the thorns of all mine iniquities. Cleanse my soul. Sanctify my thoughts . . . Ever cover me, guard me and keep me from every word and deed which may hurt the soul . . . That being made thy tabernacle through the reception of thy holy Communion every evil thing, every carnal passion may flee away from me as from fire.[132]

It is clear, then, that the Eucharist has as one of its effects the provision of assistance in the battle against sin and evil in our lives and the cultivation of the moral dimensions of the Christian life.

However, we do not worship God, either in sacrament or public prayer, with the exclusive purpose of overcoming sin and evil and doing the good. That would be a self-centered and atomistic understanding of worship. However, since evil and sin are, in fact meonic, i.e. the absence of the good who is God, worship and prayer scatter the power of evil in our lives by filling our being with the awareness, presence and relationship with God, who is the good. God's presence destroys the power of evil.

Other means which Christian experience has found useful in the combatting of evil and sin are the maintenance of *right environment,* the *sense of shame* for evil and the remembrance of *Death and the Last Judgment.* The continuing discussion among psychologists and educators on the relative influence of environment and inborn characteristics (genetic endowment) upon our behavior continues. It is reflected in ethical terms in our discussion regarding human moral capacities and *autexousion.* We have accepted neither of the extremes of the controversy and have seen that both have their place in the development of our moral life. In this case, the tradition of the Church recognizes the powerful influence of environment upon personal moral development. In personal terms (for the issue also has its social and public policy dimension) the Church conforms to the wisdom of the ancients which teaches that "bad company corrupts good character." This was one of St. Basil's arguments for the value of the monastic life. By separating one's self from the evils of the "world" one was in fact separating himself from the influences of those who could corrupt.

> Living among those who are unscrupulous and disdainful in their attitude toward an exact observance of the commandments is dangerous, as is shown by the following words of Solomon: 'Be not a friend to an angry man and do not walk with a furious man; lest perhaps thou learn his ways and take snares to thy soul (Proverbs 22, 24, 25). The words of the Apostle, "Go out from among them and be ye separate, saith the Lord,' (2 Corinthians 6:17) bear also upon this point. Consequently, that we may not receive incitements to sin through our eyes and ears and become unperceptibly habituated to it, and that the impress and form, so to speak, of what is seen and heard may not remain in the soul unto its ruin, and that we may be able to remain constant in prayer, we should before all things else seek to dwell in a retired place. In so doing, we should be able to overcome our former habits whereby we lived as strangers to the precepts of Christ.[133]

While the logic of the above passage holds for the monastic life, it is equally valid for those who are not monks. Choosing who our acquaintances and friends will be, the kinds of entertainment we select (theater, cinema, television, sports, etc.), what our reading material is (books, novels, magazines, pornographic material, etc.), the styles of life we opt for (marriage and family, committed celibacy, "swinging," singles bars, etc.) all have profound influence on our moral life. The right choices lessen the influence of sin on our life; the wrong choices increase it.

The sense of shame is also a means for avoiding evil. Shame, in this sense, means to imagine oneself doing some evil and sinful act in public view and subject to the criticism of others. It never arises unless there is a disharmony between what we profess to be, that is, what our self-image is and the particular act. Thus, if we imagine ourselves doing in public, that which we can conceive of doing only in private we are likely to be shamed into not doing the evil or sinful act. Thus, St. Paul speaks of himself as having "renounced the hidden things of shame."[134] And the Fathers instruct us "to be ashamed of our sins."[135]

There is a long history in philosophical and religious history of the contemplation of death as a means to aid in the avoidance of sin. When coupled with the Christian doctrine of the Last Judgment, it is considered to be a powerful aid in the battle against evil.

Contemplation of death tends to put our acts in perspective. What seems to be of such strong motivating force when we consider only the pleasures, desires and ambitions of this life, loses its strength when the shortness, futility and temporariness of life are measured against it. This need not be a morbid and depressing exercise. Rather it is a practice which helps us put our values in order. It is related to the Christian doctrine of the Last Judgment when the Lord will come "to execute judgment on all, and convict all the ungodly of their deeds of ungodliness which they have committed in such an ungodly way."[136] St. Basil, thus teaches that contemplation of God's judgment is a preservative against sin.

> Take note that the soul is blessed which by night and day revolves about no other concern (*merimna*) than how on the great day, on which all creation shall stand about the Judge and give account of its deeds, it also shall be able easily to discharge the reckoning of the life it has lived. For he who sets that day and hour before his eyes and ever meditates upon his defense before the tribunal which cannot be deceived, such a man will sin either not at all or very little, because sinning comes to pass in us through absence of the fear of God. But to whomsoever there is present the vivid expectation of the threatened punishments, the fear which dwells in such will give them no opportunity of falling into ill-considered actions and thoughts.[137]

Perhaps, however, the most important means for the overcoming of evil is the constant remembrance that sin separates us from God and flies in the face of our very existence as human beings. God's love has been poured out precisely so that we might be freed from the power and burden of sin and evil. To sin is to reject the loving and caring God. It is to turn away from the saving work of Jesus Christ. To violate the commandments is to reject the love of God (1 John 3). Thus, the Bible teaches "By this we may be sure that we know him, if we keep his commandments. He who says 'I know him' but disobeys his commandments is a liar, and the truth is not in him; but whoever keeps his word, in him truly love for God is perfected."[138] Ultimately, the struggle against evil and sin is waged with the strongest of all weapons, *love for God* who gave His Only begotten Son, Jesus Christ, for our redemption from sin, for the forgiveness of sins and for victory over sin. A strong, vibrant personal relationship with God is the most powerful attack against sin and evil in our lives.

Doing the Good

The struggle against evil and sin is intimately related to the struggle for good. In part, doing the good apophatically means rejecting and putting down evil. They are two sides of the same reality, and only theoretically can they be separated. The inter-relationship of the two is graphically described by St. Nilus:

God gave the commands to do good and to avoid sins, but opposing powers make us tend toward evil and it becomes difficult to do good. These sinful powers are not innate to our nature (*symphytoi*) but are brought in from the outside. For this reason the Lord orders us to uproot and plant, dig up and rebuild.[139]

The previous section of this chapter dealt with the "uprooting" and the "digging up." This section focuses, rather, on the "planting" and the "rebuilding."

Much of what is said in the preceding section needs only to be reversed for application here. For example, Holy Confession, obviously is not only negative, in that it helps us *avoid* evil; it clearly is a positive practice which helps us *do* the good. So it is with prayer and worship, askesis and agona, the choice of the proper environment, self-examination, etc. Consequently there is less need for detailed discussion. Suffice the following to be noted.

To do the good, it is necessary to strongly want to do it. Whoever wishes to "plant" and "rebuild" and to consistently do the good must *"will to do (God's) will."*[140] This is a function of our love for God—"this is love, that we follow his commandments,"[141] and this is why Jesus Christ could say to his disciples "If you love me, keep my commandments."[142] St. Basil comments,

By these words He teaches us always to place before ourselves as our goal, in undertaking a task, the will of Him who has enjoined the work and to direct our effort toward Him. . . . It is impossible to do this with exactitude unless it be done as He wills who gave (the commandments). . . . By our painstaking zeal to do the will of God in our work, we shall be united . . . with God. . . . So the Christian directs every action, small and great according to the will of God, performing the action at the same time with care and exactitude, and keeping his thoughts

256

fixed upon the One who gave him the work to do. . . . We should perform every action as if under the eyes of the Lord and think every thought as if observed by Him. . . . The soul that is truly prudent and sound and that possesses a firm conviction of the presence of God would surely not ever neglect to do what is pleasing to God . . .[143]

This love for God, translated into desire to conform one's will to God's will is not automatic. There is much that passes for piety in the form of an emotional religious thrill which remains passive and ethically uninvolved. There is need for commitment to the doing of the good. This is expressed in several ways. First there is the *pledge* given to God to do what is right and good. It is the commitment we make before God's love to live a life of righteousness and discipleship. These two themes are characteristic of the early Christian and patristic ethic (together with faith and love).[144] Thus St. Maximos the Confessor speaks of the *orkos* or pledge which the Christian gives: "He who 'swears unto the Lord' (Psalm 63:12) is to be praised; that is, we speak of each person who pledges his life to God and who, through the truth of the works of righteousness, fulfills the pledge of his good promise." Elsewhere he repeats more succinctly "He who fulfills his promises as one who pledges to God and puts it in practice, is praiseworthy."[145] The pledge we make to do the good is translated into the *offering ourselves in obedience* and conformity with the good. It is a commitment to a transfigured life, formed and reformed by life in the Spirit, leading toward the fulfillment of the divine image in us. The truly ethical Christian,

is after the image and likeness of God, who imitates God as far as possible, deficient in none of the things which contribute to the likeness as far as compatible, practicing self-control and endurance, living righteously, reigning over the passions, bestowing what he has as far as possible and doing good both by word and deed.[146]

Just as evil must be overcome by *askesis* and *agona,* so too is the good realized by them. In the ethical sense, *askesis* and *agona* are not merely the rigid and blind imposition of external rules and commandments upon our behavior. *Askesis* and the *agona* involved are much more than that, since the Christian life is the potentiality of realizing the fullness of our humanity in the divine image. It is the wholeness of true life in the Triune God, in whose image we are created. *Askesis* and *agona,* however, are means by which we "form, reform, and transform" ourselves in that image.[147] Thus, as an orientation of life which demands a continuous effort and struggle *askesis* seeks to transform the whole of our humanness into a vessel of God and to restore us to faithful conformity with the divine will and to our original and truly natural condition. Thus *askesis,* though it has a negative, denying side, is positive in its scope and purpose. Its goal is the fulfillment of the true good for human beings in conformity to the divine and transfigured life of one created in the image of the Divine Trinity. Thus,

> Askesis is an orientation of life which demands unceasing effort and constant overcoming. It is the road by which the struggling human being accomplishes the transfiguration and restoration of nature and its truly natural activity, that is, to become like Christ, to obtain the holy virtues, to receive the great gifts of God, to become an incorruptible vessel of the gifts of the Spirit, to be filled with the Holy Spirit . . . Orthodox askesis is the askesis of the commands of the Lord.[148]

This positively oriented *askesis* in the spirit of the doctrine of synergy, has two foci: force and grace. The first is the effort required by our own choice and will to opt for the good, in the face of temptation to do otherwise. In the ascetic literature, this is called *"bia"* or violence. There is a sense which the Kingdom must be taken by force (Matthew 11:12). All of the practices such as prayer and fasting require force *"bia,"* to be realized and so that they may effect our lives. So too does the obedience to the divine will and the doing of the good have its own element of hard work, including an ascetic form of forced effort. However, this is always coupled with trust in God's grace and aid. For, "without grace, there can be no good works, since they are born and are the expression and the emanation of that grace."[149]

The doing of the good, consequently, is never an isolated and totally individual experience. It is always an *ecclesial* act. The faith which maintains us as members of Christ's body, the Church, is closely tied with understanding, loving, desiring and doing the good. Some have argued, on the basis of improper interpretation of New Testament passages, that there are conflicting teachings about this subject. St. Paul is thus presented as advocating the total sufficiency of faith and St. James holding for an emphasis on good works alone.[150] Suffice it to say that the whole Patristic exegetical tradition denies such an interpretation of either author. Thus, the Fathers characterize a merely intellectual faith which is neither warmed by the heart nor expressed in good works as *apistia*, i.e., faithlessness. Faith as a living experience of the life of grace found and lived in the Church is, of necessity, expressed in good works. Thus, Prof. Karmiris states,

> Faith and good works are two inseparable elements of one and the same thing, and for this reason they cannot be separated, since the one presupposes and includes the other. Faith is closely related and acts through love, whose necessary expressions and fruits are good works, so that without question faith is an ethical work and not only a work of the intellect. Truly the true faith in Christ contains in the first instance the truth, followed then by life in Christ, i.e. good works, which when missing the faith of the Christian which is unaccompanied by good works ceases to be true and becomes false and hypocritical. Consequently the two co-exist by necessity, forming an inner and organic unity.[151]

258

Practically speaking, the doing of the good thus requires a living faith. This faith cannot exist outside the Church, where it is formed, and guided, shared and cultivated, articulated and lived in relation to others, most important of whom are the persons of the Holy Trinity, and the Saints.

Thus, all the aspects of Church life when lived faithfully are powerful aids in the doing of the good: Prayer, Worship, Scripture study, Christian fellowship, Sacramental and devotional life. We have seen in the previous section how all of these are necessary to battle evil and sin. The self-same practices have their application to positive growth in the image and likeness of God both in general and in particular acts. Rather than document by copious quotations, what is obvious in the above, we can focus on some other aspects of ecclesial life which have not been touched upon above. Our good works are not to be seen as acts of self-righteousness. "Doing the good" must never be conceived of as the mere "putting into practice" of some objective principles of ethics. Rather, the good works which we do have to be seen constantly as part of our total relationship with God. We may perceive of them as an offering of our whole existence to God.

> Positively considered, the offering of ourselves to God, understood as sanctification and progress in the virtues and accomplished only with divine grace, presupposes the "yes" of the human person by which the believer lays down and places "his whole life" at the feet of "Christ God" . . . [152]

In reference to God, this offering of ourselves expresses itself as faith, hope and love. In reference to our fellow human beings, believers and non-believers, it is an offering of our being, i.e. our self, our talents, our time and our possessions to our neighbor and through the neighbor to God Himself: "Inasmuch as you have done it unto one of these, the least of my brethren you have done it unto me," says the Lord (Matthew 25:40).

Understanding "good works" not as blind submission to a law, but rather as a self-offering to God is a powerful means for "doing the good." There is an additional aspect of this offering of self which needs to be noted, for it relates doing the good with worship. Just as worship aids in the avoidance of evil, so it is clear that worship aids in the doing of the good. Worship does this in several ways. Worship, especially sacramental worship, is a channel of grace, the realization and expression of our unity with God. As seen above, sacramental unity with God cannot be separated from our mode of behavior, our ethical life. If sin separates, doing the good unites us with God, for doing the good is not a self-righteous deed, but an expression of our fundamental relationship with God. However, there is another side of this truth which contributes to the ethical understanding of the doing of the good. This may be described as the doing of the good as an act of worship. Nicholas Mitsopoulos, in his study *The Nature and Worship-Character of Good Works* distinguishes the worship-character of good works from the sacramental worship of the

Church. The latter, he holds, is worship in its most full and complete sense.[153] But he holds, as well, that whatever good works are done, are acts of worship, as well. If the Christian perceives of his good works as acts of worship offered for God's glory then he has an additional motive for doing them. Good works, Mitsopoulos holds "are an offering and spiritual sacrifice, the rational worship of the faithful. They are so, both in the form of direct and total offering of one's self to God, and the effort to achieve bodily and spiritual purity, as well as in the form of material and spiritual good deeds directed towards other people."[154] Just as Christian love devoid of sacrifice is inconceivable, so worship if devoid of self-offering, cannot be conceived. When we view the doing of the good as a "sacrifice of praise" and a "sacrifice of thanksgiving" we are again aided in the actual doing of it.

In a previous chapter, we spoke of the *imitation of Christ* and of the Saints. It was pointed out that this is never understood to be a slavish, literal and external copying. Further, our imitation of God and Christ is not an imitation of the uncreated divine essence, an obvious impossibility for created human beings. However, "in so much as God has revealed Himself to the world and has made Himself known to human beings, he invites them to an imitation of His love and His goodness, that is, to an ethical likeness" in the words of Orthodox ethicist, G. Mantzarides.[155] "As is the case in every aspect of the Christian life, imitating Christ is never seen as a totally human endeavor. In the Patristic teaching, whenever imitation of God or Christ is commended, it depends entirely on the work of salvation present in the believer."[156] However, we will be strengthened and guided in the doing of the good if we strongly desire to "imitate Christ." Thus, we are instructed by one of the earliest documents in Christian literature "Do not wonder if it is possible for man to be an imitator of God; he can if he wills to (*thelontos autou*)."[157] By willing it we help make it—and the consequent doing of the good—a reality.

Christ thus becomes the prototype for our life "The only sure and available prototype for our life is the Theanthropos. Christ is the prototype for the believer. The Lord Himself offered Himself as a prototype, saying 'I have given you an example, that you also should do as I have done to you.'"[158]

This means that the believer must be familiar with the prototype. It means knowledge not only of the general truths about Christ, and not only a faithful devotion and love for Christ, but also of familiarity with everything about Him, every aspect of His life as a revelation guiding us in imitation of His divine-human life. Thus, St. Basil writes:

Every act and every word of our Savior Jesus Christ is a rule of piety and virtue. For this reason he became man, so that in images he might sketch out both piety and virtue for us, and so that every man and woman should look upon and strive after the prototype. For this reason he bears our body, so that we might imitate his way of life.[159]

Therefore, study of Scripture, meditation on the life of the Theanthropos, familiarity with patristic understandings of the events and actions in the life of Christ serve to heighten our ability to imitate the life of the Lord. The same holds true for the lives of the Saints. Hence, doing the good is made more likely through familiarity with their lives. We conclude these few remarks concerning the imitation of Christ with this most Orthodox and significant passage by Prof. Mantzarides,

> The Christian, as a communicant of the name of Christ, is called, as well, to appropriate into his own life, those things which characterize Christ, so that he might bear the name worthily, and not falsely (see Ignatios, *To the Romans* 3, 2). Whatever characterizes Christ, that ought to characterize the true Christian. Thus, as an imitator of Christ, he is called to a divine change and transfiguration according to the prototype of that which is imitated, in a manner so that Christ lives and acts within him.[160]

To imitate Christ is in fact then, to make sure that "God is at work in you, both to will and work for his good pleasure."[161] To want that, to desire strongly to imitate Christ is a chief way which leads to the doing of the good.

Finally, without holding that the subject has been exhausted, we note that the doing of the good in a particular case is aided by the fact that all right doing and all virtues in general are interconnected. Doing the good, one might say, is aided by doing the good! In particular cases, we are aided in doing the good if our style of life supports the doing of the good in general. The Fathers of the Church use several related words to describe this truth. They speak of *politevma,* which in its primary sense refers to government or social organization. Ethically, however, they use *politevma* as a description of one's mode of life, one's general conduct. On the positive side they thus speak of a *kata Theon politevma,* i.e. "a mode of life in accordance with God,"[162] and *to evangelikon politevma.*[163] By far, however, the most commonly used term is *politeia,* which means in its primary sense, citizenship, polity, constitution, regulation. In the ethical sense it was used widely and frequently by the Fathers to refer to a "way of life," a patterned ethos and style of living. Thus Chrysostom can say "Christianity and the correctness of doctrine demand a wholesome way of life (*hygiainousan politeian*)[164] and Cyril of Alexandria says of Christ, that "He was incarnated . . . so as . . . to teach . . . us the virtuous mode of life (*enareton politeian*)."[165] Thus, a *politeia* which is God oriented, evangelical, healthy and wholesome, Christ-like, etc. in its orientation is in itself a means for encouraging the doing of the good. It is, in fact, another way of stating the influence of a good character (see chapter above).

The Christian *Politeia* in Social Context

The doing of the good is never a private, solitary experience. It always has a communal, social dimension and it is often only that dimension that the good may be done and evil avoided.

This is true, theologically speaking, because of the ultimate nature of the good. The good is the Triune God, who is a community of persons. It is true ecclesiologically speaking because the Church is a community of persons. It is true ethically because both good and evil in practice are more often than not the outcome of the mutual interplay of the influence of people upon people and of social structures upon the individual and visa versa. Were none of this true Christian Ethics could show the necessity of the social dimension of avoiding evil and doing the good by focusing on the epitomy of Christian Ethics: love. We have seen that—from the ethical perspective—agape-love is selfless concern for the benefit and welfare of the other. To love, by definition means to be in relationship with another. Not to love—to be an enemy, to hate, to pursue another is also, by definition, to be related, but in a perverse, destructive un-God-like manner. Both, however, are communal, corporate experiences. No matter how we approach it, the doing of the good and the avoiding of evil are of necessity, social and corporate in large part.

A prototype for the ethical treatment of this reality is the coenobetic monastic system, so strongly supported by St. Basil. As we have seen above in several places, Basil argues that alone we cannot properly progress because there is no one to guide us, correct us, nor is there anyone toward whom we can show similar brotherly concern. The battle against sin and evil in our personal lives requires others in order to be actualized. Further, we deceive ourselves, and open ourselves to devilish deceit much more readily when we isolate ourselves from others, including their criticisms and brotherly correction. Alone, we often will travel mistaken paths and will be corrected only when we encounter others who care enough to correct us. Similarly, often in the doing of the good we obtain courage, strength, guidance and support from those around us. Basil was convinced that the coenobetic, communal experience is most conducive to growth in the Christian life. Orthodoxy has, by and large, agreed with that judgment and has maintained, not only in its ethics, but in its whole polity, a bias toward the corporate and the communal.

Enough has been said here and in all the pages of this study to indicate that the individual Christian is either aided or hampered in his or her ethical growth toward Theosis by the social environment in which she or he lives and acts. All which was said about the formation of character, for instance, is a case in point. But precisely because the environment in which we live impacts on and exerts a highly determinative influence upon individual behavior, the Christian is concerned about influencing *it!* Concern for the well-being of others, i.e. love, requires that we be concerned, as Christians with the social context in which others live out their lives. The coenobetic monasticism of St. Basil is one expression of this reality. Yet, lest it be thought that concern for social structures is a mere tactic, without deeper theological grounding, we need only think of the fact that God is the creator of all things and that the saving work of Christ is universal and all-inclusive in scope. The Bible teaches that "Christ is all in all."[166] The whole of life, including its social institutions

262

thus becomes the concern of the Gospel, as well as of those who wish the good done and evil avoided. There is, then, a continuity between the ascent to Theosis by the individual, the enabling power of life in the Church of God, and the powerful forces of the social institutions of this life. The forms of this life and ultimate, transcendent reality must be perceived as being, in some manner, related and in continuity. In the words of one scholar,

> If the Christian ideal is to be maintained at all as the supreme aim, and is to be brought to universal recognition, it will have to incorporate within itself the natural forms of life and the ethical ideals of this life, and this will never be possible otherwise than by means of the idea of an ascending development, which ascends from the values of the life of this world to those of the transcendent realm.[167]

As Orthodox, we know that the sacramental life in large part "incorporates the natural forms of life" in the Kingdom. Yet, often this incorporation is only realized in part. Christian marriage, for instance, is a sacrament incorporating the "natural" institution of marriage into the life of the kingdom. Yet we know that perceptions of marriage—even by Christian Hierarchs, and theologians are profoundly influenced by social norms and institutions. In our day, many Christians are confused and shaken in their marriages because the general social climate regarding marriage is so confused. Certainly, a deeper instruction and guidance by the Church in the Christian understanding of the marriage bond is required. But concurrently, we must take cognizance of the powerful social influences upon marriage today.

In large part, doing the good and avoiding evil will be influenced by social forces. This means that, of necessity, Christians will be concerned with the social institutions, influences and pressures which are exerted on the living of the Christian life. Personal striving for sexual purity, for instance, is a part of growth toward Theosis. However, a society which condones pornography, openly espouses sexual promiscuity, remains unmoved by blatant homosexuality, and encourages the breakdown of the family, as ours is increasingly doing, cannot be a matter of indifference to those concerned about the doing of the good and the avoiding of evil.

If good is to be done and evil to be avoided, then Christian Ethics must acknowledge the responsibility of dealing with social issues. This argument is made from the perspective of the individual person. It says that part of the method of persons growing in the divine image toward Theosis must use in order to avoid evil and do good, is to fight social evil and promote social good. However, this is not enough, not inclusive enough and not comprehensive enough. The institutions themselves need to be brought under Christ, as well. Eschatologically speaking it is God who will bring this about. Yet Christians, synergistically speaking, are called to share in this task, as well. It is precisely here that the distinction is made between Christian Personal Ethics and Christian Social Ethics. In as much as concern for social institutions has as its focus the development of human beings in the image and likeness of God, they are treated from the point of view of Personal Ethics. In as much as those self-same institutions are measured against the values, standards and criteria of the Kingdom of God, as institutions in and of themselves, we deal with Social Ethics. They are, of course, not sharply separable. But the focus is different.

In as much as we are concerned with the avoiding of evil and the doing of the good, we will recognize that the social dimension requires at least two things. First that the *agona* be exercised in fellowship with others: the eucharistic community, the brotherhood of the believers, the family, the father-Confessor, the Scriptures, the Tradition, etc., in general, the Church as a whole. Secondly, that society outside the Church also be perceived as an important influence in the struggle for good and against evil. That is why Christians must be concerned citizens, involved in supporting "whatever is true, whatever is honorable, whatever is just, whatever is pure, whatever is lovely, whatever is gracious"[168] and conversely in condemning and minimizing whatever is shameful, evil and unjust.

In order to do this Christians must become actively involved in the processes which influence these factors of life and must use the means available to them to influence them. In the earliest Church, St. Paul used his rights as a Roman citizen for the sake of the Church's work and during the period from 123 to about 200 A.D. a series of writers known as Apologists, not only repulsed charges against Christianity by pagan philosophers, but also made direct appeals to political authorities to change what they perceived to be unjust laws.[169]

The Church and individual Christians within the Church may limit evil and encourage the good in the social sphere in numerous ways. One is by private initiative. The strong philanthropic tradition,[170] of Eastern Christianity encourages private initiative. In Byzantium, small, locally sponsored hospices, old age homes, orphanages and similar institutions were frequently established on the basis of private initiative to meet human needs. Such efforts were the sources of much good and contributed to the alleviation of much evil. The Church was closely related to these institutions often supplying the operative and administrative personnel in the form of clergy and monks. Part of the Bishop's tasks was to oversee the operation of these institutions. In modern Greece today, many of the Metropolitans have established and maintain small philanthropic institutions for the purpose of "avoiding evil and contributing to the good." An example is the student dormitories located in and around district-wide high schools and in conjunction with the universities.

Often, however, private initiative is not enough. Alliances must be sought. The most powerful and influential force is the state, the political order. The influencing of legislation is an old tradition in the history of Orthodoxy. In a very important sense, the Church seeks to influence the state indirectly through the vision and example of its own life and teaching. This vision, for example, in Byzantium prompted Emperor Leo III to revise his compendium of laws known as the *Ecloga* "towards greater humanity."[171]

However, the Church did not limit itself to this indirect approach.

> . . . The Church also found that it could and did influence Imperial legislation "toward greater humanity" by lobbying for its causes. From the time of Eusebios of Caesaria, Christians sought to "whisper in the ear of the Emperor," and this whispering was effective. Imperial laws and practices were slowly, yet systematically modified to embody more and more Christian ideals and ethical insights. To be sure this practice never succeeded in overturning injustice completely, but it did have an ameliorating effect of Byzantine law and society.[172]

What can be done both in the area of private initiative and influence upon the laws of the state is dependent upon the climate of the environment. Byzantium and modern Greece are examples of a close tie between the Church and public life. Byzantine life, thought and culture and especially political life were imbued with an Orthodox Christian spirit,[173] which, however, did not mean that there could not be conflict and opposition between the Church and the state. Yet the Church had its role. The last remaining exclusive official Orthodox Christian state Church is in Greece. The Church can speak and act there differently than it can in other strongly Orthodox countries where there are communist regimes. In the pluralistic democratic nations of the West, another method and approach is called for. Orthodox Christians will need to evaluate the possibilities and adjust their methods to them. What no Orthodox can do consistently with the Orthodox faith and with the ethical obligation to battle against evil and to encourage good, is to remain isolated, unconcerned and uninvolved.

In the pluralistic, western democracies, the Orthodox must involve themselves in the struggle against social evil and for the civic good publically, legislatively, cooperatively and in an organized and informed manner.

Much of the indirect and direct influence on public policy is waged in the *public media:* statements, symbolic acts, conventions, publications, radio, T.V., etc. The Orthodox have not often cultivated this important aspect of influencing public policy and need to become more sensitive to its importance.

Legislatively, the Orthodox must recognize that there are now new ways of "speaking in the ear of the Emperor." By and large, that is by involvement in the legislative process for Christian goals and purposes. A heartening example of increasing Orthodox sensitivity for involvement in the law-making process, illustrating it, as well, is the recent post-script to a popular pamphlet expressing Orthodox opposition to abortion in which we find the following directives under the heading "Here's What You Can Do Now!"

Become informed — know the Orthodox position on Abortion.

Write your congressman. Urge him to support a human life amendment that will protect all human beings from their earliest beginnings until natural death.

SUPPORT PRO-LIFE ORGANIZATIONS!

Organize as a Church group to protect and defend the gift of life.

Speak Out! Become a spokesman for those who cannot speak.[174]

Such a directive indicates the need for Orthodox to become more directly involved in the political process. Three of its instructions also point to other essentials required in this environment to do battle for good and against evil.

On most issues, the Orthodox will function cooperatively with other groups, often Church groups. No Church group, for instance, in the United States is so powerful, that it can influence public legislation effectively on its own. The Orthodox will involve themselves in ecumenically structured organizations for the purpose of achieving specific social goals. Such alliances, though single-issue oriented, can also serve to foster increased understanding among Christians of different Church groups. Yet they must be perceived for what they are, temporary alliances.

This leads inexorably for the need of permanent Orthodox bodies which will serve to inform, lobby for, encourage and mobilize the Orthodox for effective involvement. These bodies need to be ecclesial, that is, they must be under episcopal supervision, for this is not a work of a few fanatics, but the work of the whole Church. As such these need direction from above, but also local initiative on the parish level. Ideally, on major, nation-wide issues all Orthodox jurisdictions will act in concert to achieve Orthodox goals.

Finally, such action requires an informed Church. All of the means available, including religious education, the Church press, Youth organizations, women's and men's associations, the sermon and so many other means need to be harnessed for this purpose.

The doing of the good and the avoiding of evil are complete tasks related to the whole Christian economy of salvation. In this chapter we have sought to clarify the specifics of how evil is to be avoided and the good accomplished. In all cases, we depend upon divine grace to accomplish the will of God. Yet we also know that there is need for our own action. The Orthodox doctrine of *synergy* assures us of that obligation.

In a subsequent volume we will deal with issues of personal ethics especially as they focus upon our relationship with God, with self, with others, with institutions and with things. The theology, ethos, problems and issues of Social Ethics must remain for separate treatment.

Those who live according to the flesh set their minds on the things of the flesh, but those who live according to the Spirit set

266

their minds on the things of the Spirit. To set the mind on the flesh is death, but to set the mind on the Spirit is life and peace.

. . . .

Do not be conformed to this age, but be transformed by the renewal of your mind, that you may prove what is the will of God, what is good and acceptable and perfect.

Romans 8:5-6, 12:2

¹ *Unseen Warfare: Being the Spiritual Combat and Path to Paradise of Lorenzo Scupoli* as edited by Nicodemus of the Holy Mountain and revised by Theophan the Recluse, translated into English from Theophan's Russian Text by E. Kadloubovsky and G. E. H. Palmer with an introduction by H. A. Hodges. London: Faber and Faber, Limited, 1952, p. 247.

² *Homily on Genesis*, 52.4.

³ *Stromata*, 1:1.

⁴ *The Long Rules*, Question 2, *op. cit.*, Vol. I, p. 20.

⁵ George Mantzarides, *Christian Community and the World*, (Greek). Thessalonika: 1967, p. 85.

⁶ St. Basil, *The Long Rules*, Question 5, *op. cit.*, pp. 27, 30.

⁷ *Paraphrasis Symeon tou Metaphrastou eis 150 Kephalaia*, 1, *Philokalia*, Volume 3, p. 171.

⁸ 2 Corinthians 1:9.

⁹ St. Cassian the Roman, *To Bishop Kastor on the Eight Evils*, 2. *Philokalia*, Vol. 1. 63, 35-36.

¹⁰ *Op. cit.*, Title of Chapter Two, p. 81.

¹¹ Matthew 16:24; Mark 8:34; Luke 9:23.

¹² *Peri Theologias*, Fifth Hekatontas, 28. *Philokalia*, Volume 2, pp. 131-132.

¹³ Michael Kardamakis, *Orthodox Spirituality*. (Greek): Athens: Genike Dieuthynsis Ekklesiastikes Paideias, 1973, pp. 43-44. He quotes St. Mark the Ascetic twice. *Concerning Those Who Believe That They Are Justified by Works*, in *Philokalia*, Vol. I, p. 113, 124.

¹⁴ Maloney, *op. cit.*, p. 65.

¹⁵ *Life of Saint Anthony*, 20.

¹⁶ Philippians 2:13.

¹⁷ Philippians 2:12.

¹⁸ 1 Timothy 4:10.

¹⁹ Kardamakis, *op. cit.*, p. 48.

²⁰ St. Mark the Ascetic, *Concerning the Spiritual Law*, 190, *Philokalia*, Vol. 1, p. 107.

²¹ St. Maximos the Confessor, "Pros Thalassion," P.G. Vol. 90, p. 336D.

²² John 15:14.

²³ Matthew 25:40, 45.

²⁴ John 14:15.

²⁵ Kardamakis, *op. cit.*, pp. 55-56.

²⁶ Galatians 5:16-21.

²⁷ Galatians 5:25.

²⁸ George I. Mantzarides, *Christian Ethics: University Lectures* (in Greek). Thessalonike, 1975, pp. 46-52.

²⁹ *Peri Theologias Hekatontas Deutera*, 71. *Philokalia*, Vol. B; pp. 82-83.

267

[30] Kardamakis, *op. cit.*, p. 30.

[31] 6:4.

[32] 6:6.

[33] 6:11.

[34] 6:12-13.

[35] 6:16.

[36] 6:17.

[37] *Peri Theologias*, 6th Hekatontas, 90. *Philokalia*, Vol. 2, p. 165.

[38] *Logos Asketikos*, in *Philokalia*, Vol. 1, p. 206, lines 8-9.

[39] Abbas Philemon, *Logos Pasy Ophelimos*, *Philokalia*, Vol. 2, pp. 250-251.

[40] *Ibid.*, p. 250, line 36.

[41] Peri *Theologias*, Hekatontas 6, 88. *Philokalia*, Vol. 2, p. 164.

[42] *Ibid.*, 87.

[43] *Ibid.*, 86.

[44] *Op. cit.*, 28. p. 131-132.

[45] Harakas, "The Local Church," *The Ecumenical Review*, Vol. 29, No. 2, April, 1977, pp. 141-153.

[46] George Mantzarides, *Christianike Ethike: University Notes* (in Greek). Thessalonike, P. Pournaras Publications, 1971, p. 121-122.

[47] See Galatians 6:4-5, 7-9.

[48] Matthew 18:6, 7.

[49] Galatians 6:1-2.

[50] 1 John 2:9-10.

[51] *The Long Rules*, Question 7, *Op. cit.*, pp. 33-38.

[52] *Logos Psychophelis*, *op. cit.*, p. 237.

[53] 34:14.

[54] 1 Peter 3:11.

[55] Romans 12.

[56] Romans 6:6.

[57] Romans 6:12-13.

[58] Stromateis, 2,13.

[59] *The Nature of Man*, MPG 40, 504.

[60] *Doctrinai Diversai* 1, 4, MPG 88, 1621 D.

[61] Kardamakis, *op. cit.*, pp. 130-131.

[62] *Concerning Discernment of the Passions and Thoughts*, *Philokalia*, Volume 1, p. 44.

[63] *Logos Psychophelis*, op. cit., p. 233.

[64] *Ibid.*, p. 233:24-26.

[65] *Ibid.*, p. 233:30-31.

[66] *Philokalia*, Vol. 1, p. 16, 85.

[67] *De Octo Vitiosis Cogitationibus*, MPG, 40:1272-1277.

[68] *Logoi synoptikoi*, 8. *Philokalia*, Vol. 3, p. 131, 24.

[69] *Kepahalaia Psychophele*, *Philokalia*, Vol. 1, 307, 19.

[70] Socrates Gikas, "Pathos" *Threskeutike kai Ethike Engyklopedia*, Volume 9. Athens: A. Martinos, 1966, p. 1037.

[71] *Philokalia*, Vol. 1, pp. 130-131.

[72] St. Anthony, *Parainesis Peri Ethous Anthropou kai Chrestes Politeias*, *Philokalia*, 1, 16, 89.

[73] Christoforos Stavropoulos, *Partakers of Divine Nature*, *Op. cit.*, pp. 50-51.

[74] *Ibid.*

[75] *Peri Theologias*, 4th Hekatontas, 40. *Philokalia* Vol. 2, p. 116.

[76] Jeremiah 4:22; Jeremiah 9:2-3, see also Isaiah, 59.

[77] Stavropoulos, *op. cit.*, p. 51.

[78] St. Anthony, *Parainesis Peri Ethous . . . Ibid.*

[79] *Peri Agapes*, 2nd Hekatontas, 33. *Philokalia*, 2, 19.

[80] *Peri Agapes kai Enkrateias*, 2nd Hekatontas.

[81] *Peri Agapes*, 3rd Hekatontas, 57. *Philokalia*, Vol. 2, p. 35.

[82] *Kephalaia Pany Ophelima*, 106; *Philokalia*, Vol. 4, p. 49.

[83] *Peri Agapes*, 3rd Hekatontas, 56. *Philokalia*, Vol. 2, 35.

[84] *Peri Agapes kai Engrateias*, 3rd Hekatontas, 7. *Philokalia*, Vol. 2, p. 217.

[85] *Physikon Kephalaion,* 2nd Hekatontas, 11. *Philokalia,* Vol. 3, p. 301.

[86] *Kephalaia Praktika kai Theologika,* 21. *Philokalia,* Vol. 3, p. 240.

[87] Kardamakis, *op. cit.,* p. 18.

[88] St. Anthony, *Parainessis* . . . 89, *Philokalia,* Vol. 1, p. 16.

[89] *Kata Eunomion* 1:1, PG 29, 500B.

[90] Homily on Philippians 5:6.

[91] Chrysostom, *Homilies on John 33:3.*

[92] *Chrysostom, Ibid.,* 70:1.

[93] *The Long Rules,* Question 6, *op. cit.,* Vol. 1, p. 32.

[94] *The Long Rules,* Question 8, *op. cit.,* Volume 1, p. 40.

[95] *Ibid.,* question 9: "Whether he who is admitted to the company of those consecrated to the Lord ought, with indifference, entrust his property to incompetent or unjust relatives." Basil's response is, obviously, in the negative.

[96] *Homily on Titus,* 2:2.

[97] Antiochos Monachos, *Pandektis Aghion Graphon,* 6.PG. 89, 1428.

[98] *Stromata* 2:18. MG 8, 1020A.

[99] 2 Kings 19:28, Job 30:11, Psalms 32:9, James 1:26, 3:2.

[100] Epistle 5, 3.

[101] *Mandata Pastoria,* 12, 1, 1.

[102] Harakas, "A Theology of the Sacrament of Holy Confession," *Greek Orthodox Theological Review,* Vol. XIX, No. 2, 1974, pp. 177-201.

[103] *Homily on Jeremiah* 20, 9. MG 13, 521D.

[104] *Asketike Logoi* 1:5. MG 31, 881A.

[105] *Oti Epikindynon* . . . *Pros Charein* 4. PG 50, 653.

[106] St. Anthony, *Parainesis Peri Ethous* . . . , 117. *Philokalia,* Vol. 1, p. 20.

[107] Diadochos, *Logos Asketikos,* 47. *Philokalia,* Vol. 1, p. 248.

[108] Maximos the Confessor, *Peri Agapes,* 1st Hekatontas, 79 *Philokalia,* Vol. 2, p. 11.

[109] *On the Statues* 3, 4. See also Abbas Dorotheos, *Doctrinae Diversae* 15, 4, MG 88, 1792D.

[110] Eusebius of Alexandria, *Sermons* 1. MG 86, 320 C, D.

[111] Matthew 17:21.

[112] Matthew 6:9 ff.

[113] Matthew 26:41.

[114] *Peri Agapes,* 2nd Hekatontas, 47, Migne 90, 1000C.

[115] Elias the Presbyter, *Antholgion Gnomikon,* 73-74. *Philokalia,* Vol. 2, p. 295.

[116] St. Gregory of Nyssa, de Vita Mosis. MG 44, 364 A.

[117] *Ephesians* XIII, in BEP Vol. 2, page 266 ff.

[118] Prayer of the Trisagion. Text from Isabel Florence Hapgood, *Service Book of the Holy Orthodox Catholic Apostolic Church.* Rev. Ed. New York Association Press, 1922, p. 85.

[119] Prayer Before Gospel, *Ibid.,* 89.

[120] Cherubic, *Ibid.,* 95.

[121] *Ibid.,* 106-107.

[122] *Ibid.,* 107.

[123] *Ibid.,* 112.

[124] *Ibid.,* 112.

[125] From Liturgy of St. Basil, *Ibid.,* p. 113.

[126] Prayer before Communion, *Ibid.,* p. 116-117.

[127] Prayer after Communion, *Ibid.,* p. 117.

[128] Prayer after Communion, *Ibid.,* p. 118.

[129] St. Basil. Prayer after Communion, *Ibid.,* p. 119.

[130] Prayers of Thanksgiving for Communion -after the D. Liturgy, *Ibid.,* p. 123.

[131] *Ibid.,* p. 123.

[132] St. Simeon Metaphrastes, *Ibid.,* p. 123-124.

[133] *The Long Rules,* Question 6, *op. cit.,* pp. 31-32.

[134] 2 Corinthians 4:2, King James Version. See also, Romans 6:21.

[135] Procopios Gazaeus, *Genesis* 4:2, MG 87, 21. See also Ignatios, *Magnesians* 12, 1, MG 5:661; Cyril of Alexandria, *On the Psalms* 17:46, MG 17:46; Ioannes Moschos, *Pratum Spirituale,* 118. MG 87:2881 D.

[136] Jude 15.

[137] *Epistle* 174, MG 32, 652 A. Translation Loeb Classical Library. Trans. Roy J. Deferrari, Vol. 2, pp. 454-455, Cambridge, Mass. Harvard Univ. Press.

[138] 1 John 1:3-5.

[139] *Sermo Asceticus,* PG 79, 1281 D. Translation, George Maloney, *op. cit.,* p. 193.

[140] John 7:17.

[141] 2 John 6.

[142] John 14:15.

[143] *The Long Rules,* Question 5. *Op. cit.,* pp. 29-31.

[144] See Eric Osborn, *Ethical Patterns in Early Christian Thought,* New York: Cambridge University Press, 1976.

[145] *Peri Theologias,* 6th Hekatontas, 67, 69.

[146] Clement of Alexandria, *Stromata* II, Ch. 19.

[147] Kardamakis, *op. cit.,* p. 94.

[148] *Ibid.,* p. 99.

[149] Nicholas E. Mitsopoulos, *Physis kai Latreutikos Charakter ton Agathon Ergon,* Athens, 1969, p. 34.

[150] Romans 3:28, Galatians 2:16, 3:11, James 2:14-18.

[151] *Synopsis tes Dogmatikes Didaskalias tes Orthodoxou Katholikes Ekklesias.* Athens, 1960, p. 75.

[152] Mitsopoulos, *op. cit.,* p. 100.

[153] *Op. cit.,* pp. 93-95.

[154] *Op. cit.,* p. 103.

[155] George Mantzarides, *Christianike Ethike: Panepestemiakai Paradoseis,* Thessalonike, 1975, p. 131.

[156] Osborn, *op. cit.,* p. 23.

[157] *Diognetos* 10, 4.

[158] John 13:15.

[159] *Asketikai Diataxeis* I. P.G. 31, 1325.

[160] *Christianike Ethike,* op. cit., p. 134.

[161] Philippians 2:13.

[162] Eusebius, *Ekklesiastike Historia* 5, proem. 4.

[163] St. Basil, *On the Holy Spirit,* 35. MPG 32, 128 D.

[164] Homily on John, 28.2.

[165] *On the Trinity,* 28, MPG 77, 1173 A.

[166] Corinthians 15:25.

[167] Erust Troeltsch, *The Social Teaching of the Christian Churches.* Translated by Olive Wyon. New York: The Macmillan Co., 1931. Volume I, p. 277.

[168] Philippians 4:8.

[169] For a detailed history of the concern and involvement of the primitive and early Church in social questions, see Demetropoulos, *The Faith of the Ancient Church as a Rule of Life and the World* (in Greek), Athens, 1959; Cecil J. Cadoux, *The Early Church and the World.* Edinburgh: T. & T. Clark, 1925; Igino Giordani, *The Social Message of the Early Fathers,* Patterson, N.J., St. Anthony Guild Press, 1944, R. A. Norris, Jr., *God and World in Early Christian Theology.* New York: Seabury Press, 1965. Social concern and activism, toward the purpose of influencing society for the better during the Byzantine period has also been documented quite thoroughly by Demetrios Constantelos, *Byzantine Philanthropy and Social Welfare,* New Brunswick, N.J.: Rutgers University Press, 1968. Ernest Barker, *Social and Political Thought in Byzantium.* Oxford: Clarendon Press, 1957. There is also a wide-spread theological affirmation among Orthodox theologians that this concern with social issues and the necessary activity related to it is an integral part of the Orthodox Christian message. (See Savvas Agourides, "The Social Character of Orthodoxy" in A. J. Philippou, ed. *The Orthodox Ethos: Studies in Orthodoxy.* Oxford: Holywell Press, 1964, pp. 209-220. Sergius Bulgakoff, *Social Teaching in Modern Russian Orthodox Theology (The Twentieth Annual Hale Memorial Sermon).* Evanston, Ill., Seabury-Western Theological Seminary, 1934. Demetrios Constantelos "Social Consciousness in the Greek Orthodox Church," *Greek Orthodox Theological Review,* Vol. XII, No. 3, Fall, 1967. Panagiotes Demetriopoulos, *Christianike Koinoniologia,* (University Lectures in Greek), Thessalonike, Greece, 1965. Christos Giannaras, *To Pronomio Tes Apelpisias,* Stanley S. Harakas, "The Orthodox Theological Approach to Modern Trends," *St. Vladimir's Theological Quarterly,* Vol. 13, No. 4, (1969), pp. 198-211. "The Church and the Secular World," *Greek Orthodox Theological Review,* Vol. XVII, 1972, No. 1. "The Meaning of the Adaptation of Orthodoxy to the Contemporary World" (Greek), *Epistemonike Epiteris,* Theologikes Scholes Panepistemious Thessalonikes, Volume 19, 1974, pp. 127-140. "Orthodox Church-State Theory and American Democracy," *Greek Orthodox Theological Review,* Vol. XXI, No. 4, 1976, pp. 399-421. *Contemporary Moral Issues Facing The Orthodox Christian,* Minneapolis: Light and Life Publishing Co., 1982. *Let Mercy Abound: Social Concern in the Greek Orthodox Church,* Boston: Holy Cross Orthodox Press, 1983. George Mantzarides, "Christianike Koinonia kai o Kosmos" (Greek), *Epistimonke Epiteris Theologikes Scholes Panepistimiou Thessalonikes,* Vol. 12, 1967. *Christianike Koinoniologia (University Notes)* (In Greek). Thessalonike: Pournaras Publications, 1973. *The Witness of Orthodoxy to the Contemporary World* (In Greek), Thessalonike, 1973. Alexander Tsirindanes, *Towards a Christian Civilization,* Athens: Damascus Press, 1950. See also, my publication regarding the development of social concern in the Greek Orthodox Archdiocese of N. & S. America, with texts of church

270

statements; *Let Mercy Abound: Social Concern in the Greek Orthodox Church.* Brookline, MA. Holy Cross Orthodox Press, 1983.

[170] Constantelos,. *Byzantine Philanthropy* . . . *Ibid.,* especially Parts one and two.

[171] Ernest Barker, *Social and Political Thought in Byzantium, Ibid.,* p. 31.

[172] Harakas, "Orthodox Church-State Theory and American Democracy," *Greek Orthodox Theological Review,* Vol. XXI, No. 4, 1976, p. 417.

[173] See Steven Runciman, *The Byzantine Theocracy,* New York: Cambridge University Press, 1977, chapter one.

[174] Rev. Fr. John Kowalczyk, *An Orthodox View of Abortion,* Minneapolis, Minn., 1977, p. 48.

SCRIPTURE REFERENCES
Old Testament

Genesis
3:8-14 — 108

Exodus
20:1-17 — 135

Leviticus
11:44-45 — 18

1 Chronicles
16:34 — 19

2 Chronicles
5:13 — 19

Job
27:5 — 108
34:18 — 18

Psalms
5:4 — 68
5:11 — 47
18:1 — 119
25:9 — 226
31:3 — 226
34:14 — 242
100:5 — 19

Isaiah
11:2 — 221
59 — 247

Jeremiah
4:22 — 246
9:2-3 — 246-7
31:33-34 — 45

Wisdom of Solomon
17:11 — 108

NEW TESTAMENT

Matthew
5:3 — 249
5:17 — 148
5:17-18 — 151
5:17-20 — 206
5:21-22 — 206
5:29 — 206
5:30 — 206
5:38-39 — 166
5:44-46 — 166
5 & 6 — 148-155
6:9ff — 252
6:24 — 179
7:1 — 18
10:10 — 193
10:33-38 — 205
11:12 — 258
15:3-6 — 138
16:19 — 86
16:24 — 233
16:27 — 201
17:21 — 252

18:6-7 — 241
18:18 — 86
19:14 — 165
19:10-21 — 207
19:21 — 206
22:36 — 151
22:36-39 — 138
22:37-39 — 164
22:37-40 — 24
23:23 — 151
23:37 — 165
24:30 — 201
25:1 — 207
25:14-30 — 193
25:31-46 — 218
25:40 — 236
25:45 — 236
26:41 — 252

Mark
7:8-9 — 138
8:34 — 233
8:34-38 — 206

INDEX

282